Oracle Database 12*c* Backup and Recovery Survival Guide

A comprehensive guide for every DBA to learn recovery and backup solutions

Francisco Munoz Alvarez

Aman Sharma

BIRMINGHAM - MUMBAI

Oracle Database 12c Backup and Recovery Survival Guide

First published: September 2013

Production Reference: 1170913

Published by Packt Publishing Ltd.
Livery Place
35 Livery Street
Birmingham B3 2PB, UK.

ISBN 978-1-78217-120-1

www.packtpub.com

Cover Image by Dilleshwar (dil.snowfire@gmail.com)

Credits

Authors

Francisco Munoz Alvarez

Aman Sharma

Reviewers

Gokhan Atil

Wissem EL Khlifi

Bjorn Naessens

Arup Nanda

Alessandro Parisi

Laurent Schneider

Acquisition Editor

Vinay Argekar

Lead Technical Editor

Azharuddin Sheikh

Technical Editors

Manan Badani

Aparna Chand

Vivek Pillai

Project Coordinator

Wendell Palmer

Proofreader

Ameesha Green

Indexers

Rekha Nair

Tejal Soni

Graphics

Abhinash Sahu

Ronak Dhruv

Production Coordinator

Shantanu Zagade

Cover Work

Shantanu Zagade

About the Author

Francisco Munoz Alvarez has over two decades of experience in consulting, analysis, support, implementation, and migration of Oracle products. He is also an expert in most phases of a database life cycle, for example, development, stabilization, security, backup and recovery, tuning, installations, and data warehouse (ETL) with excellent implementation and support methodologies. He is a popular speaker at many Oracle conferences around the world.

He is also the President of CLOUG (Chilean Oracle Users Group), LAOUC (Latin American Oracle Users Group Community, which is the umbrella organization for all of Latin America), and NZOUG (New Zealand Oracle Users Group). He worked as an Associate Technologist for Oracle in Brazil and Chile. He was an Oracle instructor for the New Horizons Centre (Chile) and for Oracle Education (Brazil and Chile). He also worked in the first team to introduce Oracle to South America (Oracle 6 and the beta version of Oracle 7). He was also the first Master Oracle 7 Database Administrator in South America, as well as the first Latin American Oracle professional to be awarded a double ACE (ACE in 2008 and ACE Director in 2009) by Oracle HQ. In 2010, he had the privilege to receive a prestigious Oracle Magazine Editor's Choice Award as the Oracle Evangelist of the Year—a huge recognition for his outstanding achievements in the Oracle world that includes the creation and organization of the already famous OTN Tours that are the biggest Oracle evangelist events in the world.

Currently, Francisco works for Revera Limited, which is a leading provider of utility computing infrastructure and enterprise data management in New Zealand, as the Oracle Professional Services Manager since June 2011. He also maintains an Oracle blog (`http://www.oraclenz.org`) and you can always contact him through this or Twitter (`@fcomunoz`) regarding any questions about this book.

Acknowledgement

Writing a book is not the accomplishment of one or two people, it involves a huge group of people behind the scenes to make it possible. Due to this, I would like to take this opportunity to acknowledge some important people in my life that without their support and help, writing this book would have been an impossible journey. I would like to start with my wonderful wife, mother of my four wonderful children; honey, without your enormous patience and support, nothing could be possible—even though at times you don't understand this fascinating journey and this fascinating world, my love, I dedicate this book to you! Secondly, my mother, my father and my well-remembered grandmother for everything you all taught me in my early years and the things I have seen because of you. And finally my good friends, Thomas Kyte, Arup Nanda, Aman Sharma (your support, help, and friendship is invaluable), Gokhan Atil, Wissem EL Khifi, Bjorn Naessens, Alessandro Parisi, Laurent Schneider, all editors, and everyone involved in the book, without your help and support throughout writing this book and even during my career, I would never have been able to finish writing this book.

About the Author

Aman Sharma is an Oracle Database consultant and instructor. He holds a Master's degree in Computer Applications and has been working with Oracle Database for over a decade. His main focus is to understand how Oracle Database works internally. Besides the core database, he has a very strong knowledge of Linux, Solaris, Oracle RAC, Data Guard, RMAN, Oracle Exadata and Oracle Enterprise Manager.

He is an Oracle Certified Professional and also an Oracle Certified Expert in Oracle RAC, SQL and Linux. He is also an Oracle Certified Implementation Specialist and a certified Solaris System Administrator. He loves to share his learning with the Oracle community, so when he is not delivering an Oracle related session, he spends a lot of his time participating in OTN (Oracle Technology Network) discussion forums. He also maintains an Oracle blog (`http://blog.aristadba.com`), is also on Twitter (`@amansharma81`), you can reach to him using either ways. He is a strong supporter of user groups and is a member of India Oracle Users Group (`http://www.aioug.org`) and has been a speaker at various Oracle conferences organized by AIOUG. He is also an associate member of IOUG (`http://www.ioug.org`). In 2010, he was awarded the prestigious Oracle ACE award from Oracle Corporation.

Acknowledgement

I dedicate this book to my entire family for their so much love, affection, and constant encouragement.

A child is just like a plain canvas. It's his parents who fill colors into it with their love, blessings, guidance, and teachings. The same is true for me as well. This book is a result of the blessings, love, affection, guidance, and support of my mom and dad. Thank you so very much mom and dad! Dad, how so I wish that you were here today, but I know you are watching over me from the heavens, your blessings are always with me and you must be very happy today! We all miss you so very much—every day, in every moment!

Writing a book is a team effort and requires a lot of hard work but every journey starts from that very first step. For me, getting aboard to work on this book became possible only because of my dear friend and co-author Francisco Munoz Alvarez, who invited me to become a co-author with him. It was a really great team effort and working with him was an absolute delight, as well as a very learning and rewarding experience. I thank him for not only making me a part of this project but also for his support, help and mentoring the entire time while we were working on this project.

Though a book is written by its authors, there are many other people who work behind the scenes and do tons of things that finally result in letting a book see the sunshine. The most important among these are the technical reviewers who do the painful job of reading the raw writing of an author, line by line and correct it. It's due to their corrections, suggestions, feedback, and questions that convert those sentences written in a Word document into the chapters of an actual book. I am so very thankful to our most excellent team of the technical reviewers which we got: Arup Nanda, Wissem EL Khlifi, Gokhan Atil, Bjorn Naessens, Laurent Schneider, and Alessandro Parisi. Without their input, feedback and corrections, it wouldn't have been possible to find out what was missing, what needed to be removed, which topics required more explanation, and above all, to spot the technical errors and correct them. So when you would be reading about a topic in any chapter and would like it, remember that a major contribution to it has come in some way or the other from the technical excellence and input given by the reviewers.

I also want to say a big thanks to the entire team at Packt who did a splendid job in every aspect of the book, especially to my editor Vinay Argekar, and Wendell Palmer, the coordinator for the entire project, for being so supportive in this entire journey. Thanks to our Lead Technical Editor Azharuddin Sheikh along with his entire team: Manan Badani, Aparna Chand, and Vivek Pillai. They all have spent a lot of time ironing out the final wrinkles from the chapters, giving them that marvellous polished look which you will see throughout. I also want to pass on my gratitude to all those people with whom I might have not interacted directly but who worked very hard behind the scenes to bring this book into your hands.

I would like to take this opportunity to say thanks to all those people in the Oracle community who were not involved in this project but who are always an inspiration and constantly motivated me—not only to correct and improve myself by learning as much as possible, but also to share that learning with others and help them. The list is far too long and I am going to miss more than I will be able to put here but still, to name a few (and in no particular order): Jonathan Lewis, Hans Forbrich, Dan Morgan, Hemant Chitale, Sam Alapati, Eddie Awad, Uwe Hesse, Syed Jaffar Hussain, Kellyn Pot'Vin, Tim Gorman, Steve Adams, Kyle Hailey, Tim Hall, Mark Bobak, Cary Millsap, Howard Rodgers, Steve Karam, Tanel Poder, Alex Gorbachev, Kai Yu, Riaz Shamsudeen, Murali Vallath, Gaja Krishna Vaidyanatha, Rama Velpuri, and so many more as the list goes on and on and on. Many thanks to all of you!

Thanks to my friend Kamran Agayev for giving me the very first writing opportunity by inviting me to be his co-author and Don Burelson, and entire team of Rampant Press for their support in the entire time of writing it. Thanks to Zahida Praveen who gave me the first opportunity to step in and prove myself in the real world. I also wish to express my gratitude and thanks to all my superordinates for their constant support and motivation: Arvind Dikshit, Gautham Malareddy, Usha George, Joann Too, Ajai Sahni, Shantnu Tandan, Latha Gangadharan, Kalyan Chakravarthy, and Ritesh Jain. I would like to offer my gratitude to all the delegates that I get to meet in person and to those whom I interact with virtually over the OTN forums, for asking their questions and doubts. It's your questions which make me learn (and many times, even re-learn) new things every single day.

Finally, thanks a ton to *you* for making this book a part of your library. I really hope and wish that you are going to like the book and it's going to be useful for you in some way.

About the Reviewers

Gokhan Atil is a Senior Applications DBA working at one of the leading IT consultancy companies in Turkey. He has a strong background in UNIX systems and hands-on experience in Oracle Database versions 11*g*/10*g*/9*i*/8*i* and Oracle E-Business Suite R12/11*i*. He is an active member of the Oracle community and a founding member of the Turkish Oracle User Group (TROUG). He has written and presented papers at various conferences. He's one of the co-authors of the book *Expert Oracle Enterprise Manager 12c*, published in 2013.

Gokhan Atil holds various Oracle certifications such as Oracle Database 10*g*/11*g* Administrator Certified Professional, Oracle E-Business Suite R12 Applications DBA Certified Professional, and Oracle Exadata Database Machine X3 Administrator Certified Expert. He was honored with the Oracle ACE award in 2011. He has a blog where he shares his experiences with Oracle since 2008. You can get in touch with Gokhan at http://www.gokhanatil.com.

Wissem El Khlifi is the first Oracle ACE in Spain and an Oracle Certified Professional DBA with over 12 years of IT experience.

He earned a Computer Science Engineer's degree from FST, Tunisia, and a Master's in Computer Science from the UPC, Barcelona.

His areas of interest are Linux System Administration, Oracle Database including high availability (RAC, Dataguard), and Oracle applications.

He has worked with Oracle Database since version 7.

His career has included the roles of Oracle programmer, Java analyst/programmer, Oracle DBA, architect, project manager, and team leader. He currently works as the Senior Oracle DBA for Schneider Electric/APC.

He writes numerous articles on his Oracle website: http://www.oracle-class.com.

Bjorn Naessens is a Senior Oracle DBA at Uptime Technologies N.V. based in Belgium. Prior to his work with Uptime, he was a system engineer/DBA at a leading Belgian media company. Most of Bjorn's projects are for new infrastructure setups, hence using RMAN for backup/recovery has been constant in these projects.

Next to Oracle databases, Bjorn is specialized in Oracle VM and Oracle Linux and has a passion for the Oracle Database Appliance.

Arup Nanda has been an Oracle DBA for the last 19 years and counting. He works as the Principal Database Architect at a New York multinational company, has co-authored four books, has written around 300 articles, and presented at 150 different conferences around the world. Honoring professional accomplishments and contributions to the user community, Oracle chose him as the DBA of the Year in 2003 and Enterprise Architect of the Year in 2012. He blogs frequently at `http://www.arup.blogpsot.com`, is a member of the Oak Table Network, is an Oracle ACE Director, and tweets with handle `@arupnanda`.

Alessandro Parisi is an Enterprise Software Architect, Data Scientist and Ethical Hacker, working as an IT Consultant for nearly 20 years now. He is keen on experimenting with non-conventional solutions to problem solving in complex and dynamic contexts, mixing new technologies with lateral thinking and a holistic approach.

Founder of InformaticaSicura.com, specializing in IT Security Consultancy, he is the curator of the Hacking Wisdom column on the blog `http://www.informaticasicura.altervista.org`.

He is also the author of *Sicurezza Informatica e Tutela della Privacy*, published by Istituto Poligrafico e Zecca dello Stato, Italy, 2006.

I would like to acknowledge Ilaria Sinisi for her support and patience. Thank you very much, Ilaria.

Laurent Schneider is working as a database administrator for a leading bank in Switzerland. He is the author of the blog http://laurentschneider.com. He has written and reviewed multiple books and articles on Oracle technologies.

Laurent loves to play chess with his friends and to hike and bike with his kids Dora and Loïc in the beautiful Swiss mountains.

www.PacktPub.com

Support files, eBooks, discount offers and more

You might want to visit www.PacktPub.com for support files and downloads related to your book.

Did you know that Packt offers eBook versions of every book published, with PDF and ePub files available? You can upgrade to the eBook version at www.PacktPub.com and as a print book customer, you are entitled to a discount on the eBook copy. Get in touch with us at service@packtpub.com for more details.

At www.PacktPub.com, you can also read a collection of free technical articles, sign up for a range of free newsletters and receive exclusive discounts and offers on Packt books and eBooks.

http://PacktLib.PacktPub.com

Do you need instant solutions to your IT questions? PacktLib is Packt's online digital book library. Here, you can access, read and search across Packt's entire library of books.

Why Subscribe?

- Fully searchable across every book published by Packt
- Copy and paste, print and bookmark content
- On demand and accessible via web browser

Free Access for Packt account holders

If you have an account with Packt at www.PacktPub.com, you can use this to access PacktLib today and view nine entirely free books. Simply use your login credentials for immediate access.

Instant Updates on New Packt Books

Get notified! Find out when new books are published by following @PacktEnterprise on Twitter, or the *Packt Enterprise* Facebook page.

Table of Contents

Preface   **1**

Chapter 1: Understanding the Basics of Backup and Recovery   **7**

Purpose of backup and recovery   **7**
  Testing backups   8
Protecting data   **9**
  Media failure   9
  Hardware failure   10
  Human error   10
  Application error   10
Types of backup   **11**
  A physical backup   11
  A logical backup   11
Backup strategies   **12**
Restore versus recovery   **13**
What is redo?   **14**
Redo generation and recoverability   **16**
The NOARCHIVELOG mode   **16**
The ARCHIVELOG mode   **18**
  Understanding the ARCHIVELOG mode   19
  Preparing for the ARCHIVELOG mode   20
  Checking the status of the ARCHIVELOG mode   22
  Specifying parameters   22
  Viewing the status of archival destinations   23
  Placing a database into the ARCHIVELOG mode   24
  Differences between redo and undo   25
  Facing excessive redo generation during an online backup?   26
Summary   **27**

Chapter 2: NOLOGGING Operations	**29**
LOGGING versus NOLOGGING	**31**
Disabling redo generation (NOLOGGING)	**34**
NOLOGGING operations	34
Indexed organized tables – an exception	40
Reducing redo generation	**44**
Tips when LOGGING is in effect (not using NOLOGGING)	44
Backups	44
Bulk inserts	44
Bulk deletes	45
Bulk updates	46
Partitioning	46
Tips for developers	48
Tips when NOLOGGING is in effect	51
Partitioning	51
Direct path inserts	54
Bulk inserts	58
Bulk deletes	58
Bulk updates	59
Backups and NOLOGGING	**60**
Redo-related wait events	**60**
The 'log file parallel write' event	60
The 'log file sync' event	62
The 'redo log space request' event	62
The 'log buffer space' event	63
Block corruption due to NOLOGGING	**63**
Repairing NOLOGGING changes on physical and logical standby databases	**64**
Finding sessions that generate lots of redo	**65**
Some other important facts	**66**
Redo and undo for DML	66
Redo and temporary tables	67
Redo generation and materialized views	67
Flashback and NOLOGGING	67
Performance and recovery considerations	68
Direct path load using SQL*Loader	68
Some useful scripts	**69**
Redo generated since instance startup	69
Redo generated since session startup	71
Redo generated by current user sessions	71
Current status for redo logs	72

Redo log group and log switch information	72
NOLOGGING objects in the database	72
Summary	**73**
Chapter 3: What is New in 12*c*	**75**
Pluggable database	**75**
RMAN new features and enhancements	**78**
Container and pluggable database backup and restore	78
Enterprise Manager Database Express	79
Backup privileges	80
SQL and DESCRIBE	84
Multi-section backups for incremental backups	86
Network-based recovery	86
Active Duplicate	87
Support for the third-party snapshot	88
Cross-platform data transport	89
Table recovery	91
Data Pump's new features and enhancements	**92**
Disabling LOGGING on Data Pump Import	92
Full transportable Export/Import	93
Exporting views as tables	94
Extended character data types	94
Encryption password	95
Compressing tables on Import	95
Exporting data from the data vault	96
Creating SecureFile LOBs on Import	96
Auditing Data Pump commands	96
Summary	**97**
Chapter 4: User-managed Backup and Recovery	**99**
Cold backup	**101**
Offline backup	**102**
Hot backups	**104**
Hot backup of a whole database	105
Hot backup of tablespaces	106
Hot backup of a container database	107
Whole container database	107
Root only or individual pluggable database	108
Check datafile status	109
Control file backup	**110**
Binary backup	111
Text file backup	111

Flashback database	**112**
Recovering from a user-managed backup	**119**
Other recovery scenarios	122
Losing all copies of the current control file	122
Losing one copy of a multiplexed control file	122
Loss of archived redo logs or online redo logs	122
Loss of SPFILE	123
Summary	**123**
Chapter 5: Understanding RMAN and Simple Backups	**125**
Why RMAN?	**126**
Getting started with RMAN	**128**
RMAN architecture	**130**
Target database	131
Target Control File	132
RMAN channels	132
Auxiliary database	132
Recovery Catalog	132
RMAN client	133
Oracle Enterprise Manager (EM) Cloud Control 12*c*	*133*
Media Management Library (MML)	134
Oracle secure backup	134
Memory requirements for RMAN	134
Configuring ARCHIVELOG mode and FRA	135
Introducing RMAN backup formats	**137**
Backup sets	138
Image copy	139
Full backup	139
Incremental backups	140
Power of one	143
Getting introduced to RMAN commands	145
Using RMAN for performing incremental backups	**151**
Fast incremental backups using the block change tracking (BCT) file	**152**
Multi-section incremental backups	**155**
Incrementally updated backups	**156**
Performing backups of the control file, the SPFILE, and archived redo logs	**158**
Using RMAN compression for backups	**161**
RMAN for multitenant container databases	**163**
Performing a full backup of a multitenant CDB	164
Partial backup of a multitenant CDB	165
Performing backup of a pluggable database and root	167
Performing backups of backups	168

Restarting RMAN backups   169
Useful RMAN views related to backups   169
Summary   **170**
Chapter 6: Configuring and Recovering with RMAN   **171**
RMAN configuration – an introduction   **171**
Using the V$RMAN_CONFIGURATION view   172
Using the SHOW ALL command   172
Configuring the backup retention policy   **174**
Redundancy retention policy   175
Recovery window retention policy   178
Using backup optimization   **178**
Configuring the device types for the backup   **180**
Configuring auto backup for the control file and SPFILE   **181**
Configuring channels   **182**
Creating duplexed backups   **184**
Configuring encrypted backups   **186**
Transparent encryption of backups   187
Creating and using Oracle Software Keystore   187
Password encryption   191
Dual-mode encryption   192
Configuring compression for backups   **193**
Configuring the snapshot control file   **194**
Configuring the archived log deletion policy   **195**
Configuring the FRA   **196**
Configuring authentication for RMAN   **199**
Operating system authentication   199
Authenticating the password file   200
Crash and media recovery   **200**
Key terms related to recovery   **202**
Overview of stages in the database startup   204
Steps involved in the crash/instance recovery   205
Instance recovery in container and pluggable databases   207
Performing media recovery   208
Recovery in the NOARCHIVELOG mode   210
Loss of a temporary file   211
Loss of non-system data files   212
Loss of system data files   214
Recovering whole CDBs, PDBs, and root container databases   215
Complete recovery of a container database   216
Complete recovery of a pluggable database   216
Complete recovery of the root container   217

Performing control file recovery   218
Performing Block Media Recovery (BMR)   221
Performing point-in-time recovery   223
  Database Point-in-time Recovery (DBPITR)   223
  Tablespace Point-in-time Recovery (TSPITR)   226
Table and table partition-level recovery from RMAN backups   227
Data recovery advisor   228
Summary   **232**

Chapter 7: RMAN Reporting and Catalog Management   **233**
Using the control file for RMAN metadata   **233**
Using the CONTROLFILE_RECORD_KEEP_TIME parameter   **236**
What is a recovery catalog   **238**
  Creating the recovery catalog   239
    Sizing and creating a database for the recovery catalog   239
    Creating the default tablespace for the catalog owner   240
    Creating the catalog owner schema   241
    Granting privileges to the catalog owner   241
    Creating the recovery catalog   242
    Using the recovery catalog   242
    Resynchronizing the recovery catalog with the control file   245
    Merging multiple recovery catalogs into one   247
  Using virtual private catalogs   252
  Creating and managing stored scripts   255
  Making a recovery catalog highly available   258
  Upgrading the recovery catalog   259
  Unregistering databases from the recovery catalog   259
  Dropping a recovery catalog   260
  Views related to the recovery catalog   260
Reporting in RMAN   **263**
  Using the LIST command   263
  Using the REPORT command   264
Summary   **265**

Chapter 8: RMAN Troubleshooting and Tuning   **267**
Getting started with RMAN troubleshooting   **268**
  Using CHECKSYNTAX   268
  Reading the RMAN error stack   270
  Debugging RMAN using the DEBUG clause   272
  Using the alert log and operating system trace files   273
RMAN tuning – an introduction   **274**
  I/O and RMAN – two sides of one coin   275
  Number and size of the input and output buffers   276
  Synchronous and asynchronous I/O modes   278

Setting the Large Pool memory   279
Monitoring RMAN I/O performance using dictionary views   281
  V$BACKUP_ASYNC_IO (for asynchronous I/O)   282
  V$BACKUP_SYNC_IO (for synchronous I/O)   282
Tuning SBT (tape) performance   283
Monitoring RMAN sessions and operations   **285**
Stopping RMAN from being uncontrollable   **290**
Using incremental, multi-section, multiplexing, and parallelism   **292**
Troubleshooting RMAN performance using tracing   **294**
Summary   **296**

Chapter 9: Understanding Data Pump   297

What is Data Pump?   **297**
The Data Pump architecture   **299**
New concepts with Data Pump   **301**
Methods to move the data   **301**
Datafile copy   301
Direct path   302
External tables   303
Conventional path   303
Network link   303
Data Pump files   **304**
Roles for Data Pump export and import   304
Directory objects   305
  Creating directory objects   305
Data Pump scenarios   **306**
Schema export and import   306
Exporting and importing tables   310
Exporting and importing a whole database/pluggable database   311
Using Export to estimate space   313
Parallel full database export and interactive-command mode   314
Importing tables with only metadata   317
Exporting views as tables   318
Importing data via a network link   320
Summary   **323**

Chapter 10: Advanced Data Pump   325

Data masking   **326**
Metadata repository and version control   **330**
Using SOURCE_EDITION and TARGET_EDITIONS   **332**
Cloning a user   **332**
Creating smaller copies of production   **333**
Creating your database in a different file structure   **335**

Moving all objects from one tablespace to another   **336**
Moving an object to a different schema   **336**
Migrating data for upgrade   **336**
Downgrading an Oracle Database   **338**
Transporting a tablespace   **340**
Data Pump flashback   **343**
Monitoring Data Pump job status   **344**
Some performance tuning tips   **345**
Summary   **346**

Chapter 11: OEM12*c* and SQL Developer   **347**
  Configuring backup, recovery, and catalog settings   **348**
    Backup settings   348
    Recovery settings   353
    Catalog settings   355
  Scheduling an RMAN backup   **357**
    Using the Oracle-Suggested Backup strategy option   358
    Using the Customized Backup option   360
  Restore points   **363**
  Export/Import with OEM12c   **365**
    Executing an export operation   365
  Monitoring the job   **368**
  SQL developer 3.2   **369**
    RMAN operations   369
    Data Pump operations   371
  Summary   **371**

Appendix: Scenarios and Examples – A Hands-on Lab   **373**
  Configuring the database   **375**
    Making sure an spfile is used to start the database   375
    Placing the database in the archivelog mode and activating Flashback   375
    Creating a new redo log group and associated files   376
  Configuring RMAN   **377**
    Creating the target DB RMAN backup account   377
    Configure RMAN using the configure command   377
    Backup database   377
    Checking and deleting obsolete backups   378
    Creating RMAN catalog user   378
    Creating recovery catalog   378
    Register your DB in the recovery catalog   378
    Create a virtual private catalog   378
    Enabling Block Change tracking   379

Playing with RMAN, FRA, and catalog views — **379**
Monitoring a backup — 379
Incremental backups — 380
Multisection backups — 380
FRA – checking number of redo switches — 380
Check for alerts — 380
Check FRA usage — 381
See the archived log generated by the DB target — 381
See the control file backups — 381
See the corrupted list that exists in datafile backups — 382
See block corruption in the DB, populated when backup
or backup validate — 382
See all RMAN configurations (equivalent to show all) — 382
Monitor backup outputs (RMAN) — 382
Offline backups with RMAN — 382
Offline backup without using configured defaults — 383
Using backup limits (duration) — 383
Modifying the retention policy for a backup set (archival backups) — 383
Archive deletion policy — 384
Using RMAN to scan DB for physical and logical errors — 384
Configuring tablespaces for exclusion from whole database backups — 384
Skipping offline, inaccessible, or read-only datafiles — 384
Forcing backups of read-only datafiles — 385
Backup of newly added datafiles — 385
Backup files not backed up during a specific period — 385
General backup examples — 385
Backup copies — 386
Advanced RMAN — **386**
Information about fully-completed backups — 386
Summary of the active session history — 386
How long does it take? — 387
V$BACKUP_ASYNC_IO — 388
Tablespace Point-in-Time Recovery (TSPITR) — 388
Reporting from a catalog — 389
Duplex backup — 389
Check if the database is recoverable — 390
Recover advisor — 390
Magic with Data Pump — **391**
Preparing Data Pump — 391
Data masking — 391
Metadata repository — 392

Cloning a user   393
Creating smaller copies of production   393
Creating your database in a different structure   394
Time-based flashback   394
Backup and recovery scenarios   **395**
Active duplication of a database to a different server with
the same structure (non-OMF and non-ASM)   395
Duplicating a PDB   399
ASM backup and restore   399
Recovering from the loss of the SYSTEM tablespace   400
Recovering a lost datafile using an image from an FRA   401
Index   **403**

Preface

Knowledge is only valuable when shared.

The three main responsibilities for a successful DBA are to ensure the availability, recoverability, and performance of any database that the DBA is accountable for. This book will focus on the recoverability set of skills, and will also include some tips and ideas regarding availability. All examples showed in the book are executed over Oracle Enterprise Linux 6.4 and Oracle Database 12.1.0.1 (also known as Oracle 12*c*), please be aware of these specific versions to ensure that you will be able to reproduce the same results, you will see reflected in this book.

To ensure the recoverability of any database, a DBA needs to have a strong backup and recovery skills set; this knowledge is essential for any good DBA. Without this knowledge, you will be in violation of my most important rule that I have used in my entire career, "The most important rule with respect to data is to never put yourself into an unrecoverable situation". If you follow this simple tip every time you work with data, I can guarantee that you will be always protected against any possible situation that could surprise you in your daily journey, including of course the unexpected ones.

My key intention by writing this book is that if you are a new DBA, introduce you to this fantastic world that is vital to your success. If you are an experienced DBA, this book will become a reference guide and will also help you to learn some possible new skills, or give some new ideas that you never knew about. It will also help you to easily find the solution to some of the most well-known problems you could find during your career, and this book will be rich with screenshots, full of scripts, examples, and tutorials that you will find more than useful and handy.

Most of the books currently available in the market only concentrate on the RMAN utility for backup and recovery; this book will be an exception to the rule and will become a must-have reference to allow you to achieve a real complete backup and recovery strategy. This is not in any case a replacement to the official Oracle documentation available at `http://www.oracle.com/pls/db121/homepage`; I will always recommend to any serious DBA to read the complete documentation set as a complement to this book.

This book contains my knowledge of more than two decades working with Oracle technologies and also shows several topics and situations that came to my attention when speaking at several conferences around the world or helping others on Oracle forums or virtual communities.

I hope you will enjoy reading this book as the same way I enjoyed writing it.

What this book covers

Chapter 1, Understanding the Basics of Backup and Recovery, covers topics such as understanding the need for creating backups, getting familiar with the different backup types, an overview of backup strategy, understanding what is redo and how it affects your database recoverability, and understanding database operational modes and redo generation.

Chapter 2, NOLOGGING Operations, covers topics such as LOGGING versus NOLOGGING, disabling redo generation, NOLOGGING operations, how to reduce redo generation, redo log wait events, practice with some interesting scripts, and much more interesting topics.

Chapter 3, What is New in 12c, covers topics such as pluggable database, RMAN's new features and enhancements, and Data Pump's new features and enhancements.

Chapter 4, User-managed Backup and Recovery, covers backup and recovery using user-managed methods. Understanding the basics involving a manual backup and recovery will help you to easily understand what is going on in the background of your database when using RMAN and it will also help you to compare and easily understand all benefits of using RMAN against any other backup method when working with Oracle.

Chapter 5, Understanding RMAN and Simple Backups, describes that being the custodians of databases, DBA's should always try to minimize the loss of data. This can be accomplished through an effective strategy that enables us to secure a backup of these databases that can be accessed in case of systemic failures. However, it is rightly said that any strategy is as good as the tool that implements it. In this chapter, we shall introduce you to a tool that's just like one of those super heroes that can fix almost any issue. So in the list of such amazing heroes such as Superman and Batman, please welcome RMAN, the Recovery Manager — Oracle's one stop solution for both backups and recoveries.

Chapter 6, Configuring and Recovering with RMAN, looks into the two abilities of RMAN, that is, how to configure it and how to use it for doing database recoveries.

Chapter 7, RMAN Reporting and Catalog Management, discusses about the topics such as benefits of recovery catalog, creation and use of recovery catalog, using the CATALOG command, and RMAN reporting using the LIST and REPORT commands.

Chapter 8, RMAN Troubleshooting and Tuning, looks at various ways to get the best performance from RMAN and also techniques to troubleshoot it when it won't behave itself.

Chapter 9, Understanding Data Pump, describes about Data Pump and its architecture, new concepts with Data Pump, methods to move data, and play with many Data Pump scenarios.

Chapter 10, Advanced Data Pump, covers topics such as data masking, build a metadata repository, create a version control, clone users (create a new user using an existent user as a template), create smaller copies of production, create your database in a different file structure, move all objects from one tablespace to another, move a object to a different schema (a simple example, change a table owner), migrate data for a database upgrade, downgrade an Oracle database, transport a tablespace, and use Data Pump with flashback.

Chapter 11, OEM12c and SQL Developer, discusses topics such as configuring our backup and recovery settings (including catalog settings) in OEM12*c*, scheduling backups in OEM12*c*, creating restore points in OEM12*c*, understanding database export/import operations in OEM12*c*, and getting familiar with the SQL developer.

Appendix: Scenarios and Examples – A Hands-on Lab, allows you to practice some of the scenarios you saw in this book (step-by-step) and learn by practice. If you have any doubt about a command of what it will be doing, please refer to the corresponding chapter in this book for more information.

What you need for this book

To be able to reproduce all scenarios in this book you will need the following software:

- Oracle VirtualBox, you can download Oracle VirtualBox (free virtualization tool) at `https://www.virtualbox.org/wiki/Downloads`

- Oracle Enterprise Linux 6.4 , you can download it (free) from `https://edelivery.oracle.com/linux`

- Oracle 12.1.0.1 database for Linux that you can download (free) from `http://www.oracle.com/technetwork/database/enterprise-edition/downloads/database12c-linux-download-1959253.html`

Who this book is for

This book is designed for Oracle DBAs and system administrators. The reader will have a basic working experience of administering Oracle databases. This book will become a reference guide and will also help you to learn some new skills, and give you some new ideas you never knew about, helping you to easily find the solution to some of the most well-known problems you could encounter as DBAs. This book is designed to be understood even by beginners who have just started with the Oracle database. Due to this, any person with a basic working experience of administering an Oracle database will be able to completely understand this book.

Conventions

In this book, you will find a number of styles of text that distinguish between different kinds of information. Here are some examples of these styles and an explanation of their meaning.

Code words in text are shown as follows: "If a directory object is not specified, a default directory object called DATA_PUMP_DIR is provided".

Any command-line input or output is written as follows:

```
SQL> GRANT DATAPUMP_EXP_FULL_DATABASE, DATAPUMP_IMP_FULL_DATABASE TO
fcomunoz;
```

New terms and **important words** are shown in bold. Words that you see on the screen, in menus or dialog boxes for example, appear in the text like this: "clicking on the **Next** button moves you to the next screen".

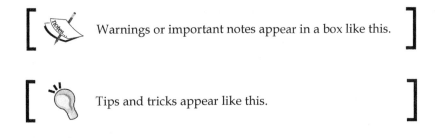

> Warnings or important notes appear in a box like this.

> Tips and tricks appear like this.

Reader feedback

Feedback from our readers is always welcome. Let us know what you think about this book—what you liked or may have disliked. Reader feedback is important for us to develop titles that you really get the most out of.

To send us general feedback, simply send an e-mail to feedback@packtpub.com, and mention the book title via the subject of your message.

If there is a topic that you have expertise in and you are interested in either writing or contributing to a book, see our author guide on www.packtpub.com/authors.

Customer support

Now that you are the proud owner of a Packt book, we have a number of things to help you to get the most from your purchase.

Downloading the example code

You can download the example code files for all Packt books you have purchased from your account at http://www.packtpub.com. If you purchased this book elsewhere, you can visit http://www.packtpub.com/support and register to have the files e-mailed directly to you.

Errata

Although we have taken every care to ensure the accuracy of our content, mistakes do happen. If you find a mistake in one of our books—maybe a mistake in the text or the code—we would be grateful if you would report this to us. By doing so, you can save other readers from frustration and help us improve subsequent versions of this book. If you find any errata, please report them by visiting http://www.packtpub.com/submit-errata, selecting your book, clicking on the **errata submission form** link, and entering the details of your errata. Once your errata are verified, your submission will be accepted and the errata will be uploaded on our website, or added to any list of existing errata, under the Errata section of that title. Any existing errata can be viewed by selecting your title from http://www.packtpub.com/support.

Piracy

Piracy of copyright material on the Internet is an ongoing problem across all media. At Packt, we take the protection of our copyright and licenses very seriously. If you come across any illegal copies of our works, in any form, on the Internet, please provide us with the location address or website name immediately so that we can pursue a remedy.

Please contact us at copyright@packtpub.com with a link to the suspected pirated material.

We appreciate your help in protecting our authors, and our ability to bring you valuable content.

Questions

You can contact us at questions@packtpub.com if you are having a problem with any aspect of the book, and we will do our best to address it.

1
Understanding the Basics of Backup and Recovery

The constant evolution of IT has, among other things, affected the role of a database administrator (DBA). Today the DBA is not merely a Database Administrator anymore, but is morphing more into the Database Architect role. If you want to become a successful DBA and be more competitive in the market, you should have a different skill set than what was normally required in the past. You need to have a wide range of understanding in architectural design, network, storage, licensing, and much more. The more knowledge you have, the better opportunities you will find.

The main idea of this chapter is to introduce you to some basic concepts regarding backup and recovery, giving you a general overview of the most important methods and tools available for you to achieve your backup goals. Therefore, in this chapter, we will cover the following topics:

- Understanding the need for creating backups
- Getting familiar with the different backup types
- An overview of backup strategy
- Understanding what is redo and how it affects your database recoverability
- Understanding database operational modes and redo generation

Purpose of backup and recovery

As a DBA, you are the person responsible for recovering the data and guarding the business continuity of your organization. Consequently, you have the key responsibility for developing, deploying, and managing an efficient backup and recovery strategy for your institution or clients that will allow them to easily recover from any possible disastrous situation. Remember, data is one of the most important assets a company can have. Most organizations would not survive after the loss of this important asset.

Testing backups

It's incredible how many corporations around the world do not have a proper **disaster recovery plan** (DRP) in place, and what is worse, many DBAs never even test their backups. Most of the time when auditing Oracle environments for clients, I ask the following question to the DBA team:

- Are you 100 percent sure that you can trust your backups? For this question I generally receive answers like:

    ◦ I'm not 100 percent sure since we do not recover from backups too often

    ◦ We do not test our backups, and so I cannot guarantee the recoverability of them

Another good question is the following:

- Do you know how long a full recovery of your database will take? Common responses to this question are:

    ◦ Probably anything between 6 and 12 hours

    ◦ I don't know, because I've never done a full recovery of my database

As you can see, a simple implementation of a procedure to proactively test the backups randomly will allow you to:

- **Test your backups and ensure that they are valid and recoverable**: I have been called several times to help clients because their current backups are not viable. Once I was called to help a client and discovered that their backup-to-disk starts every night at 10 P.M. and ends at 2 A.M. Afterwards, the backup files are copied to a tape by a system administrator every morning at 4 A.M. The problem here was that when this process was implemented, the database size was only 500 GB, but after few months, the size of the database had grown to over 1 TB. Consequently, the backup that was initially finishing before 2 A.M. was now finishing at 5 A.M., but the copy to a tape was still being triggered at 4 A.M. by the system administrator. As a result, all backups to a tape were unusable.

- **Know your recovery process in detail**: If you test your backups, you will have the knowledge to answer questions regarding how long a full recovery will take. Answering that your full recovery will take around three and a half hours, but you prefer to say five hours just in case of any unexpected problem that you will come across, you will look more professional. This will let me know that you really know what you are talking about.

- **Document and improve your recovery process**: The complete process needs to be documented. If the process is documented and you also allow your team to practice on a rotation basis, this will ensure that they are familiar with the course of action and will have all the knowledge necessary to know what to do in case of a disaster. You will now be able to rest in your home at night without being disturbed, because now you are not the only person in the team with the experience required to perform this important task.

Good for you if you have a solid backup and recovery plan in place. But have you tested that plan? Have you verified your ability to recover?

Protecting data

As being the main person responsible for the recovery and availability of the data, you need to have a full understanding of how to protect your data against all possible situations you could come across in your daily job. The most common situations you could see are:

- Media failure
- Hardware failure
- Human error
- Application error

Let's take a closer look at each of these situations.

Media failure

Media failure occurs when a system is unable to write or read from a physical storage device such a disk or a tape due to a defect on the recording surface. This kind of failure can be easily overcome by ensuring that your data is saved on more than one disk (mirrored) using a solution such as **RAID (Redundant Array of Independent Disks)** or **ASM (Automatic Storage Management)**. In the case of tapes, ensure that your backups are saved in more than one tape and as mentioned earlier, testing the recoverability from them.

Hardware failure

Hardware failure is when a failure occurs on a physical component of your hardware such as when your server motherboard, CPU, or any other component stops working. To overcome this kind of situation, you will need to have a high availability solution in place as part of your disaster and recovery strategy. This could include solutions such as Oracle RAC, a standby database, or even replacement hardware on the premises. If you are using Oracle Standard Edition or Standard Edition One and need to implement a proper standby database solution, I will recommend you to take a closer look at the Dbvisit Standby solution for Oracle databases that is currently available in the market to allow you to fulfill this need (http://dbvisit.com).

Human error

Human error, also known as user error, is when a user interacting directly or through an application causes damage to the data stored in the database or to the database itself. The most frequent examples of human error involve changing or deleting data and even files by mistake. It is likely that this kind of error is the greatest single cause of database downtime in a company.

No one is immune to user error. Even an experienced DBA or system administrator can delete a redo log file that has the extension .log as a mistake when taking it as a simple log file to be deleted to release space. Fortunately, user error can most of the time be solved by using physical backups, logical backups, and even Oracle Flashback technology.

Application error

An application error happens when a software malfunction causes data corruption in the logical or physical levels. A bug in the code can easily damage data or even corrupt a data block. This kind of problem can be solved using Oracle block media recovery, and is why it is so important to have a proper test done prior to promoting an application change to any production environment.

Always do a backup before and after a change is implemented in a production environment. A before backup will allow you to roll back to the previous state in case something goes wrong. An after backup will protect you to avoid to redo the change in case of a failure, due that it was not included in the previous backup available.

Types of backup

Now that you understand all types of possible failures that could affect your database, let's take a closer look at the definition of backup and the types of backups that are available to ensure the recoverability of our data.

A backup is a real and consistent copy of data from a database that could be used to reconstruct the data after an incident. Consequently, there are two different types of backups available, which are:

- Physical backups
- Logical backups

A physical backup

A physical backup is a copy of all the physical database files that are required to perform the recovery of a database. These include datafiles, control files, parameter files, and archived redo log files. As an Oracle DBA, we have different options to make a physical backup of our database. Backups can be taken using user-managed backup techniques or using **Recovery Manager** (**RMAN**). Both techniques will be discussed in more detail later in this book. Physical backups are the foundation of any serious backup and recovery strategy.

A logical backup

Oracle uses Oracle Data Pump to allow us to generate a logical backup that can be used to migrate data or even do a partial or full recovery of our database. The utilities available are the Data Pump Export program (expdp) and the Data Pump Import program (impdp).

Many people have a misconception of these tools in thinking that they can only be used to move data. Data Pump is a very flexible and powerful tool that if well utilized can easily become a DBA's best friend. It is not just for moving data. It can also play a crucial role in your backup and recovery strategy.

Chapter 9, *Understanding Data Pump* and *Chapter 10*, *Advanced Data Pump* will go into more detail about the use of Data Pump for logical backup and recovery.

The old Import and Export utilities

In the previous versions of Oracle we used to work with similar utilities called `exp` and `imp`. The `exp` utility is deprecated since Oracle 11*g*, but the `imp` utility is still currently supported by Oracle. The `imp` utility allows us to recover any backup generated by the old `exp` program. Just keep in mind that the use of `exp` is not supported anymore by Oracle and using it can bring future trouble to your environment.

Backup strategies

A backup and recovery strategy has the main purpose of protecting a database against data loss, and this document will contain all steps required to reconstruct the database after a disaster strikes. As the person responsible for the data of your company, it is very important to have a correct backup strategy in place to allow you to recover from any possible disaster.

Before you create a strategy, you will need to understand clearly all the **Service Level Agreements** (**SLAs**) in place with in your organization regarding this topic. To that end, you will need to ask some simple questions to the owners of the data:

- How much data can the company lose in case of a disaster? (RPO)
- How much time could the business wait to have the data restored and available again? (RTO)
- How much will it cost the company for the loss of one hour of data?
- What retention periods are required by law for the company data?

After receiving the answers to all these questions, you will be able to implement a proper backup and recovery strategy according to your real company needs and SLAs in place.

For example, if your company can only afford to lose three hours of data (RPO) but it can have the database down for up to 24 hours for a recovery process (RTO), all you will need to do to fulfill your SLA is to have a full backup of your database made daily. You will also need to make backups of all your archive logs every three hours to a tape or another network location to allow you to have all your data protected.

As part of creating a strategy, it is important to properly understand the concepts known as **Recovery Point Objective (RPO)** and **Recovery Time Objective (RTO)**. As you can see in the following figure, the RPO reflects how much data might be lost without incurring a significant risk or loss to the business, and the RTO is basically the maximum amount of time allowed to reestablish the service after an incident without affecting the company seriously.

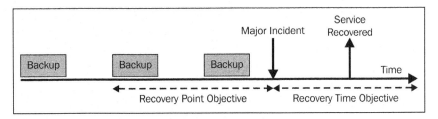

Restore versus recovery

On several occasions, people have asked me about the differences between *restore* and *recovery*. Due to these questions, I will take this opportunity to explain the difference in some simple words to make it clear:

- **Restore**: It is the act that involves the restoration of all files that will be required to recover your database to a consistent state, for example, copying all backup files from a secondary location such as tape or storage to your stage area
- **Recovery**: It is the process to apply all transactions recorded in your archive logs, rolling your database forward to a point-in-time or until the last transaction recorded is applied, thus recovering your database to the point-in-time you need

You will see some examples of how restore and recovery work later in this book. Now let's take a closer look at what is redo log and the two possible modes your database could be operating in. This will help you understand in a bit more in depth what type of backup and recovery you could use on your environment.

What is redo?

Let's look briefly at the redo process. When Oracle blocks (the smallest unit of storage in a database) are changed, including UNDO blocks, Oracle records the changes in the form of vector changes, which are referred to as redo entries or redo records. The changes are written by the server process to the redo log buffer in the **System Global Area (SGA)**. The redo log buffer will then be flushed into the online redo logs in near real-time fashion by the **log writer (LGWR)** process (if the redo log buffer is too small, then you will start seeing log buffer space waits during bursts of redo generation).

The redo entries are written by the LGWR to a disk when:

- A user issues a commit
- The log buffer is one third full
- The amount of unwritten redo entries is 1 MB
- When a database checkpoint takes place
- Otherwise every three seconds

Redo entries are written to disk when one of the situations mentioned take place first. In the event of a checkpoint, the redo entries are written before the checkpoint to ensure recoverability.

Redo log files record changes to the database as a result of transactions and internal Oracle server actions. Redo log files protect the database from loss of integrity due to system failures caused by power outages, disk failures, and so on. Redo log files must be multiplexed using different disks (use of fast disk is preferred) to ensure that the information stored in them is not lost in the event of a disk failure.

The redo log consists of groups of redo log files. A group consists of a redo log file and its multiplexed copies. Each identical copy is said to be a member of that group, and each group is identified by a number. The LGWR process writes redo records from the redo log buffer to all members of a redo log group until the file is filled or a log switch operation is requested. Then, it switches and writes to the files in the next group. Redo log groups are used in a circular fashion as shown in the following figure:

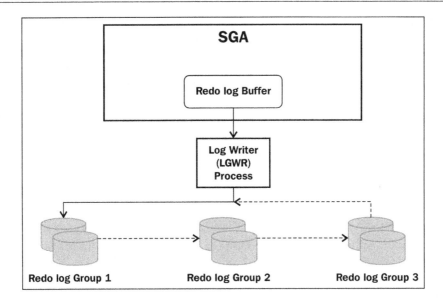

Redo log Group 1   Redo log Group 2   Redo log Group 3

 Redo log groups need to have at least two files per group, with the files distributed on separate disks or controllers so that no single disk failure destroys an entire log group. Also, never rely exclusively on your ASM disk group or the file system if they have mirrored disks underneath. Remember that mirroring will not protect your database in the event of your online redo log file being deleted or corrupted.

The loss of an entire log group is one of the most serious possible media failures you can come across because it can result in loss of data. The loss of a single member within a multiple-member log group is trivial and does not affect database operation, other than causing an alert to be published in the alert log.

Remember that redo logs heavily influence database performance because a commit cannot be completed until the transaction information has been written to the logs. You must place your redo log files on your fastest disks served by your fastest controllers. If possible, do not place any other database files on the same disks as your redo log files.

 It's not advisable to place members of different groups on the same disk. That's because the archiving process reads the online redo log files and will end up competing with the LGWR process.

As a resume about redo log files and redo log groups, it is important always to:

- Have a minimum of three redo log groups. If your database switches too often and you do not have an appropriate number of redo log groups, the LGWR process will need to wait until the next group is available before being able to overwrite it.

- All online redo logs and standby redo logs are equal in size.

- Tune your redo log files size to allow redo log switches to happen at no less than 20 minutes from each other at peak times.

- Remember to place the redo log files on high performance disks.

- Remember to have a minimum of two redo log members per group to reduce risk, and place them in different disks away from the data.

- Do not multiplex standby redo logs to prevent additional writes in the redo transport.

Remember as mentioned earlier that it is important to note that not all Oracle databases will have the archive process enabled.

Redo generation and recoverability

The purpose of redo generation is to ensure recoverability. This is the reason why Oracle does not give the DBA a lot of control over redo generation. If the instance crashes, then all the changes within the SGA will be lost. Oracle will then use the redo entries in the online redo log files to bring the database to a consistent state. The cost of maintaining the redo log records is an expensive operation involving latch management operations (CPU) and frequent write access to the redo log files (I/O). You can avoid redo logging for certain operations using the NOLOGGING feature. We will talk more about the NOLOGGING feature in *Chapter 2, NOLOGGING Operations*.

The NOARCHIVELOG mode

When your database is created by default, it will be created using the NOARCHIVELOG mode. This mode permits any normal database operations but will not provide your database with the capability to perform any point-in-time recovery operations or online backups of your database.

When the database is using this mode, no hot backup is possible (hot backup is any backup done with the database open, causing no interruption for the users). You will only be able to perform backups with your database down (shutdown, also known as the offline backup or the cold backup), and you will only be able to perform a full recovery up to the point that your backup was made. You can see in the following example what will happen if you try to make a hot backup of your database when in the NOARCHIVELOG mode:

```
SQL> SELECT log_mode FROM v$database;


LOG_MODE
------------
NOARCHIVELOG


SQL> ALTER DATABASE BEGIN BACKUP;
ALTER DATABASE BEGIN BACKUP
*
ERROR at line 1:
ORA-01123: cannot start online backup; media recovery not enabled
```

The error shown in the preceding code is the result you will receive after trying to place your database in backup mode to make a hot backup of your database files. The example to follow shows the result you will receive when trying to make a backup of your open database when in the NOARCHIVELOG mode using RMAN. As you can see, neither approach is possible:

```
RMAN> BACKUP DATABASE;


Starting backup at 04-DEC-12
using target database control file instead of recovery catalog
allocated channel: ORA_DISK_1
channel ORA_DISK_1: SID=36 device type=DISK
channel ORA_DISK_1: starting full datafile backup set
channel ORA_DISK_1: specifying datafile(s) in backup set
RMAN-03009: failure of backup command on ORA_DISK_1 channel at
12/04/2012 15:32:42
ORA-19602: cannot backup or copy active file in NOARCHIVELOG mode
continuing other job steps, job failed will not be re-run
channel ORA_DISK_1: starting full datafile backup set
channel ORA_DISK_1: specifying datafile(s) in backup set
including current control file in backup set
including current SPFILE in backup set
```

```
channel ORA_DISK_1: starting piece 1 at 04-DEC-12
channel ORA_DISK_1: finished piece 1 at 04-DEC-12
piece handle=/home/oracle/app/oracle/flash_recovery_area/ORCL/
backupset/201
2_12_04/o1_mf_ncsnf_TAG20121204T153241_8cx20wfz_.bkp
tag=TAG20121204T153241 comment=NONE
channel ORA_DISK_1: backup set complete, elapsed time: 00:00:01
RMAN-00571: ===========================================================
RMAN-00569: =========== ERROR MESSAGE STACK FOLLOWS ===============
RMAN-00571: ===========================================================

RMAN-03009: failure of backup command on ORA_DISK_1 channel at
12/04/2012 15:32:42
ORA-19602: cannot backup or copy active file in NOARCHIVELOG mode
```

Downloading the example code

You can download the example code files for all Packt books you have purchased from your account at http://www.packtpub.com. If you purchased this book elsewhere, you can visit http://www.packtpub.com/support and register to have the files e-mailed directly to you.

To make a full backup of your database when in the NOARCHIVELOG mode, you will need to:

1. First shut down your database completely in a consistent mode.
2. Backup all your datafiles, parameter files, a control file, and your redo logs manually to a tape or a different location.
3. Re-start your database.

If a recovery is required, all you will need to do is to restore all files from your last backup and start the database, but you need to understand that all transactions made in the database after your backup will be lost.

The ARCHIVELOG mode

Oracle lets you save filled redo log files to one or more offline destinations to improve the recoverability of your data by having all transactions saved in case of a crash, reducing any possibility of data loss. The copy of the redo log file containing transactions against your database made to a different location is known as an ARCHIVELOG file, and the process of turning redo log files into archived redo log files is called archiving.

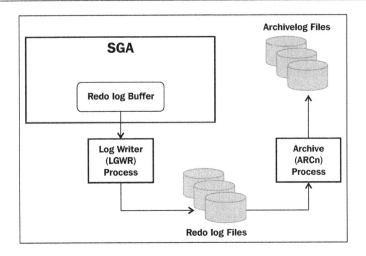

Understanding the ARCHIVELOG mode

An archived redo log file is a physical copy of one of the filled members of a redo log group. Remember that redo log files are cyclical files that are overwritten by the Oracle database and are only archived (backup copy of the file before being overwritten) when the database is in the ARCHIVELOG mode. Each redo log file includes all redo entries and the unique log sequence number of the identical member of the redo log group. To make this point more clear, if you are multiplexing your redo log file (recommended to a minimum of two members per group), and if your redo log group 1 contains two identical member files such as redolog_1a.rdo and redolog_1b.rdo, then the archive process (ARCn) will only archive one of these member files, not both. If redo log file redolog_1a.rdo becomes corrupted, then the ARCn process will still be able to archive the identical surviving redo log file redolog_1b.rdo. The archived redo log generated by the ARCn process will contain a copy of every group created since you enabled archiving in your database.

When the database is running in the ARCHIVELOG mode, the LGWR process cannot reuse and hence overwrite a given redo log group until it has been archived. This is to ensure the recoverability of your data. The background process ARCn will automate the archiving operation and the database will start multiple archive processes as necessary (the default number of processes is four) to ensure that the archiving of filled redo log files does not fall behind.

You can use archived redo logs to:

- Recover a database
- Update and keep a standby database in sync with a primary database
- Get information about the history of a database using the LogMiner utility

In the ARCHIVELOG mode, the Oracle Database engine will make copies of all online redo log files via an internal process called ARCn. This process will generate archive copies of your redo log files to one or more archive log destination directories. The number and location of destination directories will depend on your database initialization parameters.

To use the ARCHIVELOG mode, you will need to first set up some configuration parameters. Once your database is in the ARCHIVELOG mode, all database activity regarding your transactions will be archived to allow your data recoverability and you will need to ensure that your archival destination area always has enough space available. If space runs out, your database will suspend all activities until it becomes able once again to back up your redo log files in the archival destination. This behavior happens to ensure the recoverability of your database.

Never use the extension .log for redo log files. As mentioned earlier, use a different extension such as, for example, .rdo. This is because anyone, including you, can delete .log files by mistake when running out of space.

Preparing for the ARCHIVELOG mode

When setting your database to work in the ARCHIVELOG mode, please never forget to:

1. Configure your database in a proper way. Some examples of what to do when configuring a database are:

   ○ **Read the Oracle documentation**: It's always important to follow Oracle recommendations in the documentation.

   ○ **Have a minimum of three control files**: This will reduce the risk of losing a control file.

   ○ **Set the** CONTROL_FILE_RECORD_KEEP_TIME **initialization parameter to an acceptable value**: Doing so will set the number of days before a reusable record in the control file can be reused. It will also control the period of time that your backup information will be stored in the control file.

   ○ **Configure the size of redo log files and groups appropriately**: If not configured properly, the Oracle Database engine will generate constant checkpoints that will create a high load on the buffer cache and I/O system affecting the performance of your database. Also, having few redo log files in a system will force the LGWR process to wait for the ARCn process to finish before overwriting a redo log file.

- ○ **Multiplex online redo log files**: Do this to reduce the risk of losing an online redo log file.

- ○ **Enable block checksums**: This will allow the Oracle Database engine to detect corrupted situations.

- ○ **Enable database block checking**: This allows Oracle to perform block checking for corruption, but be aware that it can cause overhead in most applications depending on workload and the parameter value.

- ○ **Log checkpoints to the alert log**: Doing so helps you determine whether checkpoints are occurring at a desired frequency.

- ○ **Use fast-start fault recovery feature**: This is used to reduce the time required for cache recovery. The parameter FAST_START_MTTR_TARGET is the one to look over here.

- ○ **Use Oracle restart**: This is used to enhance the availability of a single instance (non-RAC) and its components.

- ○ **Never use the extension** .log **for redo log files**: As mentioned earlier, anyone including you, can delete .log files by mistake when running out of space.

- ○ **Use block change tracking**: This is used to allow incremental backups to run to completion more quickly than otherwise.

2. Always be sure to have enough available space in the archival destination.

3. Always make sure that everything is working as it is supposed to be working. Never forget to implement a proactive monitoring strategy using scripts or Oracle Enterprise Manager (OEM). Some important areas to check are:

   - ○ Database structure integrity
   - ○ Data block integrity
   - ○ Redo integrity
   - ○ Undo segment integrity
   - ○ Transaction integrity
   - ○ Dictionary integrity

Checking the status of the ARCHIVELOG mode

You can determine which mode or if archiving, is being used in your instance by issuing an SQL query to the `log_mode` field in the `v$database` (`ARCHIVELOG` indicates archiving is enabled and `NOARCHIVELOG` indicates that archiving is not enabled) or by issuing the SQL `archive log list` command:

```
SQL> SELECT log_mode FROM v$database;


LOG_MODE
-------------------
ARCHIVELOG


SQL> archive log list

Database log mode              Archive Mode
Automatic archival             Enabled
Archive destination            USE_DB_RECOVERY_FILE_DEST
Oldest online log sequence     8
Next log sequence to archive   10
Current log sequence           10
```

Specifying parameters

When in the `ARCHIVELOG` mode, you can choose between generating archive redo logs to a single location or multiplexing them. The most important parameters you need to be familiar with when setting your database to work in this mode are:

- `LOG_ARCHIVE_DEST_n`: Use this parameter to specify from one to ten different archival locations (*n* can be a number between 1 and 10).

- `LOG_ARCHIVE_FORMAT`: This parameter will specify the default filename format when archiving the redo log files. The following variables can be used to format the file:
    - `%s` — log sequence number
    - `%S` — log sequence number, zero filled

- ○ %t — thread number
- ○ %T — thread number, zero filled
- ○ %a — activation ID
- ○ %d — database ID
- ○ %r — resetlogs ID

One example of how to make use of these parameters could be something like this: `alter system set log_archive_format="orcl_%s_%t_%r.arc" scope=spfile`. This command will create archive log files with a name that will contain the word `"orcl"` that is the database ID, the log sequence number, the thread number, and the resetlogs ID.

- LOG_ARCHIVE_MIN_SUCCEED_DEST: This defines the minimum number of archival destinations that must succeed in order to allow a redo log file to be overwritten

Viewing the status of archival destinations

You can also check the status of your archival destinations by querying the V$ARCHIVE_DEST view, in which the following variable characteristics will determine the status:

- **Valid/Invalid**: This indicates whether the disk location or service name specified is valid or not
- **Enabled/Disabled**: This indicates the availability state of the location and if the database can use it
- **Active/Inactive**: This indicates whether there was a problem accessing the destination

The **FRA** (called **Flashback Recovery Area** before Oracle 11*g* R2, and now called **Fast Recovery Area**) is a disk location in which the database can store and manage all files related to backup and recovery operations. Flashback database provides a very efficient mechanism to rollback any unwanted database change. We will talk in more depth about FRA and Flashback database in *Chapter 4, User Managed Backup and Recovery*.

Placing a database into the ARCHIVELOG mode

Now let's take a look at a very popular example that you can use to place your database in the ARCHIVELOG mode, and use the FRA as a secondary location for the archive log files. To achieve all this you will need to:

1. Set up the size of your FRA to be used by your database. You can do this by using the command:
   ```
   SQL> ALTER SYSTEM SET DB_RECOVERY_FILE_DEST_SIZE=<M/G>
   SCOPE=both;
   ```

2. Specify the location of the FRA using the command:
   ```
   SQL> ALTER SYSTEM SET DB_RECOVERY_FILE_DEST=
   '/u01/app/oracle/fast_recovery_area' scope=both;
   ```

3. Define your archive log destination area using the command:
   ```
   SQL> ALTER SYSTEM SET log_archive_dest_1=
   'LOCATION=/DB/u02/backups/archivelog' scope=both;
   ```

4. Define your secondary archive log area to use the FRA with the command:
   ```
   SQL> ALTER SYSTEM SET log_archive_dest_10=
   'LOCATION=USE_DB_RECOVERY_FILE_DEST';
   ```

5. Shutdown your database using the command:
   ```
   SQL> SHUTDOWN IMMEDIATE
   ```

6. Start your database in mount mode using the command:
   ```
   SQL> STARTUP MOUNT
   ```

7. Switch your database to use the ARCHIVELOG mode using the command:
   ```
   SQL> ALTER DATABASE ARCHIVELOG;
   ```

8. Then finally open your database using the command:
   ```
   SQL> ALTER DATABASE OPEN;
   ```

When in the ARCHIVELOG mode, you are able to make hot backups using RMAN. You are able to perform some user-managed backups using the alter database begin backup command (used to allow you to make a consistent backup of your entire database files). You may also use the alter tablespace <Tablespace_Name> begin backup command to make a backup of all datafiles associated to a tablespace.

Now that you know everything you are supposed to know about the ARCHIVELOG mode, let's take a deeper look in what is redo and why it is so important to the recoverability of our database.

Differences between redo and undo

Another common question relates to the difference between redo log entries and undo information saved as part of transaction management. While redo and undo data sound almost like they could be used for the same purpose, such is not the case. The following table spells out the differences:

	undo	**redo**
Record of	how to undo a change	how to reproduce a change
Used for	rollback, read-consistency	rolling forward database changes
Stored in	undo segments	redo log files
Protect Against	inconsistent reads in multiuser systems	data loss

In the end, an undo segment is just a segment like any other (such as a table, an index, a hash cluster, or a materialized view). The important point here is in the name, and the main rule you need to understand is that if you modify part of a segment (any segment, regardless of its type), you must generate redo so that the change can be recovered in the event of a media or instance failure. Therefore, if you modify the table EMPLOYEE, the changes made to the EMPLOYEE blocks are recorded in the redo log buffer, and consequently to the redo log files (and archive log files if running in the ARCHIVELOG mode). The changes made to EMPLOYEE also have to be recorded in UNDO because you might change your mind and want to rollback the transaction before issuing a commit to confirm the changes made. Therefore, the modification to the table EMPLOYEE causes entries to be made in an undo segment, but this is a modification to a segment as well. Therefore, the changes made to the undo segment also have to be recorded in the redo log buffer to protect your data integrity in case of a disaster.

If your database crashes and you need to restore a set of datafiles from five days ago, including those for the UNDO tablespace, Oracle will start reading from your archived redo, rolling the five day old files forward in time until they were four, then three, then two, then one. This will happen until the recovery process gets to the time where the only record of the changes to segments (any segment) was contained in the current online redo log file, and now that you have used the redo log entries to roll the data forward until all changes to all segments that had ever been recorded in the redo, have been applied. At this point, your undo segments have been repopulated and the database will start rolling back those transactions which were recorded in the redo log, but which weren't committed at the time of the database failure.

I can't emphasize enough, really, that undo segments are just slightly special tables. They're fundamentally not very different than any other tables in the database such as EMPLOYEE or DEPARTMENT, except that any new inserts into these tables can overwrite a previous record, which never happens to a table like EMPLOYEE, of course. If you generate undo when making an update to EMPLOYEE, you will consequently generate redo. This means that every time undo is generated, redo will also be generated (this is the key point to understand here).

Oracle Database stores the before and after image in redo because redo is written and generated sequentially and isn't cached for a long period of time in memory (as mentioned in the *What is redo* section in this chapter). Hence, using redo to rollback a mere mistake, or even a change of mind, while theoretically possible, would involve wading through huge amounts of redo sequentially, looking for the before image in a sea of changes made by different transactions, and all of these will be done by reading data off disk to memory as a normal recovery process. UNDO, on the other hand, is stored in the buffer cache (just as the table EMPLOYEE is stored in the buffer cache), so there's a good chance that reading the information needed will require only logical I/O and not physical. Your transaction will also be dynamically pointed to where it's written in UNDO, so you and your transaction can jump straight to where your UNDO is, without having to navigate through a sea of undo generated by all other transactions.

In summary, you need redo for recovery operations and undo for consistency in multiuser environments and to rollback any changes of mind. This in my personal opinion, is one of the key points that makes Oracle superior to any other database in the market. Other databases merely have transaction logs which serve both purposes, and suffer in performance and flexibility terms accordingly.

Facing excessive redo generation during an online backup?

One of the most common questions I see on the **Oracle Technology Network (OTN)** forums is why so much redo is generated during an online backup operation. When a tablespace is put in the backup mode, the redo generation behavior changes but there is not excessive redo generated. There is additional information logged into the online redo log file during a hot backup the first time a block is modified in a tablespace that is in the hot backup mode. In other words, as long as the tablespace is in the backup mode, Oracle will write the entire block to disk, but later it generates the same redo. This is done due as Oracle cannot guarantee that a block was not copied while it was being updated as part of the backup.

In the hot backup mode, only two things are different:

- The first time a block is changed in a datafile that is in the hot backup mode, the entire block is written to the redo log file, and not just the changed bytes. This is because you can get into a situation in which the process copying the datafile and the **database writer** (**DBWR**) are working on the same block simultaneously. Hence, the entire block image is logged so that during recovery, the block is totally rewritten from redo and is consistent with itself.

- The datafile headers which contain the **System Change Number** (**SCN**) of the last completed checkpoint are *not* updated while a file is in the hot backup mode. The DBWR process constantly writes to the datafiles during the hot backup. The SCN recorded in the header tells us how far back in the redo stream one needs to go to recover the file.

To limit the effect of this additional logging, you should ensure to place only one tablespace at a time in the backup mode and bring the tablespace out of the backup mode as soon as you have finished backing it up. This will reduce the number of blocks that may have to be logged to the least possible.

Summary

In this chapter, we refreshed some very important topics regarding backup and recovery basics. We started with understanding the purpose of backup and recovery, all the way to types of backups and the differences between redo and undo. If you are still a little confused about some of these topics, don't worry as most of them will be explained in more detail in the following chapters of this book.

In the next chapter, we will see in more depth why redo is so important to the recoverability of our data, why the NOLOGGING operations can be dangerous, and how to use them.

2
NOLOGGING Operations

You could be asking yourself why I want to talk about NOLOGGING operations in a backup and recovery book. The answer is simple: NOLOGGING operations will affect the recoverability of a database and due to this, it is very important for a DBA to understand this concept. It is the most visited topic on my blog `www.oraclenz.org`.

Many DBAs and developers use NOLOGGING operations when doing bulk inserts and massive deletion of data to reduce redo generation but many do not know that these statements will always generate redo, in other words, `UPDATE` or `DELETE` will always be logged. Later in this chapter, we will see some techniques that will reduce redo generation for massive updates and deletes.

In this chapter, we will cover the following topics:

- LOGGING versus NOLOGGING
- Disabling redo generation
- NOLOGGING operations
- How to reduce redo generation
- Redo log wait events
- Practice with some interesting scripts

NOLOGGING operations do not generate redo records in the redo log files (only a notification that a NOLOGGING operation was made is registered, but not the changes). Consequently, such operations are a very helpful option to reduce the amount of redo to be generated in a transaction, which might make the transaction run faster and also reduce any unnecessary stress on the database.

You need to understand that NOLOGGING operations are direct path—they bypass the buffer cache. If you direct path load say 100 MB of data and that all fits in the buffer cache—a conventional path load might be much faster than a non-logged direct path load (you don't want the blocks to be written to disk and the redo streamed to disk in the background by the LGWR process).

On the other hand, if you are loading gigabytes of data, more than what can be buffered in the cache, then you might benefit from direct path writes since you'd be waiting for the DBWR process to empty the cache.

However, a problem arises due to misconceptions in the use of these operations. In particular, many people forget that NOLOGGING operations will affect the recoverability of the database.

Also it's incredible how many questions I receive regarding this topic when speaking at conferences or when connected in forums and technical chats. Some of the main questions I hear all the time are:

- Does creating a table with the `NOLOGGING` option mean there is no generation of redo ever, or just that the initial creation operation has no redo generation, but does that DML down the road generate redo?
- How and when can the `NOLOGGING` option be employed?

All these questions and many more will be answered as this chapter develops.

You need to remember that redo generation is a crucial part of the Oracle recovery mechanism. NOLOGGING operations only affect the recovery from a media failure perspective (due that you then will need to recover from a backup and apply all the available archive logs in the recover process), but will not affect a database in case of an instance failure. On the other hand, excessive generation of redo is the result of an excessive workload of update, insert, and DML operations in the database.

 A very important rule with respect to data is to never put yourself into an unrecoverable situation. The importance of this guideline cannot be stressed enough, but it does not mean that you can never use time saving or performance enhancing options.

LOGGING versus NOLOGGING

Despite the importance of the redo entries, Oracle gives users the ability to limit redo generation on tables, partitions, tablespaces, and indexes by setting them in the NOLOGGING mode. NOLOGGING affects the recoverability of a database and before going into how to limit the redo generation, it is important to clear the misunderstanding that NOLOGGING is the way out of redo generation.
The following are some interesting points regarding this topic:

- NOLOGGING is designed to handle bulk inserts of data which can be easily reproduced. (Remember that the UPDATE and DELETE operations will always be logged.)

- Regardless of the LOGGING status, writing to the UNDO blocks will always cause generation of redo.

- LOGGING should not be disabled on a primary database if it has one or more standby databases. For this reason, Oracle introduced the ALTER DATABASE FORCE LOGGING command to place the database in the FORCE LOGGING mode—meaning that the NOLOGGING attribute will not have any effect on the segments. The FORCE LOGGING mode can also be used at the tablespace level using the ALTER TABLESPACE <Tablespace_Name> FORCE LOGGING command. Use of this option results in some performance degradation, but ensures the recoverability of your primary database and the integrity of your standby database.

 Using FORCE LOGGING in the initialization parameter file in a **Multitenant Container Database** will always place all the pluggable databases using that **CDB** in the FORCE LOGGING mode.

- Any change to the database dictionary will always cause redo generation. This will happen to protect the data dictionary integrity. For example, if Oracle allocates a space above the **high water mark (HWM)** for a table, and the system fails in the middle of an INSERT /*+ APPEND */ command, then Oracle will need to rollback the data dictionary change that was made. There will be a redo generated, but it is only to protect the data dictionary, not your newly inserted data (Oracle will undo the space allocation if it fails, and your newly inserted data will also disappear).

- Objects should be set back to the LOGGING mode when the NOLOGGING mode is no longer required.

- NOLOGGING is unnecessary for direct path inserts if the database is in the NOARCHIVELOG mode (see the following table).

- Operations involving data that cannot be easily reproduced should always use LOGGING operations; avoid NOLOGGING in such cases! If data is loaded using NOLOGGING, the data will not be able to be recovered in a situation of media recovery if no backup is made after the load.

- NOLOGGING does not apply to normal UPDATE, DELETE, and INSERT operations.

- NOLOGGING will work during specific situations only, but subsequent DML operations over the data will always generate redo (we will see a list of the specific commands that will work in the NOLOGGING mode a little bit later in this chapter).

- If the LOGGING or NOLOGGING clause is not specified when creating a table, partition, or index, the default to the LOGGING attribute will be the LOGGING attribute of the database, or if not set, the tablespace in which it resides.

Table Mode	Insert Mode	Archive Log Mode	Result
LOGGING	APPEND	ARCHIVELOG	REDO GENERATED
NOLOGGING	APPEND	ARCHIVELOG	NO REDO
LOGGING	NOAPPEND	ARCHIVELOG	REDO GENERATED
NOLOGGING	NOAPPEND	ARCHIVELOG	REDO GENERATED
LOGGING	APPEND	NOARCHIVELOG	NO REDO
NOLOGGING	APPEND	NOARCHIVELOG	NO REDO
LOGGING	NOAPPEND	NOARCHIVELOG	REDO GENERATED
NOLOGGING	NOAPPEND	NOARCHIVELOG	REDO GENERATED

 When doing the insert mode APPEND, it isn't APPEND really, it is the fact that you are doing a direct path operation that will bypass undo (hence reducing redo) and may bypass redo when in NOLOGGING.

Only a few operations cannot make use of the NOLOGGING mode benefits. They are:

- Table redefinition cannot be done in NOLOGGING, in other words, it will need to be in the LOGGING mode and will always generate redo.

- Temp files are always set to the NOLOGGING mode, but any non-direct path operation on them such as INSERT/UPDATE/DELETE will generate redo since they do generate undo.

In Oracle 12*c*, temporary tables record their undo into temp, removing all redo!

 Always remember to do a backup of your database after a NOLOGGING operation is made.

The database mode FORCE LOGGING (introduced with 9*i* R2) when set is a persistent attribute for the database (initialization parameter), meaning that the NOLOGGING operations will not have any effect if used. If the database is shut down and restarted, it remains in the same logging mode state (FORCE LOGGING).

 FORCE LOGGING only needs to be configured again if a control file is re-created.

If your database has a physical or logical standby database and is not set in the FORCE LOGGING mode, then NOLOGGING operations in the primary database will render data blocks in the standby database to become *logically corrupt* because of the missing redo log entries. If the standby database ever switches to the primary role, errors will occur when trying to access data in objects that were previously written with the NOLOGGING option. In this case, you will see an error like the following:

```
ORA-01578: ORACLE data block corrupted (file # 3, block # 2527)
ORA-01110: data file 1: '/u1/oracle/dbs/stdby/tbs_nologging_1.dbf'
ORA-26040: Data block was loaded using the NOLOGGING option"
```

This doesn't sound good and I certainly can't imagine a happy DBA when called at 3:00 A.M. if this kind of error message has come up.

 A DBA can then move the datafiles over to the standby, manually making it consistent. People do this all of the time for massive loads or re-orgs to avoid generating, shipping, and applying a ton of redo; it is easier to just move the datafiles.

You can check if your database is using the FORCE LOGGING mode with the following command:

```
SQL> SELECT force_logging FROM v$database;


FORCE_LOGGING

----------------------------------------

NO
```

> The options UNRECOVERABLE (introduced in Oracle 7) and NOLOGGING (introduced in Oracle 8) can be used to avoid the redo log entries being generated for certain operations that can be easily recovered without using the database recovery mechanism. Do remember that the UNRECOVERABLE option is deprecated and is replaced by the NOLOGGING option.

Disabling redo generation (NOLOGGING)

The NOLOGGING attribute tells Oracle that the operation being performed does not need to be recoverable in the event of a failure. In this case, the database will generate only a small set of metadata that is written to the redo log, and the operation will probably run faster. Oracle is relying on the user to recover the data manually in the event of any failure. In other words, the NOLOGGING option skips the generation of redo for the affected object, but will still log many things such as data dictionary changes caused by space management.

NOLOGGING operations

At the tablespace level, the LOGGING clause specifies the default LOGGING attribute for all tables, indexes, and partitions created in the tablespace and also for all objects subsequently created on it. When the tablespace LOGGING attribute is changed by the ALTER TABLESPACE statement, then all objects created after the ALTER statement will have the new LOGGING attribute; but be aware that all previously existing objects in the tablespace will not change their LOGGING attributes. The tablespace level LOGGING attribute can be overridden by the specifications at the table, index, or partition level.

A table, index, or partition can be created with the NOLOGGING option, or it can be altered later using the ALTER NOLOGGING command. It is important to note that just because an object was created with the NOLOGGING option, that does not mean no redo for that segment will ever be generated. When a segment is in the NOLOGGING mode, any direct path operation against that segment can skip redo generation, but all conventional path operations will always generate redo—regardless of the NOLOGGING attribute. The NOLOGGING option will work while running one of the following direct path operations, but not afterwards:

- DIRECT LOAD (SQL*Loader)
- DIRECT LOAD INSERT (using the APPEND hint)
- CREATE TABLE ... AS SELECT
- CREATE INDEX
- ALTER TABLE MOVE
- ALTER TABLE ... MOVE PARTITION
- ALTER TABLE ... SPLIT PARTITION
- ALTER TABLE ... ADD PARTITION (if HASH partition)
- ALTER TABLE ... MERGE PARTITION
- ALTER TABLE ... MODIFY PARTITION
- ADD SUBPARTITON
- COALESCE SUBPARTITON
- REBUILD UNUSABLE INDEXES
- ALTER INDEX ... SPLIT PARTITION
- ALTER INDEX ... REBUILD
- ALTER INDEX ... REBUILD PARTITION

LOGGING is stopped only while one of the previous commands is running. For example, imagine that a user runs the following commands:

```
SQL> ALTER INDEX new_index NOLOGGING;
SQL> ALTER INDEX new_index REBUILD;
```

The actual rebuild of the index does not generate redo (only all data dictionary changes associated with the rebuild will do). Lack of clarity, any DML operation on the index will generate redo, including a direct load insert on the table to which the index belongs. Here is another example to make this point more clearer:

```
SQL> CREATE TABLE table_nolog_test (a number) NOLOGGING;
```

First let's check if the table we just created is really in NOLOGGING mode:

```
SQL> SELECT table_name, logging
  2    FROM user_tables
  3    WHERE table_name='TABLE_NOLOG_TEST';


TABLE_NAME                      LOGGING
----------------                -------
TABLE_NOLOG_TEST     NO


1 row selected.
```

Now that you know that the table was created with NOLOGGING, you need to understand that all the following statements will always generate redo despite the fact that the table is in the NOLOGGING mode. For example:

```
SQL> INSERT INTO table_nolog_test values (1);
SQL> UPDATE table_nolog_test SET a = 2 WHERE a = 1;
SQL> DELETE FROM table_nolog_test WHERE a = 2;
```

However, the following statements will *not* generate redo (except from dictionary changes and indexes associated with the table):

- INSERT /*+APPEND+/ ...

> The APPEND command does not always have to be obeyed as it does not ensure a direct path load. A trigger — a foreign key — can prevent the APPEND hint from working.

- ALTER TABLE table_nolog_test MOVE ...
- ALTER TABLE table_nolog_test MOVE PARTITION ...

Now that you know which commands will work with the NOLOGGING option, let's create a scenario to show the difference in redo generation when using different statements.

First we will need to build our test environment as follows:

```
SQL> CREATE TABLESPACE example
DATAFILE   '/u01/app/oracle/oradata/cdb1/pdb1/EXAMPLE01.DBF' SIZE 200M
EXTENT MANAGEMENT LOCAL
SEGMENT SPACE MANAGEMENT AUTO;


Tablespace created.


SQL> CREATE USER test IDENTIFIED BY test12c
  2    DEFAULT TABLESPACE example
  3    TEMPORARY TABLESPACE temp;


User created.


SQL> ALTER USER test QUOTA UNLIMITED ON example;


User altered.


SQL> GRANT RESOURCE, CONNECT, SELECT ANY DICTIONARY TO test;


Grant succeeded.


SQL> CONNECT test/test12c


Connected.


SQL> CREATE TABLE test1 AS SELECT *
  2    FROM dba_objects
  3    WHERE rownum=0;


Table created.
```

Remember that our database is currently operating in the NOARCHIVELOG mode. As per the table in the *LOGGING versus NOLOGGING* section, a normal INSERT command should generate a normal amount of redo, and an INSERT /*+ APPEND */ command should not generate redo (only data dictionary changes). Let's see if that is really true. The following are two inserts:

```
SQL> SET AUTOTRACE ON STATISTICS
```

 The SET AUTOTRACE ON STATISTICS statement will show only the SQL statement execution statistics after the execution of one SQL DML statement (SELECT, DELETE, UPDATE, or INSERT).

```
SQL> INSERT INTO test1 SELECT * FROM dba_objects;

88012 rows created.

Statistics
-----------------------------------------------------------
    11560972   redo size
       88012   rows processed

SQL> INSERT /*+ APPEND */ INTO test1 SELECT *
  2    FROM dba_objects;

88012 rows created.

Statistics
-----------------------------------------------------------
       36772   redo size
       88012   rows processed
```

Yes, redo generation is behaving as expected. You can see in the example that the amount of redo generated via the simple insert was 11 MB while a direct insert generates only 36 KB.

 You never need to set NOLOGGING in the NOARCHIVELOG mode — everything that can skip redo will skip redo already. NOLOGGING doesn't apply in the NOARCHIVELOG mode — it doesn't change any behavior.

To activate the NOLOGGING mode when using an ALTER command, you will need to add the NOLOGGING clause at the end of the ALTER command. For example:

```
SQL> ALTER TABLE test1
  2   MOVE PARTITION parti_001 TABLESPACE new_ts_001 NOLOGGING;
```

The same applies for a CREATE INDEX command and the CREATE TABLE command. An exception is that if your CREATE TABLE command has the clause AS SELECT and you use NOLOGGING at the end of the command, then the operation will not use the NOLOGGING mode and instead will generate an alias called NOLOGGING. For example:

```
SQL> CREATE TABLE table_nolog_test2 NOLOGGING AS SELECT *
  2   FROM dba_objects;


Table created.


SQL> CREATE TABLE table_nolog_test3
  2   AS SELECT *
  3   FROM dba_objects NOLOGGING;


Table created.


SQL> SELECT table_name, logging
  2   FROM user_tables;



TABLE_NAME            LOGGING
------------------    -------
TABLE_NOLOG_TEST      NO
TABLE_NOLOG_TEST2     NO
TABLE_NOLOG_TEST3     YES


3 rows selected.
```

 It is a common mistake to add the NOLOGGING option at the end of the SQL when using the AS SELECT statement (if done, Oracle will consider it as an alias and the table will generate normal LOGGING).

Indexed organized tables – an exception

One exception to my previous examples is when trying to use NOLOGGING with an **index-organized table (IOT)**. It is not possible to place an IOT in the NOLOGGING mode, but we can place an index associated with such a table in the NOLOGGING mode when doing a **CTAS** (CREATE TABLE AS SELECT) operation. Doing so will help us to reduce redo generation in the creation process of the IOT; any intent to use INSERT /*+APPEND*/ later will not give any redo reduction advantage.

Let's test to see if what I'm saying is true. We will test the amount of redo generated when inserting bulk data in a normal table in the NOLOGGING mode and then compare the same operation against an IOT table in NOLOGGING.

First, create the tables for this exercise:

```
SQL> CREATE TABLE iot_test
(object_name,object_type,owner,
CONSTRAINT iot_test_pk PRIMARY KEY(object_name,object_type,owner))
ORGANIZATION INDEX
NOLOGGING
AS
SELECT DISTINCT object_name, object_type,owner
FROM dba_objects
WHERE rownum = 0
/


Table created.


SQL> CREATE TABLE test5 NOLOGGING
AS
SELECT object_name, object_type,owner
FROM dba_objects
WHERE rownum = 0
/


Table created.
```

Now that we have both tables created, let's generate a bulk insert of 87,887 records into each table and compare the amount of redo each transaction generates:

```
SQL> set autotrace on statistics
SQL> INSERT /*+ APPEND */ INTO test5
  2    SELECT DISTINCT object_name, object_type, owner
  3    FROM dba_objects;


87887 rows created.


Statistics
----------------------------------------------------------
      51460   redo size
      87887   rows processed


SQL> INSERT /*+ APPEND */ INTO iot_test
  2    SELECT DISTINCT object_name, object_type, owner
  3    FROM dba_objects;


87887 rows created.


Statistics
----------------------------------------------------------
   16391704   redo size
      87887   rows processed
```

The amount of redo generated by the INSERT /*+APPEND*/ command in the normal table with NOLOGGING is 51,460 bytes and the amount generated when doing the same INSERT /*+APPEND*/ in the IOT table with NOLOGGING is 16,391,704 bytes. Clearly, the first statement used the NOLOGGING option, but the second one did not.

Now let's take a deeper look and see why the different behaviors happened. Take a look at user_tables and user_indexes to see if both tables and the IOT index are in the NOLOGGING mode:

```
SQL> SELECT table_name, logging FROM user_tables;


TABLE_NAME                           LOGGING
------------------------------------ -------
```

```
TEST5                                   NO
IOT_TEST


2 rows selected.


SQL> SELECT index_name, logging FROM user_indexes;


INDEX_NAME                              LOGGING
----------------------------------     -------
IOT_TEST_PK                             NO
```

As a result of the queries discussed, we can easily see that the normal table (TEST5) is set to NO (indicating that no logging should occur), but the IOT table (IOT_TEST) value for LOGGING is null. We can also see that the index associated with the IOT table is in the NOLOGGING mode. Now we will compare the amount of redo that will be generated when using the bulk insert in the CTAS statement.

We will use the CTAS statement to create the table TEST5 in the NOLOGGING mode and load all data at the same time. After this, we will check the DB amount of redo again after the table was created:

```
SQL> connect /


Connected.


SQL> CREATE TABLE test5 NOLOGGING
  2    AS
  3    SELECT DISTINCT object_name, object_type,owner
  4    FROM dba_objects
/


Table created.


SQL> SELECT a.name, b.value
  2      FROM v$statname a, v$mystat b
  3    WHERE a.statistic# = b.statistic#
  4      AND a.name = 'redo size';
```

```
NAME                                 VALUE
------------------------------   ----------
redo size                            119700
```

We can see that the amount of redo generated by the CTAS was 119,700 bytes. Now we will do the same, but using the IOT:

```
SQL> connect /

Connected.

SQL> CREATE TABLE iot_test
(object_name,object_type,owner,
CONSTRAINT iot_test_pk PRIMARY KEY(object_name,object_type,owner))
ORGANIZATION INDEX
NOLOGGING
AS
SELECT DISTINCT object_name, object_type,owner
FROM dba_objects
/

Table created.

SQL> SELECT a.name, b.value
  2      FROM v$statname a, v$mystat b
  3    WHERE a.statistic# = b.statistic#
  4      AND a.name = 'redo size';

NAME                                 VALUE
------------------------------   ----------
redo size                            136828
```

For this second example, the amount of redo generated was 136,828 bytes. This shows us that when using CTAS and NOLOGGING, it will be more efficient and generate less redo using NOLOGGING than a normal table. However, the downside is that we will not be able to make use of the NOLOGGING operation after the CTAS is done.

Reducing redo generation

This section shows you how to reduce redo generation using the LOGGING and NOLOGGING operations. The discussion is divided into two parts. In one part, you'll learn about things to do when LOGGING is in effect. In the other, you'll learn what to do when NOLOGGING is enabled.

Tips when LOGGING is in effect (not using NOLOGGING)

This section will cover some interesting tips to reduce redo generation without the need to use NOLOGGING.

Backups

As I mentioned earlier in the *Redo generation and recoverability* section in *Chapter 1, Understanding the Basics of Backup and Recovery*, user-managed backups can generate more redo. The best way to eliminate this problem is to use RMAN. RMAN does not need to write entire blocks to redo because it knows when a block is being copied. If you need to use the user-managed backup technique, then you can follow these steps to reduce redo generation:

- Do not back up all the tablespaces at once (using the ALTER DATABASE BEGIN BACKUP command). Doing so will put every tablespace into the BACKUP mode for longer than it really needs to be, and therefore generating redo for longer. Instead, back up one tablespace at the time using the ALTER TABLESPACE <Tablespace_name> BEGIN/END BACKUP command.

- Generate automatic backups on the busy tablespaces during a time when they are least busy in terms of DML.

Bulk inserts

I use the term *bulk inserts* in this section to mean loading a large percentage compared to the existing data. To reduce or eliminate the amount of redo generated in a bulk data load, you first need to disable the indexes (when making a direct load to a table that has indexes, the indexes will also produce redo) before the load, and then rebuild them again as follows:

```
SQL> ALTER INDEX index_name UNUSABLE ; # Do this for every index

SQL> INSERT /*+ APPEND */ INTO table_name SELECT …

SQL> ALTER INDEX index_name REBUILD;
```

Please ensure that the initialization parameter skip_unusable_ indexes is set to TRUE before making an index unusable. If set to FALSE and a user tries to access data from a table with an index unsuable, it will return an error to the user session. It is also important to know that prior to Oracle 10g, skip_unusable_indexes was needed to be set at session level.

Bulk deletes

To reduce redo generation in a bulk delete in the LOGGING mode, you should:

1. Create a new table with the same structure as the table you want to bulk delete from, with only the rows you want to keep as in the following example:

```
SQL> CREATE TABLE new_table
  2    AS SELECT *
  3    FROM test1
  4    WHERE … ;
```

2. Create indexes on the new table.
3. Create constraints, grants, and so on.
4. Drop the original table.
5. Rename the new table to the original name.

If the data remaining after step 2 is small, or if there are a lot of dependencies on the table in the form of views, procedures, functions, and so on, then following steps can be used after step 1 to move forward:

1. Truncate the original table, thus deleting all its data.
2. Disable all constraints on the original table.
3. Insert all data in the new table back to the original table. For example:

```
SQL> INSERT /*+ APPEND */ INTO test1
  2    SELECT *
  3    FROM new_table;
```

4. Commit your changes.
5. Enable the constraints on the original table.
6. Drop the new table that you created in step 1.

Bulk updates

Use the method described in this section if the indexes are going to be affected by a bulk update, because a massive update on indexes is more expensive than rebuilding them. If a small portion of the data is updated, then use this first approach:

1. Disable all constraints.

2. Make all indexes associated with the columns to be updated, UNUSABLE. For example:

    ```
    SQL> ALTER INDEX index_name UNUSABLE;
    ```

3. Run the update on the table.

4. Commit the update.

5. Rebuild all indexes that you made unusable in step 2. For example:

    ```
    SQL> ALTER INDEX index_name REBUILD;
    ```

6. Enable all constraints you disabled in step 1.

If the update causes a change to all the data to be updated, then follow this second approach:

1. Create a new table to be used as a holding table and modify the amount in the column value at the same time:

    ```
    SQL> CREATE TABLE new_table AS
      2    SELECT (value*1.10) value, ... FROM goods;
    ```

2. Create all the same indexes on the new table as exists on the original table. For example:

    ```
    SQL> CREATE INDEX idx_test3 ON test3 (owner);
    ```

3. Create all grants, constraints, and so on, on the new table.

4. Drop the original table.

5. Finally rename the new table to become the original one.

Partitioning

Table and index partitioning are very useful in reducing redo generation. Reduction is possible because partitions divide an object into smaller manageable units. You can use partition techniques with a table if you know which partitions the new data will be inserted into, deleted from, or updated. Redo generation is reduced because only the affected partitions need to be built or rebuilt, not the entire object. (Please note that global indexes are not partitioned and thus always require a rebuild.)

The following are some examples showing how to work with indexes on a partition-wise basis. First, here is how to mark an index unusable:

- Without partitioning: ALTER INDEX index_name UNUSABLE;
- With partitioning: ...ALTER INDEX index_name PARTITION partition_name UNUSABLE;

Next is how to rebuild an index:

- Without partitioning: ALTER INDEX index index_name REBUILD ;
- With partitioning: ...ALTER INDEX index_name REBUILD PARTITION partition_name ;

You can also use the ALTER TABLE ... EXCHANGE PARTITION command to swap a work table with a partition, thus almost instantly making the data in that table a part of the partitioned table. The following is an example of how the unpartitioned approach works:

```
SQL> INSERT /*+ APPEND */ INTO current_table
2    SELECT *
3    FROM new_table;
```

In a partitioning scenario, you can simply exchange the work table for an empty partition in the target table. Here's how it works:

```
SQL> ALTER TABLE current_table
2    EXCHANGE PARTITION partition_name
3    with new table...
```

Partitioning is very useful in archiving historic data. The table that contains historic data is created with a range partition on a date field. When the data becomes old enough to remove, the partition gets dropped. This feature is so important that Oracle created a new type of range partition in Oracle 11*g* to handle this situation. The new type is called the interval partition. Here is an example that works using the older partition types in Oracle 8*i* to 10*g*:

```
SQL> CREATE TABLE hist_data( sample_date date,
....)
PARTITION BY RANGE( sample_date) (
PARTITION data201203 VALUES LESS THAN (to_date('04/01/2012','mm/dd/
yyyy')) TABLESPACE ts_201203,
PARTITION data201204 VALUES LESS THAN (to_date('05/01/2012','mm/dd/
yyyy')) TABLESPACE ts_201204,
....
) ;
```

A year down the line we want to delete all the data before April 2012. All we need to do is an `ALTER TABLE hist_data DROP PARTITION data201203` command. This is much more efficient and produces far less redo than executing the command `DELETE FROM hist_data WHERE sample_date < to_date( '04/01/2012', 'mm/dd/yyyy')`

Tips for developers

Developers also have a role to play, or at least they can choose to help. The points discussed in this section can help developers reduce the redo generation on the database. Here are some tips:

1. Run DML in as few SQL statements as you can (in other words, as simply as possible). This will reduce the generation of undo and block header updates, and therefore reduce redo generation. Consider the problem of inserting a large amount of data. First create a test table:

    ```
    SQL> CREATE TABLE test4
      2    AS SELECT owner, object_name, object_type
      3    FROM dba_objects;
    ```

2. Now think about about inserting a large amount of data into that table. Think about the difference between using an `INSERT` statement and a `PL/SQL` block. The following is the approach of using an `INSERT` statement, which is more efficient:

    ```
    SQL> set autotrace on statistics
    SQL> INSERT INTO test4
      2    SELECT owner, object_name, object_type
      3    FROM dba_objects;


    88019 rows created.


    Statistics
    ----------------------------------------------------------
        4660736   redo size
          88019   rows processed
    ```

Then execute a PL/SQL block to insert the same data as before:

```
SQL> connect /
Connected.

DECLARE
  CURSOR cur_c1 is
     SELECT owner, object_name, object_type FROM dba_objects;
     rec_c1 cur_c1%ROWTYPE;
BEGIN
    OPEN cur_c1;
    FOR rec_c1 in cur_c1
    LOOP
        INSERT INTO test4 VALUES (rec_c1.owner, rec_c1.object_
name,rec_c1.object_type);
    END LOOP;
    COMMIT;
    CLOSE cur_c1;
END;
/

PL/SQL procedure successfully completed.
```

Then let's check how much redo was generated during this session:

```
SQL> SELECT a.name, b.value
  2    FROM v$statname a, v$mystat b
  3   WHERE a.statistic# = b.statistic#
  4     AND a.name = 'redo size';
```

```
NAME                                VALUE
------------------------------ ----------
redo size                         26776640
```

The amount of redo generated was 26,776,640 bytes. The PL/SQL approach generated over 26 million bytes of redo, whereas the INSERT approach generated a mere 4,660,736 bytes. Simpler is better. The simple INSERT statement generated far less redo than even that generated by simple PL/SQL block.

3. Do not commit more than you need. By issuing the COMMIT command you are forcing Oracle to do some internal updates which produce redo. I ran the PL/SQL code from tip 1 with a COMMIT command inserted after the INSERT command (making a COMMIT command after each INSERT command, instead that once in the end of the LOOP), and the result was even more awful than before. The amount of redo generated increased to 51,917,676 bytes. You can see that excessive committing generates far more redo. By reducing unnecessary commits you will reduce the strain on the LGWR process.

4. Set sequences to cache correctly. This is important since your system generates a lot of sequence numbers using the Oracle sequences. The database keeps track of the next sequence number in the SGA, but it also keeps the starting value of the next set of sequence numbers in the data dictionary according to the sequence cache setting. This starting value is needed in case the database crashes. As a sequence nextval is acquired, the value in the SGA is updated. When the value in the SGA is the same as the one in the data dictionary, the data dictionary is updated, producing redo. If the sequence cache is small, the data dictionary will be updated more often. This is illustrated by the following examples:

SQL> CREATE SEQUENCE seq2 CACHE 2;	The data dictionary is updated every second nextval.
SQL> CREATE SEQUENCE seq20 CACHE 20;	The data dictionary is updated after every twenty nextval instances.
SQL> CREATE SEQUENCE seq1000 CACHE 1000;	The data dictionary is updated after every thousand nextval instances.

I created three identical tables, test_seq_2, test_seq_20, and test_seq_1000. They all have a number column. Then I inserted rows into test_seq_2 using seq2, into test_seq_20 using seq20, and into test_seq_1000 using seq1000. Each time, I checked how much redo was generated from inserting the same number of rows (taken from dba_objects). Here is the code I executed:

```
SQL> create table test_seq_2 (a number);
SQL> create table test_seq_20 (a number);
SQL> create table test_seq_1000 (a number);
SQL> INSERT INTO test_seq_2 SELECT seq2.nextval FROM dba_objects ;

88025 rows created.
```

```
SQL> INSERT INTO test_seq_20 SELECT seq20.nextval FROM dba_objects
;


88025 rows created.


SQL> INSERT INTO test_seq_1000 SELECT seq1000.nextval FROM dba_
objects ;


88025 rows created.
```

The following table shows the relation between the redo generated and the sequence cache size:

Cache	Redo (bytes)
2	32,077,760
20	4,494,368
1000	1,492,836

Set the cache to a higher value if the application accesses the sequence a lot. It is wrong to believe that setting the cache to 1000 means that the SGA will have 1000 numbers stored for the sequence. There is only one number stored for the sequence, so do not worry about setting the cache as high as you need to.

Managing the amount of redo generated by a database requires a partnership between a DBA and a developer. The extent to which you can work with your developers to implement the discussed tips, and to educate them about the value from implementing those tips, the more you can reduce redo, making your job easier and your database more efficient.

Tips when NOLOGGING is in effect

Now that you have seen how you can achieve a reduction in redo generation without the use of NOLOGGING, let's take a closer look at how to do the same using the NOLOGGING option.

Partitioning

As I mentioned earlier in the *Tips when logging is in effect* section, table and index partitioning are very useful to help reduce redo generation. In this section, I would like to talk about interval partitioning and the NOLOGGGING mode.

If you want to make use of the NOLOGGING mode with interval partitioning, it is very important to check whether the tablespace where the partitions will be created is in the NOLOGGING mode. If the target tablespace is not in the NOLOGGING mode, then every time Oracle creates a new partition, that partition will be created in the LOGGING mode regardless of whether the table by itself is in the NOLOGGING mode.

Here I will show you how an interval partition behaves and how the table will automatically create new partitions when required. For this scenario, the tablespace (named EXAMPLE) where the table and the partitions will be created is in the NOLOGGING mode.

First, let's ensure that our tablespace EXAMPLE is in the NOLOGGING mode:

```
SQL> SELECT tablespace_name,logging
  2    FROM dba_tablespaces;


TABLESPACE_NAME                 LOGGING
------------------------------  ---------
SYSTEM                          LOGGING
SYSAUX                          LOGGING
TEMP                            NOLOGGING
EXAMPLE                         NOLOGGING
```

Next, create the test_auto_intpart table with four initial partitions:

```
SQL> CREATE TABLE test_auto_intpart
(id number, txt varchar2(4000), col_date date)
PARTITION BY RANGE (col_date)
INTERVAL(NUMTOYMINTERVAL(1, 'MONTH'))
( PARTITION ap2008 VALUES LESS THAN (TO_DATE('1-1-2009', 'DD-MM-YYYY')),
  PARTITION ap2009 VALUES LESS THAN (TO_DATE('1-1-2010', 'DD-MM-YYYY')),
  PARTITION ap2010 VALUES LESS THAN (TO_DATE('1-1-2011', 'DD-MM-YYYY')),
  PARTITION ap2011 VALUES LESS THAN (TO_DATE('1-1-2012', 'DD-MM-YYYY')));


Table Created
```

Check that all initial partitions were created using the NOLOGGING option:

```
SQL> SELECT TABLE_NAME, PARTITION_NAME, LOGGING, tablespace_name
FROM user_tab_partitions;


TABLE_NAME          PARTITION_NAME LOGGING TABLESPACE_NAME
------------------- -------------- ------- ---------------

TEST_AUTO_INTPART   AP2008         NO      EXAMPLE

TEST_AUTO_INTPART   AP2009         NO      EXAMPLE

TEST_AUTO_INTPART   AP2010         NO      EXAMPLE

TEST_AUTO_INTPART   AP2011         NO      EXAMPLE
```

As you can see, all four partitions are stored in the tablespace EXAMPLE and are in the NOLOGGING mode. Now insert some data in the initial partitions using the INSERT /*+APPEND*/ command:

```
SQL> set autotrace on statistics
SQL> INSERT /*+ APPEND */ INTO test_auto_intpart
SELECT OBJ#*LINE,SOURCE,sysdate-365*mod(rownum,4)
FROM sys.source$;


Statistics
----------------------------------------------------------
     59020   redo size
     26988   rows processed


SQL> COMMIT;
```

You can see that NOLOGGING was respected and the command generated only 59,020 bytes of redo.

Next, insert more data as in the following example. I've written the INSERT statement to force Oracle to automatically create four new partitions in the target table:

```
SQL> INSERT /*+ APPEND */ INTO test_auto_intpart
  2    SELECT OBJ#*LINE,SOURCE,sysdate+365*mod(rownum,4)
  3    FROM sys.source$;


Statistics
----------------------------------------------------------
```

```
    31908   redo size
    26988   rows processed

SQL> COMMIT;
SQL> SELECT TABLE_NAME, PARTITION_NAME, LOGGING
  2   FROM    user_tab_partitions;
```

TABLE_NAME	PARTITION_NAME	LOGGING
TEST_AUTO_INTPART	SYS_P201	NO
TEST_AUTO_INTPART	SYS_P202	NO
TEST_AUTO_INTPART	SYS_P203	NO
TEST_AUTO_INTPART	SYS_P204	NO
TEST_AUTO_INTPART	AP2008	NO
TEST_AUTO_INTPART	AP2009	NO
TEST_AUTO_INTPART	AP2010	NO
TEST_AUTO_INTPART	AP2011	NO

Yes, the INSERT command really works as expected. Oracle created four new partitions automatically, and these partitions were created in the NOLOGGING mode because the tablespace EXAMPLE was in the NOLOGGING mode.

Note: If your tablespace is in the LOGGING mode, the four new partitions would be created in the LOGGING mode, and INSERT /*+APPEND*/ would generate a normal amount of redo. If later you decided to alter the new partitions to NOLOGGING, you would need to use the following statement to achieve this goal: ALTER TABLE test_AUTO_INTPART NOLOGGING;

Direct path inserts

When using direct path inserts, the database will insert data without generation of redo or undo. Instead, Oracle logs a small number of block range invalidation redo records, and will periodically update the control file with information about the most recent direct writes.

Direct path insert without LOGGING may improve performance, but once again makes the data inserted unrecoverable in the case of a media failure.

Since the release of Oracle Database 11.2.0.2, you can significantly improve the performance of a direct path insert with NOLOGGING by disabling the periodic update of the control files. You can do so by setting the initialization parameter DB_UNRECOVERABLE_SCN_TRACKING to FALSE. However the resulting benefit comes at a price. If you perform a direct path insert with NOLOGGING and the control file is not updated, you will no longer be able to accurately determine whether any datafiles are currently unrecoverable.

To use direct path insert, use the /*+ APPEND */ hint as follows:

```
SQL> INSERT /*+ APPEND */ INTO test1
  2    SELECT *
  3    FROM dba_objects;
```

When direct path insert is used, Oracle does the following in order to bypass using the buffer cache:

1. Formats the data to be inserted as Oracle blocks.
2. Inserts the blocks above the HWM. When the commit takes place, the HWM is moved to include the newly placed block.

It is clear that direct load is useful for bulk inserts. However, using it to insert a few hundred records at a time can have a bad effect on space and performance.

The statement INSERT /*+APPEND*/ INTO <table_name> SELECT...FROM will use the NOLOGGING option if available and will not produce redo. However, since the introduction of 11.2, there is a new hint APPEND_VALUES designed to be used with bulk (array) inserts.

For example:

```
SQL> DROP TABLE t;

Table dropped.

SQL> CREATE TABLE t ( x char(2000) ) nologging;

Table created.

SQL> CONNECT /

Connected.

SQL> DECLARE
  2           type array is table of char(2000) index by binary_integer;
```

```
 3            l_data array;
 4    BEGIN
 5            for i in 1 .. 1000
 6            loop
 7                    l_data(i) := 'x';
 8            end loop;
 9            forall i in 1 .. l_data.count
10                    INSERT INTO t (x) VALUES (l_data(i));
11    END;
12    /
```

PL/SQL procedure successfully completed.

```
SQL> SELECT a.name, b.value
  2    FROM v$statname a, v$mystat b
  3    WHERE a.statistic# = b.statistic#
  4      AND a.name = 'redo size';
```

```
NAME                                 VALUE
------------------------------  ----------
redo size                          2253664
```

SQL> connect /

Connected.

```
SQL> DECLARE
  2            type array is table of char(2000) index by binary_integer;
  3            l_data array;
  4    BEGIN
  5            for i in 1 .. 1000
  6            loop
  7                    l_data(i) := 'x';
  8            end loop;
  9            forall i in 1 .. l_data.count
 10                    INSERT /*+ APPEND_VALUES */ INTO t (x) values (l_
data(i));
 11    END;
 12    /
```

```
PL/SQL procedure successfully completed.

SQL> SELECT a.name, b.value
  2    FROM v$statname a, v$mystat b
  3    WHERE a.statistic# = b.statistic#
  4      AND a.name = 'redo size';


NAME                                     VALUE
------------------------------ ----------
redo size                                 7408
```

It is very important to understand how direct path inserts affect redo generation. The operation of a direct path insert is affected by the following factors:

- The LOGGING mode (ARCHIVELOG/NOARCHIVELOG) of the database
- Using the /*+ APPEND */ hint
- The LOGGING mode of the table
- The FORCE LOGGING mode of the database

 If the database is in the FORCE LOGGING mode, then Oracle will treat the table as if it was in the LOGGING mode regardless of the table mode.

If the /*+ APPEND */ hint is not used, then the INSERT command will generate the normal amount of redo regardless of the other factors. When the hint is used, the following table shows how redo generation is affected by the mode of a database (ARCHIVELOG or NOARCHIVELOG), and whether a table is in the LOGGING or NOLOGGING mode when the direct path is used. However, it does not consider index and data dictionary changes as these are a separate matter.

LOGGING MODE	ARCHIVELOG	NOARCHIVELOG
LOGGING	Redo	No Redo
NOLOGGING	No Redo	No Redo

It is very easy to verify if our INSERT /*+APPEND*/ statement really did insert the data after the HWM. All you need to do is (without issuing a COMMIT command) run a normal SELECT command against the data just inserted. If the query works, the data was not appended. If the query returns an ORA-12838 error, then the data was appended. The error comes about because you cannot read from a table in the same transaction that a direct load was made without issuing a COMMIT command.

Bulk inserts

To further reduce redo generation when doing a bulk insert, we will make use of direct pathing. Direct path operations help to skip undo generation and maintain indexes in bulk—hence less redo.

1. Set the table in the NOLOGGING mode:

   ```
   SQL> ALTER TABLE table_name NOLOGGING;
   ```

2. Make all table indexes unusable:

   ```
   SQL> ALTER INDEX index_name UNUSABLE;
   ```

3. Insert the bulk data using the /*+ APPEND */ hint:

   ```
   SQL> Insert /*+ APPEND */ into table_name select
   ```

4. Rebuild all indexes that were set as UNUSABLE using the NOLOGGING option:

   ```
   SQL> ALTER INDEX index_name REBUILD NOLOGGING;
   ```

5. Set your table back to the LOGGING mode:

   ```
   SQL> ALTER TABLE table_name LOGGING;
   ```

6. Set your indexes back to the LOGGING mode:

   ```
   SQL> ALTER INDEX index_name LOGGING;
   ```

7. Backup the data.

There is no direct way (at the time of writing this document) of reducing redo generation for bulk update and delete.

 The creation of an index with NOLOGGING will save space in the redo log files and decrease the creation time (it will end faster when parallelizing large index creation). But do not forget to backup all affected datafiles and perhaps move them over to a standby database if necessary.

Bulk deletes

Use the following technique to reduce redo generation when doing a bulk delete:

1. Create a new table with all records you want to keep from the original table with the NOLOGGING option:

   ```
   SQL> CREATE TABLE new_table NOLOGGING
     2    AS SELECT *
     3    FROM original_table WHERE ...
   ```

2. Create the indexes on the new table with the NOLOGGING option.

3. Create all constraints, grants, and so on, as the original table.

4. Drop the original table.

5. Rename the new table as the original table.

6. Place the table and all indexes to the LOGGING mode.

7. Back up the data.

If the amount of data that will be left is very small compared to the original number of rows, or there are many dependencies on the table (views, procedures, functions, and so on), then the following steps can be used after step 2:

1. Disable constraints on the original table.

2. Truncate the original table.

3. Make indexes related to the original table UNUSABLE.

4. Place the original table in the NOLOGGING mode.

   ```
   SQL> ALTER TABLE original_table NOLOGGING ;
   ```

5. Do a direct insert of the data in new_table to original_table:

   ```
   SQL> INSERT /*+ APPEND */ INTO original_table
     2    SELECT * FROM new_table ;
   ```

6. Do a commit.

7. Rebuild all indexes using the NOLOGGING option.

8. Enable all constraints that were disabled in step 3.

9. Place the original table and all indexes in the LOGGING mode.

10. Backup the data.

11. Drop the holding table.

Bulk updates

To make a bulk update, follow the same steps you used for the bulk delete in the previous section but integrate the update within the select statement. Let's say that you want to update the value column in the goods table by increasing it by 10 percent. The steps to achieve this goal are:

1. Create a new table to be used as a holding table and modify the amount in the column value at the same time, specifying the NOLOGGING option:

   ```
   SQL> CREATE TABLE new_table NOLOGGING AS
     2    SELECT (value*1.10) value, ... FROM goods;
   ```

2. Create all indexes on the holding table as they exist in the original table. Specify NOLOGGING.

3. Create all constraints, grants, and so on.

4. Drop the original table.

5. Rename the holding table to the original name.

6. Alter the table and all related indexes to the LOGGING mode.

7. Backup the data.

Backups and NOLOGGING

If it is required that the data loaded using the NOLOGGING option needs to be recovered in the case of a disaster situation, your only solution is making a backup as soon as the NOLOGGING operation is made. Otherwise, the data cannot be recovered in the event of a media failure because it has not been logged.

Sometimes you will not be able to run a full backup of the database until later in the day. In this situation, you can make use of the following strategies:

• Hot backup

• In order to recover any additional data or modification to the table after the bulk insert using NOLOGGING is complete, you must at least perform a hot backup of the datafiles in which the objects are located. Remember that your database continues generating redo for the DML transactions over the objects, even if they are still using the NOLOGGING option, but you are strongly advised to place them in LOGGING after the NOLOGGING mode is no longer required, to avoid any possibility of unrecoverability in the future.

Redo-related wait events

There are a number of wait events that happen during redo activities and most of them are I/O related. First, I will talk about the two most important wait events: 'log file parallel write' and 'log file sync'. Then I will mention some other important ones you should know about.

The 'log file parallel write' event

Oracle foreground processes wait for 'log file sync', whereas the LGWR process waits for 'log file parallel write'. Although we usually find 'log file sync' in the *Top 5 Timed Events* or the *Wait Events* section of the **Statspack** report, in order to understand it we will first look at 'log file parallel write'.

The LGWR background process waits for this event while it is copying redo records from the memory log buffer cache to the current redo group's member log files on disk. Asynchronous I/O will be used if available to make the write parallel, otherwise these writes will be done sequentially one member after the other. However, LGWR has to wait until the I/Os to all member log files are complete before the wait is completed. Hence the factor that determines the length of this wait is the speed with which the I/O subsystem can perform the writes to the log file members.

To reduce the time spent waiting for 'log file parallel write', one approach is to reduce the amount of redo generated by the database. The following are some options for doing that:

- Make use of the UNRECOVERABLE/NOLOGGING options.

- Reduce the number of redo group members to the minimum necessary to ensure that not all members can be lost at the same time.

- Do not leave tablespaces in the BACKUP mode for longer than necessary.

- Use only the minimal level of supplemental LOGGING required to achieve required functionality, for example, in LogMiner, logical standby, or streams.

- A last approach is to make it so your applications do not wait for LGWR, who cares if LGWR is waiting for I/O if you are not waiting for LGWR. You do this by:

    ○ Committing infrequently if you are doing a large load. If you load 1 million records and commit, you will have to wait a teeny tiny amount of time for LGWR to finish writing since LGWR was writing continuously during your load (LGWR will have a lot of 'log file parallel write' waits, but you will have one tiny 'log file sync' wait). However if you load and commit 1 million records, you will have to wait 1 million times for log writer to write. That will be slow.

    ○ Looking into the ability to use asynchronous commits ('commit work write batch nowait' for example) since Oracle 10*g* R2. This has to be done with care due that in the end you are trading recoverability for speed, and consequently if buffered redo is not yet written to the redo log files and your database crashes, you will end losing your committed data.

Another approach is to tune the I/O itself:

- Place redo group members in different storage locations so that parallel writes do not contend with each other
- Do not use RAID-5 for redo log files
- Use ASM, the use of raw devices were deprecated in Oracle 11*g* and desupported in Oracle 12*c*
- Use faster disks for redo log files
- If archiving is being used, configure redo storage so that writes for the current redo group members do not contend with reads for the group(s) currently being archived

The 'log file sync' event

The `log file sync` wait event occurs in Oracle foreground processes when they have issued a COMMIT or ROLLBACK operation and are waiting for it to complete. Part (but not all) of this wait includes waiting for the LGWR process to copy the redo records for the session's transaction from the log buffer memory to disk. In the time that a foreground process is waiting for `log file sync`, the LGWR will also wait for a portion of that time on `log file parallel write`.

The key to understanding what is delaying `log file sync` is comparing the average time spent waiting for `log file sync` to that spent waiting for `log file parallel write`. You can then take action as follows:

- If the average wait times are similar, then redo log file I/O is causing the delay, and the guidelines for tuning that I/O should be followed.
- If the average wait time for `log file parallel write` is significantly smaller or larger than for `log file sync`, then the delay is caused by the other parts of the redo LOGGING mechanism that occurs during COMMIT/ROLLBACK (and are not I/O related). Sometimes there will be a latch contention on redo latches, evidenced by `latch free` or `LGWR wait for redo copy` wait events.

The 'redo log space request' event

The `redo log space request` wait event indicates how many times a server process has waited for space in the online redo log file (this is not related to the redo log buffer as many people think).

You can access the statistics information for redo log space request by querying the `v$sysstat` view, as per this example:

```
SQL> SELECT name,value FROM v$sysstat
  2   WHERE name LIKE '%redo log space requests%';


NAME                                        VALUE
------------------------------------- ----------
redo log space requests                      1375
```

Use this information plus the wait events as an indication that a tuning of checkpoints, DBWR, or archive activity is required—not in the LGWR. This is caused by the online redo log file and not by the log buffer. Thus, increasing the size of the log buffer will not solve the problem.

The 'log buffer space' event

The `'log buffer space'` event occurs when server processes are waiting for free space in the log buffer, because redo is being generated faster than the LGWR process is writing in the redo log files.

To solve this situation or conversely reduce the amount of redo being generated, you need to increase the redo log buffer size. If you have already tuned the redo log buffer size and the problem continues to happen, then the next step will be to ensure that the disks on which the online redo logs reside do not suffer from I/O contention (only if LGWR is spending a lot of time in `'log file parallel write'`).

Block corruption due to NOLOGGING

If a NOLOGGING (or UNRECOVERABLE) operation is performed on an object and the datafile containing that object is subsequently recovered, then the data blocks affected by the NOLOGGING operation are marked as corrupt and will signal an ORA-1578 error when accessed. In Oracle 8*i*, an ORA-26040 is also signaled (ORA-26040: Data block was loaded using the NOLOGGING option) which makes the cause fairly obvious, but earlier releases have no additional error message. If a block is corrupt due to recovery through a NOLOGGING operation, you need to understand that:

- Recovery cannot retrieve the NOLOGGING data
- No data is salvageable from inside the block

If this is your situation, please note that:

- The indexes with corrupt blocks can be dropped and re-created
- The corrupt tables can be dropped and built from an alternative data source
- The datafile(s) impacted by the NOLOGGING operations can be refreshed from the primary or the backup which was completed after the NOLOGGING operation
- Or a combination of the preceding points

Currently in Oracle 9*i* and Oracle 10*g* R1, only the primary database v$datafile view reflects NOLOGGING operations. In Oracle 10*g* R2, the v$datafile view was enhanced to include information regarding when an invalidation redo is applied and the aforementioned corrupted blocks are written to the corresponding datafile on a Redo Apply (or media recovery or standby) instance.

Repairing NOLOGGING changes on physical and logical standby databases

After a NOLOGGING operation on the primary is detected, it is recommended to create a backup immediately if you want to recover from this operation in the future. However, there are additional steps required if you have an existing physical or logical standby database. Executing these steps is crucial if you want to preserve the data integrity of your standby databases.

For a physical standby database, Data Guard's Redo Apply process will process the invalidation redo and mark the corresponding data blocks as corrupted. Follow these steps to reinstate the relevant datafiles:

1. Stop Redo Apply (RECOVER MANAGED STANDBY DATABASE CANCEL).
2. Take the corresponding datafile(s) offline (ALTER DATABASE DATAFILE <datafile_name> OFFLINE DROP;).
3. Start Redo Apply (RECOVER MANAGED STANDBY DATABASE DISCONNECT).
4. Copy the appropriate backup of affected datafiles over from the primary database (for example, use RMAN to backup datafiles and copy them).
5. Stop Redo Apply (RECOVER MANAGED STANDBY DATABASE CANCEL).
6. Make the corresponding datafiles online (ALTER DATABASE DATAFILE <datafile_name> ONLINE;).
7. Start Redo Apply (RECOVER MANAGED STANDBY DATABASE DISCONNECT).

For a logical standby database, Data Guard's SQL Apply process skips over the invalidation redo completely, thus the subsequent corresponding table or index will not be updated. However, future reference to missing data will result in ORA-1403 (no data found). In order to resynchronize the table with the primary table, you need to re-create it from the primary database. Follow the steps described in *Oracle Data Guard Concepts and Administration 12c Release 1 Section 11.5.5*. Basically, you will be using the DBMS_LOGSTDBY.INSTANTIATE_TABLE procedure.

Finding sessions that generate lots of redo

To find sessions generating lots of redo, you can use either of the following methods. Both methods examine the amount of undo generated. When a transaction generates undo, it will automatically generate redo as well.

- Query v$sess_io: This view contains the column block_changes, which indicates how many blocks have been changed by the session. High values indicate a session generating lots of redo.

- The query you can use is:

```
SQL> SELECT s.sid, s.serial#, s.username, s.program,
i.block_changes
  2    FROM v$session s, v$sess_io i
  3    WHERE s.sid = i.sid
  4    ORDER BY 5 desc, 1, 2, 3, 4;
```

- Run the query multiple times and examine the delta between each occurrence of block_changes. Large deltas indicate high redo generation by the session.

- Query v$transaction: This view contains information about the amount of undo blocks and undo records accessed by the transaction (as found in the used_ublk and used_urec columns).

- The query you can use is:

```
SQL> SELECT s.sid, s.serial#, s.username, s.program,
t.used_ublk, t.used_urec
  2    FROM v$session s, v$transaction t
  3    WHERE s.taddr = t.addr
  4    ORDER BY 5 desc, 6 desc, 1, 2, 3, 4;
```

- Run the query multiple times and examine the delta between each occurrence of used_ublk and used_urec. Large deltas indicate high redo generation by the session.

You use the first query when you need to check for programs generating lots of redo when these programs activate more than one transaction. The latter query can be used to find out which particular transactions are generating redo.

Some other important facts

In this section we will talk about some other important facts about redo that are important for you to know.

Redo and undo for DML

When you issue an insert, update, or delete, Oracle actually makes the change to the data blocks that contain the affected data even though you have not issued a commit. To ensure database integrity, Oracle must write information necessary to reverse the change (undo) into the redo log file to handle any transaction failure or even a rollback. Recovery from media failure is ensured by writing the information necessary to replay all database changes (redo) to the database into the redo log file. So, undo and redo information needs to be written into the transaction log of the RDBMS as a logical consequence to protect the integrity of the data.

While the RDBMS logically would only need to write undo and redo into the transaction log, the undo portion must also be kept online (on disk and accessible to the RDBMS engine) to enable rollback of failed transactions, and as importantly, for read consistency — read consistency is actually the reason we have undo and redo separate. Oracle have undo especially for read consistency and just happen to use it instead of the transaction logs to rollback. If undo data was only stored in the transaction log, the log could get archived and the RDBMS would have to try to read it from the ARCHIVELOG file or tape. On some platforms, the tape could be sitting in the DBA's desk drawer, so there are practical problems with this solution. Every RDBMS must meet the basic requirement of online access to undo data, and Oracle does this by storing the undo data in what we call **rollback segments** (where rollback means undo).

Because Oracle places the undo data into a rollback segment and also must (logically) place this data into the transaction log, it is simpler to just treat the UNDO tablespace like any other tablespace from a log generation perspective. That is why Oracle generates redo for a rollback segment, which is logically the same as undo for a data block (that is your table, index, and so on).

Oracle's transaction log is really called the redo log because it only contains redo records. There logically must be undo records stored in the log, but they are stored in the form of redo for undo segments.

Before Oracle 12*c* for temporary tables, Oracle needed to use undo to facilitate a rollback, to save point, and also for read consistency; not only to reclaim a space that was used by the temporary table, but in Oracle 12*c* all will be kept in the TEMP tablespace itself due that undo for TEMP goes into TEMP now.

Redo and temporary tables

Before Oracle 12*c*, the number of redo log entries generated by a temporary table was approximately 50% of the redo log entries generated for permanent tables. However, you must consider that an INSERT command requires only a small amount of undo data, whereas a DELETE command requires a large amount of redo data. (INSERT just stores delete+rowid in the undo, UPDATE stores the before image of the modified columns+rowid in undo, and DELETE stores the entire row+rowid in undo.) If you tend to insert data into temporary tables and don't delete the data when you're done, the relative redo log generation rate may be much lower for temporary tables than 50% of the redo log generation rate for permanent tables. Now with Oracle 12*c*, temporary tables will not generate redo.

Redo generation and materialized views

Setting the NOLOGGING option during the materialized view creation does not affect this fact as the option only applies during the actual creation and not to any subsequent actions on the materialized view.

Enhancement requests have been raised to be able to turn off redo generation during a refresh, but these were rejected as doing this could put the database into an inconsistent state and affect options such as Data Guard, as well as backup and recovery.

The amount of redo generated during a complete refresh can be reduced by setting ATOMIC_REFRESH=FALSE in the DBMS_MVIEW.REFRESH option. The complete refresh will use a TRUNCATE+INSERT /*+APPEND*/ command to refresh, and this can skip all undo and redo.

Flashback and NOLOGGING

When using Flashback Database with a target time at which a NOLOGGING operation was made, a block corruption is likely to be produced in the database objects and datafiles affected by the NOLOGGING operation.

For example, if you perform a direct path insert operation in the NOLOGGING mode and that operation runs from 9:00 A.M. to 9:15 A.M. on July 7, 2013, and later you require to use Flashback Database to return to the target time 09:07 A.M. on that date, the objects and datafiles modified by the direct path insert may leave the database with block corruption after the Flashback Database operation completes.

If possible, avoid using Flashback Database with a target time or SCN that coincides with a NOLOGGING operation. Also, always perform a full or incremental backup of the affected datafiles immediately after any NOLOGGING operation is done to ensure recoverability to a given point-in-time. If you expect to use Flashback Database to return to a point-in-time during an operation such as a direct path insert, consider to perform the operation in the LOGGING mode to ensure the recoverability of it.

Performance and recovery considerations

The NOLOGGING mode improves performance during direct path operations because it generates much less log data in the redo log files, helping eliminate the time necessary to execute the redo generation (latch acquisition, redo log writing, and so on). The user is responsible for backing up the data after a NOLOGGING insert operation in order to be able to perform media recovery.

Direct path load using SQL*Loader

To use direct path load in SQL*Loader, you must run the $ORACLE_HOME/rdbms/admin/catldr.sql script before your first load is run in the direct path mode. To run sqlldr in the direct path mode, specify the option direct=true.

To save time and space in the redo log file, use the SQL*Loader UNRECOVERABLE clause in the SQL*Loader control file when you load the data. An unrecoverable load does not record loaded data in the redo log file, instead it generates invalidation redo.

The UNRECOVERABLE clause applies to all objects loaded during the load session (both data and index segments). Therefore, media recovery is disabled for the loaded table, although database changes by other users may continue to be logged.

 Because the data loaded in this scenario is not logged, you may want to make a backup of the data after the load is completed.

If media recovery becomes necessary on the data that was loaded with the UNRECOVERABLE clause, then the data blocks that were loaded are marked as logically corrupted. To recover the data, you will need to drop and re-create the data. It is a good idea to do backups immediately after a load as this is done to preserve the otherwise unrecoverable data.

 By default, a direct path load is recoverable.

The following is an example of specifying the UNRECOVERABLE clause in the control file:

```
UNRECOVERABLE
LOAD DATA
INFILE 'example.dat'
INTO TABLE test
(name VARCHAR2(10), number NUMBER(4));
```

If a data or index segment has the NOLOGGING mode set, then full image redo logging is disabled for that segment (and of course, invalidation of redo is generated). The use of the NOLOGGING parameter allows a finer degree of control over the objects that will not generate LOGGING.

The NOLOGGING clause also specifies that subsequent direct loads using SQL*Loader and direct load insert operations are not logged. Subsequent DML statements (UPDATE, DELETE, and conventional path insert) are unaffected by the NOLOGGING attribute of the table and generate redo. In general, the relative performance improvement of specifying NOLOGGING is greater for larger tables than for smaller tables.

Some useful scripts

Now is the time to see some important scripts that could help your life become a little bit easier when dealing with redo.

Redo generated since instance startup

The script redo_since_startup.sql will show statistics regarding redo since the instance was started.

The following is an example of the output of this script:

```
                        Redo Log Statistics


Statistic                                       Statistic
Name                                            Value
------------------------------------------- ----------
redo KB read                                       209048
redo KB read (memory)                                   0
redo KB read (memory) for transport                     0
redo KB read for transport                              0
redo blocks checksummed by FG (exclusive)          205974
redo blocks checksummed by LGWR                         0
redo blocks read for recovery                        8532
redo blocks written                                367495
redo buffer allocation retries                         32
redo entries                                       277700
redo entries for lost write detection                   0
redo k-bytes read for recovery                       4266
redo k-bytes read for terminal recovery                 0
redo log space requests                                 5
redo log space wait time                               26
redo ordering marks                                     1
redo size                                       179922296
redo size for direct writes                      14202508
redo size for lost write detection                      0
redo subscn max counts                                  0
redo synch long waits                                 703
redo synch poll writes                                  0
redo synch polls                                        0
redo synch time                                       863
redo synch time (usec)                            8790494
redo synch time overhead (usec)                4.2761E+10
redo synch time overhead count (<128 msec)             10
```

```
redo synch time overhead count (<2 msec)                301
redo synch time overhead count (<32 msec)                38
redo synch time overhead count (<8 msec)                441
redo synch time overhead count (>=128 msec)              33
redo synch writes                                       879
redo wastage                                        2536524
redo write broadcast ack count                            0
redo write broadcast ack time                             0
redo write broadcast lgwr post count                      0
redo write info find                                    823
redo write info find fail                                 0
redo write time                                        5373
redo writes                                           11599

40 rows selected.
```

Redo generated since session startup

The script `redo_since_session_started.sql` shows how much redo was generated since your session started. The value it shows here is in bytes:

```
REDO_SIZE
----------
  25736452
```

Redo generated by current user sessions

The useful script `redo_generated_by_session.sql` shows how much redo is being generated by each active session in the database:

```
       SID USERNAME                          REDO_SIZE
---------- ---------------------------- ----------
        44 TEST                           25736656
```

Current status for redo logs

The following is an interesting script (`redo_current_status.sql`) showing some very important information regarding the redo log files. The script reports on the threads, number of members per group, whether a group was archived or not, size, and SCN. The following screenshot illustrates this:

```
                                                 Current Redo Log Status
                                                               First
 Th#   Grp#    Seq#     BYTES  Mem Arc? STATUS           Change# Time
 ----  ------  -------  -----  --- ---- -------      ------------ --------------------
  1     1        13   52428800   1 NO   INACTIVE       1,851,304 02-jul-2013 19:00
        2        14   52428800   1 NO   INACTIVE       1,870,230 16-jul-2013 17:00
        3        15   52428800   1 NO   CURRENT        1,894,738 02-aug-2013 14:41
SQL>
```

Redo log group and log switch information

This section's script (`redo_switch_info.sql`) is in my opinion one of the most important scripts in this chapter. It will clearly show you how many log switches occurred by day and hour. That information helps you easily identify common hours of overload in redo generation. It also helps you spot the need to tune your redo log files size to reduce log switches. Let's have a look at the following screenshot:

```
Log Switch on hour basis

Day             00  01  02  03  04  05  06  07  05  09  10  11  12  13  14  15  16  17  18  19  20  21  22  23  TOTAL
--------------- --- --- --- --- --- --- --- --- --- --- --- --- --- --- --- --- --- --- --- --- --- --- --- --- -----
MON, 01-JUL-2013  -   .   .   -   .   .   -   .   .   -   .   .   -   .   .   -   .   .   -   6   -   2   -        8
TUE, 02-JUL-2013  -   .   .   -   .   .   -   .   .   -   2   .   -   .   .   -   2   -   1   -   .   .   .        5
TUE, 16-JUL-2013  -   .   .   -   .   .   -   .   .   -   .   .   -   .   .   -   1   -   .   -   .   .   .        1
SQL> Ttitle off
SQL>
```

NOLOGGING objects in the database

The following are some queries that will help you identify objects (tables, indexes, tablespaces, and partitions) in the database that are currently in the NOLOGGING mode:

```
SQL> SELECT owner , table_name

  2    FROM dba_tables

  3    WHERE logging='NO';

SQL> SELECT owner , table_name, index_name

  2    FROM dba_indexes

  3    WHERE logging='NO';

SQL> SELECT tablespace_name

  2    FROM dba_tablespaces
```

```
 3    WHERE logging='NOLOGGING';
SQL> SELECT TABLE_NAME, PARTITION_NAME
 2    FROM user_tab_partitions
 3    WHERE logging='NO';
```

Summary

In this chapter, you learned about the LOGGING and NOLOGGING modes and saw how to use them. You also have seen different techniques for reducing redo generation when using the LOGGING and NOLOGGING modes. Hopefully we've cleared up some misconceptions about NOLOGGING operations as well. The NOLOGGING mode is one of my favorite topics in Oracle, and I hope you have enjoyed this chapter as much I have enjoyed writing it.

In the next chapter, we will talk about what is new in Oracle 12*c* for backup and recovery. We will see many new features and enhancements that will make our life more easy and our database recoverable.

3
What is New in 12c

Oracle Database 12c has introduced many new features and enhancements for backup and recovery. This chapter will introduce you to some of them and later in this book, you will have the opportunity to learn in more detail how they could be used in real life situations. But I cannot start talking about Oracle 12c without talking first about a revolutionary whole new concept that was introduced with this new version of the database product, called **Multitenant Container Database** (CDB) that will contain two or more **pluggable databases** (PDB).

When a container database only contains one PDB it is called Single Tenant Container Database. You can also have your database on Oracle 12c using the same format as before 12c, it will be called non-CDB database and will not allow the use of PDBs.

In this chapter, we will cover the following topics:

- Pluggable database
- RMAN's new features and enhancements
- Data Pump's new features and enhancements

Pluggable database

We are now able to have multiple databases sharing a single instance and Oracle binaries. Each of the databases will be configurable to a degree and will allow some parameters to be set specifically for themselves (due that they will share the same initialization parameter file) and what is better, each database will be completely isolated from each other without either knowing that the other exists.

A CDB is a single physical database that contains a root container with the main Oracle data dictionary and at least one PDB with specific application data. A PDB is a portable container with its own data dictionary, including metadata and internal links to the system-supplied objects in the root container, and this PDB will appear to an Oracle Net client as a traditional Oracle database. The CDB also contains a PDB called SEED, which is used as a template when an empty PDB needs to be created. The following figure shows an example of a CDB with five PDBs:

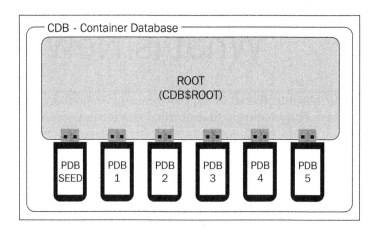

When creating a database on Oracle 12*c*, you can now create a CDB with one or more PDBs, and what is even better is that you can easily clone a PDB, or unplug it and plug it into a different server with a preinstalled CDB, if your target server is running out of resources such as CPU or memory. Many years ago, the introduction of external storage gave us the possibility to store data on external devices and the flexibility to plug and unplug them to any system independent of their OS. For example, you can connect an external device to a system using Windows XP and read your data without any problems. Later you can unplug it and connect it to a laptop running Windows 7 and you will still be able to read your data. Now with the introduction of Oracle pluggable databases, we will be able to do something similar with Oracle when upgrading a PDB, making this process simple and easy. All you will need to do to upgrade a PDB, as per example, is:

1. Unplug your PDB (step 1 in the following figure) that is using a CDB running 12.1.0.1.

2. Copy the PDB to the destination location with a CDB that is using a later version such as 12.2.0.1 (step 2 in the following figure).

3. Plug the PDB to the CDB (step 3 in the following figure), and your PDB is now upgraded to 12.2.0.1.

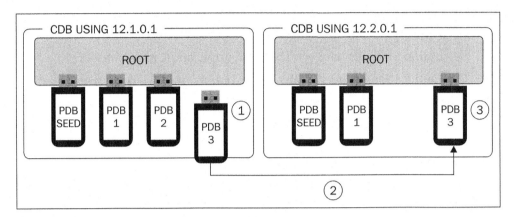

This new concept is a great solution for database consolidation and is very useful for multitenant **SaaS** (**Software as a Service**) providers, improving resource utilization, manageability, integration, and service management.

Some key points about pluggable databases are:

- You can have many PDBs if you want inside a single container (a CDB can contain a maximum of 253 PDBs)

- A PDB is fully backwards compatible with an ordinary pre-12.1 database in an applications perspective, meaning that an application built for example to run on Oracle 11.1 will have no need to be changed to run on Oracle 12*c*

- A system administrator can connect to a CDB as a whole and see a single system image

- If you are not ready to make use of this new concept, you can still be able to create a database on Oracle 12*c* as before, called non-CDB (non-Container Database)

- Each instance in RAC opens the CDB as a whole. A foreground session will see only the single PDB it is connected to and sees it just as a non-CDB

- The Resource Manager is extended with some new between-PDB capabilities

- Fully integrated with Oracle Enterprise Manager 12*c* and SQL Developer

- Fast provisioning of new databases (empty or as a copy/clone of an existing PDB)

- On Clone triggers can be used to scrub or mask data during a clone process
- Fast unplug and plug between CDBs
- Fast path or upgrade by unplugging a PDB and plugging it into a different CDB already patched or with a later database version
- Separation of duties between DBA and application administrators
- Communication between PDBs is allowed via intra-CDB dblinks
- Every PDB has a default service with its name in one Listener
- An unplugged PDB carries its lineage, Opatch, encryption key info, and much more
- All PDBs in a CDB should use the same character set
- All PDBs share the same control files, SPFILE, redo log files, flashback log files, and undo
- Flashback PDB is not available on 12.1, it expected to be available with 12.2
- Allows multitenancy of Oracle Databases, very useful for centralization, especially if using **Exadata**

 Multitenant Container Database is only available for Oracle Enterprise Edition as a payable option, all other editions of the Oracle database can only deploy non-CDB or Single Tenant Pluggable databases.

RMAN new features and enhancements

Now we can continue and take a fast and closer look at some of the new features and enhancements introduced in this database version for RMAN.

Container and pluggable database backup and restore

As we saw earlier, the introduction of Oracle 12*c* and the new pluggable database concept made it possible to easily centralize multiple databases maintaining the individuality of each one when using a single instance. The introduction of this new concept also forced Oracle to introduce some new enhancements to the already existent BACKUP, RESTORE, and RECOVERY commands to enable us to be able to make an efficient backup or restore of the complete CDB. This includes all PDBs or just one of more PDBs, or if you want to be more specific, you can also just backup or restore one or more tablespaces from a PDB.

Some examples of how to use the RMAN commands when performing a backup on Oracle 12*c* are:

```
RMAN> BACKUP DATABASE; (To backup the CBD + all PDBs)
RMAN> BACKUP DATABASE root; (To backup only the CBD)
RMAN> BACKUP PLUGGABLE DATABASE pdb1,pdb2; (To backup all specified
PDBs)
RMAN> BACKUP TABLESPACE pdb1:example; (To backup a specific
tablespace in a PDB)
```

Some examples when performing RESTORE operations are:

```
RMAN> RESTORE DATABASE; (To restore an entire CDB, including all
PDBs)
RMAN> RESTORE DATABASE root; (To restore only the root container)
RMAN> RESTORE PLUGGABLE DATABASE pdb1; (To restore a specific PDB)
RMAN> RESTORE TABLESPACE pdb1:example; (To restore a tablespace in a
PDB)
```

Finally, some example of RECOVERY operations are:

```
RMAN> RECOVER DATABASE; (Root plus all PDBs)
RMAN> RUN {
   SET UNTIL SCN 1428;
   RESTORE DATABASE;
   RECOVER DATABASE;
   ALTER DATABASE OPEN RESETLOGS; }
RMAN> RUN {
   RESTORE PLUGGABLE DATABASE pdb1 TO RESTORE POINT one;
   RECOVER PLUGGABLE DATABASE pdb1 TO RESTORE POINT one;
   ALTER PLUGGABLE DATABASE pdb1 OPEN RESETLOGS;}
```

Enterprise Manager Database Express

The Oracle Enterprise Manager Database Console or Database Control that many of us used to manage an entire database is now deprecated and replaced by the new Oracle Enterprise Manager Database Express. This new tool uses Flash technology and allows the DBA to easily manage the configurations, storage, security, and performance of a database. Note that RMAN, Data Pump, and the **Oracle Enterprise Manager Cloud Control** are now the only tools able to perform backup and recovery operations in a pluggable database environment, in other words, you cannot use the Enterprise Manager Database Express for database backup/recovery operations.

Backup privileges

Oracle Database 12*c* provides separation support for the separation of DBA duties for the Oracle Database by introducing task-specific and least privileged administrative privileges for backups that do not require the SYSDBA privilege. The new system privilege introduced with this new release is SYSBACKUP.

 Avoid the use of the SYSDBA privilege for backups unless it is strictly necessary.

When connecting to the database using the AS SYSDBA system privilege, you are able to see any object structure and all the data within the object, whereas if you are connecting using the new system privilege AS SYSBACKUP, you will still be able to see the structure of an object but not the object data. If you try to see any data using the SYSBACKUP privilege, the ORA-01031: insufficient privileges message will be raised.

Tighter security policies require a separation of duties. The new SYSBACKUP privilege facilitates the implementation of the separation of duties, allowing backup and recovery operations to be performed without implicit access to the data, so if access to the data is required for one specific user, it will need to be granted explicitly to this user.

RMAN has introduced some changes when connecting to a database such as:

* TARGET: It will require the user to have the SYSBACKUP administrative privilege to be able to connect to the TARGET database
* CATALOG: As in the earlier versions a user was required to have the RECOVERY_CATALOG_OWNER role assigned to be able to connect to the RMAN catalog, now it will need to have assigned the SYSBACKUP privilege to be able to connect to the catalog
* AUXILIARY: It will require the SYSBACKUP administrative privilege to connect to the AUXILIARY database

Some important points about the SYSBACKUP administrative privilege are:

* It includes permissions for backup and recovery operations
* It does not include data access privileges such as SELECT ANY TABLE that the SYSDBA privilege has
* It can be granted to the SYSBACKUP user that is created during the database installation process

- It's the default privilege when a RMAN connection string is issued and does not contain the AS SYSBACKUP clause:

```
$ RMAN TARGET /
```

 Before connecting as the SYSBACKUP user created during the database creation process, you will need to unlock the account and grant the SYSBACKUP privilege to the user. When you use the GRANT command to give the SYSBACKUP privilege to a user, the username and privilege information will be automatically added to the database password file.

The v$pwfile_users view contains all information regarding users within the database password file and indicates whether a user has been granted any privileged system privilege. Let's take a closer look to this view:

```
SQL> DESC v$pwfile_users
```

Name	Null?	Type
USERNAME		VARCHAR2(30)
SYSDBA		VARCHAR2(5)
SYSOPER		VARCHAR2(5)
SYSASM		VARCHAR2(5)
SYSBACKUP		VARCHAR2(5)
SYSDG		VARCHAR2(5)
SYSKM		VARCHAR2(5)
CON_ID		NUMBER

As you can see, this view now contains some new columns, such as:

- SYSBACKUP: It indicates if the user is able to connect using the SYSBACKUP privileges

- SYSDG: It indicates if the user is able to connect using the SYSDG (new for Data Guard) privileges

- SYSKM: It indicates if the user is able to connect using the SYSKM (new for Advanced Security) privileges.

- CON_ID: It is the ID of the current container. If 0, it will indicate that it is related to the entire CDB or to an entire traditional database (non-CDB): if the value is 1, then this user has the access only to root; if other value, then the view will identify a specific container ID.

To help you clearly understand the use of the SYSBACKUP privilege, let's run a few examples to make it completely clear.

Let's connect to our newly created database as SYSDBA and take a closer look at the SYSBACKUP privilege:

```
$ sqlplus / as sysdba


SQL> SET PAGES 999
SQL> SET LINES 99
SQL> COL USERNAME    FORMAT A21
SQL> COL ACCOUNT_STATUS FORMAT A20
SQL> COL LAST_LOGIN        FORMAT A41
SQL> SELECT username, account_status, last_login
  2    FROM   dba_users
  3    WHERE  username = 'SYSBACKUP';


USERNAME       ACCOUNT_STATUS       LAST_LOGIN
------------   --------------------   -------------------------
SYSBACKUP      EXPIRED & LOCKED
```

As you can see, the SYSBACKUP account created during the database creation is currently EXPIRED & LOCKED, you will need to unlock this account and grant the SYSBACKUP privilege to it if you want to use this user for any backup and recovery purposes:

> For this demo I will use the original SYSBACKUP account, but in a production environment never use the SYSBACKUP account, instead grant the SYSBACKUP privilege to the user(s) that will be responsible for the backup and recovery operations.

```
SQL> ALTER USER sysbackup IDENTIFIED BY "demo" ACCOUNT UNLOCK;


User altered.


SQL> GRANT sysbackup TO sysbackup;


Grant succeeded.
```

```
SQL> SQL> SELECT username, account_status
  2   FROM dba_users
  3   WHERE account_status NOT LIKE '%LOCKED';


USERNAME             ACCOUNT_STATUS
-------------------- --------------------
SYS                  OPEN
SYSTEM               OPEN
SYSBACKUP            OPEN
```

We can also easily identify what system privileges and roles are assigned to SYSBACKUP by executing the following SQLs:

```
SQL> COL grantee FORMAT A20
SQL> SELECT *
  2   FROM dba_sys_privs
  3   WHERE grantee = 'SYSBACKUP';


GRANTEE        PRIVILEGE                               ADM COM
-------------- --------------------------------------- --- ---
SYSBACKUP      ALTER SYSTEM                            NO  YES
SYSBACKUP      AUDIT ANY                               NO  YES
SYSBACKUP      SELECT ANY TRANSACTION                  NO  YES
SYSBACKUP      SELECT ANY DICTIONARY                   NO  YES
SYSBACKUP      RESUMABLE                               NO  YES
SYSBACKUP      CREATE ANY DIRECTORY                    NO  YES
SYSBACKUP      UNLIMITED TABLESPACE                    NO  YES
SYSBACKUP      ALTER TABLESPACE                        NO  YES
SYSBACKUP      ALTER SESSION                           NO  YES
SYSBACKUP      ALTER DATABASE                          NO  YES
SYSBACKUP      CREATE ANY TABLE                        NO  YES
SYSBACKUP      DROP TABLESPACE                         NO  YES
SYSBACKUP      CREATE ANY CLUSTER                      NO  YES


13 rows selected.


SQL> COL granted_role FORMAT A30
```

```
SQL> SELECT *
  2   FROM dba_role_privs
  3   WHERE grantee = 'SYSBACKUP';


GRANTEE          GRANTED_ROLE                        ADM DEF COM
--------------   -----------------------------       --- --- ---
SYSBACKUP        SELECT_CATALOG_ROLE                 NO  YES YES
```

Where the column ADMIN_OPTION refers to if the user has or not, the ADMIN_OPTION privilege, the column DEFAULT_ROLE indicates whether or not ROLE is designated as a default role for the user, and the column COMMON refers to if it's common to all the containers and pluggable databases available.

SQL and DESCRIBE

As you know well, you are able to execute the SQL commands, and the PL/SQL procedures from the RMAN command line starting with Oracle 12.1, do not require the use of the SQL prefix or quotes for most SQL commands in RMAN.

You can now run some simple SQL commands in RMAN such as:

```
RMAN> SELECT TO_CHAR(sysdate,'dd/mm/yy - hh24:mi:ss')
2> FROM dual;


TO_CHAR(SYSDATE,'DD)
-------------------
17/09/12 - 02:58:40


RMAN> DESC v$datafile


Name                            Null?    Type
---------------------------     -------- -----------------
FILE#                                    NUMBER
CREATION_CHANGE#                         NUMBER
CREATION_TIME                            DATE
TS#                                      NUMBER
RFILE#                                   NUMBER
STATUS                                   VARCHAR2(7)
ENABLED                                  VARCHAR2(10)
CHECKPOINT_CHANGE#                       NUMBER
```

CHECKPOINT_TIME	DATE
UNRECOVERABLE_CHANGE#	NUMBER
UNRECOVERABLE_TIME	DATE
LAST_CHANGE#	NUMBER
LAST_TIME	DATE
OFFLINE_CHANGE#	NUMBER
ONLINE_CHANGE#	NUMBER
ONLINE_TIME	DATE
BYTES	NUMBER
BLOCKS	NUMBER
CREATE_BYTES	NUMBER
BLOCK_SIZE	NUMBER
NAME	VARCHAR2(513)
PLUGGED_IN	NUMBER
BLOCK1_OFFSET	NUMBER
AUX_NAME	VARCHAR2(513)
FIRST_NONLOGGED_SCN	NUMBER
FIRST_NONLOGGED_TIME	DATE
FOREIGN_DBID	NUMBER
FOREIGN_CREATION_CHANGE#	NUMBER
FOREIGN_CREATION_TIME	DATE
PLUGGED_READONLY	VARCHAR2(3)
PLUGIN_CHANGE#	NUMBER
PLUGIN_RESETLOGS_CHANGE#	NUMBER
PLUGIN_RESETLOGS_TIME	DATE
CON_ID	NUMBER

```
RMAN> ALTER TABLESPACE users
2> ADD DATAFILE '/u01/app/oracle/oradata/cdb1/pdb1/user02.dbf' size 50M;
```

```
Statement processed
```

 Remember that the SYSBACKUP privilege does not grant access to the user tables or views, but the SYSDBA privilege does.

Multi-section backups for incremental backups

Oracle Database 11*g* introduced multi-section backups to allow us to backup and restore very large files using backup sets (remember that Oracle datafiles can be up to 128 TB in size). Now with Oracle Database 12*c*, we are able to make use of image copies when creating multi-section backups as a complement of the previous backup set functionality.

This helps us to reduce image copy creation time for backups, transporting tablespaces, cloning, and doing a **TSPITR (tablespace point-in-time recovery)**, it also improves backups when using Exadata.

The main restrictions to make use of this enhancement are:

- The COMPATIBLE initialization parameter needs to be set to 12.0 or higher to make use of the new image copy multi-section backup feature
- This is only available for datafiles and cannot be used to backup control or password files
- Not to be used with a large number of parallelisms when a file resides on a small number of disks, to avoid each process to compete with each other when accessing the same device

Another new feature introduced with multi-section backups is the ability to create multi-section backups for incremental backups. This will allow RMAN to only backup the data that has changed since the last backup, consequently enhancing the performance of multi-section backups due that they are processed independently, either serially or in parallel.

Network-based recovery

Restoring and recovering files over the network is supported starting with Oracle Database 12*c*. We can now recover a standby database and synchronize it with its primary database via the network without the need to ship the archive log files.

When the RECOVER command is executed, an incremental backup is created on the primary database. It is then transferred over the network to the physical standby database and applied to the standby database to synchronize it within the primary database. RMAN uses the SCN from the standby datafile header and creates the incremental backup starting from this SCN on the primary database, in other words, only bringing the information necessary to the synchronization process. If block change tracking is enabled for the primary database, it will be used while creating the incremental backup making it faster.

A network-based recovery can also be used to replace any missing datafiles, control files, SPFILE, or tablespaces on the primary database using the corresponding entity from the physical standby to the recovery operation. You can also use multi-section backup sets, encryption, or even compression within a network-based recovery.

Active Duplicate

The Active Duplicate feature generates an online backup on the TARGET database and directly transmits it via an inter-instance network connection to the AUXILIARY database for duplication (not written to disk in the source server). Consequently, this reduces the impact on the TARGET database by offloading the data transfer operation to the AUXILIARY database, also reducing the duplication time. This very useful feature has now received some important enhancements. In Oracle 11g when this feature was initially introduced, it only allowed us to use a push process based on the image copies. Now it allows us to make use of the already known push process or to make use of the newly introduced pull process from the AUXILIARY database that is based on backup sets (the pull process is now the new default and automatically copies across all datafiles, control files, SPFILE and archive log files). Then it performs the restore of all files and uses a memory script to complete the recovery operation and open the AUXILIARY database. RMAN will dynamically determine, based on your DUPLICATE clauses, which process will be used (push or pull).

It is very possible that soon Oracle will end deprecating the push process on the future releases of the database.

You can now choose your choice of compression, section size, and encryption to be used during the Active Duplication process. For example, if you specify the SET ENCRYPTION option before the DUPLICATE command, all the backups sent from the target to the auxiliary database will be encrypted.

For an effective use of parallelism, allocate more AUXILIARY channels instead of TARGET channels as in the earlier releases.

Finally, another important new enhancement is the possibility to finish the duplication process with the AUXILIARY database in not open state (the default is to open the AUXILIARY database after the duplication is completed).

This option is very useful when you are required to:

- Modify the block change tracking
- Configure fast incremental backups or flashback database settings
- Move the location of the database, for example, to ASM
- Upgrade the AUXILIARY database (due that the database must not be open with reset logs prior to applying the upgrade scripts)
- Or when you know that the attempt to open the database would produce errors

To make it clearer, let's take a closer look at what operations RMAN will perform when a DUPLICATE command is used:

1. Create an SPFILE string for the AUXILIARY instance.
2. Mount the backup control file.
3. Restore the TARGET datafiles on the AUXILIARY database.
4. Perform incomplete recovery using all the available incremental backups and archived redo log files.
5. Shut down and restart the AUXILIARY instance in the NOMOUNT mode.
6. Create a new control file, create and store the new database ID in the datafiles (it will not happen if the FOR STANDBY clause is in use).
7. Mount and opens the duplicate database using the RESETLOGS option, and create the online redo log files by default. If the NOOPEN option is used, the duplicated database will not be opened with RESETLOGS and will remain in the MOUNT state.

Here are some examples of how to use the DUPLICATE command with PDBs:

```
RMAN> DUPLICATE TARGET DATABASE TO <CDB1>;
RMAN> DUPLICATE TARGET DATABASE TO <CDB1>
      PLUGGABLE DATABASE <PDB1>, <PDB2>, <PDB3>;
```

Support for the third-party snapshot

In the past when using a third-party snapshot technology to make a backup or clone of a database, you were forced to change the database to the backup mode (BEGIN BACKUP) before executing the storage snapshot. This requirement is no longer necessary if the following conditions are met:

- The database crash is consistent at the point of the snapshot

- Write ordering is preserved for each file within the snapshot
- The snapshot stores the time at which the snapshot is completed

 If a storage vendor cannot guarantee compliance with the conditions discussed, then you must place your database in backup mode before starting with the snapshot.

The RECOVER command now has a newly introduced option called SNAPSHOT TIME that allows RMAN to recover a snapshot that was taken without being in backup mode to a consistent point-in-time.

Some examples of how to use this new option are:

```
RMAN> RECOVER DATABASE UNTIL TIME '10/12/2012 10:30:00' SNAPSHOT TIME
'10/12/2012 10:00:00';
```

```
RMAN> RECOVER DATABASE UNTIL CANCEL SNAPSHOT TIME '10/12/2012
10:00:00';
```

 Only trust your backups after you ensure that they are usable for recovery. In other words, always test your backup methodology first, ensuring that it can be used in the future in case of a disaster.

Cross-platform data transport

Starting with Oracle 12*c*, transporting data across platforms can be done making use of backup sets and also create cross-platform inconsistent tablespace backups (when the tablespace is not in the read-only mode) using image copies and backup sets.

When using backup sets, you are able to make use of the compression and multi-section options, reducing downtime for the tablespace and the database platform migrations.

 RMAN does not catalog backup sets created for cross-platform transport in the control file, and always takes into consideration the endian format of the platforms and the database open mode.

Before creating a backup set that will be used for a cross-platform data transport, the following prerequisites should be met:

- The compatible parameter in the SPFILE string should be 12.0 or greater
- The source database must be open in read-only mode when transporting an entire database due that the SYS and SYSAUX tablespaces will participate in the transport process
- If using Data Pump, the database must be open in read-write mode

You can easily check the current compatible value and open_mode of your database by running the following SQL commands:

```
SQL> SHOW PARAMETER compatible


NAME                      TYPE         VALUE
--------------------      ----------   ----------------------
compatible                string       12.0.0.0.0


SQL> SELECT open_mode FROM v$database;


OPEN_MODE
--------------------
READ WRITE
```

When making use of the FOR TRANSPORT or the TO PLATFORM clauses in the BACKUP command, you cannot make use of the following clauses:

- CUMULATIVE
- forRecoveryOfSpec
- INCREMENTAL LEVEL n
- keepOption
- notBackedUpSpec
- PROXY
- SECTION SIZE
- TAG
- VALIDATE

Table recovery

In previous versions of Oracle Database, the process to recover a table to a specific point-in-time was never easy. Oracle has now solved this major issue by introducing the possibility to do a point-in-time recovery of a table, group of tables or even table partitions without affecting the remaining database objects using RMAN. This makes the process easier and faster than ever before. Remember that Oracle has previously introduced features such as **database point-in-time recovery (DBPITR)**, **tablespace point-in-time recovery (TSPITR)** and Flashback database; this is an evolution of the same technology and principles.

The recovery of tables and table partitions is useful in the following situations:

- To recover a very small set of tables to a particular point-in-time
- To recover a tablespace that is not self-contained to a particular point-in-time, remember that TSPITR can only be used if the tablespace is self-contained
- To recover tables that are corrupted or dropped with the PURGE option, so the FLASHBACK DROP functionality is not possible to be used
- When logging for a Flashback table is enabled but the flashback target time or SCN is beyond the available undo
- To recover data that was lost after a **data definition language (DDL)** operation that changed the structure of a table

To recover tables and table partitions from a RMAN backup, the TARGET database should be (prerequisites):

- At the READ/WRITE mode
- In the ARCHIVELOG mode
- The COMPATIBLE parameter should be set to 12.0 or higher

 You cannot recover tables or table partitions from the SYS, SYSTEM and SYSAUX schemas, or even from a standby database.

Now let's take a closer look at the steps to do a table or table partitions recovery using RMAN:

1. First check if all the prerequisites to do a table recovery are met.
2. Start a RMAN session with the CONNECT TARGET command.
3. Use the RECOVER TABLE command with all the required clauses.
4. RMAN will determine which backup contains the data that needs to be recovered based on the point-in-time specified.

5. RMAN creates an AUXILIARY instance, you can also specify the location of the AUXILIARY instance files using the AUXILIARY DESTINATION or SET NEWNAME clause.

6. RMAN recovers the specified objects into the AUXILIARY instance.

7. RMAN creates a Data Pump export dump file that contains the objects.

8. RMAN imports the recovered objects from the dump file previously created into the TARGET database. If you want to manually import the objects to the TARGET database, you can make use of the NOTABLEIMPORT clause in the RECOVER command to achieve this goal.

9. RMAN optionally offers the possibility to rename the recovered objects in the TARGET database using the REMAP TABLE clause, or to import the recovered objects to a different tablespace using the REMAP TABLESPACE clause.

An example of how to use the new RECOVER TABLE command is:

```
RMAN> RECOVER TABLE SCOTT.test
    UNTIL SEQUENCE 5481 THREAD 2
    AUXILARY DESTINATION '/tmp/recover'
    REMAP TABLE SCOTT.test:my_test;
```

Data Pump's new features and enhancements

Now is the time to take a closer look at some of the new features and enhancements of Data Pump introduced in this database version on Data Pump. Data Pump will be covered in detail in *Chapter 9, Understanding Data Pump* and *Chapter 10, Advanced Data Pump*.

Disabling LOGGING on Data Pump Import

A new feature of Data Pump introduced with Oracle 12c has the possibility to disable logging generation during an import operation, allowing us to have faster imports due that the redo log information is not written to the disk or even archived. This is particularly useful for large data loads such as database migrations.

 When making use of a NOLOGGING option, always perform a full RMAN backup after the NOLOGGING operation is completed.

This new feature is now possible due to the introduction of a new metadata TRANSFORM parameter called DISABLE_ARCHIVE_LOGGING; It can be used on the impdp command line or even when using the DBMS_DATAPUMP.METADATA_TRANSFORM PL/SQL procedure.

Not all operations are logged when using DISABLE_ARCHIVE_LOGGING, the following operations during an import process will still be logged:

- The CREATE and ALTER statements (the only exception is the CREATE INDEX statement)
- All operations against the master table that is being used by Data Pump to coordinate its activities

 If the database is in the FORCE LOGGING mode, logging will not be disabled during an import operation that is making use of the DISABLE_ARCHIVE_LOGGING metadata TRANSFORM parameter.

Here is one example of how this new feature can be used:

```
$ impdp test/test TABLES=test.test1 DIRECTORY=datapump

DUMPFILE=test_test1.dmp   TRANSFORM=DISABLE_ARCHIVE_LOGGING:Y
```

Full transportable Export/Import

Full transportable Export/Import combines the usability of Data Pump with the speed of transportable tablespaces moving all the system, user(s), and application metadata necessary for a database migration without the need to go over a complex set of steps that was required when executing a traditional transportable tablespace operation. As a result, you will achieve a very fast migration, even for very large volumes of data.

A traditional transportable tablespace can require you to manually move user and application metadata (such as Synonyms, Triggers, Packages, and so on) to allow you to make use of the tablespace datafiles you migrated to the destination database using this technique.

Full transportable Export/Import will take care of all this, and will take advantage of many available options in Data Pump such as the ability to move metadata over a database link and combine it with the transportable tablespace mechanism to move user and application data. As a result, you will be able to accomplish a full database migration using less commands, making it all easier, faster and cleaner.

The full transportable Export exists since the database version 11.2.0.3, but the full transport Import was newly introduced within 12.1.0.1.

Full transport Export/Import allows cross-platform, cross-endian migration with the use of RMAN CONVERT of the datafiles, and also allows you to transfer dump files over NETWORK_LINK.

Exporting views as tables

Another new feature introduced to Data Pump is the option to export a view as a table. In this case, Data Pump will include in the dump file the corresponding table definition and all the data that was visible in the view, instead of only writing the view definition. This allows the Data Pump import to create it as a table with the same columns and data as the original view during the import process. All the objects, depending on the view, will be also exported as they were defined on the table. Grants and constraints that are associated with the view will now be recorded as grants and constraints on the corresponding table in the dump file.

This new ability to export views as tables can be used for:

- Exporting data subsets for development and testing
- Data Replication
- Exporting a denormalized dataset spanning multiple related tables (when moving data from an **online transaction processing (OLTP)** system to a Data Warehouse system)
- Offline archival purposes

  Here is one simple example of how to export a view as table:

  ```
  $ expdp test/test DIRECTORY=datapump
  DUMPFILE=testvwasatable.dmp VIEWS_AS_TABLES=employees_v
  ```

Extended character data types

This new version of the Oracle database extends the maximum size of the VARCHAR2 field, NVARCHAR2 field from 4000 bytes to 32,767 bytes and the row data type from 2000 bytes to 32,767 bytes. Columns with a data value of 4000 bytes or less will be stored inline. Only when they exceed 4000 bytes (called extended character data type columns) will they go out-of-line (they have enabled storage in the row in effect), leveraging the Oracle **Large Object (LOB)** technology. Data Pump utilities and the related packages DBMS_DATAPUMP and DBMS_METADATA (PL/SQL) are now modified to support the extended data types.

Your COMPATIBLE parameter in SPFILE should be 12.0 or greater and the MAX_SQL_STRING_SIZE parameter should be set to EXTENDED to allow Data Pump to support the extended character data types.

Encryption password

Previously, Data Pump allowed us to generate dump files with a password-based encryption key in the command line, making this easily to be hacked. Oracle has now enhanced this option adding to Data Pump the ability to prompt the user to add the encryption password without the value being echoed as it is entered. The new command-line parameter ENCRYPTION_PWD_PROMPT=Y can be now used silently at run-time, making it not visible by commands such as ps and the password will not be stored in the scripts.

 The concurrent use of the ENCRYPTION_PASSWORD and ENCRYPTION_PWD_PROMPT parameters is prohibited and will generate an error.

Compressing tables on Import

In earlier versions, Data Pump always performed an import operation using the same compression settings that were present during the export process. Data Pump is now enhanced to allow you to specify a compression method at import time regardless of the compression method used when the data was exported, or if you prefer, you can also now decompress tables during an import.

This new feature is now possible due to the introduction of a new metadata TRANSFORM parameter called TABLE_COMPRESSION_CLAUSE. If set to NONE, the table compression clause is ignored and it will be imported using the default compression mode for the tablespace, or you can use any valid table compression clause available such as: NOCOMPRESS, COMPRESS BASIC, COMPRESS FOR OLTP, COMPRESS FOR QUERY, or COMPRESS FOR ARCHIVE.

 If the table compression clause has more than one word, then you must use single or double quotation marks.

Here you can see an example of using compression on import:

```
$ impdp test/test DIRECTORY=datapump DUMPFILE=test.dmp
TRANSFORM=TABLE_COMPRESSION_CLAUSE:'COMPRESS FOR OLTP'
```

Exporting data from the data vault

If you are using Data Pump Export without encryption on a database where database vault is enabled, Data Pump will now generate a warning message to ensure that users are not exporting sensible data without using encryption by mistake. This is only a warning message and you can choose between continuing with the export process or to stop it and restart it enabling compression.

Creating SecureFile LOBs on Import

You are now enabled to specify a LOB storage method to be used during a Data Pump Import process regardless of the settings in the source database when the Data Pump Export was made. This provides a straightforward method that allows users to easily migrate from the BasicFile LOBs to SecureFile LOBs.

Once again, this new feature is only possible due to the introduction of a new metadata TRANSFORM parameter called LOB_STORAGE (as you can see, Oracle has introduced many enhancements to the TRANSFORM parameter on Data Pump).

Now let's take a look at an example of how to use this new TRANSFORM parameter in real life:

```
$ impdp test/test DIRECTORY=datapump DUMPFILE=test.dmp
TRANSFORM=LOB_STORAGE:SECUREFILE
```

When setting the parameter to SECUREFILE or BASICFILE, you are specifying the LOB storage method that will be applied to all the LOBs during the import session. If default is set, then the LOB clause is omitted and all the imported tables will use the DEFAULT mode associated with the destination tablespace. Finally, if you set the parameter to NO_CHANGE, the import process will use the LOB storage clauses that were created in the export dump file.

Auditing Data Pump commands

Oracle Database 12c introduced a unified and extensible audit framework that unifies various audit trails from different database components and is extensible to accommodate additional audit types and audit data fields. Data Pump utilities were extended to leverage the new audit framework, providing a comprehensive audit trail of all the invocations of Data Pump.

Here we can see some examples of the use of this new audit feature:

```
SQL > CREATE AUDIT POLICY datapump
2      ACTIONS COMPONENT=DATAPUMP EXPORT;


SQL> AUDIT POLICY datapump;


SQL> ALTER AUDIT POLICY datapump
2      ADD ACTION COMPONENT=DATAPUMP IMPORT;


SQL> DROP AUDIT POLICY datapump;
```

Summary

This chapter provided a sneak peak at some of the great new features and enhancements introduced with Oracle 12*c*. As per the previous chapter, there were very high level overviews of each feature, but we will take a deeper look in most of these features in the later chapters of this book.

In the next chapter, we will have the opportunity to read about an interesting topic, user-managed backup and recovery. The chapter will cover many different scenarios and I am sure you will enjoy reading it.

4
User-managed Backup and Recovery

This chapter will cover backup and recovery using user-managed methods. I decided to include this topic in the book due that I still receive many questions about this topic at Oracle conferences and even on my blog. User-managed backups are basically all the backups which you can take without using RMAN. Moreover, no automatic metadata record of the backup is generated anywhere in the database. Therefore, you must always keep records of what you backed up and where. Also, this method allows a DBA to make consistent backups of the entire database (cold backup), partial backups of a database making one or more tablespaces offline (inconsistent backup) or even online backups (inconsistent backup) can be performed as well if your database is running in the ARCHIVELOG mode.

The last option allows you to perform user-managed backups without affecting the availability of your database to the business, very useful when your database needs to be available 24/7, 365 days a year. RMAN was introduced in version 8.0 and is not compatible with prior releases of the database. It will make most of your work simpler when executing backups or any recovery process, consequently making your life a lot more easier and your database safer. We will learn more about RMAN in *Chapter 5, Understanding RMAN and Simple Backups*.

[A database is only in a consistent state after being shut down in a consistent way (using SHUTDOWN [NORMAL/IMMEDIATE/ TRANSACTIONAL).]

Understanding the basics involving a manual backup and recovery will help you easily understand what is going on in the background of your database when using RMAN and it will also help you to compare and easily understand all benefits of using RMAN against any other backup method when working with Oracle.

Before you start a user-managed backup, you will always need to know first:

1. Where all your datafiles are located and their names.
2. Where your archive logs are located.
3. Where your control file is located.
4. And finally where your SPFILE or PFILE is located.

 When doing user-managed backups, never backup online redo log files, because these files do not contain the end of backup marker and would cause corruption if used in a recovery process. When doing a recovery of your database, you will use the current online redo log files and it will avoid overwriting them if included in the backup.

You can easily collect all the information necessary to perform a user-managed backup using the following commands:

- To select the datafile's information you can use the following SQL*Plus command:

```
SQL> SELECT name
  2  FROM    v$datafile;
```

- Or if you prefer to see the tablespaces and all the associated datafiles, you can use the following SQL*Plus command:

```
SQL> SELECT    a.name tablespace, b.name datafile
  2  FROM      v$tablespace a, v$datafile b
  3  WHERE     a.ts# = b.ts#
  4  ORDER BY a.name;
```

- To check where your archive logs are being generated, you should use the following command:

```
SQL> SELECT destination
  2  FROM    v$archive_dest;
```

- Use the following command to see the name and location of your current control files:

```
SQL> SELECT name
  2  FROM    v$controlfile;
```

Always remember that the control file plays a crucial role in the database restore and recovery process, and you only need to make a backup of one copy of a multiplexed control file.

Also, do not forget to include a copy of your PFILE or SPFILE (these files are generally found in `$ORACLE_HOME/dbs` and contain all the initialization parameters for your database) when making a user-managed backup. `SPFILE` is a binary file and should never be manually modified (it will corrupt your SPFILE).

Now that you have all the information you need to perform a user-managed backup, let's take a close look at some of the most common user-managed backup and recovery options available.

Cold backup

As I mentioned earlier, cold backups are the only possible way for a DBA to perform a consistent backup of a database independent of the mode your database is running (`ARCHIVELOG` or `NOARCHIVELOG` as explained in *Chapter 1, Understanding the Basics of Backup and Recovery*).

If your database is running in the `NOARCHIVELOG` mode, all your backups should be made using this method to ensure that your database is always in a consistent mode. If your database is in the `ARCHIVELOG` mode, then you will be able to perform an additional recovery process to a more current point-in-time, applying all ARCHIVELOG files generated after your consistent backup was made.

You can easily perform a manual backup of your database with the database down by following these simple steps:

1. If your database is OPEN, then shut down your database completely in a consistent mode (use `SHUTDOWN [NORMAL/IMMEDIATE/TRANSACTIONAL]` only). This will ensure that all the database file headers are consistent to the same SCN.

2. Backup all the database datafiles, control files, and the PFILE or SPFILE (copying them to a stage area on the operating system level):

   ```
   $ cp $ORACLE_BASE/oradata/cdb1/*.dbf /stage/backup
   $ cp $ORACLE_BASE/oradata/cdb1/control01.ctl /stage/backup
   $ cp $ORACLE_HOME/dbs/spfilecdb1.ora /stage/backup
   ```

3. Restart the database.

4. Archive all unachieved redo logs so any redo required to recover the tablespace is archived and executes a backup of all the archive log files:

```
SQL> ALTER SYSTEM ARCHIVE LOG CURRENT;
$ cp $ORACLE_BASE/fast_recovery_area/*.arc /stage/backup
```

Always backup your archive log files generated between cold backups, this will ensure that you will not lose data when a recovery of your database is required.

Offline backup

If what you need to do is to perform an offline backup of one or more tablespaces, you should first notice that you cannot take the SYSTEM tablespace or a tablespace with any active UNDO segments offline. Also, when using this method always take into consideration whether the tablespace is completely self-contained before performing this type of backup, in other words, you should first check if any logical or physical dependencies between objects exist first, for example, if any index related to any table in the tablespace that will become offline is stored in a different tablespace, in such case both the tablespaces (DATA and INDEX) should be taken offline and backed up together.

Never perform offline backups of your database if it's running in the NOARCHIVELOG mode.

You can easily check whether a tablespace is self-contained using the very useful DBMS_TTS.TRANSPORT_SET_CHECK procedure (part of the DBMS_TTS package), and the TRANSPORT_SET_VIOLATIONS view as per the following example:

```
SQL> EXECUTE DBMS_TTS.TRANSPORT_SET_CHECK('example', TRUE);


PL/SQL procedure successfully completed.
SQL> SELECT * FROM transport_set_violations;


no rows selected


SQL>
```

For pluggable tablespaces, the user needs to switch the session to a pluggable database via the ALTER SESSION SET CONTAINER=<PDB_NAME> command and then run the command. If running the command to check a pluggable tablespace connected to the container or a different pluggable database, you will get the ORA-29304: error: tablespace does not exist.

 If not connected as SYS to the database, you must be granted the EXECUTE_CATALOG_ROLE role to be able to execute this procedure.

The example discussed will check if the tablespace EXAMPLE is self-contained or not, but you can also use the same statement to check more than one tablespace at the same time just adding all the tablespace names separated by a comma:

```
SQL> EXECUTE DBMS_TTS.TRANSPORT_SET_CHECK('example,example2',
TRUE);
```

If the query to the view TRANSPORT_SET_VIOLATIONS returns no rows, then your tablespace is self-contained.

Now that you know all the guidelines when backing up offline tablespaces, let's see how it can be done:

1. Identify all the datafiles associated with a tablespace by querying the DBA_DATA_FILES view:

   ```
   SQL> SELECT tablespace_name, file_name
     2  FROM   sys.dba_data_files
     3  WHERE  tablespace_name = 'EXAMPLE';
   ```

2. Take the tablespace offline using the NORMAL priority if possible (this guarantees that no recovery will be necessary when bringing the tablespace online later):

   ```
   SQL> ALTER TABLESPACE example OFFLINE NORMAL;
   ```

3. Backup all datafiles related to the now offline tablespace via the OS:

   ```
   $ cp $ORACLE_BASE/oradata/cdb1/pdb1/example_01.dbf /stage/backup
   ```

4. Bring the tablespaces online:

   ```
   SQL> ALTER TABLESPACE example ONLINE;
   ```

5. Archive all unachieved redo logs so any redo required to recover the tablespace is archived and executes a backup of all archive log files:

```
SQL> ALTER SYSTEM ARCHIVE LOG CURRENT;
$ cp $ORACLE_BASE/fast_recovery_area/*.arc /stage/backup
```

 Taking a tablespace offline using the TEMPORARY or IMMEDIATE priority will always require a tablespace recovery at the moment to bring the tablespace online.

Hot backups

Oracle introduced hot backups back in version 6, allowing us take hot backups of our database tablespaces without the need to shut down the database like in earlier versions. Moreover in version 10g, Oracle gave us the ability to take hot backups of the entire database, making our life a little more easy. When executing a user-managed backup online, Oracle stops recording checkpoints to all the associated datafiles.

Let's take a deeper look at what's happening internally in the database when we use the BEGIN BACKUP option:

- A hot backup flag in the datafiles header is set
- A checkpoint occurs, flashing all dirty blocks from memory to disk, synchronizing all the datafile headers to the same SCN, and freezing the headers for consistency, protection, and recoverability

Hot backups (inconsistent backups due to fractured data blocks) can be made to the whole database, a tablespace or even at container level and it will require a recovery process after the backup is restored. Due to this, it is very important to always ensure that all your archive log files are being backed up.

 When doing a hot backup of your database, do not include the temporary tablespace. This tablespace is not recorded in the control files and should be recreated when restoring and recovering a database.

Hot backup of a whole database

You can make a full backup of your database easily by placing first your database in backup mode using the `ALTER DATABASE BEGIN BACKUP;` statement at SQL*PLUS. This feature was introduced in version 10*g* of the Oracle Database. This is the most common type of user-managed backup that is used by many DBAs around the world.

Now let's go through all the steps required to perform this backup with the database open:

1. Place your entire database in backup mode:

    ```
    SQL> ALTER DATABASE BEGIN BACKUP;
    ```

     If you are using a pluggable database, you should use the `ALTER PLUGGABLE DATABASE <name> BEGIN BACKUP;` command instead of the one mentioned in the preceding statement.

2. Backup all datafiles and the PFILE or SPFILE strings. This backup is a simple physical copy of files at the OS level:

    ```
    $ cp $ORACLE_BASE/oradata/cdb1/*.dbf /stage/backup
    $ cp $ORACLE_HOME/dbs/spfilecdb1.ora /stage/backup
    ```

     For the ASM files, only RMAN can be used.

3. Take the database out of backup mode:

    ```
    SQL> ALTER DATABASE END BACKUP;
    ```

     If you are using a pluggable database, you should use the `ALTER PLUGGABLE DATABASE <name> END BACKUP;` command instead of the one mentioned in the preceding statement.

4. Archive all unachieved redo logs so any redo required to recover the database is archived:

    ```
    SQL> ALTER SYSTEM ARCHIVE LOG CURRENT;
    ```

5. Make a backup of all archived redo log files (OS level):

    ```
    $ cp $ORACLE_BASE/fast_recovery_area/*.arc /stage/backup
    ```

6. Create a copy of your control file using the `ALTER DATABASE` statement:

```
SQL> ALTER DATABASE BACKUP CONTROLFILE
TO'/stage/backup/control.ctf';
```

> Steps 4 and 5 are required due that all redo generated during
> the backup must be available to be applied in case of a recovery.
> Also, in this example I'm suggesting the backup of the control
> file using the `ALTER DATABASE BACKUP CONTROLFILE TO`
> statement to avoid any risk of overwriting the original control
> file during the recovery process.

Hot backup of tablespaces

Now it's time to learn how to do a hot backup of one or more tablespaces; in other words, do a backup of your tablespaces with your database running. This technique is still being used by many DBAs when doing a clone of a database at the storage level (snapshot). The beauty of this is that you can make an inconsistent backup of some pieces of your database at different times without affecting the availability of your database. In this option, you will need to switch each tablespace you want to make an online backup of into backup mode before manually copying all the datafiles involved to a secondary storage location on your machine, network, or tape. Every time a tablespace is placed in backup mode, the database copies all the changed data blocks into the redo stream to make all the data consistent until that point.

> Avoid parallel online tablespace backups (placing more than
> one tablespace in backup mode at the same time), as it will
> generate performance problems for your database. Also always
> make the backup of a tablespace on low load periods, never
> when it is being heavily used by the users.

To do an online backup of one or more tablespaces, you just need to follow these simple steps:

1. Identify all the datafiles associated with the tablespace by querying the `dba_data_files` view:

```
SQL> SELECT tablespace_name, file_name
  2  FROM   sys.dba_data_files
  3  WHERE  tablespace_name = 'EXAMPLE';
```

2. Place the tablespace in backup mode:

```
SQL> ALTER TABLESPACE example BEGIN BACKUP;
```

3. Backup all datafiles associated with the tablespace that you placed in backup mode. This backup is a physical copy of the datafiles at the OS level:

```
$ cp $ORACLE_BASE/oradata/cdb1/pdb1/example_01.dbf
/stage/backup
```

4. Place the tablespace back in the normal mode:

```
SQL> ALTER TABLESPACE example END BACKUP;
```

   If you need to backup another tablespace, go back to the step 1, if not then proceed to step 5.

5. Archive all unachieved redo logs so any redo required to recover the database is archived:

```
SQL> ALTER SYSTEM ARCHIVE LOG CURRENT;
```

6. Make a backup of all the archived redo log files (OS level):

```
$ cp $ORACLE_BASE/fast_recovery_area/*.arc /stage/backup
```

> If you forget to take your tablespace(s) off backup mode, it will generate performance problems and will also raise an error (ORA-01149) if trying to shut down the database.

Hot backup of a container database

With the introduction of Oracle 12*c*, you are now able to perform user-managed backup of a whole container database or only the root, or an individual pluggable database.

Whole container database

Follow these steps to make a backup of a whole container database:

1. Open SQL*Plus:

```
$ sqlplus /nolog
```

2. Connect to root as a user that has the SYSDBA or SYSBACKUP system privilege:

```
SQL> CONNECT system
```

   or

```
SQL> CONNECT userdba@cdb1
```

3. Place your entire database in backup mode:

```
SQL> ALTER DATABASE BEGIN BACKUP;
```

4. Identify all the datafiles that are a part of the whole container database (includes all the PDBs) by querying the `dba_data_files` view:

```
SQL> SELECT file_name
  2  FROM    sys.dba_data_files;
```

5. Backup all the datafiles and PFILE or SPFILE. This backup is a simple physical copy of the files at the OS level:

```
$ cp $ORACLE_BASE/oradata/cdb1/*.dbf /stage/backup
$ cp $ORACLE_BASE/oradata/cdb1/pdb1/*.dbf /stage/backup
$ cp $ORACLE_HOME/dbs/spfilecdb1.ora /stage/backup
```

6. Take the database out of backup mode:

```
SQL> ALTER DATABASE END BACKUP;
```

7. Archive all unachieved redo logs so that any redo required to recover the database is archived:

```
SQL> ALTER SYSTEM ARCHIVE LOG CURRENT;
```

8. Make a backup of all the archived redo log files (OS level):

```
$ cp $ORACLE_BASE/fast_recovery_area/*.arc /stage/backup
```

9. Create a copy of your control file using the ALTER DATABASE statement:

```
SQL> ALTER DATABASE BACKUP CONTROLFILE
TO'/stage/backup/control.ctf';
```

Root only or individual pluggable database

To do an online backup of the root or even one or more pluggable databases, you will just need to follow these simple steps:

1. Open SQL*Plus:

```
$ sqlplus /nolog
```

2. Connect to root or a specific pluggable database using a user with the SYSDBA or SYSBACKUP system privilege. In this example, we will connect to a specific pluggable database called pdb1:

```
SQL> CONNECT system
SQL> ALTER SESSION SET CONTAINER = pdb1;
```

or

```
SQL> CONNECT userdba@pdb1
```

3. Identify the datafiles that are part of the PDB you want to do the backup by querying the `dba_data_files` view:

```
SQL> SELECT file_name
  2  FROM    sys.dba_data_files;
```

4. Place the PDB in backup mode:

```
SQL> ALTER PLUGGABLE DATABASE pdb1 BEGIN BACKUP;
```

5. Back up all the datafiles associated with the PDB that you placed in backup mode. This backup is a physical copy of the datafiles at the OS level:

```
$ cp $ORACLE_BASE/oradata/cdb1/pdb1/* /stage/backup
```

6. Place the PDB back in normal mode:

```
SQL> ALTER PLUGGABLE DATABASE pdb1 END BACKUP;
```

7. Archive all unachieved redo logs so any redo required to recover the PDB is archived:

```
SQL> ALTER SYSTEM ARCHIVE LOG CURRENT;
```

8. Make a backup of all archived redo log files (OS level):

```
$ cp $ORACLE_BASE/fast_recovery_area/*.arc /stage/backup
```

 The `ALTER SESSION SET CONTAINER = <VALUE>` statement used to switch from one container to another can only be used with the following values: `CDB$ROOT` (to switch to root), `PDB$SEED` (to switch to SEED) or a PDB name to switch to a specific PDB.

Check datafile status

It's always useful to know how to check whether a datafile is part of a current online tablespace backup or even to determine whether you forgot any tablespaces in backup mode. This can be very easily accomplished by querying the `V$BACKUP` view, where the `STATUS` column value determines whether a datafile is currently in backup mode or not (`ACTIVE` means in backup mode and `NOT ACTIVE` means not in backup mode).

The V$BACKUP view is not useful if the control file currently in use by the database is a restored or newly created one, because a restored or re-created control file does not contain the information necessary to populate the V$BACKUP view accurately.

Here is a useful query that can be used over the V$BACKUP view to check the status of all the datafiles at the root or PDB level:

```
SQL> SET PAGESIZE 300

SQL> SET LINESIZE 300

SQL> COLUMN tb_name FORMAT A10

SQL> COLUMN df_name FORMAT A50

SQL> COLUMN status FORMAT A10

SQL> SELECT b.name AS "TB_NAME", a.file# as "DF#", a.name AS "DF_NAME",
c.status
  2    FROM V$DATAFILE a, V$TABLESPACE b, V$BACKUP c
  3    WHERE a.TS#=b.TS#
  4    AND c.FILE#=a.FILE#
  5    AND c.STATUS='ACTIVE';


TB_NAME   DF# DF_NAME                                     STATUS
-------   ---- --------------------------------          -------
EXAMPLE    11 /u01/app/oracle/oradata/cdb1/pdb1          ACTIVE
              /example01.dbf
```

Control file backup

Having a valid backup of the control file of a database is crucial for the successful recovery of a database. Due to this we will take a closer look at the available methods to make a user-managed backup of a control file.

 Always do a backup of the control file after making a structural change to a database operating in the ARCHIVELOG mode such as creating, deleting, or modifying a tablespace, due that this new information will not be available on previous backups of the control file.

Binary backup

You can generate a binary copy of the control file via a simple SQL statement. A binary copy of the control file contains additional information such as the archived redo log history, offline range for read-only and offline tablespaces, temp files entries (since 10.2) and RMAN backup sets, and copies of data.

Here is one example of the SQL statement used to create a binary copy of the control file:

```
SQL> ALTER DATABASE BACKUP CONTROLFILE TO
'[filename_including_location] ';
```

You can also specify REUSE at the end of the preceding statement to allow the new control file to overwrite the one that currently exists with the same name.

Text file backup

You can generate a text file that contains a CREATE CONTROLFILE statement based on the current control file in use by the database via a simple SQL statement that can be executed on a database in the MOUNT or OPEN state. This file is generated as a trace file and can be easily edited to create a proper script that can be used to create a new control file.

 Due that a multitenant (more than one PDB) or single-tenant (only one PDB) container database shares the same control file, you should run the ALTER DATABASE BACKUP CONTROLFILE command when connected to the container database, not when connected with a pluggable database.

Some examples of the SQL statements used to create a trace file based on the current control file in use are:

- To generate a trace file with the RESETLOGS and NORESETLOGS statements in the trace subdirectory (you can also easily identify the name and location of the generated file by reading the database alert log), use:

  ```
  SQL> ALTER DATABASE BACKUP CONTROLFILE TO TRACE;
  ```

- To generate a trace file in the trace subdirectory with the RESETLOGS option, only use:

  ```
  SQL> ALTER DATABASE BACKUP CONTROLFILE TO TRACE RESETLOGS;
  ```

- To generate a trace file in the trace subdirectory with the NORESETLOGS option, only use:

```
SQL> ALTER DATABASE BACKUP CONTROLFILE TO TRACE NORESETLOGS;
```

- To generate a trace file in a specific location with the RESETLOGS and NORESETLOGS statements, use:

```
SQL> ALTER DATABASE BACKUP CONTROLFILE TO TRACE AS
'/stage/backup/ctlf.sql';
```

- To generate a trace file in a specific location with the RESETLOGS and NORESETLOGS statements overwriting an existing file, use:

```
SQL> ALTER DATABASE BACKUP CONTROLFILE TO TRACE AS
'/stage/backup/ctlf.sql' REUSE;
```

- To generate a trace file with the RESETLOGS option, only use:

```
SQL> ALTER DATABASE BACKUP CONTROLFILE TO TRACE TRACE AS

 '/stage/backup/ctlf.sql' RESETLOGS;
```

- To generate a trace file with the NORESETLOGS option only use:

```
SQL> ALTER DATABASE BACKUP CONTROLFILE TO TRACE TRACE AS
'/stage/backup/ctlf.sql' NORESETLOGS;
```

Flashback database

Oracle Flashback Database is a feature introduced in Oracle 9*i* and heavily improved in Oracle 10*g* that gives you the ability to rewind your entire database to a specific point in time without the need to restore from your backups. Of course, the database flashback and the ARCHIVELOG mode needs to be enabled to allow you to perform a Flashback Database operation.

You can easily check if Flashback Database is enabled in your database by using the following statement via SQL*Plus:

```
SQL> SELECT flashback_on FROM v$database;


FLASHBACK_ON
------------------
YES
```

To enable Flashback Database, please follow these easy steps in SQL*Plus:

1. Ensure that your database is running in the ARCHIVELOG mode.

2. Configure the **Fast Recovery Area** (**FRA**) by setting values for the DB_RECOVERY_FILE_DEST and DB_RECOVERY_FILE_DEST_SIZE initialization parameters:

   ° DB_RECOVERY_FILE_DEST specifies the location of the FRA

     For example:

     ```
     SQL>ALTER SYSTEM SET DB_RECOVERY_FILE_DEST='/u01/fra';
     ```

   ° DB_RECOVERY_FILE_DEST_SIZE specifies the FRA size (bytes)

     For example:

     ```
     SQL>ALTER SYSTEM SET DB_RECOVERY_FILE_DEST_SIZE= 20G;
     ```

3. If using Oracle 11g R2 onwards (including Oracle 12c), just execute the following statement:

   ```
   SQL> ALTER DATABASE FLASHBACK ON;
   ```

> Due that the feature to flashback a pluggable database is still not available within Oracle 12c, you can only perform flashback database operations at the multitenant or single-tenant container database level. Consequently, do not run the ALTER DATABASE FLASHBACK command when connected to a PDB.

4. If using an Oracle Database version lower than 11g R2, you will need to run the statement discussed with your database in the MOUNT mode, then after activating FLASHBACK, you should open your database.

You can perform a database point-in-time recovery using the SQL*PLUS statement: FLASHBACK DATABASE (which can be also used through RMAN). This will rewind the database to a specific target time, SCN, redo log sequence, or the restore point. You can easily identify the whole range of possible Flashback SCNs and target times using the following statements:

```
SQL> SELECT current_scn, TO_CHAR(sysdate,'dd/mm/yyyy hh24:mi:ss')
CURRENT_DATE
  2   FROM   v$database;


CURRENT_SCN  CURRENT_DATE
```

```
-----------  -------------------
    1889811  22/04/2013 12:28:43


SQL> SELECT oldest_flashback_scn, oldest_flashback_time
  2    FROM v$flashback_database_log;


OLDEST_FLASHBACK_SCN OLDEST_FL
-------------------- ---------
             1806294 17-APR-13
```

In the preceding example, the first statement output shows us that the current database SCN is 1889811, and the second statement show us that the oldest SCN available for the flashback database is 1806294. The problem with the second statement is that the date field only shows us the date but not the time. Time is very important as we need to know exactly what the oldest moment of the database life we can rewind it to if required. To make all the date columns return the date and time, we need to alter the session using the NLS_DATE_FORMAT parameter, as we can in the following code:

```
SQL> ALTER SESSION SET nls_date_format='dd/mm/yyyy hh24:mi:ss';


Session altered.


SQL>
```

Now let's run the same statement and see if the result has changed:

```
SQL> SELECT oldest_flashback_scn, oldest_flashback_time
  2    FROM   v$flashback_database_log;


OLDEST_FLASHBACK_SCN OLDEST_FLASHBACK_TI
-------------------- -------------------
             1806294 17/04/2013 11:33:36
```

As you can see, knowing that you are able to rewind your database up to 17/04/2013 at 11:33:36 is significantly better than only knowing that you are able to rewind it up to 17/04/2013.

Now it's time to see some examples of the flash database statement, take note that you are only able to perform a FLASHBACK database when your database in the MOUNT mode (using a current control file, in other words, not using a backup or re-created control file). Due that this is a point-in-time recovery technique, you will also need to open your database using the RESETLOGS option:

> After a Flashback database, always open the database in read-only mode and run some queries to be sure that you have reversed the database to the correct point-in-time. If not, recover the database to the same state before the FLASHBACK DATABASE command was executed and try a new flashback. When you are sure that it is the correct point-in-time, then open the database with RESETLOGS.

```
SQL> SHUTDOWN IMMEDIATE
Database closed.
Database dismounted.
ORACLE instance shut down.
SQL>STARTUP MOUNT
ORACLE instance started.


Total System Global Area    839282688 bytes
Fixed Size                    2293304 bytes
Variable Size               557842888 bytes
Database Buffers            276824064 bytes
Redo Buffers                  2322432 bytes
Database mounted.
SQL> FLASHBACK DATABASE TO SCN 1806297;


Flashback complete.


SQL>ALTER DATABASE OPEN READ ONLY;


Database altered.


SQL>
SQL> SELECT current_scn
  2    FROM   v$database;
```

```
CURRENT_SCN
------------------
          1806297
SQL> SHUTDOWN IMMEDIATE
Database closed.
Database dismounted.
ORACLE instance shut down.
SQL> STARTUP MOUNT
ORACLE instance started.

Total System Global Area   839282688 bytes
Fixed Size                   2293304 bytes
Variable Size              557842888 bytes
Database Buffers           276824064 bytes
Redo Buffers                 2322432 bytes
Database mounted.
SQL> ALTER DATABASE OPEN RESETLOGS;

Database Altered.
```

Other options of the FLASHBACK DATABASE command are:

- TO BEFORE SCN: Revert the database back to its state to the SCN preceding the specified SCN:

  ```
  SQL> FLASHBACK DATABASE TO BEFORE SCN 1806297;
  ```

- TO RESTORE POINT: Revert the database to a specific restore point previously created:

  ```
  SQL> FLASHBACK DATABASE TO RESTORE POINT A;
  ```

- TO TIMESTAMP: Revert the database back to its state to a specific timestamp:

  ```
  SQL> FLASHBACK DATABASE TO TIMESTAMP TO_DATE(01-MAY-2013
  01:00:00','DD-MON-YYYY HH24:MI:SS');
  ```

- TO BEFORE TIMESTAMP: Revert the database back to its state to one second before a specific timestamp:

  ```
  SQL> FLASHBACK DATABASE TO BEFORE TIMESTAMP TO_DATE(01-MAY-

  2013  01:00:00','DD-MON-YYYY HH24:MI:SS');
  ```

- TO BEFORE RESETLOGS: Revert the database to just before the last resetlogs operation made:

  ```
  SQL> FLASHBACK DATABASE TO BEFORE RESETLOGS;
  ```

Another important information to know about flashback is how to monitor the FRA space usage. For this we will make use of two important views, they are:

- V$RECOVERY_FILE_DEST
- V$RECOVERY_AREA_USAGE

Let's take a closer look at each one of the views.

The V$RECOVERY_FILE_DEST view contains information regarding disk quota and current disk usage in the FRA, the columns of this view are:

- NAME: FRA location, this is the current value of the DB_RECOVERY_FILE_DEST initialization parameter

- SPACE_LIMIT: Maximum space of disk (in bytes) allocated that the database can use for the Fast Recovery Area, this is the current value of the DB_RECOVERY_FILE_DEST_SIZE initialization parameter

- SPACE_USED: Total amount of space (in bytes) used by all the files in the FRA

- SPACE_RECLAIMABLE: Total amount of disk (in bytes) that can be released by deleting obsolete, redundant, and other low priority files in the FRA

- NUMBER_OF_FILES: Total number of files in the FRA

- CON_ID: Container ID to which the data relates, possible values are:

  - 0: Entire CDB or entire non-CDB
  - 1: Only root in a CDB
  - n: Container ID

Now let's see one example of the information that we can retrieve from this view in real life:

```
SQL> SELECT *
  2  FROM v$recovery_file_dest;

NAME                   SPACE_LIMIT SPACE_USED SPACE_RECLAIMABLE NUMBER_OF_FILES     CON_ID
---------------------- ----------- ---------- ----------------- --------------- ----------
/u01/app/oracle/reco    5368709120 2914507776          37670400              13          0
very_area/orcl


SQL>
```

The preceding screenshot shows us that our FRA space limit is 5,368,709,120 bytes and that we are currently using 2,914,507,776 bytes and we have 13 files in the FRA. The CON_ID column show us that this data pertains to the entire CDB.

The V$RECOVERY_AREA_USAGE view contains information about how the recovery area is being used at the file level, the columns of this view are:

- FILE_TYPE: Type of files in the FRA, types of files can be:
    ◦ CONTROL FILE
    ◦ REDO LOG
    ◦ ARCHIVED LOG
    ◦ BACKUP PIECE
    ◦ IMAGE COPY
    ◦ FLASHBACK LOG
    ◦ REMOTE ARCHIVED LOG

- PERCENT_SPACE_USED: Percentage of space used in the FRA
- PERCENT_SPACE_RECLAIMABLE: Percentage of space that is reclaimable
- NUMBER_OF_FILES: Number of files in the FRA
- CON_ID: Container ID to which the data relates as we saw earlier in the V$RECOVERY_FILE_DEST explanation

One example of the information we can retrieve from this view is:

```
SQL> SELECT *
  2  FROM v$flash_recovery_area_usage;

FILE_TYPE                 PERCENT_SPACE_USED PERCENT_SPACE_RECLAIMABLE NUMBER_OF_FILES    CON_ID
------------------------- ------------------ ------------------------- --------------- ---------
CONTROL FILE                               0                         0               0         0
REDO LOG                                   0                         0               0         0
ARCHIVED LOG                              .7                        .7               5         0
BACKUP PIECE                           51.63                         0               6         0
IMAGE COPY                                 0                         0               0         0
FLASHBACK LOG                           1.95                         0               2         0
FOREIGN ARCHIVED LOG                       0                         0               0         0
AUXILIARY DATAFILE COPY                    0                         0               0         0

8 rows selected.

SQL>
```

Recovering from a user-managed backup

When recovering a database in the ARCHIVELOG mode, you can do it using an online or offline backup, depending on the type of backup strategy you are currently using in your environment. When recovering from a user-managed backup, you will be able to recover the database up to the point that the failure occurred, and you can choose to recover the database to a specific point in time based on date and time or using a SCN.

When doing a recovery of a database in the ARCHIVELOG mode you will be also able to make a recovery of:

- Datafiles
- Tablespaces
- Or if necessary, the entire database

Some important assumptions if you want to recover your database up to the point of failure are:

- You still have at least one member of each of the current redo log groups
- All archive logs required are available to be used

To perform a full database recovery from a backup of a database in the ARCHIVELOG mode, follow these steps:

1. Restore all the database datafiles from your backup.
2. Restore all the backed up archived redo logs.

3. Mount the database (using the STARTUP MOUNT command).

4. Recover the database (using the RECOVER DATABASE command).

5. Oracle will prompt you to apply redo from the archived redo logs. Simply enter AUTO at the prompt and it will automatically apply all the redo logs for you.

6. Once all the redo logs are applied, open the recovered database (using the ALTER DATABASE OPEN command).

The full recovery of tablespaces and datafiles can be performed with the database mounted or open. If you want to perform this type of recovery, follow these steps:

1. Make the tablespace offline (using the ALTER TABLESPACE <tablespace_ name> OFFLINE IMMEDIATE command).

2. Restore all the datafiles associated with the tablespace to be recovered.

3. Recover the tablespace (using the RECOVER TABLESPACE <tablespace_ name> command).

4. Once the recovery has been completed, make the tablespace online (using the ALTER TABLESPACE <tablespace_name> ONLINE command).

You can use the following steps to recover some specific datafiles without taking the tablespace offline:

1. Make the datafile offline (using the ALTER DATABASE DATAFILE <datafile_ name> OFFLINE command).

2. Restore all the datafiles to be recovered.

3. Recover the datafile (using the RECOVER DATAFILE <datafile_name> command).

4. Once the recovery has been completed, make the datafile online (using the ALTER DATABASE DATAFILE <datafile_name> ONLINE command).

This has the benefit of leaving the tablespace online when only the data that resides in the offline datafiles will be unavailable during the recovery process while all the other data will remain available.

A point-in-time recovery can be used to recover a database up to a specific point in time. Most of the time this is used to recover the database until just before a major failure or crash happens. It is also used to clone a database for test or development purpose.

If you want to recover a tablespace to a specific point in time, you will need to recover the entire database to the same point in time unless you perform a **tablespace point-in-time recovery (TSPITR)** which we will see later in *Chapter 6, Configuring and Recovering with RMAN*. This is a new functionality in Oracle 11*g*.

To recover your database to a point in time (**DBPITR**), you will just need to follow these steps:

1. Restore all database datafiles from a previous backup made before the point-in-time that you want to recover the database from.

2. Recover the database to the point-in-time using the `RECOVER DATABASE UNTIL TIME'April 18 2012 09:00:00'` command and apply the archive logs as required.

3. When the recovery is completed, open the database using the `ALTER DATABASE OPEN RESETLOGS` command.

You can also choose to do your DBPITR using an SCN instead of a specific date and time. If you want to do this, you just need to follow these easy steps:

1. Restore all database datafiles from a previous backup made before the point in time that you want to recover the database from.

2. Recover the database to the point-in-time using the `RECOVER DATABASE UNTIL SCN 2012` command and apply the archive logs as required.

3. When the recovery is completed, open the database using the `ALTER DATABASE OPEN RESETLOGS` command.

Here is an easy example of how this will happen in a real situation:

```
SQL> SHUTDOWN IMMEDIATE;
SQL> STARTUP MOUNT;
SQL> RESTORE DATABASE UNTIL SCN 2012;
SQL> RECOVER DATABASE UNTIL SCN 2012;
```

Another important point that we cannot forget is the backup of all the other Oracle components such as:

- The Oracle RDBMS (Binaries) Software (Oracle Home and Oracle Inventory)
- Network parameter files (`names.ora`, `sqlnet.ora`, `tnsnames.ora`, and `listener.ora`)
- Database parameter files (`init.ora`, `spfile.ora`, and so on)—note that RMAN allows you to backup your database parameter file only if you are using SPFILE

- The system `oratab` file and other system Oracle related files, for example, all `rc_startup` scripts for Oracle

Note that all these components do not have the need for frequent backups because they will rarely change.

Other recovery scenarios

In this section, I will teach you how to overcome some of the most common user managed restore operations that you could be involved in.

Losing all copies of the current control file

If you have lost all the copies of your current control file, you will need to restore a backup of the control file and perform an incomplete recovery, opening the database with the `RESETLOGS` option. If you do not have a current backup of the control file, you can attempt to re-create the control file by using a previous backup (if available) of the script generated by the `ALTER DATABASE BACKUP CONTROLFILE TO TRACE` command (and edit it to include any changes made to the database structure since the script was generated) to re-create the control file. If not available, create a new script (from another database) and match the control file structure in the script with the current database structure.

Losing one copy of a multiplexed control file

If you have lost one copy of a multiplexed control file, you will need to copy one of the surviving copies of the multiplexed control file into the location of the lost/ damaged control file and open the database. If the original location is inaccessible, then all you need to do is copy one of the surviving copies to a new location and edit the initialization parameter file to reflect the change, then open the database.

Loss of archived redo logs or online redo logs

If you need to perform a recovery of your database and discover that you have lost one or more archived redo logs that makes impossible to perform a complete recovery, then you will need to perform some form of point-in-time recovery (incomplete recovery) to allow you to recover your database with the data you have available. In the case of losing of the current online redo log file, perform the recovery using the `UNTIL CANCEL` option, then open your database using the `RESETLOGS` command.

Loss of SPFILE

If you lose your current SPFILE or PFILE and your database is up and running, then all you will need to do is execute the CREATE <SPFILE/PFILE> FROM MEMORY command to re-create it. If the database is down then you will need to restore it from a previous backup. Another option available if you have a current copy of the SPFILE as PFILE (created by using the CREATE PFILE FROM SPFILE statement in SQL*Plus) is to start the instance using the PFILE, then re-create the SPFILE using the CREATE SPFILE FROM PFILE statement, and finally re-start your database.

 If there is no available backup of the PFILE or SPFILE, you can still check the alert log file as the last solution to try to reconstruct PFILE.

Summary

In this chapter, we learned some concepts about how to perform user-managed backups and recoveries and how to ensure that a user-managed backup of a datafile is valid before executing a restore process. I would like to finish this chapter by saying that it is very important to periodically verify your backups to ensure that they can always be used for an unexpected recovery. Now is the time to understand RMAN and learn how to perform simple backups using this tool, an important and fascinating subject which is the topic of our next chapter.

5
Understanding RMAN and Simple Backups

A data center running with numerous databases is not uncommon these days. As the database becomes voluminous, it also raises the complexity of the infrastructure managing it. I am reminded of a popular adage here which says, "the bigger they are, the harder they fall". Therefore, there is a higher probability that a data center dealing with considerable databases that are crucial for business, may also become prone to failure and error. This would have an adverse impact on the business as well.

It would be naïve to deny the probability of a failure with such complex databases. Therefore, as the custodians of databases, what DBAs can do is to try and minimize the loss of data. This can be accomplished through an effective strategy that enables us to secure a backup of these databases that can be accessed in case of systemic failures. However, it is also rightly said that any strategy is only as good as the tool that implements it. In this chapter, we shall introduce you to a tool that acts like an elixir in case of failure. So, in the list of amazing heroes such as Superman and Batman, please welcome RMAN, the Recovery Manager – Oracle's one stop solution for both backups and recoveries.

In the chapter, we will be discussing the following topics:

- Salient features of RMAN
- Discussion about the architecture of RMAN
- Different types and formats of backups supported by RMAN
- Using RMAN for multitenant container databases

Why RMAN?

A frequently asked question by many DBAs who are accustomed to working on a logical backup mode is why we need to move over to using RMAN.

Well, we can weave a cogent argument in favor of moving on to RMAN through the following points:

- RMAN scales as your data center scales.
- RMAN provides a single backup standard for the entire enterprise.
- RMAN is supplied with the database software and so using it doesn't need any additional licensing to be purchased.
- Backups can easily be automated using RMAN scripts.
- RMAN is integrated with the Oracle Database kernel and thus is very efficient. This further implies that for the purpose of data recovery, you have one infrastructure application less to install before beginning recoveries.
- RMAN provides efficient backup metadata management as it is maintained within the control file of the target database itself. The control file uses parameters to mark the metadata as obsolete at respective internals, thus making space for new data.
- RMAN allows you to garner reports for backup management such as listing available backups, their status and availability, and listing the files which need to be backed up, through simple commands such as LIST, REPORT, and so forth.
- RMAN facilitates the use of the Recovery Catalog, which is an optional location to store metadata for multiple databases. The duration for which the metadata can be stored in the Recovery Catalog is also configurable.
- Though RMAN is mostly command-centric (there is a long list of RMAN commands), it is completely supported by the GUI based 12c Cloud Control (or for the previous releases, Enterprise Manager Grid Control). For a DBA, it means less typing and getting more work done, without compromising on efficiency.

Remember that it is always good to know your RMAN control commands in order to recover the Oracle Database in case your GUI applications fail. Further, in case you are in the *Disaster Recovery* situation, it will be possible to perform the restore of the Oracle database and recover it, much before the cloud control becomes available for the same. This know-how to restore and recover your database from the command line can be crucial in meeting key SLA restore times.

- RMAN enables us to secure incremental backups whereby we can take a backup of the changes made to the database rather than the entire database. This feature expedites data recovery and improves backup time, thus reducing strain on the infrastructure.

- RMAN can use multiple server sessions over the database it is working for. Thus, the backup and recovery tasks configured can gain the benefit of parallel processing. Further using load balancing capability, RMAN can segregate the work across multiple machines.

- RMAN can fasten the backup jobs of large sized data files by various techniques. This makes it a perfect tool for **Very Large Databases** (VLDB).

- RMAN has in-built compression techniques to reduce the size of the backups created through it.

- Using RMAN, you can do cross-platform database conversions for your databases and move them from an OS such as Linux to another OS such as Solaris.

- Using RMAN, advanced tasks such as cloning of databases becomes extremely easy.

- Only RMAN offers the detection and recovery of corrupted blocks without asking for any downtime either for the table or for the database. The famous DBMS_REPAIR package only allows marking of the corrupted blocks as permanently corrupt but doesn't recover them.

- Using RMAN for backups when the database is operational has far less overhead than doing the same via user-managed techniques. Being a DB tool, RMAN need not freeze the data file headers to know that the backup has begun.

- RMAN is completely supported by Exadata. By using Exadata specific features such as **Hybrid Columnar Compression** (HCC) and block filtering, RMAN can enhance the performance of backups by many folds.

- RMAN is completely RAC aware and offers full support to backups and recoveries for clustered databases. With the support of in-built load balancing for the RMAN channels for the least loaded nodes, the backup jobs can work seamlessly across multiple nodes.

- RMAN doesn't restrict you to work with only itself. It can be used along with third-party solutions such as Tivoli and Netbackup as well.

- With RMAN, backups can be configured for tape drives without any hassles.

A long list of features and benefits which would be hard for anyone to overlook, correct? Since we now know what RMAN is capable of, let's introduce you to it a little more closely in the following section.

Getting started with RMAN

To get started with RMAN, you would need to invoke the RMAN client which is actually a binary file. The best part is that to use it, you don't need to do anything except fire it like any other binary executable file of Oracle database (for example, `SQL*PLUS`), it's copied during the installation of the database in the standard path `$ORACLE_HOME/bin`. It goes without saying that before you execute it, you must have set the environment properly by including the `$ORACLE_HOME/bin` in the OS path. Failing to do so would result in the error stating **rman is not found**. If you are all set, when you issue the command `RMAN` on the OS terminal, you will be welcomed with a `RMAN` prompt by the `RMAN` client. So let's do it by firing the RMAN client executable:

```
$ RMAN

RMAN>
```

Now, we are in the `RMAN` prompt but can we do anything within it? The answer for that would be a *no* as there is no connection made by the RMAN with any (target) database. Only the `sys` user is allowed to make connections with the target database for `RMAN`, using either `SYSDBA` or `SYSBACKUP` privilege.

 `SYSBACKUP` privilege is new from the database release of 12*c*. Since it is a dedicated privilege for performing backup and recovery tasks, the use of `SYSDBA` should be avoided from the release of 12*c* onwards.

RMAN can be connected to the database by either giving the connection details over the command prompt or from within the RMAN client as well. As we have already got the RMAN prompt, we can use the `connect target` clause for making a connection with the database, as given in the following command line:

```
RMAN> connect target "sys/oracle"
```

The previous command will connect us to the target database sitting locally on our machine using the operating system authentication. If you are willing to connect to a remote target database, you will need to use the appropriate predefined TNS alias for the connection as shown in the following command line:

```
RMAN> connect target "sys/password@bkup"
connected to target database: ORCL12 (DBID=3418936258)
using target database control file instead of recovery catalog
```

The output shows us the name of the database (ORCL12 in our case) along with the **Database Identifier (DBID)** of it. DBID is an internally generated number which is assigned to the database at the time of its creation. This will be very useful in some recovery scenarios and so it is suggested to keep a note of it. If the database is lost and you haven't recorded it, it would be difficult to retrieve it.

Let's look at the command and understand its constituents:

1. The very first thing is the RMAN prompt which confirms that we are now running the RMAN client.

2. The second clause CONNECT is used to issue the connection request.

3. The third clause TARGET represents the target database that we wish to connect to, either local or remote.

   Within double quotes is the username SYS along with its password appended by the predefined TNS alias ORCL12. If you are not connecting from a remote machine to the target database and the OS authentication is not restricted, you can also just use forward slash "/". It would be treated as SYS user only. Unlike the SQL*PLUS command where forward slash must be appended with the "as SYSDBA" clause, in RMAN it implicitly means the same.

> To make the connection as SYSBACKUP, you need to explicitly mention it along with the username that has the rights for it. Also, it may be possible that due to security reasons, this kind of authentication (without username and password) won't be allowed. Thus, it would be better to use the username SYS with its valid password.

The output of the statements executed within the RMAN session are printed on the screen itself or are contained within the in-memory view V$RMAN_OUTPUT (with a restriction that it only holds 32,768 rows). As the view won't store the information if the database is restarted, if you want to have a more persistent storage of the output, you can use the option LOG while making connections. Using this option will make all the subsequent command's outputs be stored in the mentioned file. An example of using the LOG option is given as follows:

```
$ RMAN target / LOG=/some/location/rmanoutput.log
```

In this statement, the file `rmanoutput.log` would store the subsequent output of the executed statements. It's important to remember that the log file will be overridden every time it is used. Also, using the log option would not let the output be displayed over the terminal. To make use of the log file in addition to showing the output on the screen, a command such as `tee` can be used, as given in the following command line:

```
$ RMAN target sys/oracle nocatalog | tee rman.log
```

You may have noticed the use of the options `target` and `nocatalog` in the previous command. The `target` option represents the (target) database for which you are using RMAN at the moment. Using the option `nocatalog` implies that you are not using the Recovery Catalog but the target database's control file for storing RMAN metadata. To use the Recovery Catalog, the `CATALOG` option must be used along with the username and password of its owner.

> To learn more about `CATALOG`, aka the Recovery Catalog, in detail such as how to create, manage, and use it for RMAN, refer to *Chapter 7, RMAN Reporting and Catalog Management*.

Just like the Recovery Catalog, there are several important key components of RMAN which are important to understand. We shall explain these key points in the next section which is about the architectural components of RMAN.

RMAN architecture

There are a few key entities for RMAN to start with. Some of them are mandatory and the rest are optional. We will list these components along with whether they are optional or mandatory in the following list:

- Target database (mandatory)
- Target Control File (mandatory)
- Channels (mandatory)
- Recovery Catalog (optional)
- Oracle Secure Backup (optional)
- Media Management Library (optional)
- Auxiliary database (optional)
- Cloud Control 12c (optional)

Putting them all in the form of a diagram would appear as shown in the following figure:

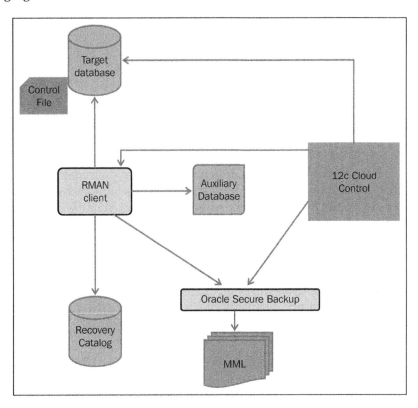

Now, let's take a closer look at each one of the components.

Target database

This is the database for which RMAN is supposed to perform all the tasks of the backup and if needed, recovery as well. Since RMAN binary is just an interface, by using a valid network service, you can make it work for all the databases of your company. The database to which RMAN would be connected and working for would be termed as the target database.

Target Control File

By default, RMAN maintains its entire backup and recovery related metadata in the control file of the target database. The duration for which the metadata is kept is controlled by the parameter CONTROL_FILE_RECORD_KEEP_TIME (default value of seven days). As the metadata occupies the physical space within the control file, it is advisable to not choose a very long duration. It would also be good to keep the metadata in the control file in sync with the recovery SLAs of your company, ensuring the backups are available when needed.

RMAN channels

Channels are the communication interface between the target database and the RMAN binary. By configuring multiple channels, you can unlock the benefits such as *parallelism* and *load balancing*. A server session is allocated in the target database for the channel. Any commands sent by RMAN binary are passed on to this server session, which subsequently executes them within the target database. There is a default disk channel that can be used for taking backups over the disks. Other than that, you can either use the pre-allocated DISK channel or manually allocate channel(s) for disk or tape drives.

Auxiliary database

This is the database which is used when doing tasks such as creating a duplicate database, doing a **tablespace point-in-time recovery (TSPITR)**, and a database conversion to a different platform. RMAN will require a connection established to this database when these tasks are being executed.

Recovery Catalog

As we just mentioned, the target database control file is the default repository for backup and recovery metadata and can make the control file grow as well. Also, some features of RMAN are not exposed if the metadata is stored only in the control file. To tide over this shortcoming, there is an optional metadata storage that can be configured called the Recovery Catalog. This is actually a schema that you have to create beforehand and then within it, configure the Recovery Catalog. This schema will hold a few views and tables that will store all the information related to backup and recovery. This schema can be created in the same target database as well but it is advisable to use a separate database specifically for it. It's worth mentioning here that even though the Recovery Catalog exists, it's still the target control file where the information gets pushed initially and from there, it is pushed into the Recovery Catalog and kept there for an infinite period.

A database used exclusively for the RMAN catalog does not need to be licensed if all the database targets managed by it are fully licensed, but if you implement a **Disaster and Recovery (DR)** solution such as the standby database, the DR database needs to be licensed.

The Recovery Catalog is a consolidated storage. So, it can be used not just for a single database but for multiple databases as well, that is, within the same catalog you can store the metadata of many databases. This is shown in the following figure where one Recovery Catalog is interacting with four different databases, namely HR, CRM, Inventory, and Finance:

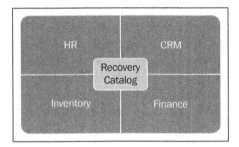

RMAN client

This is the executable client that gets invoked by the DBA. Using this, you would issue the statements which are executed within the target database.

Oracle Enterprise Manager (EM) Cloud Control 12*c*

EM Cloud Control 12*c* is the latest offering in the family of Enterprise Manager. Though this is an optional component for RMAN, it is still worth being deployed and used. Cloud Control 12*c* gives complete support to RMAN operations from simple tasks such as taking a backup to more complex ones such as creating a standby configuration. It is important to note that the GUI interface of Cloud Control does not use the RMAN client but makes internal calls to the database directly for the tasks.

Media Management Library (MML)

RMAN is not just a tool to do backups over the disk drive location, but can be used to store the backups over the tape drives as well. For this, RMAN needs to interact with the underlying tape location and for that it requires the drivers related to that tape driver, which are provided by its manufacturer. MML is an API that Oracle provides to its vendors who write an interface between that API and their product. Normally, there is a licensing cost involved for using the MML by its provider.

Oracle secure backup

This is not really a component of RMAN but can be considered as an add-on for it. As we have already said, for RMAN to take the backup over the tape drives, MML needs to contain proper drivers supplied by the vendor. Since there are so many vendors making tape drives and different types of environments in which RMAN can be used, this is where **Oracle Secure Backup** (**OSB**) comes into play. The OSB contains an in-built MML for RMAN and offers a unified management interface for not just the database but also the underlying mount points. Not only this, the OSB can seamlessly with your NAS and is completely supported by the EM, if you want a GUI interface for it.

In addition to the previous mentioned components, RMAN uses a library file `RECOVER.bsq` located at `$ORACLE_HOME/rdbms/admin`. Since RMAN executable is merely a client application, all commands executed via it are converted to PL/SQL procedure calls using **Remote Procedure Calls** (**RPC**). Within the target database, internal packages such as `DBMS_BACKUP_RESTORE`, `DBMS_RCVMAN`, and `DBMS_RCVCAT` are used for executing these procedure calls.

Memory requirements for RMAN

Before the metadata related to RMAN tasks is stored in the target database's control file, it's kept within the instance. To keep this in-memory metadata, RMAN uses Shared Pool memory structure by default. Shared Pool is actually a central repository for a very large number of memory pools (more than 800) used for different aspects of the database. Thus, it's advisable to use a separate memory area for the RMAN metadata instead of the Shared Pool. This can be done by using the memory area Large Pool, configured via the parameter `LARGE_POOL_SIZE`. This memory area is otherwise optional, but if you are using RMAN, having it in place will relieve the Shared Pool from being used for storing RMAN's metadata. The allocation of Large Pool is going to be based on the number of channels that you are allocating and the device type used for the backup disk or tape drive.

Since RMAN works using the channels which further use the dedicated server sessions in the target database, setting up the appropriate value for the channels also becomes important. Discussion of this topic in more detail along with a couple of others related to performance tuning of RMAN is covered in *Chapter 8, RMAN Troubleshooting and Performance Tuning.*

Configuring ARCHIVELOG mode and FRA

RMAN backups are typically categorized as OPEN or CLOSED depending on whether the target database is in the MOUNT or OPEN stage. RMAN needs the database to be at MOUNT to perform the backups. The ability to perform backups at the OPEN stage only occurs if your database is working in the ARCHIVELOG mode. Any backups taken at the OPEN stage are termed as inconsistent backups. This is because the database, while being backed up, would also be getting changed via the ongoing DML/DDL operations happening within it. Even at the MOUNT stage, the backup done by RMAN would be considered inconsistent only if its last shutdown was with an option such as ABORT. It's also a practice to call the backup done at the MOUNT stage as COLD backup whereas that of OPEN stage is referred to as HOT backup. Unlike the user-managed backups where a closed backup needs to be properly shut down, RMAN needs the target database to be at the MOUNT stage at the minimum. Also, if your database is working in the default NOARCHIVELOG mode, the only option for you is to take a COLD (or CLOSED) backup. It's important that the database is shut down properly before being mounted for the backup. Though it's possible to take an inconsistent backup at the NOARCHIVELOG mode (shutdown abort followed by startup mount), it would not be usable for recovery because RMAN doesn't include online redo logs in the backup.

You can put the database in the ARCHIVELOG mode using either SQLPLUS or EM. To do it by SQLPLUS, you would need to perform a consistent shutdown of the database using either IMMEDIATE, TRANSACTIONAL, or NORMAL mode. Remember that SHUT ABORT is an inconsistent shutdown and won't let you put your database in the ARCHIVELOG mode. At the next startup of the database, bring it to the MOUNT stage and issue the statement ALTER DATABASE ARCHIVELOG followed by the ALTER DATABASE OPEN statement. Let's quickly use these commands to put our database in the ARCHIVELOG mode.

For 12c multitenant databases, if you put a container database in the ARCHIVELOG mode, it will be applicable to its underlying pluggable databases as well. To learn more about multitenant databases, please refer to *Chapter 3, What's New in 12c.*

```
$ . oraenv
ORACLE_SID = [acdb] ?
The Oracle base remains unchanged with value /u01/app/oracle

$ sqlplus / as sysdba

SQL> archive log list
Database log mode              No Archive Mode
Automatic archival             Disabled
Archive destination             USE_DB_RECOVERY_FILE_DEST
Oldest online log sequence   6
Current log sequence          8
```

Currently, we don't have our database in the ARCHIVELOG mode. So, first let's bring it down and at the MOUNT stage, enable the same:

```
SQL> SHUTDOWN IMMEDIATE
SQL> STARTUP MOUNT
SQL> ALTER DATABASE ARCHIVELOG;
SQL> ALTER DATABASE OPEN;
SQL> archive log list

Database log mode              Archive Mode
Automatic archival             Enabled
Archive destination             USE_DB_RECOVERY_FILE_DEST
Oldest online log sequence      6
Next log sequence to archive    8
Current log sequence            8
```

Now we have our database in the ARCHIVELOG mode. Let's learn the difference between the NOARCHIVE and ARCHIVELOG modes and their implication in terms of backup and recovery. A database, by default, is configured to be in the NOARCHIVELOG mode. In this mode, any information of the transaction data within the redo log file is not maintained after it is checkpointed. This could prove to be fatal as you wouldn't be able to recreate any transaction data since the last backup of the database. To ensure that the database gets recovered with all the transaction data, it must be in the ARCHIVELOG mode. In this mode, after every log switch, before the redo log group is going to be made INACTIVE, that is, would lose the transaction change vectors contained in it, it would be archived in an archive log file. In the output shown previously for the command archive log list, the log sequence #8 is from the group on which the background process **Log Writer** (**LGWR**) is currently writing. At the next log switch, this sequence number would be stored as an archive log file.

In addition to putting the database in the ARCHIVELOG mode, it's also important to configure a location for the archive logs being generated. It would be even better if we could use the same location for storing backups of the entire database as well. If somehow that location could automate backup-management tasks such as purging the obsoleted backups automatically, its allocation would be completely worth it, isn't it? All of this can be achieved by configuring the **Fast Recovery Area** (**FRA**). Though usage of the FRA is optional, we would highly recommend configuring it. The FRA is located on the disk and is configured using the parameter DB_RECOVERY_FILE_DEST. The size of the FRA is controlled by the parameter DB_RECOVERY_FILE_DEST_SIZE. If the FRA is configured, it would be used as a default backup location by RMAN. To set the FRA, you can proceed as explained in the following command lines:

```
SQL> alter system set DB_RECOVERY_FILE_DEST_SIZE=10G';
SQL>alter system set DB_RECOVERY_FILE_DEST_SIZE='/u01/app/oracle';
```

Here, the first statement is defining the FRA size to be 10 GB and the second statement is setting the destination folder for it. You might have noticed that in the archive log list command's output, the archive destination is represented by the USE_DB_RECOVERY_FILE_DEST parameter which actually points to the FRA only. The FRA will be discussed in more detail in *Chapter 6, Configuring and Recovering with RMAN*.

Introducing RMAN backup formats

RMAN maintains its backups in the formats specific to it. As a result, backups taken by RMAN are usable only through it. There are two formats of backup supported in RMAN, namely:

- Backup set
- Image copy

RMAN can secure backups in the previously mentioned formats in both the consistent mode (aka COLD mode), that is, when the database is closed, as well as in the inconsistent mode (aka HOT mode), that is, when the database is in the OPEN stage.

Let's delve deeper to gain a proper understanding of the previous mentioned formats.

Backup sets

A backup set bears close resemblance to the OS directories which are used to store multiple files or the tablespaces within the database which contain one or multiple data files within them. Like an OS directory or database tablespace, a backup set is also a logical structure only. A logical backup set contains within it a physical RMAN-specific file which is considered as the real backup of its source file, that is, a data file. We can also say that the metadata related to the physical RMAN-specific backup is contained within a backup set. By default, RMAN performs all the backups in the backup set format only. A backup set can be considered as the smallest unit of a RMAN backup and using this format, RMAN supports performing incremental and compressed backups as well.

The format of backup set is applicable to all types of database backups. For example, a backup set-based backup can be created for the full database or even for a specific tablespace or a data file backup as well.

A backup set contains within it the actual backup of the source files in RMAN proprietary format. As we mentioned earlier, this file, unlike its logical container, would be a real physical file with a defined name at a defined location. This physical backup file contained within the backup is known as a Backup Piece.

Since a backup piece is going to be an actual physical file, it's important to control its size. The reason for doing so is that if a backup piece is too big, it will take much longer before it gets completely restored. Also, to preserve disk space and to save them at an offsite facility, it's a normal practice to move backup pieces over tape drives. Since the size of the tape drives will be limited, you will need to control the size allowed for a backup piece. To do so, you can use the CONFIGURE command along with the option MAXPIECESIZE. The CONFIGURE command is used to alter RMAN's default configuration settings. A detailed discussion about it will be covered in the next chapter.

A backup piece is not always the backup of a single file but can include contents from multiple input files stored within one backup set only. Backup sets containing backup pieces made by reading multiple input source files are called Multiplexed backup sets. By using them, RMAN is able to scan multiple files at the same time which will increase the performance of the backup task. For example, if there are three files constituting one backup set, the resulting backup piece would contain the chunks read from each file. The alignment of these chunks within a backup piece is internally managed by RMAN. As a result, it's not possible to segregate chunks of a specific file and restore it by any other tool other than RMAN. This explains the fact that backup pieces created by RMAN are usable only through RMAN.

Image copy

Image copy is the second type of backup that RMAN can take. This is similar to the normal copy that you can make using the OS level commands such as CP (user-managed backup) with the benefit that it will be logged in the control file and can be managed by RMAN. The biggest difference between a backup done as an image copy and the backup set is that the image copy, will always contain all the blocks within the file whether they are in use or not, which doesn't happen in the backup sets. Being a self-contained copy of the source data file, an image copy is always available to be used for restore operations. When using features such as incrementally updated image copies, the time required to recover them also can be substantial. Unlike a backup set, an image copy backup cannot be used within incremental backups.

Having gained a valuable insight into backup formats, it would be rewarding to learn about the kinds of backups possible using RMAN which are as follows:

- Full backup
- Incremental backup

Further, the incremental backups can be of two types, namely cumulative and differential backups. These incremental backup types will be discussed later in this chapter. Let's proceed to learning the know-hows of full and incremental backups.

Full backup

This backup is of the entire database and can be done either at the mount or at the open stage. This would include the data files, control file, and SPFILE. RMAN uses only the used blocks to be included in this backup. Since full backup is not recorded as an incremental backup, it can't be used as a parent for the incremental backup and so, is never a part of the incremental backup strategy.

Though RMAN backups are possible via full backup, for a voluminous database to do so would consume an enormous amount of resources and time. In light of this, it is advisable to opt for incremental backups and that's what we shall discuss in the following section.

Incremental backups

Incremental backups help in economizing time as they secure a backup of only those blocks which have been modified since the last backup done for the database. It's important to remember that a full database backup is not considered as a valid level incremental backup. Since the backup will only include those blocks that have been modified or newly formatted since the last incremental backup, the elapsed time for the backup would be significantly less, thus enabling you to do more frequent backups even of VLDBs. Some benefits of such incremental backups are as follows:

- Less consumption of the system resources such as network bandwidth and CPU
- Ability to roll forward the image copies with the incremental backups, enabling a faster recovery time
- Ability to perform more frequent backups, even of large sized databases

There are two levels used for incremental backups, level 0 and level 1. The number 0 represents the base level and 1 represents the incremental level backup. Though there are numbers supported above level 1, for example level 2, interestingly, no reference for the same would be found in the documentation. If you are going to use a level 2, it would still be treated as a level 1 incremental backup only.

A level 0 backup signifies the parent backup in an incremental backup strategy or you can consider it as the base of all subsequent incremental backups. This contains all the blocks of the source file in the backup file at the time of the backup being done.

Level 1 is the child of the level 0 backup and would contain only the blocks which are modified after level 0. As we mentioned earlier, there can be two further possible types for level 1 backup that are as follows:

- Differential incremental backup (default) contains the changed blocks from either level 0 or 1
- Cumulative incremental backup contains the changed blocks from level 0 always

[Though incremental backups are supported only for backup sets, for level 0 the backup type can either be backup sets or image copies. For level 1, the format supported is backup set only.]

Let's proceed to learning about these two types of level 1 backup.

Differential incremental backup

The rationale behind incremental backups is to save backup time. The same is true for differential incremental backups as well. In it, the level of the first incremental backup (or base backup) is going to remain as 0 and all the subsequent backups are taken using level 1. But these backups will contain only the modified blocks since the last level 0 backup or until the last incremental level 1 backup. So, if we consider that the level is N, the backup would either be N-N or N-N-1.

Let's elaborate through the following example. Let's take a weekly backup strategy where the week is supposed to start from Sunday, which is the day when we shall take a full backup at level 0 assuming that the use of the database is less. So even if there is an impact on the database performance while the backup is running, it's acceptable and the backups taken on all the subsequent days will be done using the (differential incremental backup) level 1 mode. On Sunday, the level 0 backup is taken again and this will complete the backup cycle for the entire week.

As it's rightly said, a picture is worth a thousand words. So, let's see the pictorial representation of the example given:

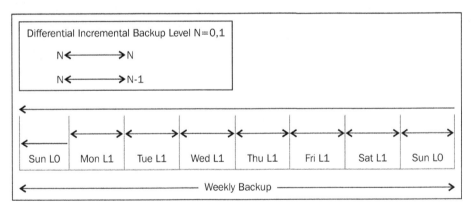

The backup comprises of the modified blocks between the two levels of the incremental backup. If the levels of the incremental backups are the same, that is, 1, the backup would be comprised of the content between the two. For levels between 0 and 1, the backup spans from the incremental level 1 to the base level 0. So in our example, the current Sunday's base level 0 backup would go up to the last Sunday's level 0 point, backing up the work done for the entire week. It would mean that with the current Sunday's level 0 backup secured, all the previous incremental level 1 backups of the week, including the last Sunday's level 0 backup, can now be safely discarded.

Since differential backups will include only the modified blocks since the last incremental level backup, the disk space occupied by them would be considerably less. Also, it would take less time to complete a differential incremental backup as the complete data file wouldn't need to get backed up.

Though differential backups seem to be the perfect choice, they do have an issue.

Since differential backups are going to result in a large number of backups, it would take a long time for you to finish restoring them. Only after restoring all the copies can you start performing the recovery of your database. This is not going to be a good thing if the recovery time is more important to you than the storage space. The solution of this issue is the second type of incremental backup, a cumulative incremental backup.

Cumulative incremental backup

This is also an incremental backup but of a different nature. Like differential backups, it also starts from level 0 and has the next level as level 1. But here, the backup is done from level 1 to level 0 every time, in other words, the cumulative incremental backup will include all the modified blocks since the last backup level 0 from the current level 1.Because of this, the space occupied by this type of backup would be larger than the corresponding differential incremental backups, but on the good side, the number of backup copies getting created would be lesser and that would be a big saving in the recovery time.

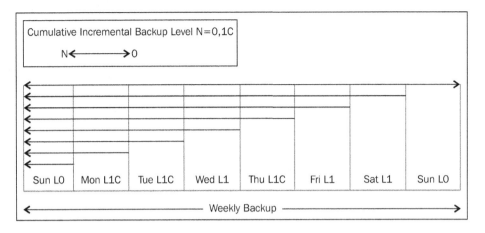

It's worth mentioning that incremental backups, either differential or cumulative, do not just improve your backup performance. These are preferred by RMAN while doing recoveries as well. To perform media recovery, RMAN will examine the files restored from the backup to check whether it can recover them using the incremental backups instead of using archived redo logs. This is going to be really helpful as using incremental backups, only specific blocks would get recovered. There is no special configuration setting required for this behavior as it's automatically done by RMAN.

Power of one

Both kinds of incremental backups discussed so far appear to have their own pros and cons. However, if we could synchronize their advantages, we could be pleasantly surprised with a higher degree of efficiency in performance. Doing so would also aid us in reducing the number of copies to be maintained.

If we look at the same example of the weekly backup given earlier, and take the level 0 backup on Sunday and the level 1 differential backup from Monday to Wednesday, it will give us the benefit of faster backups. Now, to reduce the number of copies required to be restored in the case of a crash, on Thursday we can take the cumulative incremental backup (using L1C from the following figure) which would go until the last level 0 backup done on Sunday. Since we shall have the entire work covered in these two copies of the backup, we can safely discard the intermediate backups taken from Monday to Wednesday.

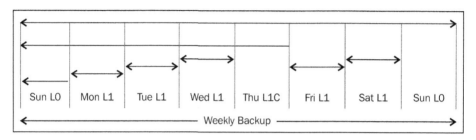

If a recovery operation is now required on Friday, all we need to do is restore and recover it using the level 0 backup from last Sunday. Then, we need to use our cumulative incremental backup generated on Thursday (that contains all the changes from Monday to Thursday) and apply all the archive logs generated since Thursday's level 1 cumulative backup up to when the failure occurred. Now, your database will be once again ready to go as lesser backups will be used in this scenario.

Even with incremental backups, you will need all the archive logs required for recovery. Therefore, it is highly recommended to do the backup of the archive logs as well to ensure that you can do a complete recovery without losing any data.

Looking at the benefits provided by incremental backups, they are surely the best possible way to perform backups, especially for large sized databases. Not only do incremental backups offer the facility of saving the elapsed backup time but also preserve disk space and provide improvements in recovery time as well. So using them as replacements for normal backups is definitely a good decision to make.

Although incremental backups are fast, can they be made faster? If this thought has crossed your mind, let us give you some good news by saying *yes*! It is indeed possible to make the already fast incremental backups speed up even more using the following two options:

- Block change tracking (10*g* and above)
- Multi section incremental backups using the SECTION SIZE clause (12.1)

We shall discuss both of these options in detail later in the chapter when we reach the section on performing backups using incremental strategies. But if you want take a backup or do a recovery or anything of that sort, as a matter of fact you would need to communicate that to the RMAN client. The only way to do this is to know the right command for that desired task. So, let's get acquainted with the RMAN commands as they will be our mode of communication with the RMAN client and from it, to the database.

Getting introduced to RMAN commands

All the tasks related to the backup, restore, and recovery of a database are performed using RMAN commands. Almost all the RMAN commands are plain English statements. That's why using them becomes very easy, even for those who are completely new to RMAN. For example, if we are willing to take the backup, the command used for it would be, of course, BACKUP! As you may want to take the backup of either the complete database or of a specific tablespace or data file, BACKUP can accommodate all these requirements. For example, if you are willing to take the backup of a tablespace, the command used would be BACKUP TABLESPACE followed by the name of the tablespace. In the similar fashion, backup of the entire database can be done using the BACKUP command with the option DATABASE. Similarly, for performing restore and recovery actions, the respective commands would be RESTORE and RECOVERY.

RMAN doesn't do object level backups, for example, backup of a table, view, and so on. If you need to do an object level recovery, you can use the option of Data Pump or TSPITR. From the database release 12*c*, we can do table level recovery using RMAN itself.

All the commands are executed in the standalone manner using the RMAN client. If you are willing to execute multiple commands together, you can do so using the RUN block. Within the RUN block, all the commands are executed as a batch, something which is very useful in creating stored scripts for scheduled executions. The following is an example of the RUN block in which first the database will be restored before being recovered:

```
RMAN> RUN
2> {
3> restore database;
4> recover database;
5> }
```

In addition to the commands for restoring, recovering, and taking the backup of databases, there are several other commands for different purposes, for example, listing the available backups. To get to know all the available commands and their options, you can use the **Backup and Recovery Reference** guide available under the **Backup and Recovery** heading found under the **High Availability** section at http://www.oracle.com/pls/db121/homepage. It may appear overwhelming to remember and use such a vast wealth of commands for the first time, but after using RMAN for some time, you will feel completely at home using it, even for its long list of available commands.

Let's pause for a moment to recall what we have discussed so far.

RMAN can take backups when the database is either in the OPEN or in the MOUNT stage. Two formats of backups are used, backup set and image copy. Using backup sets, backups can either be full or incremental backups. We perform the tasks of backup, restore, and recovery using the RMAN client. RMAN uses channels configured either over a disk or on a tape drive to connect to the target database. Channels use server sessions spawned over the target database. To perform backups, the command used is BACKUP. It is executed by the RMAN client invoked while executing the RMAN binary. So let's take some actual backups now, shall we?

Taking your first RMAN backup

Since we are now aware of the BACKUP command, let's take a full database backup using this. This backup will be stored on the FRA location. We shall explain what's happening with the execution of the command along with the output. Let's get to it right away:

```
RMAN> BACKUP DATABASE PLUS ARCHIVELOG;
```

This is the start of the command. Here, we are taking the full database backup along with its archive log files.

```
Starting backup at 10-MAY-13
```

The second line shows that the backup is beginning on the mentioned date.

```
current log archived
```

RMAN does an automatic log switch to keep the current redo log in the form of the archive log. The previous command line shows that the log switch has happened and the current redo log group is now archived.

```
using channel ORA_DISK_1
```

This line shows that we are using a disk channel. If you haven't allocated any channels by yourself, RMAN uses a DISK channel by default, which has happened in our case as well.

```
channel ORA_DISK_1: starting archived log backup set
```

From this point onwards, the backup of archived redo log files is starting. A list of the archived redo log files along with the log sequence numbers is shown in the following command lines:

```
channel ORA_DISK_1: specifying archived log(s) in backup set

input archived log thread=1 sequence=18 RECID=1 STAMP=805723744

input archived log thread=1 sequence=19 RECID=2 STAMP=805723866

input archived log thread=1 sequence=20 RECID=3 STAMP=805748939

input archived log thread=1 sequence=21 RECID=4 STAMP=805764851

input archived log thread=1 sequence=22 RECID=5 STAMP=805765088


channel ORA_DISK_1: starting piece 1 at 10-JAN-13

channel ORA_DISK_1: finished piece 1 at 10-JAN-13

piece handle=/u01/app/oracle/fast_recovery_area/ORCL/
backupset/2013_05_10/o1_mf_annnn_TAG20130510T233808_8j86w8rm_.bkp
tag=TAG20130510T233808 comment=NONE

channel ORA_DISK_1: backup set complete, elapsed time: 00:00:07

Finished backup at 10-MAY-13
```

At this point, the backup of the archived redo log files is complete. Note that RMAN doesn't do an archived redo log files backup by itself. Since we used the option PLUS ARCHIVELOG in our BACKUP command, the backup of our archived redo log files is done. The location used for the backup is the FRA which is currently configured for the normal file system. There is a tag created automatically for the backup which has a string TAG appended with the date and time when the backup is performed. There is no comment given for the backup.

> Tags can be considered as the names of the backups that you are creating, to uniquely identify them. Tags are also used to give the backups a description. For example, a weekly backup can be tagged as WEEK_BKUP. If you don't explicitly name a tag, it will be named automatically with the format TAGYYYYMMDDTHHMMSS, as we have seen in the output shown previously.

```
Starting backup at 10-MAY-13

using channel ORA_DISK_1
```

Now, the backup of the full database is starting. Like archived redo log files, this also will be done using a single disk channel only as we haven't configured multiple channels yet.

```
channel ORA_DISK_1: starting full datafile backup set
channel ORA_DISK_1: specifying datafile(s) in backup set
input datafile file number=00001 name=/u01/app/oracle/oradata/orcl/
system01.dbf
input datafile file number=00002 name=/u01/app/oracle/oradata/orcl/
sysaux01.dbf
input datafile file number=00005 name=/u01/app/oracle/oradata/orcl/
example01.dbf
input datafile file number=00003 name=/u01/app/oracle/oradata/orcl/
undotbs01.dbf
input datafile file number=00004 name=/u01/app/oracle/oradata/orcl/
users01.dbf
```

The previous given list is that of the input data files which would be getting backed up.

```
channel ORA_DISK_1: starting piece 1 at 10-MAY-13
channel ORA_DISK_1: finished piece 1 at 10-MAY-13
piece handle=/u01/app/oracle/fast_recovery_area/ORCL/
backupset/2013_01_10/o1_mf_nnndf_TAG20130510T233815_8j86wj82_.bkp
tag=TAG20130510T233815 comment=NONE
channel ORA_DISK_1: backup set complete, elapsed time: 00:01:55
```

At this point, the creation of a backup set is complete and it took only two minutes.

```
channel ORA_DISK_1: starting full datafile backup set
channel ORA_DISK_1: specifying datafile(s) in backup set
including current control file in backup set
including current SPFILE in backup set
```

The control file and the SPFILE are now being included in the backup. With the system tablespace being included in the backup, both the control file and the SPFILE will be automatically backed up too. In general, it's a good idea to configure an automatic backup of both the files.

```
channel ORA_DISK_1: starting piece 1 at 10-MAY-13
channel ORA_DISK_1: finished piece 1 at 10-MAY-13
```

```
piece handle=/u01/app/oracle/fast_recovery_area/ORCL/
backupset/2013_01_10/o1_mf_ncsnf_TAG20130510T233815_8j8704g6_.bkp
tag=TAG20130510T233815 comment=NONE

channel ORA_DISK_1: backup set complete, elapsed time: 00:00:01

Finished backup at 10-MAY-13
```

Finally, we get the message that the backup of our database is now complete:

```
Starting backup at 10-MAY-13

current log archived

using channel ORA_DISK_1

channel ORA_DISK_1: starting archived log backup set

channel ORA_DISK_1: specifying archived log(s) in backup set

input archived log thread=1 sequence=23 RECID=6 STAMP=805765213

channel ORA_DISK_1: starting piece 1 at 10-MAY-13

channel ORA_DISK_1: finished piece 1 at 10-MAY-13

piece handle=/u01/app/oracle/fast_recovery_area/ORCL/
backupset/2013_01_10/o1_mf_annnn_TAG20130510T234013_8j8705vm_.bkp
tag=TAG20130510T234013 comment=NONE

channel ORA_DISK_1: backup set complete, elapsed time: 00:00:01
```

The current redo log file is archived here and the backup for the archived log generated from it is now being backed up:

```
Finished backup at 10-MAY-13
```

The previous backup taken was in the default format of backup set. To take the same backup in the image copy format, you would need to use the `Backup` command with the option `as copy`:

```
RMAN> Backup as copy database;
```

A general question asked is that why would you want to take an image copy backup? An image copy backup would be larger in size (image copies include all the blocks of a file) and would also take more time. An image copy format of the backup can be very handy in creating a clone of the database. Each image is an exact replica of its source data file. Thus, having individual copies would certainly come in handy. Additionally, Oracle offers a fast switchover to the image copies. Doing so won't require you to spend time on restoring them to the target destination first and will offer a fast recovery.

File sections for backups of large data files

Since the advent of the database version 10*g*, there has been support for data files up to the size of 128 TB. The tablespaces made using such large sized data files are called BigFile tablespaces. For such data files, it would take an enormous amount of time to get them backed up. Since multiple channels induce parallelism, backup task can take its benefit. But the issue is that for a single large sized data file, even having multiple channels allocated would be of no use. Channels support inter-file parallelism and not intra-file parallelism. So for a data file of size 100 TB, having 100 channels configured would be actually useless since that file would still be backed up by just one channel. To resolve this issue, we can logically divide a large data file into small file chunks using the option SECTION SIZE in the BACKUP command. When a large file is broken into many smaller chunks, each chunk will be treated as an individual data file in itself. Using the same example, if we now break the data file into 100 small chunks of 1 TB each, every single chunk can be backed up by an individual channel, giving us the benefit of intra-file parallelism.

Each section is made up of contiguous blocks and is created by using the SECTION SIZE clause which can be specified in KB, MB, and GB. The backup would be created in the backup set format. You can use the SECTION SIZE clause in either a full backup of the database or for a partial backup. Let's take the backup of our SYSTEM tablespace using this clause:

```
RMAN> backup SECTION SIZE 500m tablespace SYSTEM;
Starting backup at 19-JUL-13
using channel ORA_DISK_1
using channel ORA_DISK_2
channel ORA_DISK_1: starting full datafile backup set
channel ORA_DISK_1: specifying datafile(s) in backup set
input datafile file number=00001 name=/u01/app/oracle/oradata/orcl12/
system01.dbf
backing up blocks 1 through 64000
channel ORA_DISK_1: starting piece 1 at 19-JUL-13
channel ORA_DISK_2: starting full datafile backup set
channel ORA_DISK_2: specifying datafile(s) in backup set
input datafile file number=00001 name=/u01/app/oracle/oradata/orcl12/
system01.dbf
backing up blocks 64001 through 101120
channel ORA_DISK_2: starting piece 2 at 19-JUL-13
channel ORA_DISK_2: finished piece 2 at 19-JUL-13
piece handle=/u01/app/oracle/fast_recovery_area/ORCL12/
backupset/2013_07_19/o1_mf_nnndf_TAG20130719T210445_8ylq4olx_.bkp
tag=TAG20130719T210445 comment=NONE
channel ORA_DISK_2: backup set complete, elapsed time: 00:00:08
channel ORA_DISK_1: finished piece 1 at 19-JUL-13
piece handle=/u01/app/oracle/fast_recovery_area/ORCL12/
```

```
backupset/2013_07_19/o1_mf_nnndf_TAG20130719T210445_8ylq4odr_.bkp
tag=TAG20130719T210445 comment=NONE
channel ORA_DISK_1: backup set complete, elapsed time: 00:00:16
Finished backup at 19-JUL-13
```

We can see in the output that the data file `system01.dbf` is divided into two chunks and each of them is backed up by an individual channel.

From database 12*c* onwards, the `SECTION SIZE` clause can be used for image copy format backups as well. To do so, the `BACKUP` command can use the `SECTION SIZE` clause along with the option `AS COPY` as shown in the following command line:

```
RMAN> BACKUP AS COPY SECTION SIZE 500M DATABASE;
```

The previous command would make the database backup happen in the image copy format while creating file sections of 500 MB.

Dividing a large data file into smaller sections provides a massive improvement. If you are running multi-terabyte sized databases with a BigFile tablespace, this option can provide a great improvement in reducing the backup elapsed time.

Using RMAN for performing incremental backups

For databases which are very large in size, taking a full backup daily may not be an option. Not only would such a backup take a very long time but would also be heavy on system resource consumption. Incremental backups are supposedly the best option for such large sized databases. We have already discussed incremental backups at the start of this chapter. But just to refresh your memory, incremental backups include only the modified blocks since the last full or incremental backup taken. There is a base backup level which is designated with level 0 and subsequent backups after it are labeled as level 1. For level 0, the backup format can either be a backup set or an image copy but for level 1, only the backup set format is supported. For level 1, there can be two further options, differential level 1 and cumulative level 1 incremental backups. Since we have already known how to take a full backup, it's time to perform the incremental backups now.

To take a differential backup at level 0 for the database, you can do the following:

```
RMAN> BACKUP INCREMENTAL LEVEL 0 DATABASE;
```

For level 1 incremental backup, just replace 0 with 1 in the previous command:

```
RMAN> BACKUP INCREMENTAL LEVEL 1 DATABASE;
```

If you want to take a cumulative backup, the command would appear as follows:

```
RMAN> BACKUP INCREMENTAL LEVEL 1 cumulative DATABASE;
```

To make the most of incremental backups, you can combine them with RMAN's ability to use disk and tape as backup locations. Disk backups are considerably faster than the slow tape drives. Since a level 0 backup is going to be much larger than the subsequent level 1 backups, it would be better to do this over the tape drive. The tape containing the level 0 backup can then be safely stored in an offsite data storage facility. Subsequent level 1 backups would be much smaller in size and take less time than their parent level 0 and you can choose to store them over the disk location. This mixed approach combined with other optimizations such as compression will give you a big improvement in the performance for your backups.

Fast incremental backups using the block change tracking (BCT) file

The algorithm behind the incremental backups searches for those modified blocks whose block **System Change Number (SCN)** is higher than the last incremental level backup's Incremental Start SCN. Though it's a very good workaround to skip those unchanged blocks which we don't need to back up again now, to find the list of the candidate changed blocks, it would be required to read the entire data file even when the backup type is going to be an incremental backup. That's why although the incremental backups are faster than the comparative full backups, they are not really fast enough!

An SCN within Oracle database is the internal representation of time. Using an SCN, a database keeps track of when something happened. For transactions, SCN is incremented within a block with every commit. But an SCNs are used at many different places within the database. The complete discussion about SCNs is beyond the scope of this book. You can either search on the web for numerous articles written about SCNs or you may want to read *Jonathan Lewis*'s book, *Oracle Core: Essential Internals for DBAs and Developers* which discusses them deeply.

We need to skip the scan of the entire data file to find the changed blocks since the last backup. For this purpose, Oracle Database 10*g* has introduced a more refined way using the **Block Change Tracking (BCT)** file. The purpose of this file is to keep an entry of those blocks that were modified since the last full backup. At the time of the next incremental backup, this file would be referred and the blocks mentioned in it would be the only blocks that would be included and used in the backup.

Within the BCT file, bitmap structures are used to update and maintain the information from the changed blocks. The file is populated with the information about all the blocks of the source file when the level 0 backup is done. Any subsequent level 1 backup would be able to scan the BCT file afterwards to find the list of the newly changed blocks. The internal details of the BCT file are beyond the scope of this book. If you are interested to learn more about it, you can read the Pythian group's *Alex Gorbachev*'s excellent paper at `http://www.pythian.com/documents/Pythian-oracle-block-change.pdf` and support note # 262853.1.

The BCT file is neither created by default and nor is it enabled from the start when the database gets created. You can check if it is created and enabled by querying it from the view `v$block_change_tracking`.

```
SQL> select filename, status from V$block_change_tracking;
FILENAME                STATUS
--------------------------------------- ----------
                        DISABLED
```

As expected, the BCT file is not enabled by default. Let's enable the BCT file and query this view again:

```
SQL> alter database enable block change tracking using file '/u01/rman/
blkchg';
Database altered.
SQL> select filename, status from V$block_change_tracking;
FILENAME                STATUS
--------------------------------------- ----------
/u01/rman/blkchg             ENABLED
```

The default location for the file, if not mentioned explicitly, would be `$ORACLE_HOME/dbs` or else you will have to set the location using the parameter `DB_CREATE_FILE_DEST`. It is highly recommended not to create any external file in the Oracle home, such as the BCT file. That's why we suggest that you specify a different location other than the default one. We have done this here by using a separate folder for the BCT file creation. The BCT file created would have a default size of 10 MB (typically 1/30,000 of the total database size) at the time of creation. From the default 10 MB, the file size would grow further with future backups. Note that the space allocated within the BCT file is not used right away, but is subsequently used by the bitmaps created for tracking the data block modifications of a data file. The number of updates done to the database won't have any impact on the size of the BCT file. Also, a minimum of 320,000 space per data file is used in the BCT file. So, if you have many small sized data files in your database and have the BCT file enabled, expect the BCT file to be much larger than the default 10 MB and eventually grow even bigger.

When the BCT file is enabled, Oracle databases use the background process **Change Tracking Writer (CTWR)** for recording the bitmaps of the blocks being modified for a data file. The CTWR background process uses the memory area `CTWR dba buffer` allocated from the large pool. We can see the current size of it by querying the view `v$sgastat` as shown in the following command line:

```
SQL> select pool, name, bytes from V$sgastat where  name like 'CTWR%';
POOL            NAME                      BYTES
------------    ----------------------    ----------
large pool      CTWR dba buffer              569344
```

If you are taking a large number of incremental backups, you may want to keep an eye on the space used by the CTWR dba buffer memory area and the size of the large pool. Any wait for the space in this memory area can cause the incremental backups to be slow and at times, can impact the overall database performance as well.

The BCT file helps in skipping the blocks which haven't been modified since the last incremental backup. To check how many blocks are read after the backup of data files, you can query the view `v$backup_datafile` as shown in the following command line:

```
SQL> SELECT file#, avg(datafile_blocks),
  2            avg(blocks_read),
  3            avg(blocks_read/datafile_blocks)
  4            * 100 AS PCT_READ_FOR_BACKUP,
  5            avg(blocks)
  6    FROM    v$backup_datafile
  7    WHERE   used_change_tracking = 'YES'
  8    AND     incremental_level > 0
  9    GROUP   BY file# ;
```

The following code is the output of the previous query after a level 1 incremental backup was performed which didn't use the BCT file:

```
SQL> l
  1    SELECT file#, avg(datafile_blocks),avg(blocks_read), avg(blocks_
read/datafile_blocks)*100 AS PCT_READ_FOR_BACKUP,avg(blocks)
  2    FROM    v$backup_datafile
  3    WHERE   used_change_tracking = 'NO'
  4*   AND     incremental_level > 0  GROUP   BY file#
SQL> /
```

```
       FILE# AVG(DATAFILE_BLOCKS) AVG(BLOCKS_READ) PCT_READ_FOR_BACKUP
AVG(BLOCKS)
---------- -------------------- ---------------- -------------------- ----
-------
         1               107520           106432           98.9880952         3048
         6                  640              256                   40         1
         4                16640            16448           98.8461538         2727
         3                97280            92480           95.0657895            9
```

We can see that the percentage of blocks being read is extremely high in the absence of a BCT file. That's the reason an incremental backup would still take a longer elapsed time than it ideally should. As we have now enabled the BCT file, let's check the amount of blocks being read after an incremental level 1 backup:

```
SQL> l
  1   SELECT file#, avg(datafile_blocks),avg(blocks_read), avg(blocks_
read/datafile_blocks)*100 AS PCT_READ_FOR_BACKUP,avg(blocks)
  2    FROM   v$backup_datafile
  3    WHERE  used_change_tracking = 'YES'
  4*  AND    incremental_level > 0  GROUP  BY file#
SQL> /

       FILE# AVG(DATAFILE_BLOCKS) AVG(BLOCKS_READ) PCT_READ_FOR_BACKUP
AVG(BLOCKS)
---------- -------------------- ---------------- -------------------- ----
-------
         1               107520               93          .086495536            9
         6                  640                1              .15625            1
         4                16640              125          .751201923           12
         3                97280               29          .029810855            5
```

We can clearly see that with the BCT file enabled, the percentage of blocks being read has dropped significantly. With less blocks being read, the elapsed time of the level 1 incremental backups would automatically be reduced. Thus, the BCT file speeds up the already faster incremental backups even more! Additionally, this file doesn't need to get administered by the DBA so, using it adds no additional administration overhead. Due to the improvement in performance that the BCT file can bring in the incremental backups, we strongly suggest that you include it in your backup strategy.

Multi-section incremental backups

We have discussed the section size clause and how it can help in improving the performance of the backup of large sized data files by breaking them into multiple file sections. The same behavior from database release 12c can be used in incremental backups as well.

To make use of the section size clause in level 1 incremental backups, the parameter COMPATIBLE must be set to 12.0. For level 0 incremental backups, the parameter COMPATIBLE can be 11.0. You can perform a level 1 incremental backup with multiple file sections as shown in the following command line:

```
RMAN> BACKUP INCREMENTAL LEVEL 1 SECTION SIZE 100m DATABASE;
```

It's always a challenge for DBAs to find ways to speed up their backup jobs. Using incremental backups along with the BCT file and dividing the large sized files into multiple file sections is a great step forward in the right direction.

Incremental backups are not only helpful in backups but are also preferred by RMAN when performing database recoveries. When compared, it is much faster to apply changes at the block level than applying the whole redo using archived redo logs. That's the reason RMAN prefers incremental backups over the archived redo log files for recoveries.

Incrementally updated backups

Imagine that you are a DBA working for a large company and managing a very large sized database, for example, a database of 100 TB. Now, there would be two major challenges that you would need to face. One would be how to bring down the time required for the backup of such a large sized database, and the second would be in the event of a recovery, how to ensure that the time required to get it done would be as short as possible. Before you can start recovering the file, you would need to restore it and that's where the most time is spent. So how can we reduce the restore time for a datafile which is possibly multi-gigabytes?

Most likely, for the first requirement, you may have already guessed the answer – incremental backups are the only way to go. But what about the second requirement, to reduce the elapsed time for restore and recovery processes? The answer comes from the feature – incrementally updated backups. Using this method, RMAN rolls forward the backup taken of an image copy with the subsequent incremental backups. With incremental backups applied, the image copy would now be updated with all the changes since the last incremental level backup. Using RMAN, databases can be just switched over this updated image copy, rather than restoring them back to the original file's location. Since we won't actually be restoring the file, the restore time will just be a fraction of seconds. To perform recovery, the amount of redo which would need to be applied would be only until the last incremental backup. Thus, within minutes, not hours, you will be able to restore and recover your multi-gigabyte data file or maybe even the whole database.

To make use of incrementally updated image copies, you will need to configure and use FRA. While attempting to restore the lost data file, RMAN will be looking for its updated image copy over FRA only. Since the backup format is image copy, the size of the FRA should be big enough to hold a copy of your entire database.

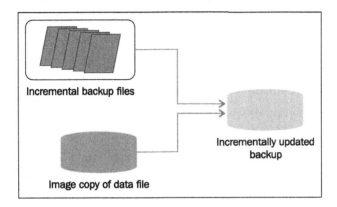

Let's discuss how incrementally updated image copies will be actually created. To create incrementally updated backups, we will need to use the BACKUP command along with the RECOVER command. Since both the commands need to run together, you can execute them using the RUN block. The following command lines show how the RUN block would look:

```
RMAN> RUN
{
  RECOVER COPY OF tablespace test_imgcpy
    WITH TAG 'testimgcpy_incr';
  BACKUP
    INCREMENTAL LEVEL 1
    FOR RECOVER OF COPY WITH TAG 'testimgcpy_incr'
    tablespace test_imgcpy;
}
```

Notice that in the BACKUP command, we have identified the backup using a tag given by us. The same tag is used in the RECOVER command as well. This is going to be mandatory as only with the help of the assigned tag, the recovery of the image copy created by the BACKUP command would be enabled by the RECOVER command.

Let's look at how this command would work. Assuming that you will be running this RUN block daily, the following steps should be performed:

1. On the first day, the RECOVER command won't do anything. To apply incremental backups, a level 0 backup is needed. Since there isn't one existing one yet, the BACKUP command will create a level 0 image copy backup of the tablespace TEST_IMGCPY.

2. On the second day, since a level 0 backup now exists, the BACKUP command will create a level 1 incremental backup. Again on this day, there won't be any work to do for the RECOVER command.

3. From the third day onwards, the RECOVER command will update the image copy with the previous day's level 1 incremental backup daily.

Since the RUN block will be executed daily, the image copy would always remain updated with the transaction data until the last incremental level. For the complete recovery (or even for a point-in-time recovery) of this image copy, you would need to apply the redo data of no more than a day.

To do a point-in-time recovery of this image copy, the available time window is only until the level 0 backup. So, if we created the level 0 backup of our tablespace on July 15, we can't recover it using incrementally updated backups till July 10 or so. To do recovery beyond the point of level 0 backup, you would need to have the backups and archive logs available up to that point.

Performing recoveries using incrementally updated image copies is much faster than doing the same using normal backup. If you are managing large sized and extremely active databases, and the SLA for the recovery time is critical, using this method to perform restores and recoveries should be favored over traditional incremental backups.

Performing backups of the control file, the SPFILE, and archived redo logs

As much as it is important to take a backup of data files, the same is true for the control file, the SPFILE, and the archived redo logs as well. A database won't halt for a lost SPFILE but losing its control file or one or more archived redo logs may prove fatal.

To take a backup of an SPFILE, you can use the command BACKUP with the option SPFILE. If you have made some significant parameter changes, this is highly recommended. If the database hasn't been shut down, you can even create the SPFILE from the instance using the statement CREATE SPFILE FROM MEMORY. But if the database has already crashed and you have lost the SPFILE (and the text parameter file) with no backup of it, then you will need to create it using the alert log file of the database. The alert log will contain the list of all the parameters with their values from the last startup.

For control file backup, there are several options. It's automatically backed up when data file #1 is backed up along with the SPFILE. Since it's very important to have the control file backed up, you can configure it permanently using the CONFIGURE command (covered in the next chapter). Enabling the automatic backup of the control file would give you two very important benefits. First, you can be assured that with any backup done, the control file would be backed up as well. Second, having a control file auto backup would be very useful while recovering the lost the control file. Thus, it's highly recommended to enable the automatic backup of the control file and the SPFILE permanently using the CONFIGURE command. You can take the control file backup individually as well using the statement BACKUP CURRENT CONTROLFILE. Although the backup of the control file would be done with this command, it won't be considered as an auto backup. That's why in the event of control file loss, this backup won't be automatically restorable by RMAN.

If the FRA is configured, it will only be used by RMAN to store the auto backup of both. If not, the auto backup would be stored under $ORACLE_HOME/dbs location. As we mentioned earlier, one must avoid using Oracle Home as the destination for any other file(s) except those of the database software itself. That's why it would be better to configure and use a non-default location for storing the auto backups in case the FRA is not configured. You can use the CONFIGURE command to set up a non-default location for the control file and SPFILE auto backups:

```
RMAN> configure controlfile autobackup format for device type disk to '/
u01/rman/%F';
```

Since this is a non-default location, Oracle won't use the Oracle-managed file naming convention for auto backup. The backup piece containing the auto backup would have the DBID and timestamp of the file creation.

You can take the image copy backup of the control file using the command BACKUP AS COPY CURRENT CONTROLFILE. You can also take the control file backup without enabling it permanently for a non-system data file or tablespace backup by using the clause INCLUDE CURRENT CONTROLFILE. For example, in the following command, we take the tablespace users' backup along with the backup of the current control file:

```
RMAN> BACKUP TABLESPACE users INCLUDE CURRENT CONTROLFILE;
```

You can also take the control file backup from within the database itself. To make an OS copy of the control file, you can use the command ALTER DATABASE BACKUP CONTROLFILE TO 'path/filename'. From this, you will get a copy of the current control file at the location you specified. To facilitate you to recover from the control file loss with no backups of it, Oracle Database allows you to recreate it as well. To recreate the control file, you will need to execute the CREATE CONTROLFILE statement. To generate this statement along with all the properties of the database as well as the name and location of the data files, you can issue the command ALTER DATABASE BACKUP CONTROLFILE TO TRACE. The resulting trace file from this command can be found under the trace folder located within the Automatic Diagnostic Repository available at $ORACLE_BASE/diag location.

To perform the backup of all the archived redo log files, you can use the BACKUP command with the option ARCHIVELOG ALL. You can also take the backup of archived redo logs using specific criteria such as sequence, time, and so on. For example, to take the backup of archived redo logs for the last two days, the statement would appear as BACKUP ARCIVELOG from time sysdate - 2. While taking a full database backup, the BACKUP command must be appended with PLUS ARCHIVELOG. So, the final command would appear as BACKUP DATABASE PLUS ARCHIVELOG.

Archived redo logs are a must for performing a successful recovery, either complete or incomplete, such as in case of a PITR. Unfortunately, unlike the control file and the SPFILE which can be configured to be backed up automatically, there is no such functionality of archived redo logs. That's why it's better to include the archived redo logs in the same schedule as that of the full database backup. To release space, you can use the option delete input to delete the archive redo logs after being backed up. So, the final statement for full database backup would appear as follows:

```
RMAN> BACKUP database plus archivelog delete input;
```

We just mentioned that to preserve space, you should delete the archived redo log files, but even backups can take a lot of space. Fortunately, RMAN offers inbuilt compression techniques to compress your backups and archive log files. Let's see how in the next section.

Using RMAN compression for backups

As the databases keep growing, so does the space occupied by their backups. Fortunately, RMAN has built-in support to compress such large sized backups which can be handy rather than using an OS utility such as TAR or so on. The following are the two kinds of compression techniques used by RMAN:

- Block Compression
- Binary Compression

RMAN uses block compression by default and that's why you can't set it off (or on either). Two modes of block compression are available, **Unused Block Compression** (**UBC**) and **Null Block Compression** (**NBC**). In NBC, all the empty blocks which were not used are skipped. This mode is always used in level 0 and for full backups. In UBC, blocks which are not used by any object are not read or included in the backups. Even the blocks which were used in the past but are empty now (for example, blocks after a truncate table or drop table operation) are skipped. Unlike NBC, which works for all the backups, UBC only works for disk-based backups and tape backups done with Oracle Secure Backup.

Since block level compression works out of the box, there is no special reason to mention it in the BACKUP command.

Binary compression is the second mode of compression and unlike block compression, needs to be explicitly enabled for the backups. To use binary compression, you would need to use the BACKUP command with the option AS COMPRESSED BACKUPSET. For example, to take a full database in compressed mode, the command would be the following:

```
RMAN> BACKUP AS COMPRESSED BACKUPSET DATABASE plus archivelog;
```

If you don't want to mention the option AS COMPRESSED BACKUPSET every time, you can configure it permanently using the CONFIGURE command. Using the same command, you can set the desired compression mode as well. The CONFIGURE command is covered in detail in the next chapter.

Binary compression allows four different modes: basic, low, medium, and high. Of the four modes, basic is the default mode and doesn't need any additional license to be purchased in order to use it. But for the other three modes, you would need to purchase an **Advanced Compression Option (ACO)** license. The difference in all the modes is in terms of the achieved compression and the amount of CPU being consumed. The following table summarizes all the compression modes:

Compression Mode	Default	ACO Required	Backup size	CPU overhead
Basic	Yes	No	Small	between Medium to High
Low	No	Yes	Small	Low
Medium	No	Yes	Medium	Medium
High	No	Yes	Smallest	Very High

On our test machine, we tested all four modes on the seed database of 1.5 GB. The virtual machine was configured with a single CPU and 4 GB RAM. To test each mode, we ran full database backups three times using each compression mode. The same was done without using any compression mode as well. The results in terms of the elapsed time and size of the backups are given as follows:

Compression Mode	DB Size(GB)	Backup Size(GB)	Elapsed Time(s)
None	1.56	1.29	30
Basic	1.56	0.36	49
Low	1.56	0.44	14
Medium	1.56	0.37	29
High	1.56	0.29	115

We can see from the results that the elapsed time for the backup was highest when the compression mode was High, but the resulting backup size was also the smallest. Between the compression modes of Basic and Medium, there was not much of a difference in the resulting backup but there was a substantial difference in the elapsed time. The Low compression mode, took the smallest elapsed time and gave a good compression ratio as well. Without using any compression method, the resulting backup size was the most similar to the actual database size.

Now, the question arises which compression mode would be a good choice to opt for. In our suggestion, we would recommend you go for medium if you are willing to pay a little extra for the ACO license. Using the High or Low compression modes will bring you to the extreme ends. If buying an additional license is not an option for you, opting for the basic mode would still be a decent choice. As shown in the table, although it took longer than the medium mode, it did result in almost the same backup size.

There are several factors which can impact the compression ratio and elapsed time for the backups. Our tests were done for a very small database. For a large sized database with data not limited to text only the results may be completely different to ours. We highly recommend that you do thorough benchmarking before opting for either of the compression modes.

RMAN for multitenant container databases

Oracle Database 12*c* has introduced the feature of creating multitenant container and pluggable databases. Now, it's possible to make a database a multitenant **container database (CDB)** with one or more user-created **pluggable databases (PDB)**. If not, you can opt for making a non-container database as well. A non-container database is actually the same database type which exists in the previous versions such as 11*g*. RMAN offers complete support for these new database types.

For more about multitenant CDB and PDB, refer to *Chapter 3, What's New in 12c.*

To support backup and recovery tasks for the new multitenant database type, some enhancements have been made to RMAN's existing commands. In the following sections, we will see how we can perform RMAN backups for the multitenant CDBs and PDBs. It's important to note that the concept of backups, their format, and types, will remain the same even for the new database type. We will now see how these concepts can be extended for the multitenant databases.

Performing a full backup of a multitenant CDB

The full backup of a CDB would include all underlying PDBs as well. In fact, there is no difference in taking a full CDB backup from a non-container database. In the previous sections, we used a non-container database for the backups discussed. So, let's take the backup of our multitenant database ACDB with the same command BACKUP DATABASE PLUS ARCHIVELOG which we have used previously as well. But we will do an additional thing before executing the BACKUP command will. In the previous outputs of the same command, we only saw the date returned to us. If we want to have the date along with the time, we can achieve this by using an OS variable NLS_DATE_FORMAT. We will be exporting it to our desired date-time format. To make it a persistent setting, you would need to enter this variable in your login profile file or within a shell script if you are using one.

```
[oracle@host5 ~]$ export NLS_DATE_FORMAT='DD-MON-YY HH24:MI:SS'
[oracle@host5 ~]$ rman nocatalog
Recovery Manager: Release 12.1.0.1.0 - Production on Tue Jul 16 23:01:00
2013
Copyright (c) 1982, 2013, Oracle and/or its affiliates.  All rights
reserved.
RMAN> connect target "sys/oracle as sysbackup"
connected to target database: ACDB (DBID=4244090852)
using target database control file instead of recovery catalog
RMAN> backup database;
Starting backup at 16-JUL-13 23:01:14
allocated channel: ORA_DISK_1
channel ORA_DISK_1: SID=65 device type=DISK
channel ORA_DISK_1: starting full datafile backup set
channel ORA_DISK_1: specifying datafile(s) in backup set
input datafile file number=00001 name=/u01/app/oracle/oradata/ACDB/
datafile/o1_mf_system_8y2tb71j_.dbf
input datafile file number=00003 name=/u01/app/oracle/oradata/ACDB/
datafile/o1_mf_sysaux_8y2t8stg_.dbf
input datafile file number=00004 name=/u01/app/oracle/oradata/ACDB/
datafile/o1_mf_undotbs1_8y2tczh3_.dbf
input datafile file number=00006 name=/u01/app/oracle/oradata/ACDB/
datafile/o1_mf_users_8y2tcy99_.dbf
channel ORA_DISK_1: starting piece 1 at 16-JUL-13 23:01:14
channel ORA_DISK_1: finished piece 1 at 16-JUL-13 23:02:09
piece handle=/u01/app/oracle/fast_recovery_area/ACDB/
backupset/2013_07_16/o1_mf_nnndf_TAG20130716T230114_8yc0v2g7_.bkp
tag=TAG20130716T230114 comment=NONE
channel ORA_DISK_1: backup set complete, elapsed time: 00:00:55
channel ORA_DISK_1: starting full datafile backup set
channel ORA_DISK_1: specifying datafile(s) in backup set
input datafile file number=00009 name=/u01/app/oracle/oradata/ACDB/
datafile/o1_mf_sysaux_8y2tr4n7_.dbf
input datafile file number=00011 name=/u01/app/oracle/oradata/ACDB/
```

```
datafile/o1_mf_example_8y2tr4nj_.dbf
input datafile file number=00008 name=/u01/app/oracle/oradata/ACDB/
datafile/o1_mf_system_8y2tr4nl_.dbf
input datafile file number=00010 name=/u01/app/oracle/oradata/ACDB/
datafile/o1_mf_users_8y2tr4nn_.dbf
channel ORA_DISK_1: starting piece 1 at 16-JUL-13 23:02:09
channel ORA_DISK_1: finished piece 1 at 16-JUL-13 23:02:54
piece handle=/u01/app/oracle/fast_recovery_area/ACDB/
E166DFDE2FBE2E26E0450000FFA80104/backupset/2013_07_16/o1_mf_nnndf_
TAG20130716T230114_8yc0wslo_.bkp tag=TAG20130716T230114 comment=NONE
channel ORA_DISK_1: backup set complete, elapsed time: 00:00:45
channel ORA_DISK_1: starting full datafile backup set
channel ORA_DISK_1: specifying datafile(s) in backup set
input datafile file number=00007 name=/u01/app/oracle/oradata/ACDB/
datafile/o1_mf_sysaux_8y2tdq2l_.dbf
input datafile file number=00005 name=/u01/app/oracle/oradata/ACDB/
datafile/o1_mf_system_8y2tdq2o_.dbf
channel ORA_DISK_1: starting piece 1 at 16-JUL-13 23:02:54
channel ORA_DISK_1: finished piece 1 at 16-JUL-13 23:03:29
piece handle=/u01/app/oracle/fast_recovery_area/ACDB/
E166C84D8F8D2B5EE0450000FFA80104/backupset/2013_07_16/o1_mf_nnndf_
TAG20130716T230114_8yc0y6o9_.bkp tag=TAG20130716T230114 comment=NONE
channel ORA_DISK_1: backup set complete, elapsed time: 00:00:35
Finished backup at 16-JUL-13 23:03:29
Starting Control File and SPFILE Autobackup at 16-JUL-13 23:03:29
piece handle=/u01/app/oracle/fast_recovery_area/ACDB/
autobackup/2013_07_16/o1_mf_s_820969409_8yc0z9xm_.bkp comment=NONE
Finished Control File and SPFILE Autobackup at 16-JUL-13 23:03:30
```

As the output clearly shows, a full backup of a CDB includes everything. We recommend scheduling a full CDB backup in your backup strategy for the situations where the entire CDB has been lost.

Partial backup of a multitenant CDB

The partial backup of a non-CDB would be of a specific tablespace(s), data file(s), and so on. For a CDB, the partial backup can be of the following types:

- Backup of the root container
- Backup of the seed container
- Backup of a specific PDB or multiple PDBs
- Backup of a particular tablespace(s) or data file(s)
- Backup of the control file and/or the SPFILE

To perform a backup of the root container and PDBs, the BACKUP command is enhanced to use the option PLUGGABLE DATABASE. For example, by using the following command, the backup of the root container would be done:

```
RMAN> BACKUP PLUGGABLE DATABASE CDB$ROOT;
```

The partial backup of a tablespace belonging to a multitenant CDB can be done using the statement BACKUP TABLESPACE followed by the name of that tablespace. But for a tablespace belonging to a specific PDB, the syntax would be different. To back up the tablespace of a specific PDB, you need to append the name of that PDB before the tablespace name with a colon. Failing to do so would lead the backup attempt to fail as a CDB can't see the tablespace belonging to a PDB. We can test it very easily:

```
[oracle@host5 ~]$ rman nocatalog
Recovery Manager: Release 12.1.0.1.0 - Production on Tue Jul 16 23:01:00
2013
Copyright (c) 1982, 2013, Oracle and/or its affiliates.  All rights
reserved.
RMAN> connect target "sys/oracle as sysbackup"
connected to target database: ACDB (DBID=4244090852)
using target database control file instead of recovery catalog
RMAN> backup tablespace example;
Starting backup at 16-JUL-13 23:21:40
using channel ORA_DISK_1
RMAN-00571: ===========================================================
RMAN-00569: =============== ERROR MESSAGE STACK FOLLOWS ===============
RMAN-00571: ===========================================================
RMAN-03002: failure of backup command at 07/16/2013 23:21:40
RMAN-20202: Tablespace not found in the recovery catalog
RMAN-06019: could not translate tablespace name "EXAMPLE"
```

So, we are shown an error that the name of the tablespace can't be translated. Let's check whether the tablespace actually exists or not and if it does, then who it belongs to:

```
SQL> show con_name
CON_NAME
-------------------------------
CDB$ROOT

SQL> select con_id, pdb_id, pdb_name,tablespace_name
  2  from dba_pdbs full outer join cdb_tablespaces on dba_pdbs.pdb_
id=cdb_tablespaces.con_id
  3  order by con_id;
   CON_ID     PDB_ID PDB_NAME                                       TABLESPACE_NAME
---------- ---------- ----------------------------------------- ----------
--------------------
        1                                   SYSTEM
        1                                   USERS
```

1				SYSAUX
1				UNDOTBS1
1				TEMP
2	2	PDB$SEED		SYSTEM
2	2	PDB$SEED		SYSAUX
2	2	PDB$SEED		TEMP
3	3	APDB	USERS	
3	3	APDB	TEMP	
3	3	APDB	SYSAUX	
3	3	APDB	EXAMPLE	
3	3	APDB	SYSTEM	

```
13 rows selected.
```

The first command `show con_name` shows us the container which we are connected to right now. As the output shows, we are in the root. The output of the join between the view `cdb_tablespaces` and `dba_pdbs` shows that the tablespace EXAMPLE actually belongs to the pluggable database APDB.

> `dba_pdbs` is a new view from Oracle Database 12c. Additionally, for every dba_* view, there is a corresponding cdb_* view to show the information about a multitenant CDB and PDB. To learn more about the new views introduced, check the reference guide available at `http://tahiti.oracle.com`.

We should alter our `backup` command now as shown in the following command line:

```
RMAN> backup tablespace APDB:EXAMPLE;
```

The previous `backup` command will perform the backup of the EXAMPLE tablespace belonging to the pluggable database APDB.

Performing backup of a pluggable database and root

A full backup of a pluggable database would include all the data files belonging only to it. As we mentioned earlier, the BACKUP command is enhanced to include the option PLUGGABLE DATABASE in order to secure the backup of a PDB. To do so, you will need to be connected to the root container and issue the command BACKUP PLUGGABLE DATABASE.

For backups of multiple PDBs, use their names separated by commas in the BACKUP command shown as follows:

```
RMAN> BACKUP PLUGGABLE DATABASE apdb, hr;
```

You can also connect to a PDB directly and perform its backup:

```
$rman target sys/oracle@apdb
```

```
RMAN> BACKUP DATABASE;
```

The previous BACKUP command would only take the backup of the pluggable database apdb.

To perform the backup of the root container, you use the statement BACKUP DATABASE ROOT.

> A full backup of a multitenant container database would take much longer than that of the underlying pluggable databases. So, prepare a backup strategy which will initiate frequent backups of PDBs.

Performing backups of backups

Besides taking care of the backups of the database, there is another thing that keeps DBAs occupied – storage usage optimization. The FRA, if configured (on the disk) would become the default destination for the RMAN backups. But it's not possible to keep the backups on FRA forever. Not only would this block space but it would also be a bad decision as the loss of FRA would eventually mean the loss of backups as well. Thus, if you would want to move the backups taken over FRA to the tape drive, you can use the command BACKUP with the option BACKUPSET. For example, to backup all the backup sets created, you can issue the following command:

```
RMAN> BACKUP BACKUPSET ALL;
```

Using a channel allocated for the tape, the backup sets would be backed up over a tape drive. Once a backup is safe over a tape drive, it can be removed from the disk and the space occupied by it can be freed. If you want to restrict the backup for specific backup sets, mention them with their backup set key. This command doesn't create any new backup sets but adds new backup pieces within the existing backup set. RMAN uses policies to mark the backups as obsolete. Thus, using RMAN for doing a backup of a backup is a better solution than doing the same at the OS level.

You can also take a backup of the image copy backups using the BACKUP command with the option COPY OF. The output can either be in the backup set format or the image copy format and the destination can either be a disk or a tape. For example, if you have to back up your full database as a copy over the disk, you can push this backup as a backup set over the tape.

Since the FRA holds all the backups, it would be a good idea to take a further backup of its contents as well. This can be done using the statement BACKUP RECOVERY AREA. To perform this backup, the destination will be a tape drive. So before attempting the backup of the FRA, set up a tape channel and a valid tape destination.

Restarting RMAN backups

If for some reason, RMAN wasn't able to finish the last backup job and some backups were left incomplete, you can restart the backup for those using the BACKUP command along with the option NOT BACKED UP which can be timed using the option SINCE TIME. For the archived redo logs, if the backup is in the backup set format, then the backup of only those archived redo logs can be done which haven't yet been backed up equivalent to the option INTEGER. Note that if you don't mention either the time or the count, the command will work to find that file among the files mentioned in the backup command which never got backed up on the same device.

For example, let's suppose that you have initiated a backup which would be completed using ten backup sets. Before the command is completed, let's say that the target device stops and you have to restart it. After the restart, which let's assume took 5 minutes, you may see that out of the ten backup sets expected, only seven are completed and three backup sets are yet to be completed. For the pending backup sets, you can write the backup command to backup only those files which were not backed up in the last 5 minutes:

```
RMAN> BACKUP NOT BACKED UP SINCE TIME 'sysdate - 5/1440' DATABASE;
```

Useful RMAN views related to backups

There are several views which provide a lot of backup-related information. The following is a list of such views with a brief description of them. To get more details about these views, refer to the **Backup and Recovery Reference guide** available at http://www.oracle.com/pls/db121/homepage.

- **V$BACKUP_FILES**: This view displays information about all the RMAN backups (both image copies and backup sets) and archived redo logs.

- **V$BACKUP_PIECE**: This view gives information about the backup pieces from the control file. Each backup set consists of one or more backup pieces.

- **V$BACKUP_REDOLOG**: This view provides information about the archived redo logs in the backup sets from the control file.

- **V$BACKUP_SET_SUMMARY**: This view gives the summary information for a backup set.

- **V$BACKUP_CONTROLFILE_DETAILS**: This view contains information about restorable control files. It will include all the control files backed up in the backup set, image copies, and proxy copies.

- **V$BACKUP_COPY_DETAILS**: This view has the information about all the available control files and data file copies.

- **V$BACKUP_DATAFILE_DETAILS**: This view contains information about restorable data files. It will include all the data files backed up in the backup set, image copies, and proxy copies.

- **V$RMAN_OUTPUT**: This view displays the messages reported by RMAN. This is an in-memory view and is not recorded in the control file. The view can hold up to 32,768 rows.

- **V$RMAN_STATUS**: This view displays the finished and ongoing RMAN jobs. For the ongoing jobs, this view displays the progress and status. The jobs which are in progress are stored only in the memory while the finished jobs are stored in the control file.

- **V$RMAN_BACKUP_JOB_DETAILS**: This view displays the details about RMAN backup jobs.

Summary

RMAN is a very vast, yet a very easy-to-use tool, making it a really good solution to do backups and recoveries. In this chapter, we listed some of the reasons why one should opt for RMAN and then proceeded to explain the different formats and backup types supported by it. Finally, we saw how to use RMAN for the new multitenant container databases of the database release 12*c*.

In the next chapter, we will talk about the possible configurations within RMAN and the recovery cases that are possible following the loss of several types of files.

6
Configuring and Recovering with RMAN

This chapter is probably going to be amongst the most ponderous chapters of the book—one that you will want to keep returning to. Any tool is only good if it has the ability to be optimized depending on the requirements of its user and the ability to perform the most important tasks that it's meant for. The same goes for RMAN as well; it can not only be customized to a great extent, but also has the ability to recover your database from a variety of crashes. In this chapter, we shall look at these two abilities of RMAN, that is, how to configure it and how to use it for database recovery. Sounds interesting, doesn't it? So let us get started, shall we?

In the chapter, we will be discussing the following topics:

- Listing the various configuration settings of RMAN
- Altering RMAN configurations using the CONFIGURE command
- Understanding the mechanics of database recovery
- Performing recoveries using RMAN

RMAN configuration – an introduction

There are numerous configurations that can be instrumental in extracting the best out of RMAN. Though RMAN is extremely flexible, the default configuration options available also fare very well in many cases.

There are two ways to list the configuration settings possible for RMAN: from the view V$RMAN_CONFIGURATION, or by executing the command SHOW ALL from the RMAN client. All the configuration settings, either default or modified, are stored in the target database's control file.

Using the V$RMAN_CONFIGURATION view

This can be one of the simplest ways to gather information about the configuration settings for RMAN. This view lists the persistent configuration settings made by the command CONFIGURE (which will be discussed later in the chapter). In other words, this view lists the non-default settings for RMAN. The following code is the output of this view:

```
SQL> SELECT * FROM V$rman_configuration;


  CONF# NAME                          VALUE                     CON_ID
------- -------------------------     --------------------      -----------

      1 CONTROLFILE AUTOBACKUP        ON                        0
SQL>
```

> If you are using the recovery catalog, you should be using the view RC_RMAN_CONFIGURATION. This is also based on V$RMAN_CONFIGURATION and shows the persistent configuration information corresponding to the databases stored in the catalog.

Using the SHOW ALL command

In case you are reluctant to write a query to list the configurations, you can derive it using RMAN itself through the command SHOW ALL. This command lists the settings that are available, either in their default or modified values. Following is the output of the command after being executed from the RMAN client. Note that the numbered bullets are not present in the default output. Here, they have been used to link the configuration with its explanation given afterwards.

```
RMAN> SHOW ALL;

using target database control file instead of recovery catalog
RMAN configuration parameters for database with db_unique_name ORCL12
are:
(1)CONFIGURE RETENTION POLICY TO REDUNDANCY 1; # default
(2)CONFIGURE BACKUP OPTIMIZATION OFF; # default
(3)CONFIGURE DEFAULT DEVICE TYPE TO DISK; # default
(4)CONFIGURE CONTROLFILE AUTOBACKUP OFF; # default
(5)CONFIGURE CONTROLFILE AUTOBACKUP FORMAT FOR DEVICE TYPE DISK TO '%F';
# default
(6)CONFIGURE DEVICE TYPE DISK PARALLELISM 1 BACKUP TYPE TO BACKUPSET; #
default
```

```
(7) CONFIGURE DATAFILE BACKUP COPIES FOR DEVICE TYPE DISK TO 1; # default
(8) CONFIGURE ARCHIVELOG BACKUP COPIES FOR DEVICE TYPE DISK TO 1; #
default
(9) CONFIGURE MAXSETSIZE TO UNLIMITED; # default
(10) CONFIGURE ENCRYPTION FOR DATABASE OFF; # default
(11) CONFIGURE ENCRYPTION ALGORITHM 'AES128'; # default
(12) CONFIGURE COMPRESSION ALGORITHM 'BASIC' AS OF RELEASE 'DEFAULT'
OPTIMIZE FOR LOAD TRUE ; # default
(13) CONFIGURE ARCHIVELOG DELETION POLICY TO NONE; # default
(14) CONFIGURE SNAPSHOT CONTROLFILE NAME TO '/u01/app/oracle/
product/12.1.0/dbhome_1/dbs/snapcf_orcl12.f'; # default
```

It is quite apparent that almost all the settings end with the comment `default`. This entails that the configured option is a default one and will work out of the box when used. A brief description of the settings listed in the previous output is as follows:

1. To configure the retention policy, that is, when the backups are marked as obsolete. The default policy is based on the number of copies which is set to `1`.

2. To configure whether the data files, archived logs, and backup set should be skipped if a copy of them is already backed up to a specific device.

3. To configure where the backup is going to be stored. The default device type for backup is a disk.

4. To enable the automatic backup of the control file and the SPFILE.

5. To configure the backup pieces' naming format for the backup of the control file.

6. To configure how many channels will be used for the backup, that is, parallelism for the tasks of backup and restore.

7. To configure how many copies of the data file backup are going to be created. The default setting allows to create a single copy.

8. To configure the number of copies for the backup of archived log files. The default option creates a single copy.

9. To configure the maximum backup piece size allowed. The default is set for an unlimited size.

10. To configure the encryption for the database backups to be either turned on or off. The default value is `OFF`.

11. To configure the default encryption algorithm for the backup encryption. The default is set to `AES128`.

12. To configure the algorithm that will be used for the compression of the backups. The default is set to the compression type `Basic`. The last option is to decide whether any processing is required to defragment the block before the backup is performed over it in the compressed format. Defragmentation is undertaken to remove the free space in the block that's going to incur the resource consumption in terms of CPU from the underlying machine. In order to avoid this from happening, this option is not enabled by default and is mentioned as `True`. If you choose `False`, it means that this optimization within the block for the space fragmentation will be executed. That will include additional resource consumption which may cause a detriment to the performance of the target database.

13. To configure when the archived logs are going to be deleted and which policy is going to be applicable to execute them.

14. To configure the name and location for the snapshot control file.

So, there are umpteen settings and each one of them will be discussed in detail in the following sections.

Configuring the backup retention policy

It is imperative that the backups taken at a specific point in time do not occupy the storage space indefinitely. There ought to be a mechanism in place to identify and delete the archaic backups once they are of no significance to the recovery. The retention policy is the configuration from which RMAN identifies the backups which are not relevant to the recovery anymore. This is extremely useful as in a dynamic database, the older backups need to be removed from the storage space because it is the latest backups, containing more recent changes to the database, that will be more useful during recovery.

Based on the configured retention policy, RMAN will mark the old backups as obsolete.

Two mutually exclusive retention policies are available:

- Redundancy (the number of copies of the backups to be kept)
- Recovery window of *n* days (the number of days for which the backups need to be kept)

Let's take a look at these two retention policies in detail.

Redundancy retention policy

The redundancy retention policy is the default retention policy and configures backup retention on the basis of the number of copies available for it. Only the most recently numbered copies mentioned by this policy would be termed as usable and the rest would be marked as obsolete. If the backups are stored on FRA and get marked as obsolete once, they will be deleted automatically to make space for the subsequent backups. But if FRA is not used, the backups will only be marked as obsolete and won't be deleted automatically.

The default value is 1 which means that only the most current copy of the backup would be used for restoring by RMAN and all the previous copies would be marked as obsolete.

To see the retention policy, we can use the SHOW command.

```
RMAN> SHOW RETENTION POLICY;


using target database control file instead of recovery catalog
RMAN configuration parameters for database with db_unique_name ORCL12
are:
CONFIGURE RETENTION POLICY TO REDUNDANCY 1; # default
```

> The SHOW command is not just for the retention policy, but also displays many of the persistent configuration settings of RMAN. We shall see it in a later part of this chapter.

So the default policy value (as expected) is REDUNDANCY and is set to 1. Let us understand the way the retention policy will affect the backup taken for our database. To display the files which will need backing up, we would use the reporting command REPORT NEED BACKUP:

```
RMAN> REPORT NEED BACKUP;


RMAN retention policy will be applied to the command
RMAN retention policy is set to redundancy 1
Report of files with less than 1 redundant backups


File #bkps Name
---- ----- -------------------------------------------------------
1    0     /u01/app/oracle/oradata/orcl12/system01.dbf
```

```
2    0        /u01/app/oracle/oradata/orcl12/example01.dbf
3    0        /u01/app/oracle/oradata/orcl12/sysaux01.dbf
4    0        /u01/app/oracle/oradata/orcl12/undotbs01.dbf
6    0        /u01/app/oracle/oradata/orcl12/users01.dbf
```

It is clear from the output that for all the files, the available backups are none, which means that we would need to take their backup. We can execute this backup through the following command:

```
RMAN> BACKUP DATABASE plus archivelog;
```

Now, we shall check how many files are required for the backup using the same REPORT command:

```
RMAN> REPORT NEED BACKUP;


RMAN retention policy will be applied to the command
RMAN retention policy is set to redundancy 1
Report of files with less than 1 redundant backups
File #bkps Name
---- ----- -----------------------------------------------------
```

Now we can see that a backup has been taken for all the files.

Since the retention policy is set to the redundancy value 1, it means only one copy of the backup has been procured. Now let's take a second copy of the backup to see how the retention policy uses it to mark the previous one as obsolete. Let's take one more backup:

```
RMAN> BACKUP DATABASE;
```

Since we have procured the second copy for the backup, it would be interesting to observe the status of the existing backups. Since the redundancy value is set to 1, the second copy would be considered useful for the recovery of the database and the first copy would be marked as obsolete. This fact is explored in the following command lines:

```
RMAN> REPORT OBSOLETE;


RMAN retention policy will be applied to the command
RMAN retention policy is set to redundancy 1
Report of obsolete backups and copies
```

Type	Key	Completion Time	Filename/Handle
Archive Log	6	08-FEB-13	/u01/app/oracle/ fast_recovery_area/ ORCL12/archivelog/2013_02_08/ o1_mf_1_14_8kb1fc51_.arc
Backup Set	2	08-FEB-13	
Backup Piece	2	08-FEB-13	/u01/app/oracle/ fast_recovery_area/ ORCL12/backupset/2013_02_08/ o1_mf_nnndf_

```
                                   o1_mf_nnndf_
TAG20130208T200133_8kb325hh_.bkp
<<output snipped>>
```

Now let's alter the retention policy and set it to 3. Once this happens, it will be interpreted that the copies that need to be retained are the latest three. Therefore, the current three copies of the file will be retained and all the prior copies will be marked as obsolete. This can be achieved through the use of the command CONFIGURE.

```
RMAN> CONFIGURE RETENTION POLICY TO REDUNDANCY 3;

new RMAN configuration parameters:
CONFIGURE RETENTION POLICY TO REDUNDANCY 3;
new RMAN configuration parameters are successfully stored

RMAN> REPORT OBSOLETE;

RMAN retention policy will be applied to the command
RMAN retention policy is set to redundancy 3
no obsolete backups found
```

So, we can see that there is no backup that's marked as obsolete now.

This retention policy works better if you are willing to keep a fixed number of copies for restoration. Using this policy may incur additional storage requirements. Also, this policy doesn't ensure that you can recover the backup copies until after a designated number of days; this is what the second type of retention policy does.

Recovery window retention policy

This retention policy can be set to a desired number of days. Rather than storing the backup for the number of days that are mentioned in the policy, it calculates the **Point Of Recovery (POR)** which includes the number of days mentioned and the current date. To illustrate this further, let's take an example of the present date, February 8, and set the recovery window to 3 days. This means that on February 11, the backup done on February 8 would be marked as obsolete. This policy won't place any restrictions on the number of copies that can be kept as usable in the POR, as is done in the case of the redundancy option.

If, for some reason, we are not satisfied with the customized retention policy and want to clear it off to return to its default value, we can use the CONFIGURE command with the option CLEAR, as shown in the following command line:

```
RMAN>CONFIGURE RETENTION POLICY CLEAR;
```

If we want to completely disable it, we can use the command CONFIGURE, as shown in the following command line:

```
RMAN> CONFIGURE RETENTION POLICY TO NONE;
```

Using backup optimization

Using this feature, the backup of files; that is, the data files, archived redo logs, and the backup sets which are already backed up to a destination device type will be skipped. Such optimization is very helpful to speed up the backups and reduce the size of the backup sets, especially for read-only tablespaces. Though this is something that should work with the normal BACKUP command, it doesn't! This option works only for the following commands:

- DATABASE
- ARCHIVELOG ALL/LIKE
- BACKUPSET ALL
- RECOVERY AREA
- RECOVERY FILES
- DATAFILECOPY

To see whether or not you have the backup optimization option ON, you can use the SHOW command as follows:

```
RMAN> SHOW BACKUP OPTIMIZATION;


RMAN configuration parameters for database with db_unique_name ORCL12
are:
CONFIGURE BACKUP OPTIMIZATION OFF;
```

Since this is the default setting, let's take the backup of the archived logs and see whether they all come under the backup or not:

```
RMAN> BACKUP ARCHIVELOG ALL;
```

Since we have taken the backups of all the archived logs, let's make the optimization ON and see its effect on the archived log backups:

```
RMAN> CONFIGURE BACKUP OPTIMIZATION ON;


old RMAN configuration parameters:
CONFIGURE BACKUP OPTIMIZATION OFF;
new RMAN configuration parameters:
CONFIGURE BACKUP OPTIMIZATION ON;
new RMAN configuration parameters are successfully stored


RMAN> SHOW BACKUP OPTIMIZATION;


RMAN configuration parameters for database with db_unique_name ORCL12
are:
CONFIGURE BACKUP OPTIMIZATION ON;


RMAN> BACKUP ARCHIVELOG ALL;
```

We can see from the output that due to backup optimization, the non-modified files were skipped in the backup. Only the new archived logs created, if any, would be backed up skipping the backup of the archived logs which were already backed up with the first BACKUP command.

If you want to override the optimization setting to forcefully include all the files, including the non-modified ones, you can use the FORCE option with the BACKUP command as follows:

```
RMAN> BACKUP DATABASE FORCE;
```

The same setting is not going to work properly if the backup media type is **Symmetric Binary Tape (SBT)**. Based on the configured retention policy, the optimization behavior will change.

Configuring the device types for the backup

The next option is to configure the device types on which the backup can be done. The default destination will be FRA, if configured. Even if FRA is not configured, the default device type will still be a disk, as a default disk channel is preconfigured for use in the RMAN. FRA can be configured only over the disk device type but if you want, another tape drive device type can also be configured.

We shall discuss FRA in an upcoming section.

To list the current device type in use, you can use the SHOW command again:

```
RMAN> SHOW DEVICE TYPE;
```

```
RMAN configuration parameters for database with db_unique_name ACDB are:
CONFIGURE DEVICE TYPE DISK PARALLELISM 1 BACKUP TYPE TO BACKUPSET; #
default
```

The second device type is the tape drive which is called as an SBT. To use it, a separate tape channel needs to be allocated along with a media manager software such as Oracle Secure Backup.

You can override the configured destination, whether it's FRA or a tape drive, to one of your own choice using the option FORMAT. To use this, you will need to specify a destination path where the backup will be created, along with a few other elements that will explain the naming of the backups. The default element is %U, which creates unique names for each backup piece.

```
RMAN> BACKUP  DATABASE format '/u01/backup/%U';
```

In the end, if you want to revert to the disk destination which comes with RMAN, you can use the following command:

```
RMAN> CONFIGURE DEVICE TYPE DISK CLEAR;
```

So, this would set the device type back to DISK if it is set to SBT.

Configuring auto backup for the control file and SPFILE

Besides the data files and archived redo log files, it's very important to take a backup of the control file and the SPFILE. Both these files are automatically backed up with the backup of data file #1, but won't when any other tablespace or file is backed up. Attainment of the control file backup is possible using the command BACKUP with the option CONTROLFILE. The default setting is OFF and we can see it using the SHOW command:

```
RMAN> SHOW CONTROLFILE AUTOBACKUP;

RMAN configuration parameters for database with db_unique_name ORCL12
are:CONFIGURE CONTROLFILE AUTOBACKUP OFF; # default
```

We can see that an automatic backup for the control file isn't enabled. Auto backup of the control file is important because having it available makes the restore operation for a lost control file very easy. A simple command like RESTORE CONTROLFILE FROM AUTOBACKUP is enough for RMAN to automatically locate the correct backup of the control file and restore it. In its absence, the same task would require a DBA to first locate and then restore the appropriate backup. So, we enable auto backup of the control file and the SPFILE using the following command:

```
RMAN> CONFIGURE CONTROLFILE AUTOBACKUP ON;

new RMAN configuration parameters:

CONFIGURE CONTROLFILE AUTOBACKUP ON;

new RMAN configuration parameters are successfully stored
```

With the previous setting, not just at the backup of the system tablespace's data file are the control file and SPFILE auto backed up, but even at that of a normal tablespace. Also, if the database is in the ARCHIVELOG mode, any structural change that is updated in the control file will also trigger an auto backup of the control file.

The naming convention of the control file's auto backup format is with the variable %F and this name translates to C-IIIIIIIIII-YYYYMMDD-QQ where C is just a literal, IIIIIIIIII is equal to DBID followed by the timestamp, and QQ is equal to the sequence number from 0 going to a maximum value of FF. You can change the format using the CONFIGURE command with many different options in place of %F, such as the following:

- **%a**: Specifies the activation ID of the database.

- **%b**: Specifies the filename stripped of directory paths. It is only valid for SET NEWNAME and backup when producing image copies. It yields errors if used as a format specification for a backup that produces backup pieces.

- **%c**: Specifies the copy number of the backup pieces within a set of duplexed backup pieces. If you did not duplex a backup, this variable is 1 for backup sets and 0 for proxy copies. If a command is enabled, the variable shows the copy number. The maximum value for %c is 256.

This is not a complete list. For the complete list, please see the *Backup and Recovery Reference guide* available at http://docs.oracle.com/cd/ E16655_01/backup.121/e17630/toc.htm.

It's important to note that the control file auto backup can only be configured on the disk and not on the tape. To override the configured settings, you will need to use the SET CONTROLFILE AUTOBACKUP FORMAT command either in the run block or directly on the RMAN prompt. Note that the format specified within the run block will take precedence over any configuration setting done on the RMAN prompt, even the persistent setting done via the CONFIGURE command.

If you want to stop the automatic backup of the control file, you can use the following command:

```
RMAN> CONFIGURE CONTROLFILE AUTOBACKUP OFF;
```

Configuring RMAN channels

Channels in RMAN perform all the tasks involving I/O, that is, backup, restore, and recover. Each channel will be responsible for the I/O stream that's going to either read from the disk while doing a backup or write to the disk while performing a restore. To make things easier, if you are taking a backup on the disk, RMAN configures a channel with the device type configured as disk by default. In addition to this, a default channel is also configured for maintenance-related commands such as CROSSCHECK, CHANGE, and so on. Let's see the nexus of the channels with RMAN via a figure:

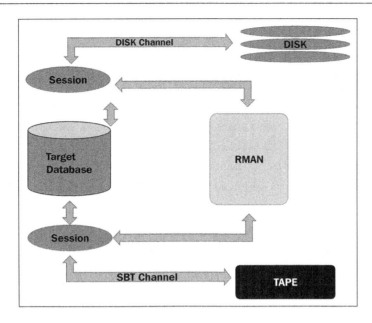

In the previous figure, we have two channels: one for disk and another for SBT, to talk to a target database and make a connection to it. As channels are essentially sessions spawned within the target database, any task executed from the RMAN client will be executed from within the database by them.

 If desired, you can still allocate the maintenance channel manually using the ALLOCATE CHANNEL FOR MAINTENANCE command. However, that's not really needed if you have an automatic channel configured for the device type on which you are taking the backup.

Additionally, not only do the channels (or the sessions corresponding to them within the database) perform tasks, they also help in achieving higher performance as multiple channels allow you to enjoy parallel processing. A backup performed by a single channel for a whole database is definitely going to be slower than if it was done by multiple channels.

According to the two device types, disk and tape, channels can be configured for them. The naming convention of each channel will also be matched with the device type using the format ORA_DEVICE_N, where N is equal to the number of channels configured, and the device type can be either disk or SBT. So, for a channel of device type disk, its name would be ORA_DISK_N and for the tape, ORA_SBT_N.

In the following statement, we will be configuring 10 channels for the disk device type:

```
RMAN> CONFIGURE DEVICE TYPE DISK PARALLELISM 10;


old RMAN configuration parameters:
CONFIGURE DEVICE TYPE DISK PARALLELISM 1 BACKUP TYPE TO BACKUPSET;
new RMAN configuration parameters:
CONFIGURE DEVICE TYPE DISK PARALLELISM 10 BACKUP TYPE TO BACKUPSET;
new RMAN configuration parameters are successfully stored
```

Besides the PARALLELISM clause, the channels can be configured using the command CONFIGURE (or ALLOCATE) with the option CHANNEL. Using this command automatically re-allocates the allocated channels. We will use the same naming convention for the PARALLELISM clause as well.

Going with the phrase "the more the merrier", a higher number of channels is assumed to give a better performance. However, there can be factors which limit the performance, that is, system resources such as the number of processors, network and device bandwidth, the size of the database files, and so on. Additionally, each channel will incur some overhead of its own over the target database as having too many would just not be optimal. Hence, the number of channels should be carefully chosen along with the other possible optimizations such as defining the number of files that can be opened at a time and so forth. We shall have a look at these aspects of RMAN in *Chapter 8*, *RMAN Troubleshooting and Performance Tuning*.

It's good practice to have the number of channels correlate with the number of devices that are going to be available. So if you have five tape drives, allocate five channels (unless your tape management system deploys automatic parallelism).

Creating duplexed backups

By default, RMAN will create only a single copy of the backup but it is always advisable to have more than one copy of the backup because, as Murphy's law says, if something can go wrong, it will. To safeguard from a situation where you have lost the one and only copy of the backup, you can create multiple copies of the backup piece within your backup set with a maximum of four copies allowed.

The option for duplexed backups is possible only for backup pieces and not for image copies. Also, the auto backup of the control file is never duplexed.

To understand this feature, let's configure the duplexed backup to two copies for a tablespace and take its backup:

```
RMAN> CONFIGURE DATAFILE BACKUP COPIES FOR DEVICE TYPE DISK TO 2;
```

The previous command configures the number of backup copies to 2 and uses DISK as the destination device.

 It is important to mention the device type which is going to store the duplexed copies of the backups. The reason for this is though it's possible to duplex on both the device types, disk and tape, it's not possible to make duplexed copies on both at the same time.

As the channel configuration is done now, let's take the backup of a non-system tablespace TESTTBS:

```
RMAN> backup tablespace testtbs format '/u01/app/oracle/%U';
Starting backup at 18-FEB-13
using channel ORA_DISK_1
channel ORA_DISK_1: starting full datafile backup set
channel ORA_DISK_1: specifying datafile(s) in backup set
input datafile file number=00005 name=/u01/app/oracle/oradata/orcl12/
testtbs.dbf
channel ORA_DISK_1: starting piece 1 at 18-FEB-13
channel ORA_DISK_1: finished piece 1 at 18-FEB-13 with 2 copies and tag
TAG20130218T102811
piece handle=/u01/app/oracle/1do2969s_1_1 comment=NONE
piece handle=/u01/app/oracle/1do2969s_1_2 comment=NONE
channel ORA_DISK_1: backup set complete, elapsed time: 00:00:01
Finished backup at 18-FEB-13
```

We can see that at the location defined by us, two backup pieces were created. But if you noticed, rather than using FRA, we used a non-default location for the backup in the FORMAT clause. This is done because if we had tried to use FRA, the backup would have failed, throwing the error–ORA-19806 can't make duplex backups in recovery area. Oracle database doesn't support the creation of duplexed backups on FRA, so it's going to be a must for you to use a non-FRA location for the duplexed backups.

Archived redo log duplexed backups can be configured using the same configuration.

Though duplexing the backups is a good option, it comes with drawbacks as well. For example, you would need more space to keep the extra copies. Also, more system resources would be utilized. That's why creating too many copies isn't a very good option.

Configuring encrypted backups

As necessary as it is to ensure that backups (and restores) are performed without spending much time, making these backups secure is also very important. You may ask why and the answer is that if someone gets their hands on the backup of a database, creating a duplicate database from it wouldn't be very tough. That's the reason why backups must be encrypted, to prevent such indirect stealing of databases. As you may have guessed already, RMAN can certainly do this.

From Version 10.2 onwards, RMAN has the option of creating the encrypted backups which will be decrypted during the restore and recover operations. To do so, the decryption keys are required which are stored individually within every backup piece. Also, for each backup set, there will be a separate key generated.

To perform encryption, you need to enable the option using the command CONFIGURE ENCRYPTION FOR DATABASE ON.

There are three modes which are available for encryption:

- Transparent encryption
- Password encryption
- Dual encryption

The default algorithm for encryption, if none is mentioned, is AES-128. The list of available algorithms can be found in the view V$RMAN_ENCRYPTION_ALGORITHM. If you want to set a non-default algorithm, you can use the CONFIGURE command to do so. For example, if you want to set the algorithm to AES256, you can do so by issuing the following command:

```
RMAN> CONFIGURE ENCRYPTION ALGORITHM TO 'AES256';
```

Since we have understood how to enable the encryption and change the algorithm for it, let's now see what each method holds and how we can use them.

Transparent encryption of backups

Transparent encryption is the default mode of encryption and probably the easiest to configure too. This uses an Oracle Software Keystore that stores the **Transparent Data Encryption** (TDE) key. It is the most optimal method if you are going to use the resulting encrypted backups in the same location. Not only does the keystore-based encryption offer better security, but there is also no need for the DBA to do anything to encrypt the backups. The same BACKUP command will result in creating encrypted backups and the RESTORE command will restore them.

 Oracle Software Keystore was known as Oracle Wallet in the earlier releases of the database.

Creating and using Oracle Software Keystore

To create a keystore, we need a common user that is granted either the role SYSKM or the ADMINISTER KEY MANAGEMENT privilege. Using this user, all the commands to create and open the keystore would be executed. So let's create this user first!

 There can be only one keystore possible for a database. It is possible to create multiple keystores which may act as redundant repositories for the one mentioned in the sqlnet.ora file.

To create the common user, we shall connect to the container database and create the administrator for the keystore:

```
$ sqlplus / as sysdba
SQL> CREATE USER c##sec_admin IDENTIFIED BY sec CONTAINER=all;
User created.
SQL> GRANT dba, syskm TO c##sec_admin;
Grant succeeded.
```

Note that the keyword CONTAINER=all represents that this user is available for all the containers including, all the existing PDBs, and even for those which will be created subsequently. Additionally, the given role SYSKM is newly introduced in 12c for keystore management.

The storage for the keystore will be either on the file system ASM or within a **Hardware Security Module (HSM)**. This information about where the keystore is located is first looked up in the `sqlnet.ora` file available under `$ORACLE_HOME/network/admin`. Within this file, the parameter `ENCRYPTION_WALLET_LOCATION` must be set to find the keystore destination. If not, the parameter `WALLET_LOCATION` is looked up in the same file. If both are missing, the default location `ORACLE_BASE/admin/DB_UNIQUE_NAME/wallet` or `ORACLE_HOME/admin/DB_UNIQUE_NAME/wallet` is looked up. The destination folder must be created earlier, the location of which will be entered into the file. For our setup, we have already modified the file with the destination folder. The final version of the file would appear as follows:

```
$ cat sqlnet.ora
ENCRYPTION_WALLET_LOCATION=
  (SOURCE=
      (METHOD=FILE)
          (METHOD_DATA=
              (DIRECTORY=/u01/app/oracle/wallet)))
```

Here, the folder named `WALLET` will contain the security certificate files.

The next step is to log in as the keystore administrator user and actually create it. There are two types of keystores available: one which needs a password to open it and another which has an auto-login and will open as soon as the database is up. To create the keystore, we shall use the command `ADMINISTER KEY MANAGEMENT`:

```
$ sqlplus c##sec_admin/sec as syskm


SQL> ADMINISTER KEY MANAGEMENT CREATE KEYSTORE  '/u01/app/oracle/wallet'
IDENTIFIED BY wallpwd;


keystore altered.
```

The previous command created a password-based keystore for us. Now, if we check the destination folder, there will be a file created in it with the name `ewallet.p12`.

To create an auto-login keystore, you need to run the following statement:

```
SQL> ADMINISTER KEY MANAGEMENT CREATE AUTO_LOGIN KEYSTORE FROM KEYSTORE
'/u01/app/oracle/wallet' IDENTIFIED BY wallpwd;
keystore altered.
```

This will create another file called `cwallet.sso`. Now with both the files created, the destination folder will look as follows:

```
$ ls -1 /u01/app/oracle/wallet
total 8
-rw-r--r-- 1 oracle oinstall 2485 May 23 17:08 cwallet.sso
-rw-r--r-- 1 oracle oinstall 2408 May 23 17:05 ewallet.p12
```

To check the attributes of the wallet such as status, type, and so on, you can query the view `V$encryption_wallet`. Let's see what status our wallet has:

```
SQL> SELECT WRL_TYPE, STATUS, WALLET_TYPE, CON_ID
  2   FROM   V$encryption_wallet;


WRL_TYPE        STATUS                WALLET_TYPE CON_ID
-------------- -------------------- ----------- ----------
FILE           OPEN_NO_MASTER_KEY   AUTOLOGIN    0
```

The keystore is now open, but there is an important component missing within it—the master key!

A master key is stored within the keystore itself. It is used to produce the special text which will generate the encryption and decryption keys. For the database release 12*c*, in a multitenant environment, the master key can be created (and managed) from either the root container or the underlying pluggable databases.

The next step is to create the master key. It's important that to create and store the master key, the password-based keystore must be open and auto-login must be disabled. If we try to open the password-based keystore followed by the auto-login, the master key will be stored in the latter as well. Since the auto-login keystore is opened by default, to close it we will need to shut down and restart the database. To save space, we have omitted the output of these steps and directly proceeded to the point where we open the keystore:

```
SQL> ADMINISTER KEY MANAGEMENT SET KEYSTONE OPEN IDENTIFIED BY wallpwd;


keystore altered.
```

Now, we shall create the master key:

```
SQL> ADMINISTER KEY MANAGEMENT SET KEY IDENTIFIED BY wallpwd WITH BACKUP;
keystore altered.
```

If we check the status of the keystore now, we will find it OPEN and its type PASSWORD:

```
SQL> SELECT WRL_TYPE, STATUS, WALLET_TYPE, CON_ID
  2    FROM    V$encryption_wallet;
WRL_TYPE    STATUS              WALLET_TYPE           CON_ID
----------  ----------------    --------------------  ----------
FILE        OPEN                PASSWORD              0
```

Excellent! So our keystore is open and ready, with the master key created within it. The next step is to check whether or not the encrypted backups can be created and, if yes, with which algorithm:

```
RMAN> SHOW ENCRYPTION ALGORITHM;


using target database control file instead of recovery catalog
RMAN configuration parameters for database with db_unique_name ACDB are:
CONFIGURE ENCRYPTION ALGORITHM 'AES128'; # default


RMAN> SHOW ENCRYPTION FOR DATABASE;


RMAN configuration parameters for database with db_unique_name ACDB are:
CONFIGURE ENCRYPTION FOR DATABASE OFF; # default
```

So the default encryption algorithm is AES128 and the option for the encrypted backups is set to the value OFF. To take an encrypted backup, we must set it to ON:

```
RMAN> CONFIGURE ENCRYPTION FOR DATABASE ON;
```

Now, as we have the encrypted backup option set to ON for our database, let's try to take the backup of the tablespace users:

```
RMAN> BACKUP TABLESPACE users;
```

You can see that the command is the same and so the output will be the same for the non-encrypted backup. This will also be the case with the RESTORE command but with one difference — the keystore containing the certificate files must be open already.

It's very important that you don't lose the certificate files that constitute your keystore. If that happens, any backups taken with the transparent encryption option will be completely unusable.

Next, we shall see the second method — password encryption!

Password encryption

This method solicits the setting up of a password for the backups to be taken which enforces the encryption of the backup; but to use this method, we do not need to create a keystore. Furthermore, this method cannot be set as a persistent one in the configuration, but it will be available when required. In order to restore the backup taken by this encryption scheme, we will need to supply the same password as that of the decryption key. If we are unable to do so, the backup won't be restorable.

To use this method, you need to use the SET command at the RMAN prompt with the desired password that will act as the encryption key for subsequent backups:

```
RMAN> SET ENCRYPTION ON IDENTIFIED BY bkppwd ONLY;
```

Perfect! So now let's take the backup of the tablespace users:

```
RMAN> BACKUP TABLESPACE users;
```

Now, just to demonstrate what will happen if we don't supply the correct password, we will make the tablespace OFFLINE and try to restore it. Any guesses? Yes, the restore will fail!

```
RMAN> ALTER DATABASE DATAFILE 6 OFFLINE;


Statement processed

RMAN> RESTORE DATAFILE 6;


Starting restore at 23-MAY-13
using channel ORA_DISK_1
channel ORA_DISK_1: starting datafile backup set restore
channel ORA_DISK_1: specifying datafile(s) to restore from backup set
channel ORA_DISK_1: restoring datafile 00006 to /u01/app/oracle/oradata/
acdb/users01.dbf
channel ORA_DISK_1: reading from backup piece
```

```
/u01/app/oracle/fast_recovery_area/ACDB/backupset/2013_05_23/o1_mf_nnndf_
TAG20130523T175017_8sw2d1gw_.bkp
```

RMAN-00571: ==

RMAN-00569: ========= ERROR MESSAGE STACK FOLLOWS =========

RMAN-00571: ==

RMAN-03002: failure of restore command at 05/23/2013 17:50:32

ORA-19870: error while restoring backup piece

```
/u01/app/oracle/fast_recovery_area/ACDB/backupset/2013_05_23/o1_mf_nnndf_
TAG20130523T175017_8sw2d1gw_.bkp
```

ORA-19913: unable to decrypt backup

And as expected, we hit the error ORA-19913.

Now, we shall re-attempt the restore but with the correct password:

```
RMAN> SET DECRYPTION IDENTIFIED BY bkppwd;
RMAN> RESTORE DATAFILE 6;


Starting restore at 23-MAY-13
using channel ORA_DISK_1


channel ORA_DISK_1: starting datafile backup set restore
channel ORA_DISK_1: specifying datafile(s) to restore from backup set
channel ORA_DISK_1: restoring datafile 00006 to /u01/app/oracle/oradata/
acdb/users01.dbf

<<output snipped>>
channel ORA_DISK_1: restore complete, elapsed time: 00:00:01
Finished restore at 23-MAY-13
```

This time, the restore worked flawlessly! Now, we can simply recover and bring the tablespace online:

```
RMAN> RECOVER DATAFILE 6;
RMAN> ALTER DATABASE DATAFILE 6 ONLINE;
```

Dual-mode encryption

The third and last option is dual-mode encryption. This option includes both the password-based and the transparent encryption methods and is a good choice if you often send your backups to be restored on remote locations with no keystore created. Thus, the password-based encryption can be used. For local sites which have the keystore in place, the transparent encryption will get the job done.

To make use of the dual-mode method, use the SET ENCRYPTION by <<password>> command while having the transparent encryption mode configured. If you noticed, this is actually where we ended up after using the SET command demonstrated previously. Since we have the transparent method in place, we have actually set up the dual-mode encryption already.

It's important to mention that there is no special configuration for archived log files when it comes to encryption. If there is a database-wide encryption being set or the option is used for any one tablespace's backup, the archived log backup will be automatically encrypted. Also, if the SET ENCRYPTION ON command is used while taking the backup of archived log files, it will be triggered.

Another important thing is that you can override the database-level encryption scheme at the tablespace level (either at the root or at the PDB level). To enable or disable the encryption at the tablespace level, you will need to use the CONFIGURE command along with the tablespace name.

Lastly, like any other setting, using the CLEAR option will switch it back to its default value OFF.

Configuring compression for backups

Compression comes in handy as it enables us to reduce the storage space for the backups taken. However, compression is a double-edged sword. Where using it enables us to save storage space, it may also burn the CPU from an acceptable percentage to a very high value, based on many factors. Because RMAN has inbuilt compression, there shouldn't be a requirement to seek this feature from any third party tool(s).

RMAN offers various types of compression schemes with different kinds of compression ratios using different amounts of system resources. The available options for compression are as follows:

- None
- Basic
- Low
- Medium
- High

You can configure the default or basic compression mode using the
CONFIGURE command:

```
RMAN> CONFIGURE COMPRESSION ALGORITH 'BASIC';
```

In order to use any other mode of compression, the same command can be used
along with the name of the mode, as shown in the following example:

```
RMAN> CONFIGURE COMPRESSION ALGORITHM 'LOW';
```

As we have already discussed and shown in the last chapter, there can be both
advantages and disadvantages with each mode. Numerous factors could have a
bearing on the compression ratio achieved such as uniqueness, CPU speed, storage
speed, and so on. Thus, the decision to use the appropriate mode should be taken
after thorough testing.

Configuring the snapshot control file

It is common knowledge that data files can be backed up when the database is
open. This option is called the hot backup or open database backup. It is possible
because even when the files are being constantly modified and are inconsistent, they
can be made consistent by using archived log files in the recovery stage. Creating a
consistent file is imperative as otherwise the database can't be opened. Archived
logs are self-contained anyway, so taking their backup with an open database is
not an issue. However, in the case of the control file that always gets updated, a
hot backup of it won't be usable at all. This presents an interesting issue, but
fortunately, a solution to tackle it is available with RMAN in the form of a
snapshot control file!

A snapshot control file is the point-in-time copy of the current control file when its
backup is initiated in the open database mode. This is not really the backup of the
control file (though it can be used as one), but a backup of the control file is created
using it, as it would contain a snapshot of the current state of the control file. We can
see the current settings for the name and location of the snapshot control file using
the SHOW command as described in the following command lines:

```
RMAN> SHOW SNAPSHOT CONTROLFILE NAME;


RMAN configuration parameters for database with db_unique_name ORCL12
are:
CONFIGURE SNAPSHOT CONTROLFILE NAME TO '/u01/app/oracle/product/12.1.0/
dbhome_1/dbs/snapcf_orcl12.f'; # default
```

You can see that the snapshot control file will not be created under FRA like other backups, but under the `dbs` folder of Oracle Home. Since nothing must be stored in this location, you need to use the `CONFIGURE` command to set up a non-default location for the snapshot control file.

It is important to note that the relevance of the snapshot control file is not limited to being a mere copy of the control file. While taking backups, RMAN uses it to synchronize the recovery catalog database as well if the target database control file can't be accessed for reasons such as several concurrent operations going on in it. If for some reason, the snapshot control file isn't available and the access of the target database control file cannot be obtained, the RMAN backup job will fail. So if you are planning to have a recovery catalog, consider creating a snapshot control file along with the target database control file. What a recovery catalog is and how to create and manage it shall be discussed in the next chapter.

Configuring the archived log deletion policy

Archived redo logs may consume a mammoth portion of the storage space. That's why it would be handy if obsolete archived logs could be identified and deleted automatically. This is possible using the archived log deletion policy.

There is no default policy to control the automatic deletion of archived logs (the default policy value is NONE). That's why, by default, archived redo logs are considered to be eligible for deletion if they are moved to a remote destination using the parameter LOG_ARCHIVE_DEST_N and, as per the recovery window retention policy, they are marked as obsolete. If FRA is configured, the stored archived redo logs must be backed up at least once, either to a tape or a disk-based location. It's important to remember that only the archived redo logs which are stored in FRA will be automatically deleted. If you are not using FRA, the files will need to be deleted manually using a deletion command such as DELETE ARCHIVELOG ALL.

There are several options available such as TO APPLIED ON STANDBY that govern the deletion of archived logs based on whether or not they are applied to the standby. Another option is TO SHIPPED TO STANDBY that takes into account whether or not the archived logs are shipped to the standby and the last option is the BACKED UP <integer> TIMES TO <device> command which considers whether or not the mentioned number of backups exist on the device. Much like other settings, the desired policy can be set using the CONFIGURE command as shown in the following command:

```
RMAN> CONFIGURE ARCHIVELOG DELETION POLICY TO BACKED UP 2 TIMES TO disk;
```

The preceding command depicts that only if the archived logs are backed up twice on the disk, they are marked as eligible to be deleted from the FRA.

Like all other settings, the current setting can be seen using the SHOW command:

```
RMAN> SHOW ARCHIVELOG DELETION POLICY;
```

If you want to reset the policy back to its default value, that is, NONE, you can use the CLEAR option:

```
RMAN> CONFIGURE ARCHIVELOG DELETION POLICY CLEAR;
```

It is important to note that these policies won't be applicable to any foreign archived redo logs.

Configuring the FRA

FRA was first introduced with the database release 10*g* as an Oracle-managed location for storing backup files and other files such as archived logs, control files, and so on. FRA simplifies the management of these files stored within it as the names of these files are auto-assigned, and those which are not needed, become candidates for auto-deletion and would be removed on a periodic basis.

There are two kinds of files that can be created in the FRA: persistent and transient. The following figure shows all the files that can be created in the FRA. In it, the dark colored circles represent the persistent file types while the rest represent the transient file types.

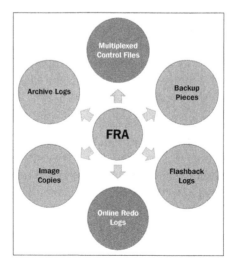

You can see that, except for the multiplexed copies of the control files and online redo logs, the rest of the files are transient in nature. Based on conditions such as space constraints in FRA and the retention policy, these transient files will be automatically deleted.

To enable FRA, you will need to set two parameters:

- DB_RECOVERY_FILE_DEST_SIZE: This parameter defines the space quota (in bytes), either on a disk or on an ASM disk group, that can be used for storing the recovery files for a database.

- DB_RECOVERY_FILE_DEST: This parameter defines the default location that will be used for FRA. The value can be a disk-based location or a dedicated ASM disk group. Also, in order to set this parameter, a valid value for the parameter DB_RECOVERY_FILE_DEST_SIZE must be previously configured.

Since FRA will be the default location for all the recovery-related files, it is important to allocate an adequate size to it. FRA should ideally be at least double the size of the database which will store its recovery-related files—though, the larger you can set it, the more useful it will be. Since going for a very large space allocation may not be practically possible, it should be able to store the backup copies of all the important tablespaces in your database and the archived redo logs for the number of days you want to keep them. Also, if you are planning to enable flashback logging for the database, based on the amount of redo generated and the retention period to keep the flashback logs, FRA would need additional space. As an example, if you have generated 30 GB of redo, you will need at least 30 GB plus 10% extra space added to FRA to manage it. Thus, we would recommend calculating the size of the entire database including all such factors to decide upon the initial size of FRA, plus about 20-25% extra space in the database.

It's also important to note that the allocation of FRA would be on a per database basis. If you are planning to use the same FRA location for multiple databases, do ensure that the available space for FRA in a file system or on an ASM disk group is big enough to cater to them all.

> FRA can't be configured on the tape drive and must be configured on the disk itself. Also, don't set the parameter value of DB_RECOVERY_FILE_DEST to match the value of either DB_CREATE_FILE_DEST or DB_CREATE_FILE_DEST_N. If you do so, a warning will appear in the alert log.

As FRA is the default location for all the backups, the archived redo logs' space usage would be constantly high. Since it's not possible to keep on adding space, it is important to take some proactive measures so that the FRA space isn't completely exhausted. If this happens, not only will the backup jobs start to fail but the database may also hang while performing a redo log switch due to unavailability of space to store the resulting archived redo logs. In order to ensure that the space within FRA will be re-used for new files, you may want to push the backups from it to a tape drive more often. Or, you may use FRA for storing the archived redo logs and schedule the backups directly over tape. If you have a large, frequently changing database, you can implement incremental backups as they will consume less space. If flashback logs are enabled, choose a smaller value for the retention period so that they won't be kept for a longer duration in FRA than needed. Last but certainly not least, implement a retention policy for your backups so that they are marked as obsolete and become candidates for deletion to free up space in FRA.

In order to monitor FRA through SQLPLUS, you can use two views. The first is V$RECOVERY_AREA_USAGE (previously known as V$FLASH_RECOVERY_AREA_USAGE), which will show the space consumption in FRA based on the types of file, the total number of each type of file and so on. The second view, V$RECOVERY_AREA_DEST will show the current location of FRA, the available space quota, used space, and reclaimable space, along with the number of files. The following is an example using the view V$RECOVERY_AREA_DEST:

```
SQL> SELECT
   NAME,
   TO_CHAR(SPACE_LIMIT, '999,999,999,999') AS SPACE_LIMIT,
   TO_CHAR(SPACE_LIMIT - SPACE_USED + SPACE_RECLAIMABLE,
'999,999,999,999')
      AS SPACE_AVAILABLE,
   ROUND((SPACE_USED - SPACE_RECLAIMABLE)/SPACE_LIMIT * 100, 1)
      AS PERCENT_FULL
   FROM V$RECOVERY_FILE_DEST;   2    3    4    5    6    7    8

NAME
-----------------------------------------------------------------------
---
----
SPACE_LIMIT SPACE_AVAILABLE   PERCENT_FULL
--------------- ---------------- ------------
/u01/app/oracle/fast_recovery_area
5,033,164,800    4,122,766,848  18.1
```

In the preceding output, we can see that very little space from the FRA space quota is consumed. Since FRA is an automatically managed area by Oracle, you will be notified if you have run out of space by the error ORA-19809. If you get this error, it means that it's time to do some housekeeping in FRA by deleting certain unnecessary files and optionally, adding more space to it as well.

Before summing up the discussion about FRA, we will suggest two not-to-be-done practices for it. Firstly, since FRA is supposed to be automatically managed, it must use the **Oracle Managed File (OMF)** format for the files stored in it. If you use the option FORMAT and manually assign formatting for the filenames, it will stop FRA from doing automatic housekeeping in files, that is, deleting them when they are not needed based on the retention policies. Secondly, don't manually delete the files stored in FRA, such as backups, archived logs, and so on using any OS command, such as RM. Just any manual operation won't update the target database's control file and even after the space is marked free by the OS, this won't be reflected by the control file. Use RMAN's DELETE command instead!

Configuring authentication for RMAN

RMAN, being a database tool, needs to connect with the user using a valid username that has proper privileges and roles to perform backups. The user needs to be authenticated as well, and RMAN supports two types of authentications:

- **Operating system (OS)** authentication
- Password file authentication

Let's see how to set up OS authentication first.

Operating system authentication

OS authentication validates the username, using the operating system user and group(s). For a RMAN connection, two things need to be set: the first is the Oracle Home and the second is the OS user which must be part of either the DBA group or the OSBACKUPDBA group; this is required for connecting to the new SYSBACKUP role. This role is designated for those who want to work on either RMAN or SQLPLUS to manage the tasks of backup and recovery only.

The default privilege used is sysdba for RMAN. If you want to connect using OS authentication and the SYSBACKUP privilege, you need to explicitly mention it as the following:

```
RMAN> connect target "/ as sysdba"
```

Authenticating the password file

To connect to the target database via a remote machine, you will need to supply the correct password for SYS along with having a valid TNS configuration set up. There isn't much difference in the connection string from RMAN compared to the normal database connection, except for some changes in the syntax. For example, if you want to connect to the remote database as sysbackup, you use a connection string as shown in the following command lines:

```
$ rman target '"sys@apdb as sysbackup"'
```

Notice the extra quotes in the connection string. If you don't mention either sysdba or sysbackup, the default connection established is with the sysdba privilege.

As we are talking about connections, it's important to mention that if you have configured a shared server mode (or MTS, for the early users of Oracle) in the database, RMAN will not be able to connect via that mode. For RMAN, you need a dedicated connection in the TNSNAMES.ora file configured using the keyword DEDICATED.

This brings us to the end of the discussion about RMAN configuration settings. It's a long list of options, but once you have set up RMAN with the options that you need, you will see RMAN performing to its highest potential.

Now, as we understand how to configure RMAN and from the last chapter, we know how to take backups, we must use all of this knowledge to recover our databases. So, in the next section, we shall discuss database recovery, starting with the following:

- Crash (instance) and media recovery
- Key terms related to recovery
- Different kinds of recovery scenarios

Crash and media recovery

In general, database recoveries can be categorized into two broad domains:

- Crash recovery
- Media recovery

Crash recovery (a.k.a. instance recovery) is a more subtle form of database recovery because all that is lost is the database instance. Since it's just the instance that's lost and not any physical file of the database, the recovery won't need any physical file(s) to be restored. The background process **SMON** will initiate the recovery automatically at the time of the next database startup. In this recovery, only the online redo logs belonging to a single thread (for a single instance) or of multiple failed threads are used for a **Real Application Cluster (RAC)** database.

> Many DBAs often use the terms instance and crash recovery interchangeably. However, it is actually wrong to do so. In a single instance, the loss of one instance is going to bring down its database as well. So a recovery in this case can be called either an instance or a crash recovery. But in an RAC database, as long as at least one instance is up and running while the rest have crashed, the subsequent recovery performed is instance recovery only. Only when all the instances are lost and the database has also gone down with their loss, would it be appropriate to call such a recovery a crash recovery.

Media recovery is a more crucial database recovery because it includes a physical loss of the mount point, including some database files such as the data file and control file. Even the deletion of any of these files or a physical corruption of them would necessitate a DBA to perform media recovery for them. To perform media recovery, firstly you must either create a new file at its source location (or at a new one if the source destination is completely damaged) and no backup of it is available, or restore the same from the backup to the source location of the lost file (or to a new location as well). The checkpoint information stored in the headers of the restored data files won't match with the existing database. Thus in the second and final step, you will need to synch these new data file(s) with the existing files of the database using the archived logs and online redo log files. The media recovery can further be of two types: complete and incomplete. In a complete recovery, applying all the archived logs and the online redo logs along with the backup files would enable you to recover without any loss of data. But if, for example, you have a missing archived log or for some reason, you can't do a complete recovery such as recovering a dropped table, then you must perform an incomplete recovery to recover from such kind of issues. Note that for the recovery of a dropped table, you can even restore it from the recycle bin (if it's still in there), or use RMAN to do an exclusive table-level recovery in the current release 12*c* (discussed later in the chapter). As the restore and recovery of backups requires explicitly executed commands by the DBA, media recovery can't be performed automatically. Also, to ensure that there is no, or minimal, data loss after the media recovery is complete, the database must be in the ARCHIVELOG mode with all the required archived logs for recovery available.

Key terms related to recovery

There are many internal structures that play a very important role in the recovery of the database and also in its internal workings. In the following list, we shall look at the most important key terms which are a must for you to understand:

- **Data block**: It is the smallest unit among the storage structures of the database and is used for storing user data. An example is the infamous table EMP which contains the employee data. Thus, for an employee AMAN, block #100, for example, would contain the data in the form of a row belonging to it.

- **Dirty block**: When a database block's content is modified by a DML, as long as that transaction is not completed with either a ROLLBACK or COMMIT command, the data is termed as inconsistent and correspondingly, that block is marked as a dirty block. A dirty block would need to have its transaction status updated with either a ROLLBACK or COMMIT command to finally become a clean block.

- **Change vectors**: The changes done over the contents of a data block are stored in a particular memory area called the Redo Log Buffer. Within the redo log buffer, these changed values are stored in an Oracle internal format known as change vector. For example, if you have updated a salary value from $1000 to $2000, the redo log buffer will receive this updated data of 2000 in the form of a change vector. A single change vector may contain different changes if they all belong to the same database. In addition to the change vector for the updated data of the block, another undo change vector that represents the changed undo block that would be formatted to store the original copy, as 1000 in our example, will also be created and stored in the same redo log buffer. The background process LGWR will subsequently write both of these change vectors into the online redo log files.

> There is confusion among many DBAs about whether or not the undo data goes into the redo logs. The answer to that is yes. It's not really the undo itself, but the undo change vector describing the change done over the undo block that is stored in the redo log. Doing so is important to ensure the recovery of the undo tablespace if it gets corrupted or lost.

- **Redo records**: These are a collection of multiple change vectors. Because there are multiple change vectors that are combined in one redo record; while using them for recovery, it's ensured by the database that either the complete redo record is applied over a data file or nothing at all! Redo records are ordered by the **System Commit Number (SCN)** arrangement. An SCN is considered an internal representation of time by the database and is used to reflect that the transaction is finally committed. Redo records within a redo log file use a special locator called **Redo Byte Address (RBA)**, which is a combination of the log file sequence number, the block number of that log file, and a position within that redo log block from where the required redo record starts.

- **Redo log buffer**: It is a memory area within the **System Global Area (SGA)** of the database where the redo records are stored. The redo records stored in it are not kept for a long duration and are flushed by the background process LGWR into the online redo log files very quickly at various events.

- **Redo log files**: These are physical, persistent files stored over the disk and grouped under the redo log groups. When we say that the recovery process will bring the backup files in sync with the rest of the database, it is the application of the redo records over the data files and increasing their SCN that brings it to the point where it matches the one's stored in the control file.

  Because log files are fixed in size, once the LGWR process fills the current redo log file (group), they will jump over to the next log group, thus initiating a checkpoint, which is more precisely called the thread checkpoint.

- **Redo thread**: All the redo log groups belonging to an instance are grouped under a thread owned and mounted by it. Thus, in simple words, the entire redo generated by an instance is owned exclusively by its own thread. The information about the redo threads and the log groups associated with them is stored within the control file.

- **Redo stream**: The entire redo that belongs to one thread will form the redo stream that is ordered based on the time the changes' occurrence. For a single instance database, the redo thread and redo stream are actually the same because there is no other thread to be managed. For a clustered database, the redo stream is the redo data that is generated by all the threads of that database.

- **Checkpoint**: A checkpoint (event) causes the dirty buffers to be written to the data files by the background process DBWR. Using checkpoints at recovery time, it is determined how many redo records need to be applied in order to bring the data files, control files, and redo logs in sync. Checkpoints occur at different events and are of many types too—thread checkpoint, file checkpoint, object checkpoint, and incremental checkpoint, to list a few. Though these are different events, the purpose of them all is to push the dirty buffers into the data files so that at the time of instance recovery, there will be as few blocks as possible that need recovering.

The complete description of checkpoints and SCN would probably require many pages, if not a book itself. To learn more about both, refer to the book authored by *Jonathan Lewis, Oracle Core: Essentials internals for DBAs and Developers*, which covers a lot of details on these two topics and many other internals related to the database.

Overview of stages in the database startup

The final goal of performing recovery is to open the database with either zero or minimal data loss. For a database to be opened, there are three stages which it has to pass: nomount, mount, and open.

In the nomount stage, an instance is allocated to the database after reading the SPFILE (or PFILE). At this stage, no permanent files, such as control files or redo logs, are opened.

At the mount stage, an attempt is made to open all the control files. In case a control file is unavailable but there is no issue with the control files, the mount phase is aborted, that is, they are located and opened. Along with this, a couple of checks are performed to ensure that it's possible to proceed to the open stage. An example of one such check is whether or not the name of the database stored in the control file's database area matches the database name used in the instance. As redo log files are also opened at the mount stage, the next step is to attempt to mount the redo thread. If all the redo log files are intact and report no issues, the mounting of the redo thread becomes successful and the alert log is updated with the message `successful mount of the redo thread`. With this, the mount stage is complete and the open stage is initiated.

At the open stage, an attempt to open all the data files listed in the control file is made and further checks are performed to determine whether or not there is a need for any sort of recovery. To ensure that the last shutdown was a proper one, two checks are performed: the first compares the checkpoint count stored in the data files to the control file (visible from the fixed table X$KCVFH) and the second compares the checkpoint SCN stored in the data file headers to the redo log file. If any data file's checkpoint SCN does not match with the redo log file's SCN range, it is a signal that media recovery is required. Also, it is confirmed that the STOP SCN parameter for the data files is set to infinity is done to ensure that the last shutdown was a clean one and all the dirty buffers are written to the data files prior to the last shutdown. If it did happen, it would mean that no updates remain pending for the data files. The reason to mark the last SCN (or STOP SCN) to infinity is that Oracle database can't decide when the data files will be properly closed the next time. Thus, the internal value for STOP SCN is set to infinity, which gets updated with the last checkpoint information at the time of the next shutdown.

The checkpoint information recorded in the data file header is the SCN generated for the last log file switch. Using this, it will be easier for the database to know from which lowest redo log file it will need to start applying the change vectors in case there is a mismatch reported. Because of the incremental checkpoint, dirty buffers get written to the data files constantly. This constant writing ensures that in the event of an instance crash, only a few dirty buffers will require recovery and, to do so, just a few of the change vectors would need to be applied. The checkpoint writes completed by the DBWR are also updated in the control file in the form of an on-disk-SCN and become a starting point for the recovery. To sum it up, using all this information, Oracle can find the appropriate redo log files which will be used in the recovery as well as the position from where to start applying the change vectors. Once the recovery is complete, a marker for the end-crash-recovery is also recorded to ensure that it avoids repeating the crash recovery if there is an instance crash right away.

If there is no problem or mismatch whatsoever, the open phase proceeds smoothly and gets completed with all the data files being opened in the read-write mode.

Steps involved in the crash/instance recovery

As we mentioned before, the crash recovery is a subtle and automatic recovery and is initiated by the DBA that issues the STARTUP command. There are two steps involved in it:

- Roll forward (crash recovery)
- Roll backward (transaction recovery)

Roll forward is the application of the change vectors to the data files. It happens at the mount stage by the process SMON that reads the redo log file from the last full checkpoint recorded in it (due to the log switch). The information about the last full checkpoint will be available in the control file. The control file stores this information in the form of an on-disk-SCN-checkpoint call made to the data files due to the last log switch. If it matches the data files that have the last checkpoint recorded in their headers, it will mean that the data files were properly shut down and no recovery is required. If this is not the case, the on-disk version becomes the starting point of the recovery and from this point until the end of the redo log (the last change vector recorded in redo log), the change vectors will be applied to the data files. Note that the change vectors will include both the committed and uncommitted data.

Because there might be a huge number of change vectors that need to be applied to the data files, it may take a lot of time to completely roll forward and eventually, the startup of the database will also be delayed. To optimize this phase, Oracle introduced an enhancement named the two-pass recovery.

The instance recovery is the recreation of the lost transactions which couldn't get written to the data files and these transactions are stored (in the form of redo records) within the online redo log files. Please recollect our mentioning that the redo log files are selected based on the last full checkpoint. It sounds quite straightforward but has one small issue: there are several types of checkpoints available. One of them is the incremental checkpoint due to which the DBWR process will always keep writing the dirty buffers to the data files after a specific time interval all the time. While writing the dirty buffers, the DBWR will also ping the LGWR process to add a little extra information to the associated change vector known as **Block Written Record** (**BWR**). This additional information will be used in the instance recovery to ensure that those change vectors which have a BWR bit associated with them won't need to be applied to the data file as their dirty buffer would be already checkpointed (or simply, written) to the data file. So, if there are a total of 100 change vectors that need to be applied over the data files and 30 of them have the BWR bit appended to them, only 70 change vectors would actually be applied at the roll forward phase, thus saving time and quickening the process.

To further optimize the duration of the roll forward phase, you can use the FAST_START_MTTR_TARGET parameter. The parameter value is set in seconds and will decide the **Mean Time To Recover** (**MTTR**) value that the instance will take to get the cache recovery done. Once this parameter is set to a non-zero value, the Oracle database tries to tune the incremental checkpoints based on the workload so that the number of the checkpoint writes matches the given target value of the parameter. It's important to mention that if you are going to set an unachievable value for this parameter, Oracle database will self-tune the given value to a more realistic one. The maximum value possible for this parameter is 3600 seconds (one hour) and the minimum is one second, though this is not really possible as many different factors will jump in.

Once the roll forward phase is completed and all the database files get in sync with each other, the database can now be opened. But since the roll forward phase applied both the committed and uncommitted data over the data files, they now contain inconsistent data in them. Thus at the open stage, the rollback of this uncommitted data will start, managed by the roll backward phase.

In the roll backward phase, the data within the undo tablespace will be applied to roll back the uncommitted changes. The SMON process will initiate the rollback of the uncommitted buffers. To make this faster, you can set the parameter FAST_START_PARALLEL_ROLLBACK which will spawn parallel slaves to make the rollback faster.

Once the roll backward phase is over, the instance recovery will be considered complete as well.

 In the case of RAC database instances, there will be additional steps to recover global cache and enqueue services.

The previous discussion on instance recovery is for database releases up to 11*g* and for non-container databases for 12*c*. If your database is a 12*c* multitenant container database, although most of the things will be the same, you still need to keep a few distinct points in mind. The next section discusses the instance recovery for container and pluggable databases in 12*c*.

Instance recovery in container and pluggable databases

The instance recovery holds the same meaning in a multitenant **container database (CDB)** as in the non-container databases. But, since the container database will contain the pluggable databases along with the control file and redo log files, the instance being exclusive to the container database only, instance recovery will be performed at the container database level. Instance recovery is impossible for the PDBs. Since the redo log files for the CDBs hold the transactional data for the underlying PDBs and themselves, they are used by all the data files whenever instance recovery is needed.

If there is an instance crash in the container database, the following steps are performed:

1. The container database is started as a whole by the DBA using the STARTUP command.

2. The data file headers are compared to the control files for the checkpoint count, as well as the SCNs.

3. If the match between the checkpoint count and the SCN is not obtained, the need for instance recovery is detected and the action is started by applying the required change vectors from the redo log files to the data files, bringing them in sync with the control files.

4. Once the data files are in sync with the control files, the CDB can be opened. Please note that the container database being open doesn't mean that the underlying PDBs are also open. All the PDBs remain at the mount stage only when the root container is open.

5. Since with the application of the redo data over the data files, both uncommitted and committed changes were pushed over them; a roll back phase will start for the data files belonging to the root, and the uncommitted transactions will revert back.

6. Since the PDBs remain at the mount stage initially, you can open them one by one by explicitly mentioning their name or open them all at once using the ALTER PLUGGABLE DATABASE ALL OPEN statement. Once the command finishes and the PDBs are opened, their data files will have the uncommitted data stored in them rolled back. Once both the CDBs and PDBs are left with committed data only, the instance recovery can be assumed to be complete.

In conclusion, crash recovery doesn't require much to be done explicitly, other than restarting the database (single instance) or one of its instances (RAC), and then it will be completed on its own. If there is no physical file loss accompanying it, things will remain simple and straightforward. But if there is physical file loss, things will become a little tricky depending on which kind of file is lost, whether or not its backup exists, whether or not the database is in the archive log mode, and so on. Hence, let's move on from crash recovery to media recovery and see what different kinds of failure can occur and how we can recover from them!

Performing media recovery

As mentioned already, media recovery is a more serious recovery category which involves the physical damage or loss of database files which may even lead to its complete crash (depending on the file type). For media recovery, unlike crash recovery, a DBA has to be involved to carry it forward manually. There are two steps that will be used in media recovery:

*   Restore of the backup files
*   Recovery of the lost or damaged files using archived logs and online redo logs

Since media recovery is performed when a physical file is lost, it's not possible to recover the damage without first restoring the lost file from the backup, which would involve copying or moving the backup files from the backup media using either OS or RMAN commands, the latter making the job much easier.

As the files restored from the backup will be lagging behind in the checkpoint information stored in them compared to the rest of the database, it's not possible to bring them online without bridging that gap. To ensure that the restored files become in sync with the control file and the rest of the database, the archived logs and online redo logs will need to be applied over them. This procedure is termed recovery or, more specifically, media recovery. To make sure that there won't be any missing transactions, the database must be in the ARCHIVELOG mode and all the archived logs must be available. Since archived logs store the transactions in them based on the SCN ordering, no gap will be allowed. In case there is a gap (caused by missing or lost archived log(s)), it will cause the recovery to stop. As such, this recovery will result in lost data and will be called an incomplete recovery.

If the database is in the NOARCHIVELOG mode and a file is lost, since there is no backup available of the previous transactions in the form of archived logs, a complete restore of not just the lost data file but all the data files and control files from the previous consistent backup would needed to be done. It is a simple task from a technical perspective as all you are doing is using an OS command such as CP to restore the files from the backup to the target location. However, this recovery will also be incomplete as you will only be able to go back into the past to recover that data which becomes available through the restored backup. So, if your backup is a month old, after the restore you will find your data pushed back a month. You will lose all the data since the backup and your users will need to enter the data generated over the entire month.

NOARCHIVELOG is the default log mode of the database. But, as we have already mentioned, it restricts your recovery of lost data. So, it's very important to have the database switched over to the ARCHIVELOG mode as soon as possible.

Now, as we have established a good understanding about the different recovery categories and also how instance and media recovery work, let us take a step forward and look at the different media recovery scenarios and what you should do when you encounter them.

Recovery in the NOARCHIVELOG mode

If you have lost a data file in the NOARCHIVELOG mode, depending on whether a redo log switch has taken place or not since the last backup, a complete or incomplete recovery will be done. For the latter case, any data entered since the last backup would need to be re-inserted by the users.

If the database has lost one of its data files and the online redo logs have not been switched since the last consistent full backup, the database can be recovered with no data loss. In this scenario, the steps are typically as follows:

1. Shut down the database.

2. Startup the database in the mount mode and restore the entire database.

3. Once the restore is complete, open the database along with all the included PDBs.

Had the online redo logs been overwritten since the last full backup (which mostly happens in a production environment), the process would be a little different. In this case, the steps are as follows:

1. Shut down the database immediately with the ABORT option.

2. Start the database in the NOMOUNT mode.

3. Restore the control file from the backup.

4. Bring the database to the mount stage.

5. Restore the entire database. Here, you might need to use the CATALOG command to update the control file about the last backup taken.

6. Recover the database using the option NOREDO which would stop RMAN from requesting the archived logs for recovery.

7. Open the database using the RESETLOGS option as it will be required to sync the online redo logs with the restored backup.

The following steps are for the same scenario where a data file named users01.dbf is removed. A consistent full backup of the database has been taken already. The following steps performed will show the (incomplete) recovery done over the database:

```
RMAN> shutdown abort

RMAN> startup nomount

RMAN> restore controlfile from '/u01/app/ORCL12/backupset/2013_08_15/o1_
mf_ncnnf_TAG20130815T210237_90sx4q9q_.bkp';

RMAN> alter database mount;

RMAN> catalog start with '/u01/app/ORCL12/backupset/2013_08_15';
```

```
RMAN> restore database;
RMAN> recover database noredo;
RMAN> alter database open resetlogs;
Statement processed
```

Since the database release 12*c*, SQL statements can be executed from the RMAN client executable without using the SQL operator. We have performed all the previous steps using the RMAN executable itself.

If you have taken an incremental backup, it is also usable for recovery, provided it is a consistent backup, that is, it was not taken when the database was open. Also, recovery is not possible for the missing transactions as there won't be any archive logs available to make that possible.

Loss of a temporary file

Temporary files are not backed up by RMAN. They are used for the operations that can't fit in the PGA memory. Since the temporary files are not considered so important, if you lose one (or even all), it wouldn't have any impact on the database itself.

There are two possible ways to get the temporary file(s) back at the CDB level:

1. Create another temporary file as a replacement for the lost file. For example, if you have lost a temporary file TEMP01 from the TEMP tablespace, you can add another file to it using the following command:

   ```
   RMAN> ALTER TABLESPACE TEMP ADD TEMPFILE TEMPFILE2 SIZE 100M;
   ```

2. After this, you can drop the lost temporary file using the following command:

   ```
   RMAN> ALTER TABLESPACE TEMP DROP TEMPFILE TEMP1;
   ```

The second option is useful only if you are allowed to restart the database. Once you restart the database, the lost temporary file will automatically be created and an entry in the alert log would be added that would appear as follows:

```
Re-creating temp file /u01/app/oracle/oradata/acdb/temp01.dbf
```

There is a difference between the loss of a temporary file in the CDB and a PDB. Unlike the CDB, the temporary file for a PDB won't be created automatically when opened. So, if there is any work that will require the temporary file, it will throw an error. Although the absence of a temporary file will not be taken care of automatically at the time of the PDB startup, it won't stop the PDB from being opened. After the PDB is opened, you can add another temporary file to the tablespace and drop the missing one while being connected to the container database.

If the temporary file for a non-container database is lost, at the next database startup, it will automatically be created. If restarting the database is not an option, a new temporary file can be created by using the ALTER TABLESPACE command and the entry of the lost file can be deleted. A lost temporary tablespace doesn't stop a non-container database startup or halt its working if the database is already in the open stage.

Loss of non-system data files

If you have lost a data file that doesn't belong to the system, sysaux, or undo tablespaces, the database will remain open and functional, except for the non-availability of the data stored in the lost data file(s). The recovery process won't be different from a non-container database and will include all the steps for the restoration and recovery of a lost file or files as described earlier in this chapter, after making it offline.

The steps for recovering a non-system data file belonging to a container (or non-container) database will be as follows:

1. If the data file has not gone offline, make it so by using the ALTER TABELESPACE command (if the database is open) or ALTER DATABASE command (if the database has gone down at the mount stage).

2. Restore the lost data file(s) from the backup by using the RESTORE command.

3. Recover the data file(s) by using the RECOVER command.

4. Bring the data file(s) (or the whole tablespace) online once the recovery is complete.

To demonstrate this, we shall forcefully remove a data file that belongs to the users tablespace in the container and then try to recover it. A backup of the whole database has already been taken and the database is in the ARCHIVELOG mode.

Let's remove the data file users01.dbf using the O/S command and then bounce the database to ensure that we get the error for the file loss:

```
SQL> !rm -rf /u01/app/oracle/oradata/acdb/users01.dbf
SQL> STARTUP FORCE


<<output snipped>>
ORA-01157: cannot identify/lock data file 6 - see DBWR trace file
ORA-01110: data file 6: '/u01/app/oracle/oradata/acdb/users01.dbf'
```

As expected, we have the error. Since this is a non-system data file, let's make it offline and proceed with opening the database. After that, we shall perform the recovery.

It's certainly possible to perform recovery at the mount stage, but in order to illustrate that the database can remain operational in such a recovery, we have chosen to do it in a slightly different way.

```
SQL> ALTER DATABASE DATAFILE 6 OFFLINE;


Database altered.
```

Since the data file has been made offline, it won't be required by the database while being opened. So, we can now bring up the database without receiving any error:

```
SQL> ALTER DATABASE OPEN;
```

Now, we shall perform the recovery at the RMAN prompt and make it online from there:

```
RMAN> RESTORE DATAFILE 6;

RMAN> RECOVER DATAFILE 6;

RMAN> ALTER DATABASE DATAFILE 6 ONLINE;
```

In case of a PDB, there is no any difference in the commands for this scenario. The implications of the file loss will vary depending on whether or not the PDB is already open. If it is already open, the loss of the non-system file won't bring it down and the PDB will remain up even for the recovery. If the CDB comes down, the PDB will be in the mount stage at the next startup and won't open because of the file loss. However, as the data file belongs to the PDB, it won't stop the CDB from opening. To open the PDB, you will need to connect to it and make the data file offline, following that with an attempt to recover the file.

The following steps are required for such a recovery:

1. Connect to the pluggable database.
2. Put the lost data file or the whole tablespace in the offline status.
3. Connect to the root container.
4. Restore the PDB specific data file(s) (or tablespace) from the backup.
5. Recover the PDB specific data file(s) (or tablespace).
6. Bring the data file(s) (or tablespace) to the online status.

To demonstrate this, we shall remove the data file that is specific to our pluggable database apdb. After that, we shall make the data file offline and attempt the recovery. So, let's first remove the file:

```
SQL> !rm -rf /u01/app/oracle/oradata/acdb/apdb/apdb_users01.dbf
```

Now, let's proceed to recover this data file:

```
[oracle@host5 ~]$ sqlplus sys/oracle@apdb as sysdba
SQL> alter tablespace users offline;
```

From RMAN, we shall now recover the tablespace users:

```
RMAN> connect target /

connected to target database: ACDB (DBID=4244090852)

RMAN> restore tablespace apdb:users;
RMAN> recover tablespace apdb:users;
SQL> alter tablespace users online;
```

For a non-container database, the commands RESTORE and RECOVER are used in the same way.

Loss of system data files

If the file that's lost belongs to a tablespaces such as system or undo, the recovery can't happen when the database is open. The steps to perform the recovery of a container and non-container database would be similar and are as follows:

1. Shut down the database.
2. At the mount stage, restore the lost file (or the whole tablespace).
3. Recover the lost file(s) (or the whole tablespace).
4. Bring the database up using the ALTER DATABASE OPEN command.

As we mentioned, a container database will require a shutdown in the event of system data file loss. Since a PDB can't be up without its container being up, all the pluggable databases will also remain closed while the recovery is going on.

To demonstrate this case, let's remove the data file system01.dbf belonging to the system tablespace of our container database acdb. To find the name of the file, you can query the CDB_DATA_FILES view which has the container #1 (CON_ID) for the CDB.

Now, we will introduce a crash by removing this file using the rm command:

```
SQL> !rm /u01/app/oracle/oradata/acdb/system01.dbf

So, the file is removed and now we shall do a bounce of the container
database and bring it to the mount stage in order to recover it:
SQL> STARTUP FORCE MOUNT
```

Now, while being connected to the root, we shall perform the restore and recovery of the file with RMAN. Once recovered, we shall open the container and the pluggable databases inside it:

```
RMAN> RESTORE DATAFILE 1;
RMAN> RECOVER DATAFILE 1;
SQL> ALTER DATABASE OPEN;
SQL> ALTER PLUGGABLE DATABASE ALL OPEN;
```

If a PDB loses a system data file, the recovery will need the pluggable database to be closed. Also, the CDB has to be closed and while the recovery is on, neither the pluggable database(s) (all of them) nor the root container will be available. The recovery must commence from the CDB, which needs to be in the mount stage.

The following steps need to be executed to recover from a system data file loss related to a PDB:

1. Shutdown the container database:

   ```
   RMAN> shutdown immediate;
   ```

2. Mount the container database. All the PDBs are closed at this stage:

   ```
   RMAN> startup mount;
   ```

3. Restore the lost system data file (or tablespace) of the PDB:

   ```
   RMAN> restore tablespace apdb:system;
   ```

4. Open the container database:

   ```
   RMAN> alter database open;
   ```

5. Open all the pluggable databases:

   ```
   RMAN> alter pluggable database open;
   ```

This will complete the recovery of a system data file belonging to a pluggable database.

Recovering whole CDBs, PDBs, and root container databases

If there are multiple data files lost for either a CDB, PDB, or a root container; it's easier to get the recovery done by recovering them as a whole. Although the overall concept is the same for the CDB, PDB, and root databases, there are some subtle differences in the commands that will be used depending on the type of the database.

Complete recovery of a container database

The complete recovery of a container database would include the recovery of its underlying seed database, root container, and all the pluggable databases. This would be required if all or most of the data files of the container database were lost. The recovery of a complete container would need to happen at the mount stage and so while the recovery is going on, any pluggable database(s) would be non-accessible. You can perform the recovery using either the SYSDBA or the SYSBACKUP privilege. To perform recovery of our container database ACDB, the following steps would be carried out:

1. Connect to the container database using either the SYSDBA or the SYSBACKUP privilege and bring it to the mount stage:

   ```
   [oracle@host5 ~]$ rman target sys/oracle
   RMAN> startup mount;
   ```

2. Restore the whole container database by using the restore database command:

   ```
   RMAN> restore database;
   ```

3. Once the entire database restore is complete, recover it using the recover database command:

   ```
   RMAN> recovery database;
   ```

4. As the recovery gets completed, open the container database using the alter database command:

   ```
   RMAN> alter database open;
   ```

5. Finally, open all the pluggable databases:

   ```
   RMAN> alter pluggable database all open;
   ```

Complete recovery of a pluggable database

If one or more data files of a pluggable database are lost, this doesn't impact its container database and other pluggable databases. The container database and other pluggable databases will remain open and functional even while the recovery of the damaged pluggable database is performed.

The recovery of one or multiple pluggable databases can be performed by the container database. While being recovered, the target pluggable database(s) will remain closed. If while closing the pluggable database, an error related to the lost data file(s) is reported, that file(s) must be made offline before closing the pluggable database.

Let's connect to the root and close our pluggable database `APDB` that requires recovery:

```
$ rman target sys/oracle@acdb
RMAN> alter pluggable database APDB close;
```

The next step is to perform a restore of the pluggable database, followed by its recovery:

```
RMAN> restore pluggable database APDB;
RMAN> recover pluggable database APDB;
```

In order to recover multiple pluggable databases, separate their names with commas when mentioning them in the preceding commands.

Since the recovery of the pluggable database is now complete, the final step is to bring it up, that is, open it! If any data files have been made offline, they can now be brought back to the online mode:

```
RMAN> alter pluggable database APDB open;
```

If a single pluggable database needs to be recovered, recovery can be performed while being connected to that specific database using a local user with the `SYSDBA` privilege. Though the procedure will remain the same, the `restore` and `recover` commands can't include the `pluggable` option, nor can they use the name of the pluggable database in them (the error `RMAN-07538` would be thrown). Similar to the method described previously, the pluggable database must be closed before undergoing recovery. The following commands perform the recovery of the pluggable database `APDB` using its local user `bkup`:

```
$ rman target bkup/bkup@apdb
RMAN> shutdown immediate
RMAN> restore database;
RMAN> recover database;
RMAN> alter pluggable database APDB open;
```

Complete recovery of the root container

If you have only lost the data files in the root container, performing its restore and recovery is still possible. To avoid any inconsistency between the underlying PDBs and the root container, you should recover all the PDBs as well, after the recovery is completed.

If you are recovering the root and all the PDBs, it's better to perform a recovery of the entire CDB itself. Doing so will save you from performing multiple restores and recovery tasks.

Recovery of the root container takes place with the container database in the mount stage. As the CDB will be down, all the pluggable databases would remain closed and so need to be brought up online.

The following steps will be carried out to recover to the root container:

1. Connect to the container database, which must be in the mount stage:

   ```
   $ rman target bkup/
   ```

2. Restore and perform the recovery of the root container, using the ROOT option with the RESTORE and RECOVER commands:

   ```
   RMAN> RESTORE DATABASE ROOT;

   RMAN> RECOVER DATABASE ROOT;
   ```

3. Optionally, perform the restore and recovery of the pluggable databases as well. It's not really required, but is advisable.

4. Open the container database and all the pluggable databases as the final step to complete the task:

   ```
   RMAN> alter database ACDB open;

   RMAN> alter pluggable database all open;
   ```

Performing control file recovery

Control files in the database release 12*c* belong to the container database only; thus, recovery of the lost control file will be done at the container database level. Depending on whether you have lost just one out of the multiple control files, or worse, all the control files, the recovery procedure will vary.

If you have just lost one or a few of the control files and still have at least one good working copy of the control file for the database, the recovery will be simple. The steps involved are as follows:

1. To speed up the recovery time, perform a checkpoint before shutting down the database:

   ```
   SQL> alter system checkpoint;
   ```

2. Shutdown the database using the `immediate` option:

    ```
    SQL> shutdown immediate;
    ```

3. While the database is down, copy one of the existing control files to the location of the lost control file(s) and rename it after the lost files.

4. Startup the database using the `STARTUP` command.

If the destination is not intact and has been corrupted, you will need to use a new location for the renamed file. As the location change needs to be updated in the control file as well, the parameter `CONTROL_FILES` will also need to be updated using either the `ALTER SYSTEM` command (if using SPFILE) or by manually editing it in the initialization parameter file (`initSID.ora`).

If all the control files are lost, restoring these files would require to be followed by their recovery. If the original location where the control files were located is intact, you can restore the control file backup there. But if due to reasons such as file system corruption or disk failure, you can't restore the control files to their old location, you will need to choose a new location for them. This must include the editing and updating of the parameter file before attempting to mount the database. To do so, you can use the `ALTER SYSTEM` command at the `nomount` stage.

For this recovery, you need to have the database ID with you. We strongly recommend that you take a note of the DBID and enable the auto backup of the control file if you are not using a recovery catalog.

 If you are using the recovery catalog, the use of the auto backup feature is not required. To learn more about the recovery catalog, refer to the next chapter.

To demonstrate the loss of control files and their recovery, we shall remove our control files and recover them using their auto backup feature.

Let's see the control files that we have in our database:

```
SQL> show parameter control_files
```

NAME	TYPE	VALUE
control_files	string	/u01/app/oracle/oradata/acdb/control01.ctl, /u01/app/oracle/fast_recovery_area/acdb/control02.ctl

```
SQL>
```

So, we have two copies of the control file. Now, we shall remove both these files in order to simulate the crash:

```
SQL> !rm -rf /u01/app/oracle/oradata/acdb/control01.ctl
```

```
SQL> !rm -rf /u01/app/oracle/fast_recovery_area/acdb/control02.ctl
```

As both the files are removed, the database instance will crash after some time, but we will not wait for that to happen and instead, shall abort the instance ourselves:

```
SQL> SHUTDOWN ABORT
```

Now, using RMAN, we shall attempt to restore the control files from their auto backup versions. For this, the database must be in the NOMOUNT stage:

```
$ rman target /
```

```
RMAN> STARTUP NOMOUNT
```

```
RMAN> RESTORE CONTROLFILE FROM AUTOBACKUP;
```

The previous command will perform the restore of both the control files to their original destinations. Since the control files are in place, we can now mount the database and issue the RECOVER command. This needs the database to be in the MOUNT stage before being submitted:

```
RMAN> ALTER DATABASE MOUNT;
```

```
RMAN> RECOVER DATABASE;
```

After we have restored the control file, we need to use the RESETLOGS option to open the database. If you don't have an auto backup of the control files, you will need to explicitly mention the backup set name which would have it. Interestingly, even though we are using it, this is not going to be an incomplete recovery as we had our redo log files intact at the time of the recovery:

```
RMAN> ALTER DATABASE OPEN RESETLOGS;
```

This completes our recovery of the lost control files.

If the data file has become more recent than the control file restored from the backup, the previously mentioned RECOVER command won't work. In this case, the RECOVER command used must be:

```
RMAN> RECOVER DATABASE USING BACKUP CONTROLFILE;
```

It may be the case that you haven't taken the backup of the control file or it is corrupted. In that case, you would need to create the control file using the CREATE CONTROLFILE command. A script to do so can be made available by using the trace file backup of the control file created using the ALTER DATABASE BACKUP CONTROLFILE TO TRACE command.

Before we conclude this section, we suggest that although it's not tough to recover from a lost control file(s), it would be better to not get into that situation. Instead of performing a recovery of the one and only control file, multiplex it and create three different copies located at different mount points. It's much faster and less error-prone to copy a control file from one of its multiplexed copies than to perform its recovery.

Performing Block Media Recovery (BMR)

RMAN, besides recovering the data files (and even the whole database), can perform the recovery of individual block(s) if they get corrupted. In such a block-level recovery, only the blocks participating in the recovery would be inaccessible. The rest of the data file and the database as a whole will remain open and functional. Not only that, the recovery time will also be less because certain specific blocks are being recovered. For BMR, the database must be in the ARCHIVELOG mode and a valid copy of the backup must be available. Another very important thing is that the BMR is an **Enterprise Edition** (EE) option. If your database is not an EE, you will receive the error RMAN-05009!

 If a flashback database is enabled, RMAN can search for a good copy of the block from the flashback logs as well.

When a block is corrupted, the database reports the user about using ORA-1578. Besides, the user who tries to access the corrupted block will receive the following error and it will be logged in the alert log file as well:

```
Error(1): ORA-00604: error occurred at recursive SQL level 1
ORA-01578: ORACLE data block corrupted (file # 2, block # 69985)
ORA-01110: data file 2: '/u01/app/oracle/oradata/ORCL12/SYSAUX01.DBF'
```

An absence of the ORA-1578 error would mean that there is no physical corruption in the blocks encountered. You can also check the database for corrupted blocks using the VALIDATE command as follows:

```
RMAN> VALIDATE DATABASE;
```

The previous statement takes all the data files as input and any blocks found to be corrupted are reported in the V$DATABASE_BLOCK_CORRUPTION view. To recover the corrupted blocks only, you can use the RMAN RECOVER command with a couple of variations:

```
RMAN> RECOVER DATAFILE 2 BLOCK 10;
```

The preceding command would recover the data file 2 and its block #10.

To recover all the blocks detected as corrupt from the V$DATABASE_BLOCK_ CORRUPTION view, you can use the following command line:

```
RMAN> RECOVER CORRUPTION LIST;
```

Since block corruption is a serious issue, Oracle database does implicit checks of the data blocks to check corruption induced by underlying disks, storage systems, and so on. This is done with the help of the DB_BLOCK_CHECKSUM parameter (with the default value as typical) that enables DBWR to compute a checksum from all the bytes stored in the block at the time of writing it. This check is enabled for every tablespace. If the value is set to full, the block is checked for corruption within the memory and not written to the disk. This check is enabled for the system tablespace by default, irrespective of the value of the parameter. The overhead of using this parameter is not more than 4-5% so, it is strongly advised that you don't stop this check.

Since 11g onwards, the database checkers keep on checking for corrupted blocks without DBA intervention and if a corrupted block is found, its entry is automatically updated in the V$DATABASE_BLOCK_ CORRUPTION view. To learn more about database checkers, see the Oracle documentation's *New Features guide* for 11g.

Besides the physical corruption check using the block header, the entire block can be checked for self-consistency using the DB_BLOCK_CHECKING parameter. The overhead of this parameter is about 15-20% for a production database and that's the reason it's not enabled by default. You should enable it only if the overhead induced by it is acceptable.

From 11g onwards, a single parameter DB_ULTRA_SAFE can control the two previously mentioned parameters.

Performing point-in-time recovery

Although data loss after recovery is unacceptable; at times, it becomes inevitable. We have already mentioned that the loss of an archived log would bring a halt to your recovery and result in the loss of data. Also, there can be cases where you need to explicitly cancel the recovery. One such example is the recovery of a table dropped permanently by the end user. Since dropping a table is actually not an incorrect action, at the time of recovery, the database will reapply the last issued DROP TABLE command from the archived logs. Because of this, even after the recovery is complete, the table won't be recovered. To stop this from happening, the recovery must stop before the DDL of dropping the table gets reapplied.

There are two variations possible for point-in-time recovery: for the whole database and for a specific tablespace. In the next sections, we shall have a look at both of these.

Database Point-in-time Recovery (DBPITR)

Database point-in-time recovery is done for the whole database and using it, the entire database is pushed back in time. You can perform this recovery using various options, for example, recovery up to a specific time in the past, such as to a particular log sequence number or a specific SCN. The typical steps that you will use for this recovery are as follows:

1. Decide which option, that is, time, SCN, or log sequence number, you will be performing the recovery by.

2. Shut down the database and bring it to the mount stage.

3. Using the desired option, set the SET UNTIL option in RMAN. For example, to use an SCN for the recovery, you will need to mention SET UNTIL SCN NNNN.

4. Restore the database.

5. Once the restore is complete, perform the recovery of the database.

6. Since it's not a complete recovery as we haven't applied all the archived logs and the online redo logs, we can't open the database normally and will have to use the RESETLOGS option which shows that the recovery performed is an incomplete one.

If you are using time as the criteria to perform the recovery, don't forget to set the environment variables `NLS_LANG` and `NLS_DATE_FORMAT` to the following values:

`NLS_LANG=american_america.us7ascii`

`NLS_DATE_FORMAT=Mon DD YYYY HH24:MI:SS`

Let's perform DBPITR for our container database `acdb`. To demonstrate that the recovery is performed and the database has gone back in time, we shall create a table with some data in it. After some time, we shall delete the data in the table and attempt to get it back using the DBPITR.

To start, we shall create a table while connected to the root:

```
SQL> CREATE TABLE t AS SELECT * FROM dba_tablespaces;
```

Now, we shall record the SCN when the table has data in it:

```
SQL> SELECT timestamp_to_scn(sysdate) FROM dual;


TIMESTAMP_TO_SCN(SYSDATE)
-------------------------
        1625048
```

At the moment, the table contains the data and this is the SCN to which we shall perform the DBPITR.

Now, we shall delete the table and commit the work in order to simulate the logical error.

```
SQL> DELETE FROM t;


4 rows deleted.


SQL> COMMIT;
```

Now the table has zero rows and we want to get the data back. For DBPITR, we will need to bring the database to the mount stage:

```
SQL> SHUTDOWN IMMEDIATE
SQL> STARTUP MOUNT
```

Now, using the RMAN prompt, the recovery can be attempted to the SCN to which we want the database to be recovered:

```
$ rman target /
```

```
RMAN> run
2> {set until scn=1625048;
3> restore database;
4> recover database;
5> }
```

```
executing command: SET until clause
```

Now the entire database has been pushed back to the given SCN in the preceding command. Since we have done an incomplete recovery, we will need to use the RESETLOGS clause to open the database:

```
RMAN> ALTER DATABASE OPEN RESETLOGS;
```

It's important to confirm that the recovery has succeeded. So, let's query the table to check for the data:

```
SQL> SELECT count(*) FROM t;

  COUNT(*)
----------
        4
```

This confirms that we have successfully done the PITR of our container database.

If you are going to perform a database-level point-in-time recovery for a PDB, the steps will be almost identical compared to a CDB recovery, except that unlike the CDB as a whole, only the candidate PDB will be closed and will undergo recovery. Also, a single PDB recovery doesn't impact the rest of the PDBs and they remain up and functional.

The steps to perform the DBPITR of a PDB are as follows:

1. Connect to the PDB using the sys user with either the sysdba or the sysbackup privilege as follows:

    ```
    $ sqlplus sys/oracle@apdb as sysdba
    ```

2. While the other PDBs and the root are open, close this PDB for recovery:

```
SQL> ALTER PLUGGABLE DATABASE apdb CLOSE;
```

3. Based on requirement, use the appropriate conditions and perform the restore and recovery of this PDB:

```
RMAN>run{
            set until SCN 1000;
            Restore pluggable database <name>;
            Recover pluggable database <name>;
        }
```

4. After the recovery is complete, open this PDB with the RESETLOGS option:

```
RMAN>alter pluggable database APDB open resetlogs;
```

It is important to note that a pluggable database can't be opened in the read-only mode. So to open a pluggable database in the read-write mode, the RESETLOGS option must be used. The existing backups of the pluggable database that have already undergone recovery will remain valid after the recovery as well.

Tablespace Point-in-time Recovery (TSPITR)

TSPITR is the recovery of a specific tablespace at a particular point in time in the past and, unlike the DBPITR, this method only affects the tablespace that undergoes recovery. For example, you can use TSPITR to recover a table from the TRUNCATE or ALTER command and to revert from a logical user error, when more than one table is dropped. In addition to these, this method can also be used to recover a dropped tablespace.

To perform the TSPITR, you will need the same things that were required for the DBPITR, that is, valid backup, archived logs, and the criteria using which you would do the recovery, that is, time or SCN. Depending on whether or not you are using FRA, you may or may not need to define the location for the auxiliary database. If you are using the FRA, RMAN will use it to perform the recovery, but if not, you will need to create a location for the automatically maintained auxiliary database and will also need to supply this destination in the RECOVER TABLESPACE command while doing the TSPITR, as shown in the following sample command:

```
RMAN> RECOVER TABLESPACE test_pdb UNTIL SCN 162189
AUXILIARY DESTINATION '/tmp/auxdir';
```

The target tablespace for the recovery must be a self-contained tablespace, that is, the objects inside it must not refer to any objects in another tablespace. To confirm this, you can use the DBMS_TTS.TRANSPORT_SET_CHECK package. RMAN performs this check at the start of the TSPITR itself. The results of this package check will be populated in the TRANSPORT_SET_VIOLATIONS view. If any errors are reported, ensure that they are resolved before you proceed to the TSPITR.

The recovery of a tablespace that's contained within a PDB requires the name of the PDB to be appended before the tablespace's name. So in the previous example, our pluggable database's name is apdb, and the command will be written as follows:

```
RMAN>RECOVER TABLESPACE apdb:test_pdb UNTIL SCN 1234 AUXILIARY
DESTINATION '/tmp';
```

It's better to use the recovery catalog when attempting the TSPITR if you are planning to do it over the tablespace more than once. In the absence of a recovery catalog, the recovery of the same tablespace can be done only with its backup created after its recovery. This is because the control file loses all the information about the tablespace's previous metadata when it goes through TSPITR.

If you do not have a recovery catalog but still want to do multiple TSPITR operations on the same tablespace, you will need to drop the tablespace each time before proceeding.

Since both DBPITR and TSPITR have their imitations as well as benefits, it's better to avoid both and use an alternative, if possible. For example, to recover from a dropped table or logical user error, it's easier to use flashback technology. Still, if you are committed to recovering the table without using flashback, there is a better alternative to DBPITR and TSPITR which we shall see in the next section.

Table and table partition-level recovery from RMAN backups

If you can't use any other technique to recover a table more easily, you can carry out a table-level recovery using RMAN backups without affecting the entire database or any other objects. In this technique, RMAN applies the backups to the tables, recovers them within the desired time frame, and then imports the recovered table into the target (main) database using the Data Pump.

To perform the recovery, you will be using the following command:

```
RMAN> RECOVER TABLE AMAN.
TESTTAB1 OF PLUGGABLE DATABASE APDB UNTIL TIME "to_date('2013-08-
15:20:10:00','YYYY-MM-DD:HH24:MI:SS')" AUXILIARY DESTINATION '/
tmp' DATAPUMP DESTINATION '/tmp' DUMP FILE 'testtab_dump.dmp';
```

In the previous RECOVER TABLE statement, we recovered the table TESTTAB1 using a specific date and time value. The command works by creating an auxiliary database at the mentioned auxiliary destination. The clone database created is opened by an in-memory script in the read-only mode. The tablespace that used to contain the table is restored and recovered using the read-only data dictionary. The last step will be the import of the table back into the database using the export DUMP FILE mentioned in the RECOVER TABLE command. If you don't want the table to be automatically imported, you can use the NOIMPORT option in the previous command.

Data recovery advisor

Although performing recovery is not really tough, with a little practice and understanding how various database components work with each other, it can go smoothly even for advanced scenarios. Still, almost every time I take a session on RMAN, the same question arises from the delegates of why recovery isn't being automated when almost everything else in the database is. Well, their wish has been granted and since the database release 11*g*, a simple yet efficient tool is now available that can actually perform recoveries automatically. Please say hello to **Data Recovery Advisor (DRA)**.

DRA is available in both the CLI (via RMAN) and GUI mode (via Cloud Control). In the RMAN, DRA is maintained through the following commands:

- LIST FAILURE
- ADVICE FAILURE
- REPAIR FAILURE PREVIEW
- CHANGE FAILURE

A failure is a persistent issue that has occurred in the database, for example, permanent file loss. Oracle database can detect a failure by itself or you can look for the details of one if you sense something is wrong. Marked with a unique ID, each failure's details will be stored in the ADR of the database. DRA can only work if a failure is stored in the ADR. The status of OPEN and CLOSED is given to each failure, where OPEN means that the failure still needs to be resolved and the CLOSED status shows that it's already taken care of. A priority rank of CRITICAL, HIGH, or LOW is also maintained and the failures with the rank CRITICAL or HIGH are attended to by the DRA.

You can change the rank between LOW and HIGH using the CHANGE FAILURE command manually as well. Please note that if for a failure, the rank is already marked as CRITICAL, you can't downgrade it to either HIGH or LOW.

The LIST command will be the first one to be executed and lists the existing failures stored in the ADR along with checking for new ones that may have come up.

The ADVICE command will generate an automated script containing the instructions that need to be carried out in order to solve the issue. This script will be stored under the **Health Monitor (HM)** folder in the ADR. You can either execute the steps listed in the script on your own or ask DRA to execute them using the REPAIR command.

The REPAIR command will execute the autogenerated script. This also has an option called PREVIEW which will show you what is being executed. The PREVIEW option doesn't do any repairs as such. Once you are satisfied, you can use the REPAIR command.

Let's remove some files to simulate a data file loss and use DRA to help us in its recovery:

```
SQL> !rm /u01/app/oracle/oradata/acdb/users01.dbf
```

Now it's time to fire up the DRA to see the details of this failure. From the RMAN client, we shall execute the LIST FAILURE command along with the DETAIL option that will give us elaborate details of the issue:

```
RMAN> LIST FAILURE DETAIL;


Database Role: PRIMARY


List of Database Failures
=========================


Failure ID Priority Status     Time Detected Summary
---------- -------- ---------- ------------- -------
8          HIGH     OPEN        31-MAY-13     One or more non-system
datafiles are missing
   Impact: See impact for individual child failures
   List of child failures for parent failure ID 8
   Failure ID Priority Status     Time Detected Summary
   ---------- -------- ---------- ------------- -------
   505        HIGH     OPEN        31-MAY-13     Datafile 6: '/u01/app/
oracle/oradata/acdb/users01.dbf' is missing
      Impact: Some objects in tablespace USERS might be unavailable
```

Since we know the reason for the failure, let's get advice on how we can resolve it by using the ADVISE command:

```
RMAN> ADVISE FAILURE;

Database Role: PRIMARY

List of Database Failures
=========================

Failure ID Priority Status     Time Detected Summary
---------- -------- ---------  ------------- -------
8          HIGH     OPEN       31-MAY-13     One or more non-system
datafiles are missing
  Impact: See impact for individual child failures
  List of child failures for parent failure ID 8
  Failure ID Priority Status     Time Detected Summary
  ---------- -------- ---------  ------------- -------
  505        HIGH     OPEN       31-MAY-13     Datafile 6: '/u01/app/
oracle/oradata/acdb/users01.dbf' is missing
    Impact: Some objects in tablespace USERS might be unavailable

analyzing automatic repair options; this may take some time
allocated channel: ORA_DISK_1
channel ORA_DISK_1: SID=36 device type=DISK
analyzing automatic repair options complete

Mandatory Manual Actions
========================
no manual actions available

Optional Manual Actions
========================

1. If file /u01/app/oracle/oradata/acdb/users01.dbf was unintentionally
renamed or moved, restore it


Automated Repair Options
========================

Option Repair Description

------ ------------------

1      Restore and recover datafile 6

  Strategy: The repair includes complete media recovery with no data loss
  Repair script: /u01/app/oracle/diag/rdbms/acdb/acdb/hm/reco_2490080082.
hm
```

We can see a script name in the output. We can also see the details of this script using the PREVIEW option of the REPAIR command:

```
RMAN> REPAIR FAILURE PREVIEW;


Strategy: The repair includes complete media recovery with no data loss
Repair script: /u01/app/oracle/diag/rdbms/acdb/acdb/hm/reco_2490080082.hm


contents of repair script:
    # restore and recover datafile
    sql 'alter database datafile 6 offline';
    restore ( datafile 6 );
    recover datafile 6;
    sql 'alter database datafile 6 online';
```

Now, we can ask DRA to solve this issue for us without asking us anything:

```
RMAN> REPAIR FAILURE NOPROMPT;


Strategy: The repair includes complete media recovery with no data loss
Repair script: /u01/app/oracle/diag/rdbms/acdb/acdb/hm/reco_2490080082.hm


contents of repair script:
    # restore and recover datafile
    sql 'alter database datafile 6 offline';
    restore ( datafile 6 );
    recover datafile 6;
    sql 'alter database datafile 6 online';
```

So, the repair is now complete and the data file has been brought to the online status, which shows that it has been recovered successfully.

Even though DRA is extremely helpful, in the current release it is still only meant for a single instance and not for RAC databases. Also, there is no support for the PDB in the current release and DRA can work only for the non-CDB and container databases.

Summary

In this chapter, we took a look at the numerous options for RMAN configurations and also the recovery scenarios of different kinds of possible crashes. Although it's not tough to perform recovery, when there is an actual crash, it's quite possible that panic may strike if you are not comfortable with the process to resolve the issue. Thus, I would strongly suggest that you don't wait for the crash to happen in your production database, but that you practice recovery for these cases more than once, such that you can recover from either of them, even with your eyes closed.

The next chapter will discuss two very important concepts: how to use RMAN for reporting the metadata that it has collected, and the creation, management, and usage of RMAN's recovery catalog.

7

RMAN Reporting and Catalog Management

The previous chapter covered probably the most important aspect of RMAN— using it to perform various kinds of recoveries. One could find it confounding to see the importance attached to reporting and maintaining the information about the backups taken because it is a widely held belief that the crucial entity is the backup itself. Well, though this is an undisputed fact, you need to ascertain whether or not the backup secured is useful. In order to restore the backup and use it in a recovery scenario, the DBA must know its whereabouts as quickly as possible. As a consequence, the metadata and structures that hold the relevant information are as instrumental as the backup itself. In addition to this, a DBA may also be required to create some scripts related to redundant tasks such as taking backups. This chapter promises to explore all these interesting aspects and much more!

In this chapter, we will discuss the following topics:

- Benefits of a recovery catalog
- Creation and use of a recovery catalog
- Using the CATALOG command
- RMAN reporting using the LIST and REPORT commands

Using the control file for RMAN metadata

RMAN maintains the repository of its metadata within the target database's control file. Being the default option, the control file acts as the primary location for RMAN. The control file maintains many internal structures, each with its own importance. For RMAN-related metadata within the control file, you can query the V$CONTROLFILE_RECORD_SECTION view (based on the fixed table X$KCCRS).

This view contains many different types of metadata sections, including the one specifically related to backup. Let's check how many total sections we have within the control file:

```
SQL> select count(distinct type) from v$controlfile_record_section;
COUNT(DISTINCTTYPE)
-------------------
        41
```

So, there are 41 unique sections available in the control file. Let's now restrict our query to show only those which are related to the backup:

```
SQL> select TYPE,RECORD_SIZE,RECORDS_TOTAL,RECORDS_USED
  2  from v$controlfile_record_section
  3  where type like '%BACKUP%';
```

TYPE	RECORD_SIZE	RECORDS_TOTAL	RECORDS_USED
BACKUP SET	96	742	231
BACKUP PIECE	780	909	262
BACKUP DATAFILE	200	1065	281
BACKUP REDOLOG	76	215	15
BACKUP CORRUPTION	44	371	0
BACKUP SPFILE	124	131	66

```
6 rows selected.
```

In the preceding output column, RECORD_SIZE shows the size in bytes for a record within the control file. The RECORDS_TOTAL and RECORDS_USED columns display the total and used record slots for a specific section within the control file. For example, in the preceding output, we can see that for the mentioned backup set there are 742 total slots allocated, of which 231 are used. Each section within the control file is further linked to its own internal structure (using the X$ fixed table) and is exposed using a public view (V$). For example, the BACKUP PIECE section is maintained by the fixed table X$KCCBP (**Kernel Cache Control Backup Piece**). The public view for the same is V$BACKUP_SET.

A complete listing and explanation of all the internal contents of the control file is beyond the scope of this book. If you are interested, you can dump the contents of the control file into a trace file using the following command:

```
SQL> alter session set events 'immediate trace name controlf level
  N';
```

Here, N is the level of the dump and can have values such as 1,2,3,4, and 5. With each increasing level, the amount of information dumped will become more elaborate. The `alter session` statement will create a trace file within the ADR. You can find the name of the resulting trace file after dumping the control file using the `V$DIAG_INFO` view, as shown in the following command:

```
SQL> alter session set events 'immediate trace name controlf level
5';

Session altered.

SQL> select value
  2    from V$diag_info
  3  where name='Default Trace File';

VALUE
--------------------------------------------------------------------
----------
/u01/app/oracle/diag/rdbms/orcl12/orcl12/trace/orcl12_ora_7191.trc
```

So, the name of our trace file is `ORCL12_ORA7191.trc`. Another way to retrieve a similar trace is by using Oracle's internal (and undocumented) debugging utility **Oracle Debugger (oradebug)**. A quick example of dumping the control file at level 5 using `oradebug` is given in the following command lines:

```
SQL> oradebug setmypid
Statement processed.
SQL> oradebug dump controlf 5
Statement processed.
SQL> oradebug tracefile_name
/u01/app/oracle/diag/rdbms/orcl12/orcl12/trace/orcl12_ora_2361
.trc
```

The following is a small excerpt from the preceding trace file for the section related to the backup piece:

```
***************************************************************************
***
BACKUP PIECE RECORDS
***************************************************************************
***
(size = 780, compat size = 780, section max = 909, section in-
use = 262)
```

We can see that the preceding snippet exactly matches the output of the same section from the V$CONTROLFILE_RECORD_SECTION view. It's worth mentioning that oradebug is meant to be primarily used by Oracle support staff who are equipped with the complete knowledge of it. To learn more about oradebug, read the excellent paper written by *Mladen Gogla*, available at http://mgogala.byethost5.com/oradebug.pdf.

Using the CONTROLFILE_RECORD_ KEEP_TIME parameter

A control file, as the name suggests, is just a file and is made at the time of the database creation with a finite size. The size of a control file is mainly based on the following parameters:

- MAXDATAFILES

- MAXINSTANCES

- MAXLOGFILES

- MAXLOGMEMBERS

- MAXLOGHISTORY

The initial size of the control file is determined based on the values of these parameters. To accommodate subsequent changes to these parameters after the database creation, the control file will be expanded dynamically. Unlike the default block size (determined by the DB_BLOCK_SIZE parameter), the block size of a control file will be fixed and hardcoded for a specific database release; for database release 12*c*, it is fixed for 16 KB. You can check the block size and the total size of the control file (in blocks) using the V$CONTROLFILE view (or the fixed table X$KCCCF), as shown in the following command lines:

```
SQL> select file_size_blks, block_size
  2  from V$controlfile;


FILE_SIZE_BLKS BLOCK_SIZE
-------------- ----------
           720      16384
```

There are two categories of records maintained within the control file: circular re-use records and non-circular re-use records. For both categories, (record) slots are allocated within the control file, but the space management would be different for each. For circular re-use records, if all the allocated record slots are occupied, either the number of record slots is increased to the required number (the maximum limit is 65,535), resulting in the size of the control file increasing, or the allocated space gets reused. Examples of sections from the previous code that are of the circular re-use records type are the archived redo logs and the sections which are related to the RMAN backup. If the control file expands to accommodate the increase in record slots, you will see the following message in the alert log file:

```
kccrsz: expanded controlfile section 11 from 721 to 1603 records
requested to grow by 721 record(s); added 3 block(s) of records
```

The preceding message means that for `section 11`, that is the archived log, the control file is expanded by three blocks and now the allocated record slot count is 1,603.

If the control file overwrites the oldest records to make space for the new entries in a section, the following text appears in the alert log file:

```
kccwnc: following control file record written over
```

Non-circular re-use records, contrary to circular re-use records, are never overwritten automatically. An example of such a record is the location of data files within the database.

For circular re-use records, the decision whether to overwrite the old records or to increase the allocated record slot count is made on the basis of the CONTROLFILE_RECORD_KEEP_TIME parameter. This parameter sets the minimum number of days (the default value is seven days) which must pass before the records can be overwritten. If the minimum day limit has not been crossed and all the record slots for a section are already occupied, the record slot count increases dynamically.

If you are considering using the CONTROLFILE_RECORD_KEEP_TIME (**CFRKT**) parameter, do check the configured time of the retention policy as well. A retention policy configuration time lesser than that of CFRKT won't do any harm. However, if it is the other way round, the metadata records might be overwritten before they are marked as obsolete. If the backup type is incremental, having its metadata being overwritten would leave the entire backup as unusable. That is why we would recommend always setting the value of the CFRKT parameter higher than that of the retention policy.

Do not set the value of the `CONTROLFILE_RECORD_KEEP_TIME` parameter to 0 since by doing so, you won't have any control over the frequency of the metadata being overwritten. If you are not using the recovery catalog, leave the parameter to its default value of seven days.

In addition to the control file's dynamic expansion, there are a few more drawbacks of using it as the sole repository for RMAN metadata.

Since the control file can only belong to one database, a single control file can't act as the central repository if you are using RMAN for multiple target databases. Also, if you lose all the control files in your database, performing a recovery will be tough since the RMAN metadata will also be lost! Moreover, certain very useful features of RMAN such as creating stored scripts for scheduled backups or using RMAN for a Data Guard environment simply won't be available if the control file is the sole option for metadata repository. For reasons and issues such as these, RMAN needs something more than just the control file; it needs a secondary catalog for its metadata — a *recovery catalog*.

What is a recovery catalog

A recovery catalog is a very useful option for storing the repository data of all of RMAN's operations. Though the name says catalog, it is actually a schema with views and tables inside it that will store the metadata. A recovery catalog offers some very distinct features, such as:

1. The default repository and the control file can overwrite the RMAN metadata by default after seven days. A recovery catalog, on the other hand, is a far more persistent repository.

2. Using a recovery catalog, you can create RMAN-stored scripts which can be used in repeated executions of the tasks. These scripts can be created globally by enabling them to be used by any RMAN client that can connect to a target database and to the recovery catalog.

3. If you are willing to use RMAN in Data Guard, a recovery catalog is required.

4. A single recovery catalog acts as the central repository for multiple target databases. There are features to provide privacy for the management of different databases' metadata within one catalog.

5. Only by using the recovery catalog can you report on a database at a specific time in the past.

Creating the recovery catalog

Often, after hearing that a recovery catalog is required, configuring it might seem an arduous task for some. However, this perception is not true because the creation of a catalog involves a few simple steps, Let's take a look at the list of steps required to achieve this goal:

- Sizing and creating a database for the recovery catalog
- Creating a tablespace for the recovery catalog's owner schema
- Creating the recovery catalog owner
- Granting required permissions to the catalog owner
- Creating the recovery catalog

So, let's look at each of these steps in detail in the following sections.

Sizing and creating a database for the recovery catalog

Since a recovery catalog is a schema, a database is required for it. You can either create a dedicated database for the recovery catalog or use the target database itself. But, using the target database isn't an ideal choice since losing it will make you lose your backup metadata as well. That's why I recommend a dedicated database for the recovery catalog, preferably on a machine different to the one running the target database.

> Although losing the database holding the recovery catalog would not present a good situation to be in, not all would be lost either. Using the CATALOG command, you can use the existing backup pieces: the data file, control file, and archive log copies.

In terms of creation, there is no difference between the recovery catalog database and its target database. Depending on whether you like **Graphical User Interface (GUI)** or **Command Line Interface (CLI)**, you can create the database using either the **Database Configuration Assistant (DBCA)** or the CREATE DATABASE command. Whether you choose to create a new database or use an existing one for the catalog owner, choosing an appropriate size for the database is important in order to avoid insufficiency. There are several factors which affect the size of the recovery catalog database and these are as follows:

- Frequency of the backups
- Size of the target databases

- Number and size of the files which will be backed up in one backup job
- Total number of databases maintained by the same recovery catalog database
- Number of additional entities maintained within the catalog, such as the backup scripts

So, all of the discussed points will be a deciding factor in estimating the size of the catalog database. As per Oracle documentation, if you backup 100 data files, the estimated space taken up in the catalog will be 62 MB per backup. If you are going to include the metadata from more than one database, you must also include the number of target databases in this estimation. Additionally, the frequency at which the backups will be taken is also an important factor. The more backups you perform, the more metadata gets generated, which will eventually need more space. For example, if you perform daily backups, the space occupied will certainly be different to that required by weekly or quarterly backups. Also, the backups of the archived redo logs and stored RMAN scripts will occupy space in the recovery catalog. Since the recovery catalog is going to be owned by its owner, this sizing estimation will be helpful to create its default tablespace.

Creating the default tablespace for the catalog owner

The recovery catalog owner will require a tablespace. This tablespace will store the tables, views, and so on, that will constitute the recovery catalog. Since all the metadata will be stored in this tablespace only, it should be of an adequate size, about 500 MB. Since this isn't a special kind of tablespace, the usual command CREATE TABLESPACE will be used. In this step, we will create a tablespace in a database dedicated to the RCATDB recovery catalog. So, let's proceed by first connecting to the database as the sys schema:

```
$sqlplus sys/oracle@rcatdb as sysdba


SQL> create tablespace rcat_tbs
  2    datafile '/u01/app/oracle/oradata/rcatdb/rcattbs.dbf' size 500m;


Tablespace created.
```

In the preceding output, we created a tablespace named RCAT_TBS along with a single data file RCATTBS.dbf. It's important to mention that the chosen name of the tablespace has no special meaning, so choosing any unique name will be just fine.

Creating the catalog owner schema

As we mentioned earlier, a recovery catalog is a collection of tables and views owned by a schema and will need to be explicitly created. In order to create it, like any other non-default schema, a unique name and a default permanent tablespace will need to be available beforehand. Since we already created the RCAT_TBS tablespace in the previous section, let's create the recovery catalog schema now:

```
SQL> create user rcat_adm identified by rcat
  2   default tablespace rcat_tbs
  3   quota unlimited on rcat_tbs temporary tablespace temp;

User created.
```

Now, we have created the catalog owner schema RCAT_ADM with the RCAT_TBS tablespace assigned to it.

Granting privileges to the catalog owner

Before the catalog owner can be used to create the recovery catalog, it will need a few mandatory privileges assigned to it. Besides the normal privileges such as creating a session, a mandatory role RECOVERY_CATALOG_OWNER needs to be assigned to the catalog owner:

```
SQL> grant connect, resource, recovery_catalog_owner to rcat_adm;

Grant succeeded.
```

 connect, resource, and recovery_catalog_owner are predefined roles within the database. Besides these, any other privilege or role is not needed for the catalog owner.

Since we now have all we need for creating the recovery catalog, let's proceed to actually creating it.

Creating the recovery catalog

To create a recovery catalog, the CREATE CATALOG command will need to be executed while connected as the catalog owner. It's important to note that to create the catalog, no connection to a target database is required:

```
[oracle@host5 ~]$ rman catalog rcat_adm/rcatpwd@rcatdb

Recovery Manager: Release 12.1.0.1.0 - Production on Sun Aug 4
14:26:41 2013

Copyright (c) 1982, 2013, Oracle and/or its affiliates.   All
rights reserved.

connected to recovery catalog database

RMAN> create catalog;

recovery catalog created
```

We have now created a recovery catalog. We used the option catalog in the command. This is to indicate that the username and password mentioned after it are those of the recovery catalog owner. Now we are ready to use this catalog for the target database.

Using the recovery catalog

RMAN, by default, doesn't use the recovery catalog; but the control file of the target database. To make RMAN use the catalog, you have to explicitly mention the catalog option while initiating a connection to the target database. Failing to do so (even with a recovery catalog already created) will cause RMAN to skip using the recovery catalog and still use the control file. As mentioned earlier, a recovery catalog, should ideally be in a separate database, preferably created on a different node from the one hosting the target database. If this is the case, you will need to configure the tnsnames.ora file sitting on your target database's machine to the machine hosting the recovery catalog database. The tnsnames.ora file can be found under $ORACLE_HOME/network/admin and can be edited either manually or using your preferred GUI tool, such as **Network Configuration Assistant** (**NETCA**), **Network Manager** (**NETMGR**), or even Cloud Control. An updated tnsnames. ora file along with an entry of the recovery catalog database will appear like the following code:

```
rcatdbsrv =
(DESCRIPTION =
(ADDRESS_LIST =
(ADDRESS = (PROTOCOL = TCP) (HOST = rcatserver) (PORT=1521))
```

```
)
(CONNECT_DATA =
(SERVICE_NAME = rcatdb)
)
)
```

In the preceding command lines, we have set up a **Transparent Network Substrate**
(TNS) alias `rcatdbsrv` which connects to our catalog database `rcatdb`, which sits on
the host, `rcatserver`. The port number `1521` belongs to the listener running on the
same server.

To use the recovery catalog with RMAN, we will need to execute the RMAN client as
shown in the following command lines:

```
[oracle@host5 ~]$ rman target sys/oracle@orcl12 catalog
rcat_adm/rcatpwd@rcatdbsrv

Recovery Manager: Release 12.1.0.1.0 - Production on Sun Aug 4
14:29:04 2013

Copyright (c) 1982, 2013, Oracle and/or its affiliates.  All rights
reserved.

connected to target database: ORCL12 (DBID=3418936258)
connected to recovery catalog database
```

Though it is required to specify the correct TNS alias for the recovery catalog
database, for the target database you can use either the OS authentication or the
TNS alias; whether the target database will be located on the local machine or over
a remote host will depend on this factor. For the sake of clarity, we have configured
and used a TNS alias even for our target database, ORCL12, besides using `rcatdbsrv`
for the recovery catalog. The output shows the name of the target database and also
mentions that the recovery catalog is used.

Since we have now created the recovery catalog, the immediate thought would be to
actually use it. But can the target database(s) (in our case, ORCL12) be managed using
this newly created recovery catalog just by connecting to it? The answer would be
no for the reason that before a catalog can be used for any target database, it must be
registered within the recovery catalog. If you haven't registered your target database
within the recovery catalog yet, any RMAN operation would fail, showing the error
RMAN-06004, as shown in the following command lines:

```
RMAN> backup tablespace users;

Starting backup at 04-AUG-13
RMAN-00571:
```

```
============================================================
RMAN-00569: =============== ERROR MESSAGE STACK FOLLOWS
===============
RMAN-00571:
============================================================
RMAN-03002: failure of backup command at 08/04/2013 14:29:19
RMAN-03014: implicit resync of recovery catalog failed
RMAN-06004: ORACLE error from recovery catalog database: RMAN-20001:
target database not found in recovery catalog
```

Since our target database is not yet registered, the backup command fails. So, now we will register the ORCL12 database with the recovery catalog using the RMAN command REGISTER DATABASE, while connected to the target database and using the recovery catalog database. The following command lines illustrate this:

```
RMAN> REGISTER DATABASE;

database registered in recovery catalog
starting full resync of recovery catalog
full resync complete
```

 When registering a target database with a catalog, it will load and sync all the information available in the target control file to the catalog repository.

Now that the database is registered in this catalog, we can confirm whether it can be accessed via the recovery catalog or not using a simple command, REPORT SCHEMA, which lists all the data files and temporary files of the target database:

```
RMAN> report schema;


Report of database schema for database with db_unique_name ORCL12


List of Permanent Datafiles
===========================
File Size(MB) Tablespace           RB segs Datafile Name
---- -------- -------------------- ------- -----------------------
1    840      SYSTEM               YES     /u01/app/oracle/oradata/
orcl12/system01.dbf
3    820      SYSAUX               NO      /u01/app/oracle/oradata/
orcl12/sysaux01.dbf
```

```
4     130      UNDOTBS1              YES      /u01/app/oracle/oradata/
orcl12/undotbs01.dbf

6     5        USERS                NO       /u01/app/oracle/oradata/
orcl12/users01.dbf


List of Temporary Files

=========================

File Size(MB) Tablespace           Maxsize(MB) Tempfile Name

---- -------- -------------------- ----------- ---------------

-----

1     426      TEMP                 32767
/u01/app/oracle/oradata/orcl12/temp01.dbf
```

And there we go! Finally we have a working catalog that shows us the contents of the registered database in it.

> If you want to register any other database to the catalog, all you need to do is repeat all the registration statements mentioned in this chapter and change the code that follows the / symbol for the corresponding connection string of the target DB to be registered, such as `username/password@sid`.

Resynchronizing the recovery catalog with the control file

The metadata that is stored in the catalog comes from the control file. Any operations done from the RMAN client executable would automatically sync the recovery catalog with the target database's control file. However, a resync may also be required at times to refresh the information stored in the catalog. In this process, a comparison is done between the current contents of the recovery catalog and the target database's control file or even a backed up control file, and any piece of metadata that's missing in the catalog is recompiled.

There are two types of resync performed and they are:

- Partial resynchronization
- Full resynchronization

The following diagram is a pictorial representation of both types of resync:

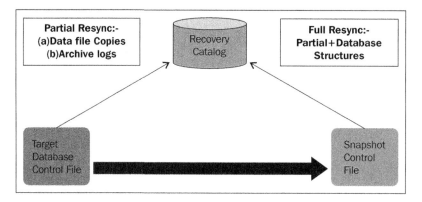

In a partial resync, RMAN will compare the metadata stored in the catalog with the target database control file and update it with any missing metadata in the data file copies, archive log files, and so on. The full resync includes the metadata related to the partial resync, along with any kind of structural changes that might have happened in the target database such as adding a new tablespace, or any kind of changes related to the data file such as renaming or changing their location. To have a full resync done, a snapshot of the target database's control file is created, which itself is actually a copy of the control file.

A full resynchronization can also be done by a DBA by issuing the RESYNC CATALOG command explicitly. Because the syncing of the catalog and the control file is supposed to happen without any explicit intervention by the DBA, this command does not really require being executed on a routine basis. Still, there are several situations where doing so would be required, for example:

- You didn't use the CATALOG option to include the recovery catalog while performing RMAN operations. This could be a situation when either the catalog database was not available for some reason, or updating the catalog could possibly take a much longer time due to issues such as the distance between the target database and the catalog database. Also, it's important to note that an automatic resync of the metadata will be done by RMAN before any backup. So, doing a manual resync will also avoid risks of latency with respect to the metadata between the control file and the recovery catalog.

- Your database is in the `ARCHIVELOG` mode and there are a huge number of redo log switches that may take place between a sync operation. Because the information about the log switches and archive logs is not updated in the catalog and only in the target database control file, a manual resync will be required to bring the catalog to the same location as the control file.

- You have made significant changes to the database structure and want to ensure that this information is updated in the catalog properly.

Following are the steps that a DBA would need to take to do a full manual resync:

1. Start RMAN and connect to the target database and the recovery catalog.

2. Mount or open the target database if it is down:

   ```
   RMAN> STARTUP MOUNT;
   ```

3. Resynchronize the recovery catalog using the `RESYNC CATALOG` command at the RMAN prompt:

   ```
   RMAN> RESYNC CATALOG;
   ```

 For a Data Guard environment, you will have to use the `DB_UNIQUE_NAME` command to specify the required database whose control file you want to use to perform the sync. There is no need to use the database name if the environment doesn't include any Data Guard setup.

Merging multiple recovery catalogs into one

At times, when we have many databases of different releases available, it becomes tough to maintain their metadata information which is scattered around in different catalog databases. To make the management of this easier, the releases since Oracle 11*g* have made it possible to create a parent catalog and import the other catalogs' information into it using the `IMPORT CATALOG` command. Using this feature, the metadata related to multiple catalogs can be stored in a single catalog, thus reducing the overhead.

Though the procedure for importing catalogs into a base catalog is a very straightforward one, it still needs some attention. To ensure that the import works successfully, the source catalog database version and the version of the RMAN executable must be the same. If both match, the catalog import will work without any issues; but if they don't, the source catalog must be upgraded to the version matching the RMAN executable.

Since it is easy to import a catalog of the same release as that of the target RMAN client, we will demonstrate the catalog of a database release 11*g* being imported into the catalog of a target database release 12*c*. The 11*g* database is already registered with a catalog created locally within itself with the catalog owner RCATADM11. Since the releases are not the same, the catalog import will fail. The following command lines illustrate this:

```
[oracle@host5 admin]$ rman target / catalog
rcat_adm/rcatpwd@rcatdbsrv


Recovery Manager: Release 12.1.0.1.0 - Production on Sun Aug 4
20:45:36 2013


Copyright (c) 1982, 2013, Oracle and/or its affiliates.  All rights
reserved.


connected to target database: RCATDB (DBID=475235813)
connected to recovery catalog database


RMAN> import catalog rcatadm11/rcatadm@orcl11gsrv
2> ;


Starting import catalog at 04-AUG-13
connected to source recovery catalog database
PL/SQL package RCATADM11.DBMS_RCVCAT version 11.02.00.03 in IMPCAT
database is too old
RMAN-00571:
===============================================================
RMAN-00569: =============== ERROR MESSAGE STACK FOLLOWS
===============
RMAN-00571:
===============================================================
RMAN-03002: failure of import catalog command at 08/04/2013 20:45:57
RMAN-06429: IMPCAT database is not compatible with this version of
RMAN
```

We can see that the catalog available in the database release 12*c* has thrown the error that the source database is not compatible. We can confirm the catalog schema version of the source database from the view RCVER under the catalog schema, as shown in the following command:

```
[oracle@host5 dbs]$ . oraenv
ORACLE_SID = [orcl11g] ?
The Oracle base remains unchanged with value /u01/app/oracle
[oracle@host5 dbs]$ sqlplus rcatadm11/rcatadm@orcl11gsrv

SQL*Plus: Release 11.2.0.3.0 Production on Sun Aug 4 21:01:03 2013

Copyright (c) 1982, 2011, Oracle.  All rights reserved.


Connected to:
Oracle Database 11g Enterprise Edition Release 11.2.0.3.0 - 64bit
Production
With the Partitioning, OLAP, Data Mining and Real Application Testing
options

SQL> select * from rcver;

VERSION
------------
11.02.00.03
```

As expected, the catalog schema release is of version 11.2.0.3. This can also be seen if we connect to the database release 11*g* using the RMAN client of the release 12*c*, as shown in the following command:

```
[oracle@host5 admin]$ rman catalog  rcatadm11/rcatadm@orcl11gsrv

Recovery Manager: Release 12.1.0.1.0 - Production on Sun Aug 4 21:03:10
2013

Copyright (c) 1982, 2013, Oracle and/or its affiliates.  All rights
reserved.

connected to recovery catalog database
PL/SQL package RCATADM11.DBMS_RCVCAT version 11.02.00.03 in RCVCAT
database is too old
```

To make the source catalog schema version match with the target database RMAN client, we will need to upgrade it.

A database upgrade does not upgrade the catalog schema. Also, an upgrade of the recovery catalog does not upgrade the databases it manages.

The recovery catalog is upgraded using the UPGRADE CATALOG command. As shown in the following output, you will need to execute the command twice before it finally does its job:

```
RMAN> upgrade catalog;


recovery catalog owner is RCATADM11
enter UPGRADE CATALOG command again to confirm catalog upgrade


RMAN> upgrade catalog;


recovery catalog upgraded to version 12.01.00.01
DBMS_RCVMAN package upgraded to version 12.01.00.01
DBMS_RCVCAT package upgraded to version 12.01.00.01
```

Since we now have the source recovery catalog upgraded, let's re-execute the same IMPORT CATALOG command which previously failed to execute:

```
[oracle@host5 admin]$ rman target / catalog rcat_adm/rcatpwd@rcatdbsrv

Recovery Manager: Release 12.1.0.1.0 - Production on Sun Aug 4 21:05:51
2013

Copyright (c) 1982, 2013, Oracle and/or its affiliates.  All rights
reserved.

connected to target database: RCATDB (DBID=475235813)
connected to recovery catalog database

RMAN> import catalog rcatadm11/rcatadm@orcl11gsrv;


Starting import catalog at 04-AUG-13
connected to source recovery catalog database
import validation complete
database unregistered from the source recovery catalog
Finished import catalog at 04-AUG-13
```

As we can see, the command was executed successfully and the catalog of our database release 11*g* has now been imported into the catalog of the database release 12*c*. We can confirm this by querying a catalog view RC_DATABASE while being connected as the catalog owner RCAT_ADM. The output of the view will list all the databases stored within the catalog:

```
[oracle@host5 Desktop]$ sqlplus rman_vpc/rmanpwd@rcatdbsrv


SQL*Plus: Release 12.1.0.1.0 Production on Mon Aug 5 00:52:23 2013


Copyright (c) 1982, 2013, Oracle.  All rights reserved.


Last Successful login time: Mon Aug 05 2013 00:47:26 +05:30


Connected to:
Oracle Database 12c Enterprise Edition Release 12.1.0.1.0 - 64bit
Production
With the Partitioning, OLAP, Advanced Analytics and Real Application
Testing options


SQL> select name from rc_database;


NAME
--------

ORCL11G

ORCL12
```

Using this option for importing catalogs, not only can multiple catalogs be merged into one, but they can also be moved from one catalog database to another. All that it will require is the creation of a new database and the import of the source catalog into it. The import of the catalog can also be done for a selective list of databases from the source catalog by specifying the database names along with the option DB_NAME in the IMPORT CATALOG command.

> Once a catalog is imported, the databases' IDs are unregistered from the source catalog. To keep the database IDs in the source catalog after the import process, you have to use the NO UNREGISTER option along with the IMPORT CATALOG command.

Using virtual private catalogs

A recovery catalog is not restricted to being used as a metadata repository for a single database. Multiple databases can be (and are) registered within one catalog database. Even with the option of importing catalogs, a base catalog becomes a repository for multiple catalogs. For such a consolidated environment, there is a requirement to enforce some sort of security. This is required to ensure that no unauthorized person is able to access or, worse, delete the metadata of any database that he doesn't manage. Using the option of virtual private catalogs, such catalog privacy can be implemented. A virtual catalog, along with using a virtual catalog owner, limits the accessibility of the databases to be managed. The databases not accessible to the virtual catalog owner will still remain with the base catalog and be accessible to the base catalog owner. A base catalog will be the one holding multiple virtual catalogs within it.

To create a virtual catalog, a separate owner also needs to be created for it. Let's create a virtual catalog owner with the name RMAN_VPC in our base catalog database RCATDB:

```
[oracle@host5 Desktop]$ sqlplus sys/oracle@rcatdbsrv as sysdba

SQL*Plus: Release 12.1.0.1.0 Production on Mon Aug 5 00:41:27 2013

Copyright (c) 1982, 2013, Oracle.  All rights reserved.


Connected to:
Oracle Database 12c Enterprise Edition Release 12.1.0.1.0 - 64bit
Production
With the Partitioning, OLAP, Advanced Analytics and Real Application
Testing options
SQL> create user rman_vpc identified by rmanpwd default tablespace rcat_
tbs temporary tablespace temp;

User created.

SQL> grant connect, resource , recovery_catalog_owner to rman_vpc;

Grant succeeded.
```

You may have noticed that the predefined role RECOVERY_CATALOG_OWNER (along with the other two roles) is granted to the virtual catalog owner. Granting this role is mandatory since the virtual catalog owner will be the owner of the databases that it is managing.

Once the virtual catalog owner is created, we will grant it the privilege to manage a specific database from the base catalog. Though we have two databases in the base catalog, the virtual catalog owner will only be able to manage one database, ORCL11g, as illustrated in the following command:

```
[oracle@host5 Desktop]$ rman target / catalog rcat_adm/rcatpwd@rcatdbsrv

Recovery Manager: Release 12.1.0.1.0 - Production on Mon Aug 5 00:44:26
2013

Copyright (c) 1982, 2013, Oracle and/or its affiliates.  All rights
reserved.

connected to target database: ORCL12 (DBID=3418936258)
connected to recovery catalog database
RMAN> grant catalog for database orcl11g to rman_vpc;

Grant succeeded.
```

The final step will be to create a virtual catalog using this virtual catalog owner, as shown in the following code:

```
[oracle@host5 Desktop]$ rman target / catalog rman_vpc/rmanpwd@rcatdb
Recovery Manager: Release 12.1.0.1.0 - Production on Mon Aug 5 00:46:20
2013

Copyright (c) 1982, 2013, Oracle and/or its affiliates.  All rights
reserved.

connected to target database: ORCL12 (DBID=3418936258)
connected to recovery catalog database

RMAN> create virtual catalog;

found eligible base catalog owned by RCAT_ADM
created virtual catalog against base catalog owned by RCAT_ADM
```

We can confirm that the granted database only is accessible from this virtual catalog owner using the catalog view rc_database. The output of this view will be only the databases available within the virtual catalog:

```
[oracle@host5 Desktop]$ sqlplus rman_vpc/rmanpwd@rcatdbsrv

SQL*Plus: Release 12.1.0.1.0 Production on Mon Aug 5 00:52:23 2013

Copyright (c) 1982, 2013, Oracle.  All rights reserved.
```

```
Last Successful login time: Mon Aug 05 2013 00:47:26 +05:30


Connected to:
Oracle Database 12c Enterprise Edition Release 12.1.0.1.0 - 64bit
Production
With the Partitioning, OLAP, Advanced Analytics and Real Application
Testing options


SQL> select name from rc_database;


NAME
---------
ORCL11G
```

In this demonstration, we have given the `catalog` privilege to the virtual catalog owner. This privilege will enable the virtual catalog owner to work with the already registered databases and the base catalog. If you want the virtual catalog owner to be able to register new databases as well, grant it the `register` privilege, as shown in the following command line:

```
RMAN> grant register database to rman_vpc;
```

To revoke the rights of the virtual catalog owner to manage any database, use the `revoke` command:

```
RMAN> revoke catalog for database ORCL11g from rman_vpc;
```

Finally, if you want to drop the virtual catalog, use the DROP CATALOG command. It's important to note that this command must be executed while being connected as the virtual catalog owner only. If the same command gets executed by the base catalog owner by mistake, it will drop the complete catalog and not just the virtual one:

```
[oracle@host5 ~]$ rman target / catalog rman_vpc/rmanpwd@rcatdbsrv


Recovery Manager: Release 12.1.0.1.0 - Production on Mon Aug 5 16:22:25
2013


Copyright (c) 1982, 2013, Oracle and/or its affiliates.  All rights
reserved.


connected to target database: ORCL12 (DBID=3418936258)
connected to recovery catalog database


RMAN> drop catalog;
```

```
recovery catalog owner is RMAN_VPC
enter DROP CATALOG command again to confirm catalog removal


RMAN> drop catalog;


virtual catalog dropped
```

With the help of the virtual catalog and import catalog procedures, a very transparent yet secure management environment can be created for multiple databases hosted under a single catalog. Also, this will relieve the DBA from hopping from one database to another so they can manage many catalog schemas.

Creating and managing stored scripts

As we mentioned at the beginning of this chapter, one of the major advantages of the recovery catalog, which is not provided by the control file, is the ability to create stored scripts. By using stored scripts, it will become very easy for a DBA to store the routine tasks in a script and then simply call that script whenever they need to execute those tasks, even on a repeated basis.

Using recovery catalog, two kinds of scripts can be created; they are:

- Local scripts
- Global scripts

As the name suggests, the local scripts (created by default) are usable only in the target database to which RMAN is connected while creating the local script. This script won't be visible and usable to any other database in the same recovery catalog. On the other hand, a global script created by the keyword GLOBAL will be visible and usable to all the databases in that recovery catalog.

To create a script, you will be required to use the command CREATE SCRIPT. If you don't mention the keyword GLOBAL, this script will become a local script by default. Let's create a simple script that has the command to back up the tablespace system:

```
RMAN> CREATE SCRIPT test_scr{
2> BACKUP TABLESPACE system;
3> }


created script test_scr


RMAN>
```

Now the script is there with us, but how will we know about the scripts that have already been created? We can use the command LIST with the option SCRIPT NAMES. This will show us the script(s) that have been created so far. So, let's see if we have any other scripts available in our catalog database:

```
RMAN> LIST SCRIPT NAMES;


List of Stored Scripts in Recovery Catalog


    Scripts of Target Database ORCL12


      Script Name       Description
      - - - - - - - -   - - - - - - - - - - - - - - - - - - - - - - - - - -
      test_scr
```

As expected, this is our only script. So we have the name, but how do we see what this script contains? For this, we can use the command PRINT SCRIPT along with its name:

```
RMAN> PRINT SCRIPT test_scr;


printing stored script: test_scr
{
backup tablespace system;
}


RMAN>
```

So, this script will take the backup of the tablespace system for us, but how will we execute it? To execute the script, we will need to use the run block and pass the script name to the execute command:

```
RMAN> run{execute script test_scr;}


executing script: test_scr


Starting backup at 03-MAY-13


<<output snipped>>
```

RMAN offers us the option to change a script by using the REPLACE SCRIPT command. Using this command, we can edit the contents of the script without deleting and recreating it. So, let's edit our script and replace the tablespace system with sysaux:

```
RMAN> REPLACE SCRIPT test_scr
2> {backup tablespace sysaux;}


replaced script test_scr


RMAN> PRINT SCRIPT test_scr;


printing stored script: test_scr
{backup tablespace sysaux;}


RMAN>
```

Now, the script's content is replaced with that of the new tablespace.

Finally, if we don't want the script, we can delete it using the DELETE SCRIPT command:

```
RMAN> DELETE SCRIPT test_scr;


deleted script: test_scr


RMAN> LIST SCRIPTS NAME;


List of Stored Scripts in Recovery Catalog


        No scripts in recovery catalog
RMAN>
```

You can even call the OS scripts from the RMAN binary as shown in the following example:

```
$ rman TARGET / CATALOG rcat_adm@rcatdbsrv SCRIPT '/u01/app/oracle/fbkp.
cmd';
```

Using scripts, it becomes very easy to maintain a reusable set of instructions which can be used by either a specified target database or any other target database registered in the catalog as a global script. As per the example, simple tasks such as doing backups or crosschecking their status are supposed to be routine and on-going and having them scripted in the stored scripts in the recovery catalog would make the life of a DBA much easier as they won't need to retype the same commands over and over again.

Making a recovery catalog highly available

Since the recovery catalog stores crucial information that is required to execute any recovery operation on the target databases, it becomes as important as those databases it hosts within itself. So, it's necessary to ensure that you have the catalog backed up to prevent any kind of issues that may lose it; in which case, the recovery of your protected databases within will become very tough.

You can use different methods to protect the recovery catalog, such as the following:

- Take a backup of the whole catalog database frequently, using either RMAN or via a user-managed backup. If the catalog database does not contain anything except the catalog, having fewer tablespaces in it is advisable as it will complete the backup job of the catalog database quicker and won't consume much storage space.

- Execute logical backups of the catalog schema at frequent intervals. In case the catalog database is lost, you can simply import this schema in a new database and you will then be able to access all the metadata stored in it without any issues.

As good practice, it is also advisable to have the catalog database in the ARCHIVELOG mode so that you can do a complete recovery in the case of loss of the tablespace or data file related to the catalog schema. Also, while making backup copies, don't just take one, but at least two copies to make sure that at least one is available when you need it. Ensure that at least one copy of the backup is not stored on the same disk where the catalog database is stored, but on a separate media device such as a tape. Last but certainly not least, do not store the recovery catalog in the same database which it protects; instead, use a separate database for storing the catalog. Storing the recovery catalog in the same database as the one it protects could result in losing stored scripts, repositories for other databases, and any metadata older than what the target control file is holding.

Upgrading the recovery catalog

Upgrading the recovery catalog is independent of upgrading its underlying database. As we saw in the section on importing catalogs, there are restrictions when it comes to version compatibility among the RMAN client, the target database, and the recovery catalog. To use a recovery catalog with an RMAN client of a higher release, an upgrade of it must be done. Also, the version of the recovery catalog database must be equal to or higher than that of the databases it is managing. So, it's better to upgrade the catalog if any of its registered databases is being upgraded to a release higher than it.

To upgrade a recovery catalog, you can use the UPGRADE CATALOG command. Upgrading to the current release of the catalog schema is possible by querying a view RCVER while being connected as the owner of the recovery catalog. This command needs to be executed twice before the upgrade of the recovery catalog is finally done.

Unregistering databases from the recovery catalog

If you don't want a client database to be protected from the recovery catalog anymore, you can easily unregister it from the recovery catalog using the UNREGISTER command. Unregistering a database from the catalog wipes out its metadata. Since the metadata is stored in the target database's control file by default, it would be resynced with the catalog if you register the database again. But, metadata of more than seven days (the default value) won't be available so before proceeding to unregister a database from the recovery catalog, it is recommended to keep a note of the metadata, that is, the backups of that database.

 You can get the list of all the backups done so far by using the LIST BACKUP command before issuing the UNREGISTER command.

Let's unregister our database ORCL11g from the catalog. For unregistering, you just need to connect to the catalog database using the catalog owner:

```
[oracle@host5 ~]$ rman catalog rcat_adm/rcatpwd@rcatdbsrv

Recovery Manager: Release 12.1.0.1.0 - Production on Mon Aug 5 18:52:15
2013

Copyright (c) 1982, 2013, Oracle and/or its affiliates.  All rights
reserved.
```

```
connected to recovery catalog database


RMAN> unregister database orcl11g;


database name is "orcl11g" and DBID is 929485328


Do you really want to unregister the database (enter YES or NO)? yes
database unregistered from the recovery catalog
```

The output confirms that the database ORCL11g is no longer registered with
the catalog.

[For standby environments, it is important to mention the
DB_UNIQUE_NAME for the same command.]

Dropping a recovery catalog

If you do not want to use the recovery catalog for any database, you can go ahead
and drop the entire catalog using the DROP CATALOG command:

```
$ rman target / catalog=rcat_adm/rcatpwd@rcatdbsrv


RMAN> DROP CATALOG;


recovery catalog owner is RCAT_ADM
enter DROP CATALOG command again to confirm catalog removal


RMAN> DROP CATALOG;


recovery catalog dropped
```

Views related to the recovery catalog

There are several views owned by the recovery catalog schema that store the
metadata for the target database(s). The information stored within these views can be
accessed using RMAN reporting commands such as LIST and REPORT (discussed in
the next section), but, can be accessed by querying the catalog views directly, too.

The views belonging to the recovery catalog are appended with RC, thus making the name of the views appear like RC_name of the view. For example, if you want to query the databases registered within the catalog, you can query the RC_DATABASE view. These views will be available under the owner schema of the catalog. In order to access these views, you will need to log in into the catalog owner's schema stored within the catalog database.

The following is a list of all the catalog views that are available only when the recovery catalog is present:

- RC_ARCHIVED_LOG
- RC_BACKUP_ARCHIVELOG_DETAILS
- RC_BACKUP_ARCHIVELOG_SUMMARY
- RC_BACKUP_CONTROLFILE
- RC_BACKUP_CONTROLFILE_DETAILS
- RC_BACKUP_CONTROLFILE_SUMMARY
- RC_BACKUP_COPY_DETAILS
- RC_BACKUP_COPY_SUMMARY
- RC_BACKUP_CORRUPTION
- RC_BACKUP_DATAFILE
- RC_BACKUP_DATAFILE_DETAILS
- RC_BACKUP_DATAFILE_SUMMARY
- RC_BACKUP_FILES
- RC_BACKUP_PIECE
- RC_BACKUP_PIECE_DETAILS
- RC_BACKUP_REDOLOG
- RC_BACKUP_SET
- RC_BACKUP_SET_DETAILS
- RC_BACKUP_SET_SUMMARY
- RC_BACKUP_SPFILE
- RC_BACKUP_SPFILE_DETAILS
- RC_BACKUP_SPFILE_SUMMARY
- RC_CHECKPOINT
- RC_CONTROLFILE_COPY
- RC_COPY_CORRUPTION

- RC_DATABASE
- RC_DATABASE_BLOCK_CORRUPTION
- RC_DATABASE_INCARNATION
- RC_DATAFILE
- RC_DATAFILE_COPY
- RC_LOG_HISTORY
- RC_OFFLINE_RANGE
- RC_PROXY_ARCHIVEDLOG
- RC_PROXY_ARCHIVELOG_DETAILS
- RC_PROXY_ARCHIVELOG_SUMMARY
- RC_PROXY_CONTROLFILE
- RC_PROXY_COPY_DETAILS
- RC_PROXY_COPY_SUMMARY
- RC_PROXY_DATAFILE
- RC_REDO_LOG
- RC_REDO_THREAD
- RC_RESTORE_POINT
- RC_RESYNC
- RC_RMAN_BACKUP_JOB_DETAILS
- RC_RMAN_BACKUP_SUBJOB_DETAILS
- RC_RMAN_BACKUP_TYPE
- RC_RMAN_CONFIGURATION
- RC_RMAN_OUTPUT
- RC_RMAN_STATUS
- RC_SITE
- RC_STORED_SCRIPT
- RC_STORED_SCRIPT_LINE
- RC_TABLESPACE
- RC_TEMPFILE
- RC_UNUSABLE_BACKUPFILE_DETAILS

Since the list is quite long, we recommend that you search for the descriptions of these within the *Backup and Recovery Reference Guide* from the online Oracle documentation available at http://www.oracle.com/pls/db121/homepage.

Reporting in RMAN

As much as it is important to backup your database, it is equally important that you know what you have done already and what is still pending. For example, you must know which data files you have already backed up and which still require backing up. For this kind of reporting in RMAN, there are two commands available: LIST and REPORT. Though both the commands are meant to be used for reporting purposes, they solve two very distinct purposes. In this section, we will have a look at RMAN's reporting commands.

Using the LIST command

The LIST command is primarily used to list the existing backups and image copies of the database. There are several other variations of this command as well, for example, listing the failures (like a data file is deleted) or the stored scripts, and so on. The following are a few examples using the LIST command:

```
RMAN> LIST BACKUP SUMMARY;


List of Backups
===============
Key     TY LV S Device Type Completion Time #Pieces #Copies Compressed
Tag
------- -- -- - ----------- --------------- ------- ------- ----------
---
4       B  F  A DISK        03-MAY-13        1       1       NO
TAG20130503T223931
```

The preceding command lists a summary of the backup sets created.

The following command groups the backups based on their source file types:

```
RMAN> LIST BACKUP BY FILE;


List of Datafile Backups
========================
```

```
File Key      TY LV S Ckp SCN    Ckp Time   #Pieces #Copies Compressed Tag
---- -------  -  -- - ---------- --------- ------- ------- ---------- ---
6    4        B  F  A 1709105    03-MAY-13 1       1       NO
TAG20130503T223931
<<output snipped>>
```

The following command lists all the existing backups:

```
RMAN> LIST BACKUP;


List of Backup Sets
===================


BS Key  Type LV Size        Device Type Elapsed Time Completion Time
------- ---- -- ----------  ----------- ------------ ----------------
4       Full    1.61M       DISK        00:00:00     03-MAY-13
        BP Key: 4   Status: AVAILABLE  Compressed: NO  Tag:
TAG20130503T223931
        Piece Name:  /u01/app/oracle/fast_recovery_area/ORCL12/
backupset/2013_05_03/o1_mf_nnndf_TAG20130503T223931_8r7vtc93_.bkp
   List of Datafiles in backup set 4
   File LV Type Ckp SCN    Ckp Time   Name
   ---- -- ---- ---------- --------- ----
   6       Full 1709105    03-MAY-13 /u01/app/oracle/oradata/orcl12/
users01.dbf
```

Using the REPORT command

Unlike the LIST command which creates a listing of all the available backups,
the REPORT command is used to provide an analysis of the metadata repository.
There are several options supported and the following are a few examples of it:

```
RMAN> report schema;
```

The preceding command will generate a detailed output of all the data and
temporary files of a database.

```
RMAN> report need backup;
```

The need backup option will create a report based on the retention policy (covered
in the previous chapter) of those files which are yet to be backed up.

Another example of the `REPORT` command being used is in reporting those backups which are marked as obsolete based on the configured retention policy:

```
RMAN> report obsolete;
```

Though we have mentioned a few examples for both the `LIST` and `REPORT` commands, there are various other options available for both. To check all of them, refer to the *Backup and Recovery Reference Guide* available at `http://docs.oracle.com/cd/E16655_01/backup.121/e17631/toc.htm`.

Summary

The recovery catalog is an optional repository, but its importance cannot be denied. As we have shown, there are a couple of things which are completely impossible if you are not using the catalog and a few areas which work better once the catalog is in place. Although you may find using the control file easier, creating and using the recovery catalog is something that you must do to get the best out of RMAN.

Now we understand RMAN and have learned how to configure it and use it for performing backups and recoveries. So, it is time to go to the next step which is to dive deeper and understand two very important aspects: how to troubleshoot any issues related to RMAN and optimize its performance using several techniques. Let's proceed to the next chapter in which both requirements are discussed at great length.

8

RMAN Troubleshooting and Tuning

When it comes to any tool or utility, there are inevitably going to be aspects related to them. One, it is always expected that the tool must perform at its best; and two, whenever there is any issue with the tool, we should be able to troubleshoot and resolve it easily. A DBA looks forward to the same with RMAN as well. Therefore, in this chapter, our objective is to look at the various ways to get the best performance from RMAN and also learn some techniques to troubleshoot it when it acts mischievously.

Throughout the chapter, we will be discussing the following topics:

- Using CHECKSYNTAX
- Using the DEBUG option
- I/O modes and their impact on RMAN
- Memory management related to RMAN
- Monitoring RMAN
- Using tracing for RMAN performance tuning

Getting started with RMAN troubleshooting

Irrespective of the fact that RMAN is a very mature tool since its inception, it might still require troubleshooting at times. There are many areas which may require your timely attention. In some instances, it could be basic things such as correcting the wrong syntax of a command, while at other times, there can be even tougher challenges, for example, solving errors such as ORA-4031 causing a backup job to fail. So, there are various possible issues depending on what you are doing with RMAN.

 Oracle Database error codes start with the text ORA followed by the error code, for example, ORA-4031 is an insufficient memory error. This is reported when a memory pool fails to provide the required memory for an operation, resulting in the failure of the operation. To learn more about this error, check the support note 1088239.1.

Since using RMAN involves many distinct infrastructure layers such as storage, database, tapes, and managing the software, it thereby expands the scope of troubleshooting. As it is not possible to discuss all of these issues here, we will be looking at a few of the most important aspects, starting with the most basic one: writing the correct commands of RMAN.

Using CHECKSYNTAX

RMAN has the GUI face from the Enterprise Manager, but many DBAs still prefer to use RMAN using the command line only and the biggest issue with it is to remember the correct syntax of the commands. Though RMAN commands are well documented in the online documentation, what if you don't have access to that? Fortunately, the CHECKSYNTAX option comes to the rescue. Using this, you can verify the correct syntax of the command before actually executing them over RMAN. The CHECKSYNTAX option, when used with RMAN, gives you the message whether the syntax is correct and reports the RMAN-00558 error, which represents the syntax error

To use the CHECKSYNTAX option, you don't need to log in to the target database. You can just fire up RMAN along with the option CHECKSYNTAX option and in the session, type your command to test whether it's correct. For example, if we want to check which command would be the correct command to take the backup of a tablespace using the DURATION clause, we can do so as shown in the following example:

```
$ rman checksyntax
```

Since we have the RMAN prompt now, we can test our desired command by executing it:

```
RMAN> BACKUP DURATON 2:00 TABLESPACE users;

RMAN-00571: ===========================================================

RMAN-00569: =========== ERROR MESSAGE STACK FOLLOWS ==========

RMAN-00571: ===========================================================

RMAN-00558: error encountered while parsing input commands

RMAN-01009: syntax error: found "identifier": expecting one of:
"archivelog, as, auxiliary, backupset, backup, channel, check,
controlfilecopy, copies, copy, cumulative, current, database,
datafilecopy, datafile, db_file_name_convert, db_recovery_file_dest,
device, diskratio, duration, filesperset, force, format, for, from, full,
incremental, keep, maxsetsize, nochecksum, noexclude, nokeep, not, pool,
proxy, recovery, reuse, section, skip readonly, skip, spfile, tablespace,
tag, to, validate, ("

RMAN-01008: the bad identifier was: duraton

RMAN-01007: at line 1 column 8 file: standard input
```

So, we are told that the command is wrong and that's correct indeed as we deliberately did a typo there. Had the command been correct, the output would be as follows:

```
RMAN> BACKUP DURATION 2:00 TABLESPACE users;

The command has no syntax errors
```

There is also another way to get an idea about the command that you are trying to execute: by asking RMAN itself. What's that supposed to mean? Well, if you enter a keyword, for example, ALLOCATE or CONFIGURE (or any command's starting keyword), and press the *Enter* key thrice, RMAN will list the next available options for the command. Use the command you are looking for and if that's not the complete command, again do the same thing and you will finally have the complete syntax with you. For example, let's use the keyword BACKUP and see the options that are available to use with it:

```
RMAN> BACKUP

2>

3>

RMAN-00571: ===========================================================

RMAN-00569: ============= ERROR MESSAGE STACK FOLLOWS ============

RMAN-00571: ===========================================================

RMAN-00558: error encountered while parsing input commands
```

```
RMAN-01009: syntax error: found "end-of-file": expecting one of:
"archivelog, as, auxiliary, backupset, backup, channel, check,
controlfilecopy, copies, copy, cumulative, current, database,
datafilecopy, datafile, db_file_name_convert, db_recovery_file_dest,
device, diskratio, duration, filesperset, force, format, for, from, full,
incremental, keep, maxsetsize, nochecksum, noexclude, nokeep, not, pool,
proxy, recovery, reuse, section, skip readonly, skip, spfile, tablespace,
tag, to, validate, ("
RMAN-01007: at line 3 column 1 file: standard input
```

So, RMAN has listed all the options available to us for the BACKUP command. Let's assume we want to take a backup of the archived logs, so the next keyword we will choose is the ARCHIVELOG to make the command appear as BACKUP ARCHIVELOG and shall see what options are available for it:

```
RMAN> BACKUP ARCHIVELOG
2>
3>
RMAN-00571: ===========================================================
RMAN-00569: =========== ERROR MESSAGE STACK FOLLOWS =============
RMAN-00571: ===========================================================
RMAN-00558: error encountered while parsing input commands
RMAN-01009: syntax error: found "end-of-file": expecting one of: "all,
from, high, like, low, scn, sequence, time, until"
RMAN-01007: at line 3 column 1 file: standard input
```

So, we can see that the next available options are ALL, FROM, HIGH, and so on. Now if you recall, to take the backup of the all the archive logs, the command is BACKUP ARCHIVELOG ALL. So now we know the command and the help we got with it came from none other than RMAN itself!

Reading the RMAN error stack

RMAN's error output comprises a long stack of error codes along with their messages. Because there are a couple of messages piled up one after the other, it often becomes confusing to troubleshoot the exact issue that has occurred. Well, it's not so confusing actually. All you need to do is remember one simple rule, that is, read from the bottom up in the error stack! Yes, for RMAN error stack, the most relevant error message code will be at the end which will reveal the exact issue that has occurred. There can be a mix of ORA and RMAN error codes shown, with the former showing the error codes from the database and the later displaying the error codes from RMAN.

The error messages above the first message from the bottom to top would be either the supporting error codes or may be from other components that also got an error. The following is an example of the error stack from the failed RMAN command:

```
RMAN-03002: failure of recover command at 06/16/2013 00:56:29
ORA-00283: recovery session canceled due to errors
RMAN-11003: failure during parse/execution of SQL statement: alter
database recover if needed
 datafile 1
ORA-00283: recovery session canceled due to errors
ORA-01124: cannot recover data file 1 - file is in use or recovery
ORA-01110: data file 1: '/u01/app/oracle/oradata/orcl/system01.dbf'
```

Now to read this error message, following the bottom-up rule, we can see that the reported error is ORA-01110 which is showing that the file 1 has thrown the error. The message immediately above it is also an ORA error and is saying that for this data file 1, the recovery is cancelled as it is currently in use. This is true as the error is reported because we kept the data file 1 online when we issued this command in the OPEN stage of the database. Next message shows that the recovery session is cancelled. Now the fourth message is from the RMAN category, that is, RMAN-11003, and though we already know what's wrong, let's check with RMAN as well. The description of this error message says that the command didn't get parsed and the command preceding it says that the recovery session is cancelled. The highest command in the error stack says that a RECOVER command has failed, which we knew already!

Now in the preceding example, although you knew why the command failed after reading the first message itself, at times for certain issues you would need to read all the way up till the starting of the error stack. In that case, if you knew (briefly) what the reported error code meant, you would probably be able to find the cause of the issue simply by looking at the error code itself. RMAN error codes are categorized under different categories and each category represents a specific error section. For example, error codes from 1000-1999 are for the wrong keyword, 2000-2999 are for the wrong syntax, and so on. If you look back at the example that we used when reading the error stack, the error code shown for the wrong keyword, DURATON, is RMAN-01008.

It is not possible to remember all the error codes and the categories, but seeing the codes from time to time will make you remember most of them. An easy way to find the explanation of them would be in the online Oracle documentation, which has all the error codes listed along with their causes and possible solutions.

Debugging RMAN using the DEBUG clause

RMAN doesn't offer any kind of tracing or debugging by default when being initiated, but it does have the option to enable this if required, for example, to debug the performance issues when RMAN has stopped working, or a channel has died suddenly, and so on. Using debugging, very detailed information will be collected which can be very helpful in troubleshooting the issue.

You can enable debugging at various layers with multiple levels. For example, you can enable RMAN debugging either at the time of the connection or along with any command executed within RMAN. For example, in the following statement, debugging is enabled in the starting itself:

```
$ rman target / trace=/tmp/rmantrc.trc debug
```

All the debugging information will be entered into the RMANTRC.trc trace file. In the next command, it's enabled for a specific statement from within the RMAN:

```
RMAN> run{debug on;
2> BACKUP TABLESPACE users;
3> debug off;}
RMAN-03036: Debugging set to level=9, types=ALL
RMAN-03090: Starting backup at 16-JUN-13
RMAN-06009: using target database control file instead of recovery
catalog
<<output trimmed>>
RMAN-03091: Finished backup at 16-JUN-13
Debugging turned off
```

You can see that debugging is initiated at the start of the execution and once the command is complete, it's switched off. Interestingly, the output reveals that debugging is set to level 9, which is the default level with all the types. This is important as there are different categories which the debugging can be enabled for, along with higher levels (a maximum of 15), which will generate an even more detailed and lengthy output. The types which the debugging can be enabled for are:

- IO
- SQL
- PLSQL
- RCVMAN
- RPC

So if you want to enable debugging for an I/O type with trace level 10, you can do it as follows:

```
$ rman target / trace=/tmp/rman.trc debug=io level=10
```

Though debugging is a great way to obtain very detailed information, it's important to keep in mind that it also impacts the consumption of system resources while being enabled along with the normal executions of the commands. Also, the information captured is vast and includes a lot of internal functions, packages, and APIs that RMAN uses. Without completely knowing their meaning, it can be hard to use the enormous amount of information collected in a useful manner. That's why it's better to use this option with the help of Oracle Support and for the best analysis, let the trace file be analyzed by a support engineer.

Using the alert log and operating system trace files

Since RMAN works, by connecting to the database, at times it may have issues which are initiated by the database itself, for example, an internal database error such as ORA-600.

 ORA-600 is a generic error code representing an issue within the Oracle Database kernel. Mostly this error is due to some bug and it's highly recommended that you involve Oracle Support to solve it. Oracle Support provides a lookup tool to search the reason for the error which can be found at support note 153788.1.

These error messages will be reported in the database's alert log and for some, there may be a separate trace file created. So if you received an error while working with RMAN, it will be helpful to look at these files under the **Automatic Diagnostic Repository** (**ADR**) destination (controlled by the parameter DIAGNOSTIC_DEST).

For RMAN, besides disks, tape drives can also be used which are configured by their media management software. Several errors can arise from the **Media Management Library** (**MML**) whenever RMAN is going to do some operation over a tape drive. For such errors, RMAN ORA-19511 would be reported along with the additional error information related to the MML error. For example, this is a partial output of such an error:

```
ORA-19511: Error received from media manager layer, error text:
RPC receive operation failed.  A network connection could not be
established with the host.
```

The error message indicates that a connection to the host containing the tapes was not able to get established. So to troubleshoot, the next step will be to look into this direction. Just like RMAN error codes, MML errors also have categories and error codes related to them. (Refer to the Oracle documentation for a complete list of such errors. Additionally, you can also check the Oracle Support note 604143.1 for this).

It's also important to verify that once the installation is done, the MML reports no issues. If there are any, you may receive the ORA-27211 error. To confirm the installation of your MML software, the SBTTEST utility can help. It should be available under the $ORACLE_HOME/bin folder, but if it's not, you can ask Oracle Support for it. (Additionally, details regarding the usage of the SBTTEST utility can also be found in Oracle Support note 942418.1). RMAN normally won't have any issues that will require you to apply a patch or engage Oracle Support because it's a binary and if there are any errors, they would arise from its configuration or if using tapes, from its media management software. But if you think you have tried enough to fix the error, you can raise a ticket with Oracle Support to get help. There are various notes related to RMAN available on **My Oracle Support** (**MOS**) which can be of immense help to you.

So, this brings us to the end of the troubleshooting section of RMAN. As we said at the start of this chapter, it's not possible to mention every error in this chapter. But if you face an issue while working with RMAN, you can take lead from the tips mentioned here. If you have all your backups in place, all you archive logs available, MML installed and working properly, RMAN will hardly ever give you any trouble. Unfortunately, there can be no guarantee that you won't encounter any bugs but even in that case, Oracle Support is there to help.

Now let's take a look at how can we make RMAN perform at its best in our next section.

RMAN tuning – an introduction

To start with, RMAN performance tuning is related to when it's doing operations such as backup and restore. Anything can make such operations slower and if that happens, you will need to detect the bottleneck and use optimizations which can enhance the performance. It becomes even more important that RMAN can deliver a great performance because nowadays, the size of an average database is in multiterabytes and as backups work on 24/7 basis, any slowness won't be acceptable to the management.

There are several factors which can appear as a bottleneck for RMAN performance. For example, an I/O bottleneck from the storage, the type of backup that you have configured, whether the backup or restore job involves parallelism, and so on. In addition to these factors, RMAN may not be performing well even due to factors which are not under your direct control, such as a slow network or less bandwidth from the storage device. In the next section, we will first look at the aspects which you as a DBA can assess and then try to optimize I/O bottlenecks.

I/O and RMAN – two sides of one coin

All the work that RMAN does is related to I/O, whether it's a backup job or a restore job. Therefore, it's important to understand how RMAN deals with the IO related tasks internally. If you remember our discussion from *Chapter 6, Configuring and Recovering with RMAN*, we mentioned that RMAN performs all the backup, restore, and recovery operations using the channels which act as an I/O stream that talks to the underlying device and performs either the reading(for taking the backup) or writing(for restoring the backups). Each channel does an I/O operation in three different phases:

- **Read Phase**: In this phase, a channel reads the source data files and copies its content to the input buffers

- **Copy Phase**: Is the phase in which the input buffers are copied to the output buffers after doing any sort of processing, such as validation or compression of the contents in them

- **Write Phase**: In this phase, the output buffers are moved to the underlying device which would be either a tape drive or a disk

Input buffers and output buffers are allocated from the **Program Global Area (PGA)** memory (if using asynchronous I/O) and will be used for the storage and processing of blocks read from the files stored over the disk. The processing of these blocks can include compressing the data, making it encrypted, and so on. If you have configured I/O slaves (for synchronous I/O), the same is done from the Shared Pool or Large Pool (if set) within the **System Global Area (SGA)**.

 If you are wondering what asynchronous and synchronous are, we shall be it discussing this in a subsequent section.

RMAN uses these buffers for both the backup and restore operations. When a backup job is started, the blocks are read from the disk and copied into the input buffers and from there, are written to the destination location: either a disk or a tape drive. Similarly, while restoring the backup, the content is read into the input buffers and copied to the output buffers, and from there it's written to the location where it is needed. To detect from where the buffers are allocated, with the size allocated to them, you can query the views V$SESSTAT and V$STATNAME. The following output shows the PGA memory used by the buffers while a full database backup was going on:

```
SQL>  SELECT s.sid, n.name , s.value/1024/1024 session_pga_mb
   2   FROM    v$statname n, v$sesstat s
   3   WHERE   s.sid = (SELECT sess.SID
   4                        FROM   V$PROCESS p, V$SESSION sess
   5                        WHERE  p.ADDR = sess.PADDR
   6                        AND    CLIENT_INFO LIKE '%rman%')
   7   AND     n.name = 'session pga memory'
   8*  AND     s.statistic# = n.statistic#
       SID NAME                                      SESSION_PGA_MB
---------- --------------------------------- --------------
        39 session pga memory                          23.0314026
```

Here SID 39 is for the channel which is used to perform the backup. We can see that the memory is allocated in the PGA.

The V$SGASTAT view from which you can find out the amount of PGA memory allocated for the buffers, you can also use for finding out the amount of memory allocated for either the Large Pool or Shared Pool.

Number and size of the input and output buffers

The size and count of the buffers allocated will depend on the type of the backup, that is, whether the backup format is a backup set or an image copy; and how many buffers per file will be allocated will depend on the number of files that are being backed up. The allocation of the input buffers for the backup set type backups would depend on multiplexing, that is, how many files one RMAN channel is able to read at the same time. The level of multiplexing will be further dependent on how many files are configured to be part of one backup set and how many files available for RMAN to open at the same time for reading.

These factors would be configured by the parameters MAXOPENFILES (default=8) and FILESPERSET (default=64). Multiplexing is set to the minimum of the values of these two parameters so the level of multiplexing would be based on the following formula:

```
Multiplexing= Min (MAXOPENFILES, FILESPERSET)
```

 RMAN doesn't use multiplexing when the backup is done using the multi-section backups.

So as per the preceding formula, that is, how many files are allowed to be read by one channel at one time, Oracle would be allocating the input buffers. The following chart explains the relation between multiplexing and the size of the input buffers for the device type disk and the backup type as backup set:

Multiplexing level	Input disk buffer size
>= 4	Size of 1 buffer=1 MB, total buffer size per channel=16 MB
>4 But < 8	Size of 1 buffer=512 KB, total buffer size per channel=16 MB
> 8	Total buffer size per channel=512 KB with 4 buffers(128 KB each)

For example, if you have configured one channel for the backup with MAXOPENFILES=4 and FILESPERSET=4, the level of multiplexing would become 4. As there are 4 files; for each file, 4 buffers of 1 MB size would be allocated which would make the total buffer size for the channel 16 MB.

 If you are using ASM as the storage type, the number of input buffers would be based on the **Allocation Unit** (**AU**) size of the disk group and the number of physical disks within it. For example, if you have a disk group DATA with 4 disks, then the number of input buffers becomes 4.

Based on the different factors such as whether the backup or a restore operation is done on either a tape or a disk, and whether the format is backup set or image copy, the count and the size of the output buffers will vary.

- For disk-based backups, the number and the size of the output buffers would be set to 4 and 1 MB, making the total buffer size for each channel 4 MB.

- For tape backups, the number and size of the output buffers would be 4 and 256 KB. So if you are going to be using a single channel for the backup over a tape drive, the total size of the output buffers would become 4*256 KB*1=1024 KB.

- For a restore, either from the backup sets or image copies, the output buffer size would be set to 1 MB and the number of the buffers would be set to 4.

I/O is the most important and integral aspect of a backup or recovery job. This fact would immensely affect the performance whether it's carried out as *asynchronous* or *synchronous* I/O. As we have briefly mentioned these terms in the preceding sections, now let's get to know these two I/O modes in detail and see how they impact the performance.

Synchronous and asynchronous I/O modes

With synchronous I/O, whenever a process requests I/O to be done over the OS, it has to wait for the acknowledgement to come from the same before it can do any other work. This means that until the OS sends an acknowledgement to declare that the given request is complete, the requesting process will just sit idle doing nothing. Imagine this happening when, for example, the **DBWR** process, for completing a checkpoint would send the dirty buffers to the disk and is now sitting idle because there is no response from the OS. Wouldn't it slow down the DBWR? If you answered a yes, you should also note that because of this behavior, the synchronous IO mode is also considered to be slow.

When compared to the synchronous I/O; in asynchronous, the server process which gave the I/O request doesn't wait for the acknowledgement to come but keeps on doing other tasks. When the acknowledgement is ready to arrive, it's received, thus making the process work almost all the time. Nowadays, most of the OSs natively support asynchronous I/O. If you are using Linux, to confirm that asynchronous I/O is configured and working for you, you can refer to the MOS documents 370579.1 and 237299.1. For raw volumes, asynchronous I/O is enabled by default. If you have configured your **FRA** on an ASM disk group, since ASM is also based on the principle of **SAME** (`http://www.miracleas.com/BAARF/oow2000_same.pdf`), it uses asynchronous I/O out of the box. From a database perspective, Oracle Database sets the parameters `DISK_AYNCH_IO` for disks and `TAPE_ASYNCH_IO` for tape drives and both are set to the default value `TRUE`. If you have the asynchronous I/O working for you by default, leave these parameters unchanged.

Please note that we have only mentioned the MOS documents for the Linux OS to check asynchronous I/O. For other OSs, refer to their specific documentation to confirm whether they use asynchronous or synchronous I/O.

If you are taking the backup over disk and your OS does not support asynchronous I/O, you can use the DBWR_IO_SLAVES parameter to simulate the similar I/O behavior. Using this parameter, multiple I/O slaves for the DBWR process can be allocated which won't be quite as fast as allocating multiple DBWR processes but will still be able to improve the performance to some level. The memory allocation will be done from the SGA for these IO slaves.

 If your operating system supports asynchronous I/O, allocate multiple DBWR processes.

If you are using a tape drive, the tape management software along with the performance of the hardware (tape) will play a combined role in affecting the performance. Since with tapes, the I/O mode is always synchronous, if you want to mimic the I/O behavior as asynchronous, you can use the BACKUP_TAPE_IO_SLAVES parameter. When set to TRUE, this parameter makes use of the I/O slaves (one slave per tape drive) to do either a read or write operation from the tape drives. If this parameter is set to FALSE (default), then the I/O behavior would be left to its default setting, that is, synchronous.

If synchronous I/O is used, the SGA is used for the memory allocation, either within the Shared Pool or the Large Pool. Large Pool is an optional parameter but it's still better to allocate the Large Pool for the allocation of the memory buffers by setting the LARGE_POOL_SIZE parameter rather than using the Shared Pool because its memory management is quite different in two ways. One, the Shared Pool allocates memory in 5 kilobits chunks and if it doesn't find free memory available in 5 kilobits chunks, it will throw the famous ORA-4031 error, but this is not the case with the Large Pool. Two, the **Least Recently Used (LRU)** algorithm of the Shared Pool will keep on flushing the memory more aggressively than the Large Pool. Also, the Shared Pool is the repository for many other data structures. That's why it's better not to fill it up with the additional memory of the RMAN memory buffers, instead setting a good value for Large Pool for this.

Setting the Large Pool memory

The adequate value for the Large Pool can be derived using the following formula:

```
LARGE_POOL_SIZE = number_of_allocated_channels* (16 MB + (4 * size_of_
tape_buffer))
```

In the preceding formula, if you are using a tape drive, the size of the tape buffer would be set to 256 KB and based on that, along with the number of the channels, you should set the value for it. For example, for 4 tape drives, the number of channels would be 4 and for each channel, the value for the output buffers will be 1 MB. Thus the total value for the Large Pool should be 4*(16+4)=80 MB. If you modify the size of the tape buffer according to the given value, you would need to calculate the value.

For disk buffers, the value of the tape buffer is used in the formula. So leaving it out of the formula and using the same assumption but this time for 4 disks, the value of the Large Pool should be 64 MB. It's worth mentioning that if the Large Pool is not set to the required limit, even then, ORA-4031 error would be reported.

 Instead of setting the values manually, configure **Automatic Memory Management (AMM)** and let the database set the optimal size for the Shared Pool and the Large Pool based on the workload. If you are using Oracle Database 10*g*, you can also use **Automatic Shared Memory Management (ASMM)**.

It's important to note that if the Large Pool is not configured and there is insufficient memory in the Shared Pool, the slaves will not be used and the following error will be reported:

```
ksfqxcre: failure to allocate shared memory means sync I/O will be used
whenever
async I/O to file not supported natively
```

Another important thing to keep in mind is that merely having the Large Pool parameter set may not bring it into use. Large Pool would only be used if:

- DBWR_IO_SLAVES is set to a non-zero value
- BACKUP_TAPE_IO_SLAVES is set to the value TRUE
- DISK_ASYNCH_IO is set to the value FALSE

If these conditions are not met, even though the Large Pool is configured, still the Shared Pool will be used and if it doesn't have enough free memory in it, the operation would receive the error ORA-4031.

Monitoring RMAN I/O performance using dictionary views

To monitor the performance of the RMAN backup and restore jobs and to check the size and number of the memory buffers, Oracle uses either the view V$BACKUP_ASYNC_IO (if using asynchronous I/O) or V$BACKUP_SYNC_IO (if using synchronous I/O). These views would also be able to help in identifying the bottlenecks related to I/O as well. Both the views contain following categories of rows within them:

- One row for each data file, read and written
- One row for each backup piece, read and written
- One aggregated data file row for overall performance

The following is an output from the view V$BACKUP_ASYNC_IO, which we took while taking the backup on our test system:

```
SQL>  SELECT type, status, filename, buffer_size, buffer_count
  2   FROM    v$backup_async_io  WHERE type <> 'AGGREGATE'
  3   AND     status = 'IN PROGRESS';


TYPE     STATUS       FILENAME               BUFFER_SIZE BUFFER_COUNT
-------  -----------  ---------------------  ----------- ------------
INPUT    IN PROGRESS  +DATA/orcl/datafile/      1048576            4
                      system.256.737196671
OUTPUT   IN PROGRESS  +DATA/orcl/backupset/     1048576            4
                      2013_06_12/nnndf0_tag
                      20130612t153821_0
                      .273.8179701
```

In the preceding output, you can see that there are 4 buffers; both the input and output are allocated 1 MB size each for the system tablespace backup.

Though both the views contain couple of columns, to determine the I/O performance, just a few will be useful. You can see the complete column listing of these views from the Oracle documentation at http://www.oracle.com/pls/db121/homepage.

V$BACKUP_ASYNC_IO (for asynchronous I/O)

While using the asynchronous I/O, the output of the I/O-related job is recorded in the V$BACKUP_ASYNC_IO view. The view will collect the information while the underlying backup or restore job is going on. Though the view contains several columns, to measure the I/O performance, you should concentrate on the following 5 columns:

- IO_COUNT: This is the total number of I/O's performed on the file
- LONG_WAITS: This is the total number of times the backup or restore job asked the OS to wait until the I/O gets completed
- SHORT_WAITS: This is the total number of times the backup or restore job made an OS call to poll for I/O completion in non-blocking mode
- SHORT_WAIT_TIME_TOTAL: This is the total time (in hundredths of seconds) taken by non-blocking polls for I/O completion
- LONG_WAIT_TIME_TOTAL: This is the total time (in hundredths of seconds) taken by blocking wait for I/O completion

To find the bottleneck while using the asynchronous I/O, divide the LONG_WAITS column with IO_COUNT while querying the view to identify the file that is being read slowly and is causing the bottleneck. Additionally, the columns LONG_WAIT and SHORT_WAIT should both report zero wait time.

V$BACKUP_SYNC_IO (for synchronous I/O)

If you are using synchronous I/O, use V$BACKUP_SYNC_IO view. Since the I/O is only unidirectional, it is relatively easy to deduce the bottleneck. In the view, pay attention to the DISCRETE_BYTES_PER_SECOND column and compare its value with the vendor-supplied value of the device. If the derived output of the column is less than that mentioned by the device, you may want to look deeper.

If the underlying device is a tape drive and you are either using asynchronous or synchronous I/O, for either of the views you may want to keep a check on the column EFFECTIVE_BYTES_PER_SECOND and compare it with the performance of the tape. The value should be matching or at least, should be very close to the value of the tape. If it's not, there may be some additional wait happening which will probably cause the degradation in performance.

Since a backup or restore job involves both reading from the source and writing to the destination, to find out where the bottleneck is, you can use the option VALIDATE along with the BACKUP command to find where the bottleneck is: in the reading phase or the writing phase. The BACKUP VALIDATE command only reads the source data files. Since using the VALIDATE option doesn't actually create any backups on the destination device, by using this option you can measure the performance of only the read phase without involving the write phase overhead in it. If the time taken by the using the VALIDATE option command is the same as that of the actual backup, you can very well assume that the reading is being done slowly as the time taken for BACKUP VALIDATE should be almost half of the actual backup performed. To further check, you can concentrate on those large files which have a longer wait ratio (LONG_WAITS/IO_COUNT). It may be that the disks are slow or the files are stored on the inner side of the disks, thus making the access slower.

If you are using ASM, try to see if there are any disk(s) which are underperforming and causing this bottleneck. If you have the option, you may do a rebalance of the ASM disk group and see if that gives any improvement in the performance. On the other hand, if the BACKUP command takes significantly longer than the BACKUP VALIDATE, this means that while copying the data into the buffers and/or writing them to the disk, there is some wait or bottleneck. In this case, depending on where you are taking the backup—either disk or tape—you will need to choose the appropriate action to do the troubleshooting. For example, if it's a disk, rather than using basic compression, try to use the advanced compression settings so that you can achieve a higher compression ratio and lesser data is sent for the backup. If encryption is configured, try to use an algorithm such as AES128. For the tape drive, refer to the areas mentioned in the next section.

If you have checked thoroughly and have concluded that the media is working fine, you may have to play with the configuration of the memory buffers. This will involve changing the size and number of the buffers explicitly using some undocumented parameters, something which should only be done with the involvement of Oracle Support.

Tuning SBT (tape) performance

As tape drives are going to involve many other things with them and also may not be a direct component of that machine which hosts the database, there is very little room for you as a DBA to tweak anything related to them. Still, there are a few options from the database side that can help:

- If you are configuring parallelism, set the number of the tape (SBT) channels equivalent to the number of the tape drives that you have in the configuration.

- RMAN automatically filters out the unused blocks in the data files so they are not included in the backup. Also, if you have used **Oracle Secure Backup (OSB)** for backing up the tape drives, the undo data for any uncommitted transactions also won't become part of the backup.

- With OSB, you can take advantage of Linux direct I/O which with the use of **Direct Memory Access (DMA)** reduces the consumption of CPU very significantly.

 OSB is a separately downloadable and installable tool. You can download it from `http://www.oracle.com/goto/osb`. OSB is not covered in this book.

The previous points are applicable from the database side or if you are using OSB, but if OSB is not your media manager software then you can look at the following configuration areas in general for the tape drives which will be helpful in improving performance:

- **Network throughput**: This represents the amount of data that can travel through the underlying network. This factor is probably the biggest impact maker when the tape drives are attached remotely to another host.

- **Native transfer rate**: This is the speed of writing to the tape without involving compression. The upper limit of the aggregated total transfer rate should match with the overall performance that you are achieving from all your tape drives.

- **Tape compression**: This is the compression provided by the media manager software. If you are getting a good compression ratio through it, the available backup rate will be also good. Also, we won't advice to use RMAN's binary compression along with the tape compression if the performance achieved using the tape compression is acceptable.

- **Tape streaming**: Tape streaming will happen if the data transfer rate of the disk, network, and the CPU is either matching or higher than the native transfer rate of the tape. If it doesn't and if there is no data in the tape buffer to push over the media, the tape moves ahead and will be required to be rewound to the point from where the writing stopped. To control this behavior, ensure that the streaming doesn't break or use tape drives with varying speeds.

- **Physical tape block size**: This is set by the media management software only. As this is the data written over the tape in one call, if it's larger, the backup speed will also be good. To alter the block size, you can use the option `BLKSIZE` in the `CONFIGURE` or `ALLOCATE` commands.

You must remember that when compared to the disks, tapes will be slower anyway. That's why it's better to configure FRA, preferably on an ASM disk group and use that as the first destination to do the backup.

In the next section, we will look at some views which are helpful to track the RMAN session and the backup and recovery tasks.

Monitoring RMAN sessions and operations

As RMAN performs the tasks using the channels which work by maintaining a session within the database as any other normal user session, it's easy to track its working using the standard database views V$SESSION and V$PROCESS. Using these two views together, we can identify the server processes that are used by RMAN channels and use that information for performance bottleneck troubleshooting as we would do for a normal database session, for example, by enabling tracing on it.

The easiest way to find information about the **System ID (SID)** of the channel is to look at the RMAN prompt. For example, the following is a partial output from a backup command:

```
allocated channel: ORA_DISK_1

channel ORA_DISK_1: SID=55 device type=DISK
```

You can see that the SID for the channel is in the output itself along with the device type that would be used by it.

If you are using a single session of RMAN, you can track the details of the channel(s) used by it with the following query:

```
SQL> SELECT s.sid,p.spid,s.client_info
  2    FROM   V$process p, V$session s
  3    WHERE p.addr=s.paddr AND client_info like '%rman%';


       SID SPID                    CLIENT_INFO
---------- ----------------------- --------------------------
        55 3580                    rman channel=ORA_DISK_1
```

The preceding output shows that we have one disk channel. The SID derived from the V$SESSION is the session ID of the server process within the database and the SPID from the V$PROCESS is the process ID from the OS.

For multiple RMAN sessions working at the same time, it's better to use the SET COMMAND ID and use it while executing the commands within a RUN block. If you would be using it, you would need to modify the preceding query and mention the CLIENT_INFO to search to the literal that you would be using in the SET command. For example, if we use the literal "session" appending with different numbers to denote different sessions such as "session1" and "session2" then the query would become:

```
SQL> SELECT s.sid,p.spid,s.client_info
  2    FROM   V$process p, V$session s
  3    WHERE  p.addr=s.paddr AND client_info like '%sess%'


  SID  SPID       CLIENT_INFO
  ---- --------   -----------------------
   45     3563    id=session1
   55     3580    id=session1,rman channel=ORA_DISK_1
```

Within RMAN, the RUN block for both sessions would look like the following:

```
RMAN> run{
2> set command id to 'session1';
3> backup tablespace users;}


RMAN> run{
2> set command id to 'session2';
3> backup tablespace users;}
```

The next question that comes is to track the backup jobs that you have scheduled using RMAN. Not only do you want to know the scheduling statistics about the backup jobs, but also to compare how much time each job actually took. For this, the V$RMAN_BACKUP_JOB_DETAILS view (you can also use RC_RMAN_BACKUP_JOB_DETAILS) is helpful to list and compare the backup jobs created in one RMAN session. Let's see the output from this view:

```
SQL>  SELECT session_key S_KEY,session_recid S_RECID,start_time,
  2      end_time, round(output_bytes/1048576) as OUTPUT_MB,
        elapsed_seconds
  3      FROM   V$RMAN_BACKUP_JOB_DETAILS
  4      WHERE  start_time >= sysdate-180 and status='COMPLETED'
  5      AND    input_type='DB FULL';
```

S_KEY	S_RECID	START_TIM	END_TIME	OUTPUT_MB	ELAPSED_SECONDS
7	7	26-JAN-13	26-JAN-13	1143	125
13	13	26-JAN-13	27-JAN-13	4321	8757

It's important to keep in mind that this view doesn't get reset with database shutdown and at times, even accessing this view becomes slow.

From the view, have a look at the ELAPSED_SECONDS for each backup job. From the output of this column, you can deduce which backup job took longer to be completed.

Just as there is a view to monitor the backup jobs, there is a dedicated view to monitor the recovery jobs as well. The name of the view, is unsurprisingly, V$RECOVERY_PROGRESS. To monitor the progress of a recovery operation, you can query the view as follows:

```
SQL>SELECT type, item, units, sofar, total
2    FROM    V$RECOVERY_PROGRESS;
```

The output of this view will show that for each ITEM, which can be LOG FILES, REDO APPLIED and so on, how much out of total work (TOTAL) has been completed (SOFAR). From this view, you can find whether your recovery is going on or is stuck and can get an estimate of the time required for it to be completed.

In addition to the preceding RMAN-specific views, you can use the standard database V$SESSION_LONGOPS view, which is designed to track any long running operation in the database, for example, a long running query. For RMAN, such an operation can be either a long running backup or a restore operation. Two types of rows from this view are going to be used, *aggregate* and *detail*. Aggregate rows shows the files processed at the completion of a RMAN-related task such as the creation of a backup set and image copy or for the restore of the same. Detail rows shows the ongoing progress of the same tasks at one job step. For analysis of the performance, the aggregate rows is more useful.

To use the view, you need to find the process ID from the V$SESSION view:

```
SQL> COLUMN program FORMAT a30
SQL> SELECT sid, serial#, program,status
2    FROM    v$session WHERE lower(program) LIKE '%rman%';
```

```
    SID    SERIAL# PROGRAM                            STATUS
---------- ---------- ------------------------------ --------
     20         35 rman@machine2 (TNS V1-V3)         INACTIVE
     44         97 rman@machine2 (TNS V1-V3)         INACTIVE
```

So we have two RMAN sessions as shown in the preceding code. This will always be the case as at the start of the RMAN, there are two sessions allocated for it. A third session is also allocated with the configuration of the channel that's going to perform the actual I/O. So with it allocated, we will see one more row added to the preceding query's output as follows:

```
SQL> SELECT sid, serial#, program,status
  2   FROM   v$session WHERE lower(program) LIKE '%rman%';


    SID    SERIAL# PROGRAM                            STATUS
---------- ---------- ------------------------------ --------
     20         35 rman@machine2 (TNS V1-V3)         INACTIVE
     39        149 rman@machine2 (TNS V1-V3)         ACTIVE
     44         97 rman@machine2 (TNS V1-V3)         INACTIVE
```

According to the preceding output, we have a channel activated right now which is in the ACTIVE status. This is true because we ran a database backup command before querying this view which actually configured this channel. If you will query status of this channel when the job gets over, it will be shown as INACTIVE.

If you want to confirm that it is indeed a channel, you can map the V$SESSION view with the V$PROGRAM view:

```
SQL> SELECT s.sid,p.spid,s.client_info
  2   FROM   V$process p, V$session s
  3   WHERE  p.addr=s.paddr  and client_info like '%rman%';


    SID SPID                    CLIENT_INFO
---------- ------------------------ ------------------------
     39 9567                    rman channel=ORA_DISK_1
```

Now, since we initiated a database backup job as we mentioned earlier performed by this channel, let's quickly look at the output from the V$SESSION_LONGOPS view for this:

```
SQL> SELECT sid, serial#, opname, time_remaining
  2    FROM   v$session_longops Where sid||serial# in (39149)
  3    AND    time_remaining > 0;


       SID    SERIAL# OPNAME                               TIME_REMAINING
---------- ---------- ----------------------------- --------------
        39        149 RMAN: full datafile backup                155
```

So the backup is going on and there is an estimated 155 seconds remaining before the backup job is completed.

You can customize the output from V$SESSION_LONGOPS further to show a percentage of the backup job completion as follows:

```
SQL> SELECT SID, SERIAL#, CONTEXT, SOFAR, TOTALWORK,
  2    ROUND(SOFAR/TOTALWORK*100,2) "%COMPLETE"
  3    FROM   V$SESSION_LONGOPS WHERE OPNAME LIKE 'RMAN%'
  4    AND    OPNAME NOT LIKE '%aggregate%'
  5    AND    TOTALWORK != 0 AND SOFAR <> TOTALWORK
  6  /


  SID    SERIAL#    CONTEXT      SOFAR  TOTALWORK  %COMPLETE
---- ---------- ---------- ---------- ---------- ----------
  39        149          1      46648     491600       9.49
```

Now, if you keep executing the query, you can see how much work is done and how much is still pending:

```
SQL> /


       SID    SERIAL#    CONTEXT      SOFAR  TOTALWORK  %COMPLETE
---------- ---------- ---------- ---------- ---------- ----------
        39        149          1      49080     491600       9.98


SQL> /


       SID    SERIAL#    CONTEXT      SOFAR  TOTALWORK  %COMPLETE
---------- ---------- ---------- ---------- ---------- ----------
        39        149          1      53048     491600      10.79
```

You will need to keep querying this view and watching the output in the %COMPLETE column until it shows 100 percent, as this would indicate that the job is complete. If you don't see the job moving forward and it appears to be hung for longer than two or three minutes with the %COMPLETE column showing no progress, it's a sign of a bottleneck somewhere. To troubleshoot it, you can look into the database view V$SESSION_WAIT to find out which wait event for RMAN is waiting for. For example, the following output was taken when the backup job was going on:

```
SQL> SELECT sid, event, seconds_in_wait AS sec_wait
  2  FROM    V$session_wait WHERE wait_time= 0
  3  AND     sid in(SELECT sid FROM V$session
  4              WHERE lower(program) like '%rman%')
  5  /

     SID EVENT                                      SEC_WAIT
---------- ------------------------------------- ----------
      34 RMAN backup & recovery I/O                      0
      40 SQL*Net message from client                     3
      47 SQL*Net message from client                    58
```

Stopping RMAN from being uncontrollable

In terms of performance, it's going to be very important that RMAN doesn't consume a lot of I/O bandwidth. It's also required that with the backup going on, the impact on the overall performance of the database shouldn't get impacted much. To control this, the following options are useful:

- RATE parameter
- MAXPIECE parameter
- DURATION parameter

Configuring the RATE parameter sets an upper level over the I/O that RMAN can do. This would be configured for a channel since the I/O would be done by the channel only. This parameter controls how much data can be read by one channel in terms of bytes, kilobytes, megabytes, or gigabytes. Using this parameter will restrict RMAN from doing a lot of I/O which causes an adverse impact on the underlying database's performance by exhausting the complete or maximum bandwidth of the disks. There is no defined optimal setting for this parameter, but you should set it to such a value that the disks will have some bandwidth left after giving away the bandwidth that you would ask by setting it. For tape backups, you should watch carefully because if the tape is not streaming, it would actually be better to remove this parameter from the CONFIGURE or ALLOCATE commands.

Setting the MAXPIECE parameter will restrict the maximum allowed backup piece size for RMAN since the given value would be the upper value for it. Because RMAN takes backups physically in the form of backup pieces, having control over their size would allow RMAN not to create large sized backup pieces and spend too much time doing it.

Setting the DURATION parameter gives you control over how long it takes for RMAN to complete the job. The format used to specify the duration is HH:MM. For example, using the following RMAN configuration will ensure that the backup job takes two hours:

```
RMAN> BACKUP DURATION 2:00 TABLESPACE users;
```

Not only can you can set the total duration of the job but also you can control how the job is going to affect the database. There are two configurations that can be set with DURATION:

- MINIMIZE TIME
- MINIMIZE LOAD

The following is an example of how you can use MINIMIZE TIME along with the DURATION parameter:

```
RMAN> BACKUP DURATION 2:00 MINIMIZE TIME TABLESPACE users;
```

Using MINIMIZE TIME will make RMAN perform to its fullest potential and eventually will also affect the performance of the database as resource consumption will be quite high. The other option, MINIMIZE LOAD, would make RMAN balance the performance of the job in comparison to the given time period in the DURATION clause. So in the preceding example, RMAN would estimate what the chances are of getting the job completed in the given time of two hours. If the estimate comes out that the job will finish in the required time, it will make the job run slower so that there isn't excessive consumption of system resources. Thus, using MINIMIZE LOAD will prove to be a good option when you want your RMAN jobs not to impact the performance of your database. But remember, using this option for tape drives may not be optimal as to limit the resource consumption, RMAN may restrict the rate of the data streaming offered by the tape. This would make the tape backups run slower. Also, since the tape won't be released as long as the job won't be complete, it would not be good if the tape would be required to get accessed by another job. For these factors, it is better not to use the MINIMIZE LOAD option when using the tapes as the backup storage.

It's important to mention that if the given job is not yet complete and the assigned duration is complete, RMAN will not continue with the backup and will abort it. It would also report about this. If you have executed multiple commands using a RUN block, any commands which are yet pending to run, won't get executed. To avoid this, with DURATION you can also use another option called PARTIAL which will make RMAN complete the command rather than interrupting it.

Using incremental, multi-section, multiplexing, and parallelism

In general, the biggest concern for DBAs is those long running backup jobs which take hours to complete and they want to bring the backup time down by any means. If you see the same issue and want to improve the time elapsed for your RMAN backup jobs, you can use a few features that are inbuilt to RMAN. The RMAN features that can help greatly are:

- Incremental backups
- Multi-section backups
- Multiplexing
- Parallelism

A full backup would definitely take a very long time compared to incremental backups. Because incremental backups only consider the modified blocks to be included in the backup, the time taken for them to complete is far lower than the normal backups. Using a block change tracking file keeps the information of the modified blocks, lets the incremental backup read that information, skips reading the entire data file, and makes the incremental backup even more efficient and time saving.

For large sized files, multi-section backups can be a great help as you can use multiple channels to do a parallel backup of a single file to achieve intrafile parallelism as well. In Oracle Database 12c, since multi-section backups are possible for incremental backups as well as for image copy backups also, so that's going to take a good feature even one step ahead.

Multiplexing offers RMAN the capability to read more than one datafile or archived redo logs at one time by a single channel. As we mentioned earlier, it's set using the minimum out of the setting of `FILESPERCET` and `MAXOPENFILES` with the former set to value 64 by default, thus making the multiplexing value equivalent to 8, implying that 8 files would be read by a single channel at one time. As we have shown previously with the different levels of multiplexing, there is a distinct configuration of the size and count of the memory buffers which would be affecting the performance. Therefore, you must ensure that you do a complete benchmarking before suggesting any value for it.

A serial process is always going to be slower than a parallel one and the same is applied for the RMAN backups as well. To improve backup performance, you should play with the number of channels that you set for optimal performance. Though it would be good to have more channels to get as much parallelism as possible, since each channel is going to a separate process and entering the database as a separate session, you must be careful as allocating too many will burn out your system resources. Depending on the channels you are going to plan, a suitable adjustment will be required for the `PROCESS` parameter as well. If you are taking a backup on the disks which are configured using the concept SAME or are a part of a disk group, set the number of channels equal to the number of the disks you have. For backup jobs using a tape drive as the storage type, the number of channels should be equivalent to the tape drives used. For example, if an array of 10 tape drives is used, then 10 SBT channels should be allocated.

There is one last option that we have not listed in the preceding list of features because it's actually really not a feature, though it can but still help. If you have a physical standby configured, you can offload the backups over it. By doing so, you can also benefit from incremental backups as well. This won't be any different from doing the same on your primary database but at least the burden on the server will be reduced. Since the physical standby won't be as busy as your primary database, there will be more system resources available that you can give to RMAN to optimize its performance.

Troubleshooting RMAN performance using tracing

Enabling tracing on RMAN can be done in a couple of ways. As with any other trace file, the information collected will be huge and won't be very well formatted. This option should be used as the last option and in extreme cases only, for example, when RMAN has become completely non-responsive. As it won't be easy to find the relevant bottleneck from reading the raw trace files, you should let Oracle Support staff read and analyze it to find the actual reasons for the bottleneck. It's certainly not going to be a good idea to generate RMAN trace files on a regular practice.

There can be three possible ways to enable tracing for RMAN:

- Using the DEBUG option
- Using the 10046 trace event
- Using the SQLNET tracing

The DEBUG command, as we discussed at the start of this chapter, is meant to debug various categories. Since for RMAN, the biggest reason for bottlenecks would be I/O, you can enable debugging using the following category:

```
$ rman target / log=/tmp/rman.log trace=/tmp/rmantrc.trc debug=IO
```

The preceding command will generate the log file and trace file under the /tmp folder. The following is a very small snippet of the trace file created:

```
DBGSQL:        CHANNEL> alter session set events '19737 trace name context
off'
DBGSQL:        sqlcode = 0
DBGMISC:    EXITED krmksimronly [20:50:32.297] elapsed time
[00:00:00:00.010]
DBGMISC:    ENTERED krmksimronly [20:50:32.510]
DBGMISC:    EXITED krmksimronly [20:50:32.510] elapsed time
[00:00:00:00.000]
DBGMISC:    ENTERED krmkgetdb [20:50:32.591]
```

As you can see, there is a lot of information in the file and it is constituted by the internal information. The details of these internal function calls and API's is beyond the scope of this book. That is why it is best for you to generate this information at the request of the Oracle Support staff and let them analyze the trace file generated in order to troubleshoot the issue, if any.

The 10046 trace event will generate the wait event information related to RMAN's processing. You can combine it with the debugging information. To set the trace event, you need to execute commands as follows:

```
$ rman target / catalog <connection> debug trace=/tmp/rmantrc.trc log=/
tmp/rmanlog.txt

RMAN> sql "alter session set tracefile_identifier=''rman_10046''";

RMAN> sql "alter session set events ''10046 trace name context
forever,level 12''";

RMAN> BACKUP DATABASE;

RMAN> exit;
```

The resulting trace file can be formatted using any trace file formatting tool such as **Trace Kernel Profiler** (**TKPROF**). The analysis of the trace file will help to find those problems, for example, if there is an I/O bottleneck or not. But as the information collected can be very vast, it's better to send the file to Oracle Support for analysis.

> TKPROF is a free database utility used for formatting the trace files for a better read. This is bundled with the database software itself. To learn more about it, refer to the support note 760786.1. You may also make use of another tool, that is, **Trace Analyzer** (**TRCA**) for the formatting of trace files (support note 224270.1).

It is the last option useful to eliminate any network related bottlenecks. Because RMAN connects and works with the target database using the underlying network only, enabling tracing would be helpful to debug slow performance. You can enable the SQLNET tracing using the parameter TRACE_LEVEL_SERVER or TRACE_LEVEL_CLIENT in either the server-side or client-side SQLNET.ora file. It goes without saying that this should be done only on an on-demand basis of Oracle Support staff and the resulting trace files should be sent to them for the correct analysis.

Summary

In this chapter, we saw how we can troubleshoot some RMAN-related issues and also took a glance at the factors which can affect its performance. As with any performance or troubleshooting activity, there is no defined way to do either of them. At times, even some basic things such as doing numerous backup jobs at the same time or scheduling the backup job when your database's workload is at its peak can make RMAN work slowly.

On the other hand, there can be more crucial issues, for example, slow hardware or a nasty bug which might be affecting performance. The same goes for troubleshooting. So the next time you are trying to make RMAN perform faster or are solving a failed backup job, try to look at the areas mentioned in this chapter. Additionally, there are many very useful online resources available as well. To start with, you can search knowledge base of Oracle's Support portal My Oracle support (`https://support.oracle.com`). Note that you will need a valid support license to login into this portal. If you don't have it, you can search the **Oracle Technology Network (OTN)** RMAN forum, a place where members from all over the globe interact and try to solve each other's issues as much as possible. Last but certainly not least, the online documentation of Oracle Database and Google can always come to the rescue.

In the next chapter, we will introduce you to Data Pump, a simple yet very powerful utility which makes tasks such as moving data (or even metadata) from one database to another so easy. Not only that, this tool can be used for more advanced tasks such as making a duplicate database from your production database.

9

Understanding Data Pump

Data Pump is one of the most preferred utilities by DBAs in the Oracle space. The motive of this chapter is to introduce you to this amazing world without wasting too much time on understanding the internal working of it, but to provide specific examples that will make it easier for us to understand how flexible it is.

In this chapter we will learn about:

- What is Data Pump?
- The Data Pump architecture
- New concepts with Data Pump
- Methods to move the data
- And, play with many Data Pump scenarios

What is Data Pump?

The Data Pump utility is a fully integrated feature of the Oracle database that was introduced within Oracle 10*g* as a replacement to the original export and import utilities. Data Pump is more powerful and flexible than the old utilities and provides, for example, high speed, fast object recovery, parallel read and write, data transformation (such as scrubbing sensible data), and compression. It also provides bulk data and metadata movement of Oracle database content, and also enables an efficient movement of data and metadata between Oracle databases independent of database versions and the OS platform involved.

In previous versions of Oracle, we used to work with similar utilities named exp and imp. The exp utility was deprecated since Oracle 11*g*, but the imp utility is still supported by Oracle for migration purpose. The imp utility allows us to recover any backup generated by the old exp program. Just keep in mind that the use of exp is no longer supported by Oracle, and using it can bring future trouble to your environment.

Oracle uses the Oracle Data Pump to allow us to generate logical backups that can be used to migrate data or even to do a partial or full recovery of our database. These utilities are also very useful after upgrading an Oracle database. The following are some of the most important points about Data Pump:

- It supports different modes for unloading or loading portions of a database, such as:
  - Full database mode
  - Schema mode
  - Table mode
  - Tablespace mode
  - Transportable tablespace mode

- The Data Pump export and import utilities are much faster than the original export and import Utilities due to the use of data access methods, direct path, and external tables, which are much faster than the conventional SQL. Data Pump also does all the processing on the server, rather than on the client (as a consequence, the dump files are located on the database server and not on the client), and the speed can be intensely improved by using the PARALLEL parameter (Data Pump uses parallelism to build indexes and load package bodies).

- It allows you to perform point-in-time logical backups of your entire database or even subsets of it.

- It enables you to specify how partitioned tables should be handled during import operations, allowing multiple worker processes to perform inter-table and inter-partition parallelism to load and unload tables in multiple, parallel, direct-path streams.

- Data Pump jobs can be restarted without any loss of data whether or not the stoppage was voluntary or involuntary; you can also easily modify, stop, or restart jobs manually, if necessary.

- Data Pump is the most flexible utility available in the market that allows you to easily perform on-the-fly changes to your database metadata, including data transformation. And what's better, there's no extra cost for using it.

- It provides support for the full range of data types in an Oracle database.

- Data Pump jobs support fine-grained objects' selection. Virtually any type of object can be included or excluded in a Data Pump job.

- Data Pump supports the ability to load one database directly from another (network import) without the need to generate a dump file, and also the possibility to unload a remote database (network export).

- Data Pump utilities were extended to leverage the new audit framework, providing a comprehensive audit trail of all invocations of Data Pump.

- The possibility to disable logging generation during an import operation, allowing us to have faster imports. Due to this, the redo log information is not written to disk or even archived. This is particularly useful for large data loads like database migrations (new in Oracle 12*c*).

- It provides an option to export a view as a table. In this case, Data Pump will include in the dump file, the corresponding table definition and all the data that was visible in the view, instead of only writing the view definition. This allows the Data Pump import to create it as a table with the same columns and data as the original view during the import process. All objects depending on the view will also be exported as if they were defined on the table. Grants and constraints that are associated with the view will be now recorded as grants and constraints on the corresponding table in the dump file (new in Oracle 12*c*).

After learning about all the reasons to use Data Pump, it is now time to learn about how it works internally and its components.

The Data Pump architecture

Data Pump has a very simple mechanism that can interact with many other interfaces such as, Oracle Enterprise Manager and custom interfaces, and it is basically made up of three unique parts; they are:

- The command-line interfaces, `expdp` and `impdp`

- The `DBMS_DATAPUMP` package, also known as the Data Pump API

- The `DBMS_METADATA` package, also known as the Metadata API

As you can easily see in the following figure, the command-line interfaces, `expdp` and `impdp`, uses the `DBMS_DATAPUMP` package to execute the export and import operations using all the parameters passed in by the user in the command line. When metadata needs to be manipulated, it uses the `DBMS_METADATA` package to extract, manipulate, and also to recreate the dictionary metadata. Furthermore, due to this, the Data Pump packages are stored in the Oracle database by itself (`DBMS_DATAPUMP` and `DBMS_METADATA`). They can be directly accessed by any external application using PL/SQL, the Oracle Enterprise Manager Cloud Control Transportable Tablespaces, or even by SQL*Plus.

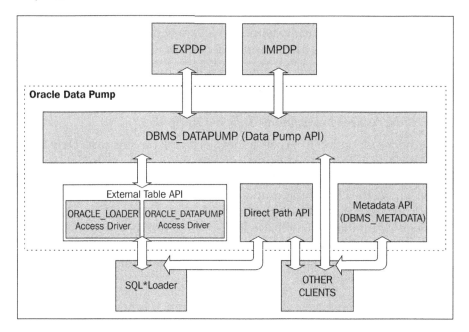

The other two parts in the diagram that are worth mentioning are the **External Table API** and the **Direct Path API**. The External Table API (`ORACLE_DATAPUMP` access driver), which is responsible for allowing Oracle to read and write the data in an external table (an external table is an OS level file that resides outside of the database). The Direct Path API is responsible for passing the data loaded directly to the load engine in the server using direct-path operations such as using direct-path `INSERT` statements instead of using conventional insert statements.

 It is important to know that all the processing, including the reading and writing of dump files created by Data Pump will be done on the system (server) selected by the specified database connection string used when invoking the utility.

New concepts with Data Pump

Some new concepts were introduced with Data Pump when comparing it with the original export and import utilities; they are:

- **Directory objects**: In order to use Data Pump, the DBA must create a directory object that defines the location where it will create or locate the dump, log, or SQL files during an import or export operation, and grant privileges to the user on that directory object (such as READ and WRITE). If a directory object is not specified, a default directory object called DATA_PUMP_DIR is provided. This default DATA_PUMP_DIR is available only to privileged users unless access is granted by the DBA.

- **Interactive command-line mode**: This mode allows you to take full control of all Data Pump jobs running in the database. You can easily monitor and manage the jobs running, and do things such as stop, re-start, or kill a job. This also gives you the ability to detach from a running job and later reconnect to it, if necessary.

Methods to move the data

Data Pump uses different methods to move the data in and out of a database; it can use the following methods:

- Datafile copy
- Direct path
- External tables
- Conventional path
- Network link

Now let's take a closer look at each one of these methods.

Datafile copy

This is the quickest way to transport an entire tablespace to a target system; all you will need to do is transfer the tablespace's underlying files to the target environment. With this method, Data Pump export is used to unload only structural information (metadata) into the dump file.

When using this option, firstly always check if the database character set is the same in the source and target databases and they must also be at same time zone version.

For a tablespace to be transported to a target system, it must be self-contained. Use the TRANSPORT_SET_CHECK procedure in the DBMS_TTS package to determine whether you are moving a self-contained tablespace (or tablespaces). You must have been granted the EXECUTE_CATALOG_ROLE role to be able to execute this procedure.

Here is an example of how to use this procedure. Here, we will check if the tablespace test_1 is self-contained:

```
SQL> EXECUTE DBMS_TTS.TRANSPORT_SET_CHECK('test_1', TRUE);
```

If you need to check two or more tablespaces, all you will need to do is name all the tablespaces separated by a comma as shown in the following example:

```
SQL> EXECUTE DBMS_TTS.TRANSPORT_SET_CHECK('test_1,test_2', TRUE);
```

After executing the procedure, you should query the TRANSPORT_SET_VIOLATIONS view to check if any violation exists. If the view does not return any rows, the tablespace is self-contained.

```
SQL> SELECT * FROM TRANSPORT_SET_VIOLATIONS;
```

If the source and target platform are using different endian formats, you must convert the data being transported (using RMAN CONVERT to change endianness) to become the same format as the target platform. Please refer to http://en.wikipedia.org/wiki/Endianness for more information about endian formats.

We will see more about this method including its examples in *Chapter 10, Advanced Data Pump*.

Direct path

Because the direct path operation can bypass undo (hence reducing redo), the load and unload process of the data will be faster. Data Pump uses by default the direct path method when the structure of a table allows it.

Data Pump does not load tables with disabled unique indexes. When loading data into a table in this situation, the indexes should be either dropped or renamed.

External tables

When not using datafile copy (transportable tablespace), and the data cannot be moved using direct path, the external table method is used. The external table method creates an external table that maps to the dump file data for the database table, then the SQL engine is used to move the data. This uses the access driver that was introduced with Oracle 10*g* called ORACLE_DATAPUMP, which allows Oracle to READ and WRITE to external tables. Data Pump might use external tables for the export, but direct path for the import.

In particular, Data Pump uses external tables in the following situations:

- When loading and unloading very large tables and partitions in situations where it is advantageous to use parallel SQL capabilities
- When loading tables with global or domain indexes defined on them, including partitioned object tables
- When loading tables with active triggers or clustered tables
- When loading and unloading tables with encrypted columns
- When loading tables with fine-grained access control enabled for inserts
- When loading tables that are partitioned differently at load time and unload time
- When loading a table not created by the import operation (the table exists before the import starts)

 It is important to understand that files that Data Pump creates, when it uses external tables, are not compatible with files created when manually creating an external table using a SQL statement.

Conventional path

When Data Pump is not able to use either the direct path or external table method, then the conventional path will be used. This method can affect the performance of your Data Pump operation.

Network link

When specifying the parameter NETWORK_LINK in Data Pump import, an INSERT SELECT statement will be used to move the data through the network without the need to generate a dump file.

When specifying the parameter NETWORK_LINK in Data Pump export, the data from the source database is written directly to a dump file in the target database.

> To export from a read-only database, the NETWORK_LINK parameter is required.

Data Pump files

Data Pump jobs manage few types of files; they are:

- Dump files; these files contain all the data and metadata that is being moved (generated as per the DUMPFILE parameter input).
- A log file that records all outputs related with an import or export operation (when using the LOGFILE parameter).
- SQL files that contain the results of a SQLFILE operation (when using the SQLFILE parameter). In other words, this file will enclose a dump of all SQL DDL statements that import operations would execute without really executing the real import.
- Datafile copies that will be used during a transportable import operation (specified in the DATA_FILE parameter).

Roles for Data Pump export and import

If you are required to perform export and import operations using Data Pump, you will need to have the following roles assigned to the user account that will be used with the expdp and impdp utilities:

- DATAPUMP_EXP_FULL_DATABASE
- DATAPUMP_IMP_FULL_DATABASE

The DATAPUMP_EXP_FULL_DATABASE role gives you the privilege to perform export operations, and the DATAPUMP_IMP_FULL_DATABASE role gives you the privilege to perform import operations (including import operations with the use of the SQLFILE parameter).

For example, the following will be the statement to grant previously mentioned roles to the user `fcomunoz` (when connected as `sysdba`):

```
SQL> GRANT DATAPUMP_EXP_FULL_DATABASE, DATAPUMP_IMP_FULL_DATABASE TO
fcomunoz;


Grant succeeded.
```

 These are powerful roles, and as the DBA is responsible for the database, you should use caution when granting these roles to users.

Directory objects

Data Pump differs from the original export and import utilities. In them, all jobs run principally on the server using server processes. These server processes access files for Data Pump jobs using directory objects that identify the location where Data Pump will read and write to these files. In other words, because Data Pump runs from inside the database, it needs to have the file's location path to be internally specified as a directory object.

Creating directory objects

Let's start this scenario by creating a directory object called `datapump` at SQL*Plus connected as `sysdba`, and then grant privileges for read and write on it to the user `fcomunoz`. This can be easily done by using the CREATE DIRECTORY and GRANT statements.

 If a directory object is not specified, a default directory object called `DATA_PUMP_DIR` is provided. The default `DATA_PUMP_DIR` will be available only to privileged users unless access is granted by the DBA.

```
SQL> CREATE OR REPLACE DIRECTORY datapump AS '/u01/db_backups';


Directory created.


SQL> GRANT READ, WRITE ON DIRECTORY datapump to fcomunoz;


Grant succeeded.
```

When granting READ and WRITE privileges to fcomunoz, we are only granting privileges via the Oracle Database, not at OS level.

We can verify if the directory object was created successfully by executing the following query:

```
SQL> SELECT * FROM DBA_DIRECTORIES WHERE DIRECTORY_NAME =
  'DATAPUMP';


OWNER DIRECTORY_NAME DIRECTORY_PATH  ORIGIN_CON_ID
----- -------------- --------------- -------------

SYS   DATAPUMP       /u01/db_backups 3
```

Now that we are all set, let's start playing with Data Pump.

Data Pump scenarios

As I have mentioned earlier, the best way to learn how to use Data Pump is practicing scenarios to see by yourself how it works and what you can do with it. In this chapter, we will see the following scenarios:

- Schema export and import
- Table export and import
- Exporting and importing a whole database/pluggable database
- Using export to estimate space
- Parallel full database export and interactive command mode
- Importing tables with only metadata
- Export views as tables
- Import data via network link

Now, let's start playing with Data Pump!

Schema export and import

In this scenario, we will first create a schema named test, and then create a table named EMPLOYEES that will hold our employees' data, followed by inserting a few rows in it. Then, we will execute an export operation to backup this schema, delete it, and then recover it through an import operation. Have a look at the following command:

```
SQL> CREATE USER test IDENTIFIED BY test DEFAULT TABLESPACE users
     QUOTA UNLIMITED ON users;


User created.


SQL> GRANT CREATE SESSION, RESOURCE TO test;


Grant succeeded.


SQL> CREATE TABLE TEST.EMPLOYEE
( EMP_ID   NUMBER(10) NOT NULL,
  EMP_NAME VARCHAR2(30),
  EMP_SSN  VARCHAR2(9),
  EMP_DOB  DATE
)
/


Table created.

SQL> INSERT INTO test.employee VALUES (101,'Francisco
  Munoz',123456789,TO_DATE('30-JUN-73','DD-MON-YY'));


1 row created.


SQL> INSERT INTO test.employee VALUES (102,'Gonzalo
  Munoz',234567890,TO_DATE('02-OCT-96','DD-MON-YY'));


1 row created.


SQL> INSERT INTO test.employee VALUES (103,'Evelyn
  Aghemio',659812831,TO_DATE('02-OCT-79','DD-MON-YY'));


1 row created.


SQL> COMMIT;
```

Now that the table is created, we will execute the export (from command line) to back up this schema:

```
$ expdp fcomunoz/alvarez@pdborcl directory=datapump dumpfile=test.dmp
  logfile=test.log  schemas=test reuse_dumpfiles=y


Export: Release 12.1.0.1.0 - Production on Thu May 30 15:13:45 2013


Copyright (c) 1982, 2013, Oracle and/or its affiliates.  All rights
  reserved.


Connected to: Oracle Database 12c Enterprise Edition Release
  12.1.0.1.0 - 64bit Production
With the Partitioning, OLAP, Advanced Analytics and Real Application
  Testing options
Starting "FCOMUNOZ"."SYS_EXPORT_SCHEMA_01":
  fcomunoz/********@pdborcl directory=datapump dumpfile=test.dmp
  logfile=test.log schemas=test
Estimate in progress using BLOCKS method...
Processing object type SCHEMA_EXPORT/TABLE/TABLE_DATA
Total estimation using BLOCKS method: 64 KB
Processing object type SCHEMA_EXPORT/USER
Processing object type SCHEMA_EXPORT/SYSTEM_GRANT
Processing object type SCHEMA_EXPORT/ROLE_GRANT
Processing object type SCHEMA_EXPORT/DEFAULT_ROLE
Processing object type SCHEMA_EXPORT/TABLESPACE_QUOTA
Processing object type SCHEMA_EXPORT/PRE_SCHEMA/PROCACT_SCHEMA
Processing object type SCHEMA_EXPORT/TABLE/TABLE
Processing object type
  SCHEMA_EXPORT/TABLE/STATISTICS/TABLE_STATISTICS
Processing object type SCHEMA_EXPORT/STATISTICS/MARKER
. . exported "TEST"."EMPLOYEE"                6.468 KB        3 rows
Master table "FCOMUNOZ"."SYS_EXPORT_SCHEMA_01" successfully
  loaded/unloaded
******************************************************************
Dump file set for FCOMUNOZ.SYS_EXPORT_SCHEMA_01 is:
  /u01/db_backups/test.dmp
Job "FCOMUNOZ"."SYS_EXPORT_SCHEMA_01" successfully completed at Thu
  May 30 15:14:19 2013 elapsed 0 00:00:31
```

As seen in the previous example, we should specify the username and password of the user executing the export (plus the database service name that will be used to connect to the database, in this case `@pdborcl`). After this, we used the parameter `DIRECTORY` to stipulate the directory object that `datapump` would use to generate the export files. We then used the `DUMPFILE` parameter to state the name of the dump file that will be created. The parameter `LOGFILE` will define the name of the log file of this operation, the `SCHEMAS` parameter is used to tell the export that only the test schema should be exported, and finally the `REUSE_DUMPFILES` parameter is used to overwrite a dump file, if it exists. If wanted to execute a full export of the database, all you will need to do is to replace the `SCHEMAS` parameter and the valued assigned to `FULL=y`.

Now it's time to check if all Data Pump files were created successfully before we proceed to the next step:

```
$ ls -lrt /u01/db_backups

total 340

-rw-r-----. 1 oracle oinstall 221184 May 30 15:14 test.dmp

-rw-r--r--. 1 oracle oinstall   1517 May 30 15:14 test.log
```

As you can see in the preceding result, all files were created successfully (one dump file and one log file). The next step would be to DROP the schema test, and then proceed with the recovery of the schema using the import utility as shown in the following command:

```
SQL> DROP USER test CASCADE;


User dropped.


$ impdp fcomunoz/alvarez@pdborcl directory=datapump dumpfile=test.dmp
  logfile=imp_test.log


Import: Release 12.1.0.1.0 - Production on Thu May 30 15:21:31 2013


Copyright (c) 1982, 2013, Oracle and/or its affiliates.  All rights
  reserved.


Connected to: Oracle Database 12c Enterprise Edition Release
  12.1.0.1.0 - 64bit Production
With the Partitioning, OLAP, Advanced Analytics and Real Application
  Testing options
```

```
Master table "FCOMUNOZ"."SYS_IMPORT_FULL_01" successfully
   loaded/unloaded
Starting "FCOMUNOZ"."SYS_IMPORT_FULL_01":   fcomunoz/********@pdborcl
   directory=datapump dumpfile=test.dmp logfile=imp_test.log
Processing object type SCHEMA_EXPORT/USER
Processing object type SCHEMA_EXPORT/SYSTEM_GRANT
Processing object type SCHEMA_EXPORT/ROLE_GRANT
Processing object type SCHEMA_EXPORT/DEFAULT_ROLE
Processing object type SCHEMA_EXPORT/TABLESPACE_QUOTA
Processing object type SCHEMA_EXPORT/PRE_SCHEMA/PROCACT_SCHEMA
Processing object type SCHEMA_EXPORT/TABLE/TABLE
Processing object type SCHEMA_EXPORT/TABLE/TABLE_DATA
. . imported "TEST"."EMPLOYEE"                6.468 KB       3 rows
Processing object type SCHEMA_EXPORT/TABLE/STATISTICS/TABLE_STATISTICS
Processing object type SCHEMA_EXPORT/STATISTICS/MARKER
Job "FCOMUNOZ"."SYS_IMPORT_FULL_01" successfully completed at Thu May
   30 15:21:51 2013 elapsed 0 00:00:17
```

Finally, let's verify if the schema was successfully recovered:

```
$ sqlplus test/test@pdborcl


SQL> SELECT * FROM test.employee;


    EMP_ID EMP_NAME                       EMP_SSN   EMP_DOB
---------- ------------------------------ --------- ---------
       101 Francisco Munoz                123456789 30-JUN-73
       102 Gonzalo Munoz                  234567890 02-OCT-96
       103 Evelyn Aghemio                 659812831 02-OCT-79
```

Exporting and importing tables

In this scenario, we will first execute an export operation to back up the table
EMPLOYEE, and then delete and recover it through an import operation. Have a
look at the following command:

```
$ expdp fcomunoz/alvarez@pdborcl directory=datapump
   dumpfile=employee.dmp logfile=employee.log  tables=test.employee
```

The main difference between this example and the previous one is that now we are using the TABLES parameter to export only the table that we want to backup.

The next step would be to DROP the table employee, and then proceed with the recovery of the table using the import utility:

```
SQL> DROP TABLE test.employee PURGE;


Table dropped.


SQL>exit


$ impdp fcomunoz/alvarez@pdborcl directory=datapump
  dumpfile=employee.dmp logfile=imp_employee.log
```

Finally, let's verify if the table was successfully recovered:

```
SQL> SELECT * FROM test.employee;


    EMP_ID EMP_NAME                      EMP_SSN   EMP_DOB
---------- ----------------------------- --------- ---------
       101 Francisco Munoz               123456789 30-JUN-73
       102 Gonzalo Munoz                 234567890 02-OCT-96
       103 Evelyn Aghemio                659812831 02-OCT-79
```

Exporting and importing a whole database/ pluggable database

In this example, we will export a pluggable database named pdborcl, drop it, recreate a new pluggable database from seed, and import all the data and metadata on it (these are the same steps to use on a non-container database). Have a look at the following command:

```
$ expdp fcomunoz/alvarez@pdborcl directory=datapump dumpfile=full_
pdborcl.dmp logfile=full_pdborcl.log  full=y
```

Once again, the FULL parameter indicates that the export will be made using the full database mode export, and all data and metadata in the database will be exported.

Now we will close the pluggable database to be able to drop it:

```
$ sqlplus / as sysdba


SQL> ALTER PLUGGABLE DATABASE pdborcl CLOSE;


Pluggable database altered.


SQL> DROP PLUGGABLE DATABASE pdborcl INCLUDING DATAFILES;


Pluggable database dropped.
```

Now let's create the new pluggable database from seed:

```
SQL> CREATE PLUGGABLE DATABASE pdborcl ADMIN USER pdb_admin
  IDENTIFIED BY oracle
  2      STORAGE (MAXSIZE 2G MAX_SHARED_TEMP_SIZE 100M)
  3      DEFAULT TABLESPACE Users
  4        DATAFILE
    '/u01/app/oracle/oradata/orcl/pdborcl/datafile1.dbff' SIZE 250M
      AUTOEXTEND ON
  5      PATH_PREFIX = '/u01/app/oracle/oradata/orcl/pdborcl/'
  6      FILE_NAME_CONVERT = ('/u01/app/oracle/oradata/orcl/pdbseed/',
    '/u01/app/oracle/oradata/orcl/pdborcl/');


Pluggable database created.


SQL> ALTER PLUGGABLE DATABASE pdborcl OPEN;
```

Even though this new environment does not contain the Data Pump environment set yet, we will now connect to our pluggable database and create the Data Pump environment (User, Privileges, and the Directory object) for the generation of log, SQL, and dump files:

```
SQL> ALTER SESSION SET CONTAINER=pdborcl;


Session altered.


SQL> CREATE USER fcomunoz IDENTIFIED BY alvarez DEFAULT TABLESPACE users
QUOTA UNLIMITED ON users;
```

```
User created.


SQL> GRANT CREATE SESSION, RESOURCE, DATAPUMP_EXP_FULL_DATABASE,
DATAPUMP_IMP_FULL_DATABASE TO fcomunoz;


Grant succeeded.


SQL> CREATE OR REPLACE DIRECTORY datapump AS '/u01/db_backups';


Directory created.


SQL> GRANT READ, WRITE ON DIRECTORY datapump to fcomunoz;


Grant succeeded.
```

Now we will be able to proceed with the import of the source pluggable database in the target server:

```
$ impdp fcomunoz/alvarez@pdborcl directory=datapump dumpfile=
  full_pdborcl.dmp logfile=imp_full_pdborcl.log
```

Using Export to estimate space

We can use Data Pump to estimate the amount of disk space consumed in a schema mode export. For this, we will use the ESTIMATE_ONLY parameter. This operation will not execute the normal export (only a simulation), and we will be able to see the estimation in the log file and in the information displayed on the client's expdp output.

 The estimation is for the table row data only; it does not include metadata.

The following command at OS level will execute an export operation that will calculate the estimation of the amount of space that will be required for the schema test:

```
$ expdp fcomunoz/alvarez@pdborcl directory=datapump schemas=test
  estimate_only=y logfile=est_test.log


Export: Release 12.1.0.1.0 - Production on Thu May 30 15:57:42 2013
```

```
Copyright (c) 1982, 2013, Oracle and/or its affiliates.  All rights
   reserved.


Connected to: Oracle Database 12c Enterprise Edition Release
   12.1.0.1.0 - 64bit Production
```

With the Partitioning, OLAP, Advanced Analytics and Real Application
   Testing options

```
Starting "FCOMUNOZ"."SYS_EXPORT_SCHEMA_01":
   fcomunoz/********@pdborcl directory=datapump schemas=test
      estimate_only=y logfile=est_test.log
```

Estimate in progress using BLOCKS method...

```
Processing object type SCHEMA_EXPORT/TABLE/TABLE_DATA
.  estimated "TEST"."EMPLOYEE"                                 64 KB
Total estimation using BLOCKS method: 64 KB
```

Job "FCOMUNOZ"."SYS_EXPORT_SCHEMA_01" successfully completed at Thu
   May 30 15:57:50 2013 elapsed 0 00:00:05

As you can see, Data Pump has estimated that it will need 64 KB to recreate the schema test. You can also replace the parameter SCHEMAS=test for FULL=y and it will now estimate how much space will be required to import the whole database, or even use it at other levels such as the tablespace level using the TABLESPACES parameter, or object level by using the TABLES parameter or the INCLUDE and EXCLUDE parameters.

Parallel full database export and interactive-command mode

Data Pump is much faster than the old exp and imp client commands. Data Pump has a feature that helps to make it even faster by trading performance for resource consumption (CPU); this feature is called the **parallel** option. With this option, Data Pump will dump data and metadata using as many threads as specified by the PARALLEL parameter, having each thread exclusively writing to one file at the time.

 The parallel option should be used in conjunction with the %U wildcard in the DUMPFILE parameter to allow multiple dump files to be created simultaneously.

Let's test to see if this really works as promised. In the following example, we will run a whole database export using four parallel threads:

```
$ expdp fcomunoz/alvarez@pdborcl directory=datapump
  dumpfile=full_%U.dmp parallel=4 logfile=full.log full=y
```

If we compare the time taken to finish the export (3 minutes and 50 seconds) against time taken by the normal export previously generated (5 minutes and 20 seconds), you can clearly see that the export operation was faster using the PARALLEL parameter. Also, it is important to know that this option can also be used in the import operation as shown the in the following example:

```
$ impdp fcomunoz/alvarez@pdborcl directory=datapump
  dumpfile=full_%U.dmp parallel=4 logfile=imp_full.log
```

 The PARALLEL parameter is valid only in the Enterprise Edition of the Oracle database.

You can also increase or decrease the value of PARALLEL or even stop or start the job when it is running in the background by using the interactive-command mode that is described in the following example. In this example, we will use the FILESIZE parameter to limit the maximum size of each dump file to 5 GB and play with the interactive-command mode.

```
$ expdp fcomunoz/alvarez@pdborcl dumpfile=full2_%U.dmp filesize=5g
  parallel=4 logfile=imp_full2.log job_name=expfull full=y
    directory=datapump
```

Now that the job is running, we will play with the interactive-command mode by pressing *Ctrl + C* to leave the execution mode output, and you will see the Export> prompt appear. From this prompt, you will be able to enter various commands to manage the job in execution; for example, you will be able to do the following:

- Stop the job as shown in the following command:

  ```
  Export> STOP_JOB=immediate
  ```

- Re-attach to the job to restart it using the following command.

  In this example, we will use the ATTACH parameter to attach to the client session of an existing export job, placing you automatically into the interactive-command interface as shown in the following command:

  ```
  $expdp fcomunoz/alvarez@pdborcl attach=expfull
  ```

Notice that we are using the `job_name` used in the export operation we previously executed, stopped, and now we want to restart; after being attached to the job, you can restart it as shown in the following command:

```
Export> START_JOB
```

- Change the parallel level used as shown in the following command:
```
Export> PARALLEL=10
```

- Display the cumulative status of the job, description of the current operation, and an estimated completion percentage. The amount entered specifies how frequently (in seconds) this status should be displayed in the logging mode as shown in the following command:
```
Export> STATUS=15
```

- Return to the client output mode as shown in the following command:
```
Export> CONTINUE_CLIENT
```

The following table shows a complete list of all commands available when in interactive export/import mode:

Command	Description	Export	Import
ADD_FILE	Add a dump file to the dump file set	No	Yes
CONTINUE_CLIENT	Return to logging mode. Job will be restarted if idle	No	No
EXIT_CLIENT	Quit client session and leave job running.	No	No
FILESIZE	The default file size (in bytes) for subsequent ADD_FILE commands.	No	Yes
HELP	Summarize interactive commands.	No	No
KILL_JOB	Detach and delete a job.	No	No
PARALLEL	Change the number of active workers for current job.	No	No
REUSE_DUMPFILES	Overwrite destination dump files if it exists.	No	Yes
START_JOB	Start or resume the current job.	No	No
STATUS	The job status will be displayed to monitor the job running (within seconds). The default 0 shows job status when available.	No	No

Command	Description	Export	Import
STOP_JOB	Orderly shuts down the job execution and exits the client; if using STOP_JOB=IMMEDIATE, it will perform an immediate shut down of the Data Pump job. You can also restart the job later by using the START_JOB command.	No	No

You can query the DBA_DATAPUMP_JOBS view to see a summary of all active Data Pump jobs on the system.

Importing tables with only metadata

The CONTENT parameter enables you to filter the data and metadata when executing an export or import operation, and it has the following values specified to this parameter:

- ALL: Loads table row data, and object definitions (metadata) are recreated
- DATA_ONLY: Loads only table row data; no database object definitions (metadata) are recreated
- METADATA_ONLY: Database object definitions (metadata) are re-created, but it doesn't load any data

Now we will see this in action by first exporting the whole schema test on the pluggable database pdborcl, and then import the schema test metadata_only in the pluggable database pdborcl2 as follows:

```
$ expdp fcomunoz/alvarez@pdborcl directory=datapump schemas=test
   dumpfile=shema_test.dmp logfile=schema_test.log


$impdp fcomunoz/alvarez@pdborcl2 directory=datapump
   dumpfile=shema_test.dmp logfile=imp_schema_test.log
     content=metadata_only table_exists_action=replace
```

As you can see, it does not matter if we export all the data and metadata on the export operation. This is because we can also specify on the import operation that we only want the metadata to be imported. You can also notice that I have used the TABLE_EXISTS_ACTION parameter to specify that if the object already exists in the target database (in this case, the pluggable database pdborcl2), it will be replaced during the import (by dropping the existing table and then creating it, and loading the data from the source). Other options that can be used with the TABLE_EXISTS_ ACTION parameter are:

- APPEND: It loads rows from the source and leaves existing rows unchanged.
- SKIP: It leaves the table as it is and moves on to the next object. This is not a valid option if the CONTENT parameter is set to DATA_ONLY.
- TRUNCATE: It deletes existing rows and then loads rows from the source.

Exporting views as tables

Data Pump introduced a new feature within Oracle 12c, the option to export views as tables. In this situation, Data Pump will include in the dump file the corresponding table definition and all the data that was visible in the view, instead to only write the view definition. This allows the Data Pump import to create it as a table with the same columns and data as the original view during the import process. All objects depending on the view will also be exported if they are defined on the table, grants, and constraints that are associated with the view; and will now be recorded as grants and constraints on the corresponding table in the dump file.

In this scenario, we will connect to the pluggable database pdborcl and create a view named employee_view in the schema test as follows:

```
$ sqlplus fcomunoz/alvarez@pdborcl


SQL>   CREATE VIEW test.employee_view AS
  2      SELECT *
  3      FROM employee;


View created.


SQL> SELECT * FROM test.employee_view;


    EMP_ID EMP_NAME                            EMP_SSN    EMP_DOB
---------- ------------------------------ --------- ---------
```

```
101 Francisco Munoz              123456789 30-JUN-73
102 Gonzalo Munoz               234567890 02-OCT-96
103 Evelyn Aghemio              659812831 02-OCT-79


SQL> exit
```

Now that we have the view created, let's export it using the parameter VIEWS_AS_TABLES:

```
$ expdp fcomunoz/alvarez@pdborcl directory=datapump dumpfile=
  employee_view.dmp logfile=employee_view.log
    views_as_tables=test.employee_view


Export: Release 12.1.0.1.0 - Production on Wed Jun 5 11:15:12 2013


Copyright (c) 1982, 2013, Oracle and/or its affiliates.  All rights
  reserved.


Connected to: Oracle Database 12c Enterprise Edition Release
  12.1.0.1.0 - 64bit Production
With the Partitioning, OLAP, Advanced Analytics and Real Application
  Testing options
Starting "FCOMUNOZ"."SYS_EXPORT_TABLE_01":  fcomunoz/********@pdborcl
  directory=datapump dumpfile= logfile=employee_view.log
    views_as_tables=test.employee_view
Estimate in progress using BLOCKS method...
Processing object type TABLE_EXPORT/VIEWS_AS_TABLES/TABLE_DATA
Total estimation using BLOCKS method: 16 KB
Processing object type TABLE_EXPORT/VIEWS_AS_TABLES/TABLE
. . exported "TEST"."EMPLOYEE_VIEW"          6.476 KB        3 rows
Master table "FCOMUNOZ"."SYS_EXPORT_TABLE_01" successfully
  loaded/unloaded
******************************************************************
Dump file set for FCOMUNOZ.SYS_EXPORT_TABLE_01 is:
  /u01/db_backups/employee_view.dmp
Job "FCOMUNOZ"."SYS_EXPORT_TABLE_01" successfully completed at Wed
  Jun 5 12:02:28 2013 elapsed 0 00:46:14
```

To check if it works, we will execute an import operation using the parameter SQLFILE. This parameter forces the import to dump all metadata in a file without really executing the import to a target database as shown in the following command:

```
$ impdp fcomunoz/alvarez@pdborcl directory=datapump
  dumpfile=employee_view.dmp sqlfile=employee_view.sql
```

Now that we have the employee_view.sql file created, let's check if it will create a table (as expected) or a view (as in the source database). For this we will use the CAT command shown as follows:

```
$ cat employee_view.sql
-- CONNECT FCOMUNOZ
ALTER SESSION SET EVENTS '10150 TRACE NAME CONTEXT FOREVER, LEVEL 1';
ALTER SESSION SET EVENTS '10904 TRACE NAME CONTEXT FOREVER, LEVEL 1';
ALTER SESSION SET EVENTS '25475 TRACE NAME CONTEXT FOREVER, LEVEL 1';
ALTER SESSION SET EVENTS '10407 TRACE NAME CONTEXT FOREVER, LEVEL 1';
ALTER SESSION SET EVENTS '10851 TRACE NAME CONTEXT FOREVER, LEVEL 1';
ALTER SESSION SET EVENTS '22830 TRACE NAME CONTEXT FOREVER, LEVEL 192
  ';
-- new object type path: TABLE_EXPORT/VIEWS_AS_TABLES/TABLE
CREATE TABLE "TEST"."EMPLOYEE_VIEW"
   (    "EMP_ID" NUMBER(10,0) NOT NULL ENABLE,
        "EMP_NAME" VARCHAR2(30 BYTE),
        "EMP_SSN" VARCHAR2(9 BYTE),
        "EMP_DOB" DATE
   ) SEGMENT CREATION DEFERRED
  PCTFREE 10 PCTUSED 40 INITRANS 1 MAXTRANS 255
 NOCOMPRESS LOGGING
  TABLESPACE "USERS" ;
```

We can see that it really works and the view was exported as a table.

Importing data via a network link

By using Data Pump, we are able to import metadata and data directly to a target database using a database link to connect to the source database and pull all information through the network.

The main benefits of using this method are:

- No dump file is generated. And consequently, no dump file needs to be copied.

- No need to execute an export command.

- It exports from the source, then imports into the target immediately.

In this scenario, we will basically import the whole schema test from `pdborcl` to `pdborcl2` using the network. Our first step will be to connect to our pluggable database, define a database link object to identify the source database, and provide login credentials.

The import operation must be performed by a user on the target database with the DATAPUMP_IMP_FULL_DATABASE role, and the database link must connect to a user on the source database with the DATAPUMP_EXP_FULL_DATABASE role. The user on the source database cannot be a user with SYSDBA system privilege. If the database link is a connected user database link, the user on the target database cannot be a user with SYSDBA system privilege.

```
sqlplus fcomunoz/alvarez@pdborcl2
```

```
SQL> CREATE DATABASE LINK pdborcl_lnk CONNECT TO fcomunoz IDENTIFIED by
alvarez USING 'pdborcl';
```

```
Database link created.
```

To ensure that the database link is working properly, we will issue a query that will use the newly created database link `pdborcl_lnk` to retrieve the employee table rows from the source database (`pdborcl`) schema test:

```
SQL> SELECT * FROM employee@pdborcl_lnk;
```

```
    EMP_ID EMP_NAME                        EMP_SSN   EMP_DOB
---------- ------------------------------- --------- ---------
       101 Francisco Munoz                 123456789 30-JUN-73
       102 Gonzalo Munoz                   234567890 02-OCT-96
       103 Evelyn Aghemio                  659812831 02-OCT-79
```

It works great, but just to be sure let's check if the table `employee` exists on the target environment we are connected to (`pdborcl2`):

```
SQL> SELECT * FROM test.employee;
select * from test.employee
              *
ERROR at line 1:
ORA-00942: table or view does not exist
```

Now it's time to make the magic happen; we will execute a normal import operation on the target environment using the parameter NETWORK_LINK to use the database link that we have created to directly access the remote data and metadata. The command we would use to achieve this goal is:

```
$ impdp fcomunoz/alvarez@pdborcl2 schemas=test directory=datapump
  network_link=pdborcl_lnk logfile=pdborcl_lnk.log
```

 This method does not work with LONG/LONG RAW and object types with nested tables.

Now let's connect to `pdborcl2` and check if the table `employee` is now in the database using the following command:

```
$ sqlplus fcomunoz/alvarez@pdborcl2


SQL> SELECT * FROM test.employee;
```

EMP_ID	EMP_NAME	EMP_SSN	EMP_DOB
101	Francisco Munoz	123456789	30-JUN-73
102	Gonzalo Munoz	234567890	02-OCT-96
103	Evelyn Aghemio	659812831	02-OCT-79

```
SQL>
```

Summary

In this chapter, we learned about the Data Pump architecture, how to configure it, and how to use it through some interesting hands-on scenarios. Furthermore, in the next chapter we will learn about playing with some advanced hands-on scenarios that will make you fall in love with Data Pump. Some examples of what we will see are data masking with Data Pump, creating smaller copies of production, migrating data for upgrade, downgrading an Oracle database, Data Pump flashback, and monitoring and performance tuning of Data Pump jobs.

10
Advanced Data Pump

Many people don't know about several powerful functionalities that are available when using Data Pump (expdp/impdp). Most of the people only use these tools to export and import data (in other words, only to move data), and never notice that it can be used, for example, to help us to do:

- Data masking
- Build a metadata repository
- Create a version control
- Work with different object editions in a database
- Clone users (create a new user using an existent user as a template)
- Create smaller copies of production
- Create your database in a different file structure
- Move all objects from one tablespace to another
- Move an object to a different schema (a simple example, change a table owner)
- Migrate data for a database upgrade
- Downgrade an Oracle database
- Transport a tablespace
- Use Data Pump with Flashback

As you can see, Data Pump is very flexible; now let's see how each of the examples that I have mentioned here can be used in real life.

Data masking

In many organizations (I hope so), the DBAs have the obligation for a security and compliance purpose to mask (scramble) all sensible information that leaves the production environment; as an example, when refreshing or creating a QA/ TEST or DEV environment. To help us to address those requirements, we could use the Enterprise Manager Data Masking Pack (Remember it is an extra pack, and consequently you need to pay extra to be able to use it. This pack allows you to make use of premade masking templates and executes the process for you.) or as a different approach, use the REMAP_DATA parameter available in Data Pump to help us with this requirement.

 The REMAP_DATA parameter was introduced within Oracle 11*g*!

Let's use the classic **SSN (Social Security Number)** example to illustrate how it works:

1. In the previous chapter, we created a table named EMPLOYEE with three records. We would use this table to run our data masking scenario shown as follows:

```
SQL> SELECT * FROM test.employee;


    EMP_ID EMP_NAME                              EMP_SSN   EMP_DOB
---------- ------------------------------- --------- ---------
       101 Francisco Munoz                      123456789 30-JUN-73
       102 Gonzalo Munoz                        234567890 02-OCT-96
       103 Evelyn Aghemio                       659812831 02-OCT-79
```

2. The second step will be to create the remap function:

```
$ sqlplus fcomunoz/alvarez@pdborcl

SQL> CREATE OR REPLACE PACKAGE pkg_masking
  2    AS
  3      FUNCTION mask_ssn (p_in varchar2) RETURN varchar2;
  4    END;
  5    /

Package created.
```

```
SQL> CREATE OR REPLACE PACKAGE BODY pkg_masking
 2    AS
 3       FUNCTION mask_ssn (p_in varchar2)
 4       RETURN varchar2
 5    IS
 6    BEGIN
 7      IF p_in IS NOT NULL then
 8          RETURN lpad (
 9                round(dbms_random.value
   (001000000,999999999)),9,0);
10      END IF;
11    END;
12    END;
13    /
```

`Package body created.`

This function will take a VARCHAR2 argument and returns a random VARCHAR2(9) value. We will use this function to mask all SSN information inside our employee table shown as follows:

```
SQL> DESC test.employee
```

Name	Null?	Type
EMP_ID	NOT NULL	NUMBER(10)
EMP_NAME		VARCHAR2(30)
EMP_SSN		VARCHAR2(9)
EMP_DOB		DATE

For this example, all you want to mask is the column EMP_SSN that contains the SSN of each employee.

3. Now we are going to export the table employees using the expdp tool, and while exporting, we will use the parameter REMAP_DATA to mask the data for us in the dump file using the function we have previously created.

You can invoke REMAP_DATA during an export or import operation, but I will recommend it to be used during the export operation to avoid the raw data to be available in a dump file (for security reasons).

```
$expdp fcomunoz/alvarez@pdborcl tables=test.employee
  dumpfile=mask_ssn.dmp directory=datapump
    remap_data=test.employee.emp_ssn:pkg_masking.mask_ssn


Export: Release 12.1.0.1.0 - Production on Wed Jun 19 12:49:14
  2013


Copyright (c) 1982, 2013, Oracle and/or its affiliates.  All
  rights reserved.


Connected to: Oracle Database 12c Enterprise Edition Release
  12.1.0.1.0 - 64bit Production
With the Partitioning, OLAP, Advanced Analytics and Real
  Application Testing options
Starting "FCOMUNOZ"."SYS_EXPORT_TABLE_01":
  fcomunoz/*******@pdborcl tables=test.employee
    dumpfile=mask_ssn.dmp directory=datapump
      remap_data=test.employee.emp_ssn:pkg_masking.mask_ssn
Estimate in progress using BLOCKS method...
Processing object type TABLE_EXPORT/TABLE/TABLE_DATA
Total estimation using BLOCKS method: 64 KB
Processing object type TABLE_EXPORT/TABLE/TABLE
Processing object type
  TABLE_EXPORT/TABLE/STATISTICS/TABLE_STATISTICS
Processing object type TABLE_EXPORT/TABLE/STATISTICS/MARKER
. . exported "TEST"."EMPLOYEE"                    6.468 KB
  3 rows
Master table "FCOMUNOZ"."SYS_EXPORT_TABLE_01" successfully
  loaded/unloaded
******************************************************************
********
Dump file set for FCOMUNOZ.SYS_EXPORT_TABLE_01 is:
  /u01/db_backups/mask_ssn.dmp
Job "FCOMUNOZ"."SYS_EXPORT_TABLE_01" successfully completed at
  Wed Jun 19 12:49:47 2013 elapsed 0 00:00:30
```

By default, the `REMAP_DATA` parameter will use the user doing the export as the owner of the remap function. If the schema owner of the function is different, you will need to explicitly enter the user owner of the remap function in the `expdp` instruction shown as follows:

```
$ expdp fcomunoz/alvarez@pdborcl tables=test.
employee dumpfile=mask_ssn.dmp directory=datapump
remap_data=test.employee.emp_ssn:owner.pkg_
masking.mask_ssn
```

4. Now all we need to do is to import `mask_ssn.dmp` in our QA/TEST or DEV database and it will automatically have the new values there. For this example we will import the data back on the same pluggable database and truncate the data on the table during the import shown as follows:

```
$ impdp fcomunoz/alvarez@pdborcl table_exists_action=truncate
  directory=datapump dumpfile=mask_ssn.dmp


Import: Release 12.1.0.1.0 - Production on Wed Jun 19 12:57:25
  2013


Copyright (c) 1982, 2013, Oracle and/or its affiliates.  All
  rights reserved.


Connected to: Oracle Database 12c Enterprise Edition Release
  12.1.0.1.0 - 64bit Production
With the Partitioning, OLAP, Advanced Analytics and Real
  Application Testing options
Master table "FCOMUNOZ"."SYS_IMPORT_FULL_01" successfully
  loaded/unloaded
Starting "FCOMUNOZ"."SYS_IMPORT_FULL_01":
  fcomunoz/********@pdborcl table_exists_action=truncate
    directory=datapump dumpfile=mask_ssn.dmp
Processing object type TABLE_EXPORT/TABLE/TABLE
Table "TEST"."EMPLOYEE" exists and has been truncated. Data
  will be loaded but all dependent metadata will be skipped
    due to table_exists_action of truncate
Processing object type TABLE_EXPORT/TABLE/TABLE_DATA
. . imported "TEST"."EMPLOYEE"                     6.468 KB
  3 rows
Processing object type
  TABLE_EXPORT/TABLE/STATISTICS/TABLE_STATISTICS
```

```
Processing object type TABLE_EXPORT/TABLE/STATISTICS/MARKER
Job "FCOMUNOZ"."SYS_IMPORT_FULL_01" successfully completed at
   Wed Jun 19 12:57:35 2013 elapsed 0 00:00:07
```

Now let's check if the data changed on the table EMPLOYEE:

```
$ sqlplus fcomunoz/alvarez@pdborcl


SQL> SELECT * FROM test.employee;
```

EMP_ID	EMP_NAME	EMP_SSN	EMP_DOB
101	Francisco Munoz	356245915	30-JUN-73
102	Gonzalo Munoz	842801230	02-OCT-96
103	Evelyn Aghemio	072963035	02-OCT-79

> You can use it to mask almost everything, but please take into consideration your application requirements and data integrity requirements when using it!

Metadata repository and version control

As a DBA, I'm always looking for proactive ways to allow me to be prepared in case of a disaster strike or if an emergency release rollback is required (I always love to use the "what if" methodology); and due to these reasons, having a metadata repository and version control of it is always useful.

But, how can I easily create it? Easy; first do a full backup of your database using Data Pump as shown in the following command:

```
$ expdp fcomunoz/alvarez@pdborcl content=metadata_only full=y
   directory=datapump dumpfile=metadata_06192013.dmp
```

> If you want to create a repository only for objects such as procedures, packages, triggers, and so on, all you need to do is add the parameter INCLUDE=<procedure,package,trigger,...> to your expdp command; I usually include the date of the dump in the dump filename for reference purpose and best practice.

Then use the `impdp` tool to create the SQL file that will allow you to create all objects in your database. It will be something like the following command:

```
$ impdp fcomunoz/alvarez@pdborcl directory=datapump dumpfile=
metadata_06192013.dmp sqlfile=metadata_06192013.sql
```

This simple technique will allow you to create your metadata repository easily and also keep a version of your database objects as an extra; also if you create your repository (DB) and you want to refresh an object definition (as an example let us use once again the table EMPLOYEE from the schema TEST), all you will need to do is an export of the new table definition from your source database, and then import it on your target database (your repository) as shown in the following command:

```
$ expdp fcomunoz/alvarez@pdborcl content=metadata_only
   tables=test.employee directory=datapump dumpfile=
     refresh_of_table_employee_06192013.dmp
```

```
$ impdp fcomunoz/alvarez@pdborcl table_exists_action=replace
   directory=datapump dumpfile= refresh_of_table_name_06192013.dmp
```

Notice that the parameter TABLE_EXISTS_ACTION will inform to the import operation that if the table exists on the target database, it will be replaced on import.

Another good example of what you can do using this technique is detecting changes in the database that you didn't know about. The next time you receive a call from a user complaining that an application is not performing as it did yesterday, and after checking for all changes applied to the database in the past 24 hours you found nothing, you can generate a full export of the database and then generate a new SQL file using the SQLFILE parameter to compare it with yesterday's SQL file (on Linux you can use the DIFF command for this). It will show any changes done to the database since yesterday, and if someone made any change to an index, package, or any objects on the database, it will show up, and it will help you to easily solve the problem.

Add a full daily export of your database to your backup strategy to allow you to always have a dump file available when required.

Using SOURCE_EDITION and TARGET_EDITIONS

With the introduction in Oracle 11gR2 of editions (Edition-Based Redefinition) that allow us to play with different versions (editions) of an object in an Oracle Database, Data Pump was forced to introduce new parameters to allow us to work within different editions available in the database. The parameters introduced were:

- SOURCE_EDITION to be used within expdp

- TARGET_EDITIONS to be used within impdp

A good example of the use of these new parameters is when we have multiple versions (editions) of an object in our development environment for different releases of an application, and we want to migrate a code from one version to a different version within a database or even across multiple databases.

In the following example, we will migrate a view (from our development database) called TEST from the schema TEST in the edition called NEW_EDITION to our production database schema TEST and to the edition called ORA$BASE:

```
$ expdp fcomunoz/alvarez@pdbdevorcl schemas=test
  dumpfile=exp_edition_09082013.dmp logfile=exp_edition_09082013.log
    include=view:"= 'TEST'"

source_edition=NEW_EDITION directory=datapump


$ impdp fcomunoz/alvarez@pdborcl dumpfile= exp_edition_09082013.dmp
  logfile= imp_edition_09082013.log TARGET_EDITION=ORA\$BASE
    directory=datapump
```

Cloning a user

In the past when a DBA had the need to create a new user with the same structure (all objects, tablespaces quota, synonyms, grants, system privileges, and so on) using the old exp/imp, it was a very painful experience. This is because not all the metadata was included, and it was a very slow process when moving a big volume of data. Now this can be done very easily using Data Pump. Let's use an example where you want to create the user TEST2 exactly like the user TEST. In order to achieve this goal, all you will need to do is first export the schema TEST definition, and then import it again asking the Data Pump to change the schema TEST for the new schema named TEST2 using the REMAP_SCHEMA parameter available with impdp:

```
$ expdp fcomunoz/alvarez@pdborcl schemas=test content=metadata_only
  directory=datapump dumpfile= test_06192013.dmp
```

If you want to clone a schema including the data, all you need to do is repeat the preceding example, removing the parameter CONTENT of it.

```
$ impdp fcomunoz/alvarez@pdborcl remap_schema=test:test2
  directory=datapump dumpfile= test_06192013.dmp
```

And, your new user TEST2 is now created like your existing user TEST, that easily!

Creating smaller copies of production

Creating a smaller copy of a production environment is a very common task for a DBA (for development or test purpose), but many times your destination server doesn't have enough space to create a full copy of it! This can be easily solved using Data Pump, for example, let's say that you only have space for 70 percent of your production database. Now to know how to proceed, we need to decide if the copy will contain metadata only (no data/rows) or if it will include the data also. Let's see how to do this each way:

- Metadata-only:

    1. First, do a full export of your source database:

        ```
        $ expdp fcomunoz/alvarez@pdborcl content=metadata_only full=y
          directory=datapump dumpfile=metadata_06192013.dmp
        ```

    2. Then, let's import the metadata and tell Data Pump to reduce the size of all objects extent to 70 percent; you can do this using the parameter TRANSFORM available with impdp; it represents the percentage multiplier that will be used to alter extent allocations and datafile sizes:

        ```
        $ impdp fcomunoz/Alvarez@pdborcl3 transform=pctspace:70
          directory=datapump dumpfile=metadata_06192013.dmp
        ```

    3. Let's do a test and see if this is really true; firstly, let's export any table of my test database (metadata only) and generate the SQL script to see the normal size of it:

        ```
        $ expdp fcomunoz/alvarez@pdborcl content=metadata_
        only tables=test.employee directory=datapump
        dumpfile=example_206192013.dmp
        ```

        ```
        $ impdp fcomunoz/alvarez@pdborcl content=metadata_
        only directory=datapump dumpfile=example_206192013.dmp
        sqlfile=employee_06192013.sql
        ```

```
CREATE TABLE "TEST"."EMPLOYEE"
    (    "EMP_ID" NUMBER(10,0) NOT NULL ENABLE,
         "EMP_NAME" VARCHAR2(30 BYTE),
         "EMP_SSN" VARCHAR2(9 BYTE),
         "EMP_DOB" DATE
    ) SEGMENT CREATION IMMEDIATE
 PCTFREE 10 PCTUSED 40 INITRANS 1 MAXTRANS 255
 NOCOMPRESS LOGGING
 STORAGE(INITIAL 65536 NEXT 1048576 MINEXTENTS 1 MAXEXTENTS
2147483645
 PCTINCREASE 0 FREELISTS 1 FREELIST GROUPS 1
 BUFFER_POOL DEFAULT FLASH_CACHE DEFAULT CELL_FLASH_CACHE
DEFAULT)
 TABLESPACE "USERS";
```

The preceding code is the SQL code generated by Data Pump, and you can see that the table is going to be created using 65536 for the initial extent and 1048576 for the next extent.

4. Now let's generate it again, but using the transform parameter to reduce the size of it to 70 percent of the original size:

```
$ impdp fcomunoz/alvarez@pdborcl transform=pctspace:70
content=metadata_only directory=datapump dumpfile=
example_206192013.dmp sqlfile=transform_06192013.sql
```

```
CREATE TABLE "TEST"."EMPLOYEE"
    (    "EMP_ID" NUMBER(10,0) NOT NULL ENABLE,
         "EMP_NAME" VARCHAR2(30 BYTE),
         "EMP_SSN" VARCHAR2(9 BYTE),
         "EMP_DOB" DATE
    ) SEGMENT CREATION IMMEDIATE
 PCTFREE 10 PCTUSED 40 INITRANS 1 MAXTRANS 255
 NOCOMPRESS LOGGING
 STORAGE(INITIAL 45875 NEXT 734003 MINEXTENTS 1 MAXEXTENTS
2147483645
 PCTINCREASE 0 FREELISTS 1 FREELIST GROUPS 1
 BUFFER_POOL DEFAULT FLASH_CACHE DEFAULT CELL_FLASH_CACHE
DEFAULT)
 TABLESPACE "USERS";
```

The preceding code is the SQL code generated by Data Pump, and you can see that the table is now going to be created using 45875 for the initial extent and 734003 for the next extent, clearly reduced 30 percent of the original size; in other words, it works.

Please refer to the Oracle documentation for more ways to use the transform parameter, you will not regret it.

- Metadata and data:

    1. Firstly, do a full export of your source database using the export parameter SAMPLE. This parameter specify a percentage of the data rows to be sampled and unload from your source database; in this case, let's use 70 percent.

    ```
    $ expdp fcomunoz/alvarez@pdborcl sample=70 full=y
      directory=datapump dumpfile=expdp_70_06192013.dmp
    ```

    2. Then, all you need to do as the preceding example is to import it telling the Data Pump to reduce the size of extents to 70 percent, and that's it!

    ```
    $ impdp fcomunoz/alvarez@pdborcl3 transform=pctspace:70
      directory=datapump dumpfile=expdp_70_06192013.dmp
    ```

Creating your database in a different file structure

Duplicating your database using a different structure is very easy to be done using Data Pump; all you need to do is use the parameter REMAP_DATAFILE on your import command as shown in the following example:

```
$ impdp fcomunoz/alvarez@pdborcl directory=datapump
  dumpfile=diff_structure_06192013.dmp
   remap_datafile='/u01/app/oracle/oradata/pdborcl/datafile_01.dbf':'
   /u01/app/oracle/oradata/pdborcl2/datafile_01.dbf'
```

Moving all objects from one tablespace to another

Moving all objects in one tablespace to another tablespace is something very easy to be done. As shown in the previous example, all you need to do is to use the parameter REMAP_TABLESPACE on your import command as shown in the following example:

```
$ impdp fcomunoz/alvarez@pdborcl directory=datapump
  dumpfile=mv_tablespace_06192013.dmp remap_tablespace=test:test2
```

 Please ensure that the destination tablespace exists before executing this example.

Moving an object to a different schema

To be able to move objects in one schema to a different schema, all you need to do is to use the parameter REMAP_SCHEMA when importing it, as shown in the following command:

```
$ expdp fcomunoz/alvarez@pdborcl tables=test.employee
  directory=datapump dumpfile=employee_06192013.dmp
```

```
$ impdp fcomunoz/alvarez@pdborcl directory=datapump dumpfile=
  employee_06192013.dmp remap_schema=test:test2
```

 If all you want to do is to move a table or a group of tables, remember to use the parameter TABLES to achieve this goal; you can also use the INCLUDE and EXCLUDE parameters to filter the data to be moved even more.

Migrating data for upgrade

We can easily use Data Pump expdp and impdp to help us to migrate data from one database to another when, for example, upgrading a database. This can be easily done by exporting the data from the source database (in this example using the 11.2.0.3 version of Oracle), and then import it into the target database (in this example, there will be a database using the 12.1.0 version of Oracle).

Let's go over all the steps required to achieve this goal:

1. Install the new version of the Oracle database to which you want to upgrade your data; in this example, we have installed Oracle database 12.1.0 and created a new database.

 If the new database (target) will have the same name and will be located in the same server, the source database will not forget to shutdown it before creating the new database in step 2.

2. Create (using ORAPWD) or migrate your password file from the source database to the target database.

3. Create or migrate the initialization parameter file (SPFILE or PFILE) and do not forget to adjust the initialization parameters for Oracle 12c such as enabling the new extended data type capability on the target database (12.1.0) to make use of the 32767 byte limit for VARCHAR2, NVARCHAR2, and RAW data types that were introduced with Oracle 12c. You can do it by setting the initialization parameter MAX_STRING_SIZE to EXTENDED. And, do not forget to set the COMPATIBILITY parameter to 12.0.0.0 or higher.

 The new limit is not set by default, and you need to ensure that the COMPATIBILIY initialization parameter is set to 12.0.0.0 or higher to make use of it. Also, you need to be aware that downgrading an Oracle 12c database with the EXTENDED capability to a version lower than 12.1.0 will possibly end up with truncated data.

4. Connect to the newly created database via SQL*Plus (SYS as SYSDBA) and start the instance.

5. Export all data and metadata from the 11.2.0.3 database (source database) using the following command.

 To ensure that this export is consistent, the source database must not be available for modifications during and after the export operation. If the source database needs to be fully available to the user's modifications after the export operation is completed, you will need to put some procedures in place that will copy all changes made in the source database to the target database after the import operation is completed.

```
$ expdp fcomunoz/alvarez dumpfile=full_11_06192013.dmp
  logfile=full_11_06192013.log full=y
```

6. Import all data and metadata exported in step 1 in the target database using the following command:

```
$ impdp fcomunoz/alvarez@pdborcl dumpfile=full_11_06192013.dmp
  logfile=imp_full_11_06192013.log
```

> If importing in the same server, you should make use of the parameter REMAP_DATAFILE to tell Oracle that it needs to create the datafiles in a different location when creating the new tablespaces during the import operation, if not it will fail as the source database datafiles are still there. Or, you can even precreate the tablespaces and use the parameters REUSE_DATAFILES=N and DESTROY=N when executing the import.

7. Check the logfile of the import operation to ensure that it is completed successfully.

8. If the database contains a RMAN CATALOG, do not forget to connect to it via RMAN, and execute the UPGRADE CATALOG command twice.

9. Refer to *Chapter 4, Post-Upgrade Tasks for Oracle Database*, in the *Oracle Database Upgrade Guide 12c Release 1* document to ensure that you are not missing any required post-upgrade task to your environment.

Downgrading an Oracle Database

You can also use Data Pump to downgrade an Oracle Database; for example, move all data and metadata from Oracle 12.1 to a database using 11.2.0.3.

To achieve this goal, you need to obtain a downward compatible dump file by setting the export (expdp) parameter VERSION to 11.2.0.3 (the target database release) as shown in the following command:

```
$ expdp fcomunoz/alvarez@pdborcl directory=datapump
  dumpfile=version_full_06192013.dmp full=y version=11.2.0.3
```

> The import utility (impdp) cannot read dump files created by a later release unless it was created using the VERSION parameter to set the release number of the target database.

This is the error message I got when trying to import data exported from a 12.1.0 database into an 11.2.0.3 database without using the VERSION parameter when executing the export operation:

```
Import: Release 11.2.0.3.0 - Production on Wed Jun 19 15:57:58 2013


Copyright (c) 1982, 2011, Oracle and/or its affiliates.  All rights
  reserved.


Connected to: Oracle Database 11g Enterprise Edition Release
  11.2.0.3.0 - 64bit Production
With the Partitioning, OLAP, Data Mining and Real Application Testing
  options
ORA-39001: invalid argument value
ORA-39000: bad dump file specification
ORA-39142: incompatible version number 4.1 in dump file
  "/u01/app/oracle/admin/dpdump/version_full_06192013.dmp"
```

Just keep in mind the following information when using export and import to move data between different database releases:

- If specifying a database release that is older than the current database release when using the VERSION parameter, you need to be aware that certain features that are exclusive to the current version of the source database may be unavailable.

- When executing an export operation using the VERSION parameter to identify a migration of data to an older release, the dump file generated will not contain any objects that the older database release does not support. Consequently, allowing it to be imported in the target database.

- Data Pump Import can always read any dump file created by older releases of the database.

- Data Pump Import cannot read a dump file created by a database release (source database) that is newer than the current database release unless the export operation was done using the VERSION parameter set to the same release as the target database.

- When operating across a network link, Data Pump requires that the source and target databases differ by no more than two versions, not taking into consideration the release numbers.

- A full-mode export of an Oracle 11g (11.2.0.3) database can specify the Data Pump VERSION=12 parameter when the target database is using Oracle 12c (12.1) or later.

Transporting a tablespace

You can use Data Pump to transport tablespaces between databases, or even transport a complete database. This method prior to the introduction of Oracle 12*c* was the faster way to migrate data; now in Oracle 12*c*, the faster way to migrate a complete Oracle Database is using Full Transportable Export/Import as detailed in *Chapter 3, What is new in 12c.*

The following list of steps summarizes the process of transporting a tablespace from one database to another:

1. Pick a self-contained set of tablespaces.

2. As we have seen in *Chapter 9, Understanding Data Pump,* we can use the TRANSPORT_SET CHECK procedure to verify if a tablespace is self-contained. For this scenario we will transport the tablespace EXAMPLE from a database 11.2.0.3 that contains the schema TESTx to our pluggable database pdborcl in 12.1.

3. Let's start checking if this tablespace is self-contained.

> Remember that you should have EXECUTE_CATALOG_ROLE granted to be able to execute the TRANSPORT_SET_CHECK procedure.

```
SQL>  EXECUTE DBMS_TTS.TRANSPORT_SET_CHECK('example', TRUE);

PL/SQL procedure successfully completed.

SQL> SELECT * FROM transport_set_violations;
no rows selected
```

As you can see, the query over the view TRANSPORT_SET_VIOLATIONS did not return any results; it means that the tablespace EXAMPLE is self-contained and consequently, we are able to continue.

4. At the source database, place the tablespace EXAMPLE in read-only mode and generate a transportable tablespace set.

> A transportable tablespace set (or transportable set) consists of a group of datafiles that are related to all tablespaces being transported and an export dump file that contains all the structural information (metadata only) for the set of tablespaces.

On the source, database executes shown as follows:

```
SQL> ALTER TABLESPACE example READ ONLY;


Tablespace altered.


$ expdp fcomunoz/alvarez dumpfile=transp_example_06192013.dmp
  directory=datapump transport_tablespaces=example logfile=
    transp_example_06192013.log
```

 You can also make use of a NETWORK_LINK to avoid the need for generation of an export operation; consequently, no need to generate a dump file.

 You can also verify if the tablespace(s) are self-contained at the same export operation by using the parameter TRANSPORT_FULL_CHECK=Y; if the tablespace(s) are not self-contained, the export operation will fail.

5. Copy the transportable tablespace set created (the export dump file and all datafiles associated with the tablespace EXAMPLE) to the target database using any file transfer method, for example, using SFTP on Linux.

 If the source platform's endian format is different from the target platform's endian format, you can use one of the following methods to convert the datafiles:

Use the GET_FILE or PUT_FILE procedure in the DBMS_FILE_TRANSFER package to transfer the datafiles. These procedures will convert the datafiles to the target platform's endian format automatically.

Use the RMAN CONVERT command to convert the datafiles to the target platform's endian format.

Remember that you can query the view V$TRANSPORTABLE_PLATFORM to check the endian format of each platform.

6. (Optional step) You can place the tablespace EXAMPLE back to read/write mode on the source database after step 3 is completed using the following command:

```
SQL> ALTER TABLESPACE example READ WRITE;


Tablespace altered.
```

7. Now at the target database, import the tablespace set.

First, we need to import the metadata exported as follows.

> If the schema in the exported tablespace does not exist on the target database, you should create it before executing the following import, or you can use the REMAP_SCHEMA parameter to migrate the ownership to an existing schema.

```
SQL> CREATE USER testx IDENTIFIED BY alvarez;


User created.


SQL> GRANT CREATE SESSION, RESOURCE TO testx;


Grant succeeded.


$ impdp fcomunoz/alvarez@pdborcl
  dumpfile=transp_example_06192013.dmp directory=datapump
    transport_datafiles='/u01/app/oracle/oradata/pdborcl/ts_
example_01.dbf'
```

> If transporting multiple datafiles, separate them on the TRANSPORT_DATAFILES parameter by using comma, for example:
> TRANSPORT_DATAFILES='/u01/app/oracle/oradata/pdborcl/ts_example_01.dbf', '/u01/app/oracle/oradata/pdborcl/ts_example_02.dbf'

After the import operation is completed, all tablespaces imported will remain in the read-only mode as they were in the source database when exported.

8. Place the imported tablespace in read and write mode if required using the following command:

```
SQL> ALTER TABLESPACE example READ WRITE;
```

```
Tablespace altered.
```

Oracle Database 12c Release 1 comes with the possibility to use backup sets and image copies to transport data between platforms.

The new clause ALLOW INCONSISTENT in a BACKUP or CONVERT command creates a cross-platform inconsistent backup of one or more tablespaces. You can create an inconsistent backup of the tablespace when the tablespace is still in read/write mode.

The first inconsistent backup is a level 0 incremental backup. Then, you can create multiple cross-platform level 1 incremental backups. The final cross-platform incremental backup must be a consistent backup that requires to bring the tablespace in read-only mode.

Data Pump flashback

When exporting data we can also use Data Pump with flashback to make a point-in-time export by using the parameter FLASHBACK_TIME assigning a timestamp to it, or FLASHBACK_SCN to assign a specific SCN, if using this option, the database will look for the SCN that most closely matches the specified time, and this SCN will be used to enable the Flashback utility and the export operation will be performed with the data that is consistent up to this SCN. In this scenario, we will export the data of the table EMPLOYEE from the schema TEST up to 30 minutes ago shown as follows:

```
$ expdp directory=datapump dumpfile=employee_flashback_06192013.dmp
flashback_time="to_timestamp('19-06-2013 14:30:00', 'dd-mm-yyyy
  hh24:mi:ss')"
```

Some restrictions to this kind of operation are:

- FLASHBACK_TIME and FLASHBACK_SCN are mutually exclusive.

- The FLASHBACK_TIME parameter pertains only to the flashback query capability of Oracle Database. It is not applicable to Flashback Database, Flashback Drop, or Flashback Data Archive.

- When using it in an impdp operation, it needs to be used in conjunction with the NETWORK_LINK parameter.

- Not possible to use a point-in-time prior to a DDL operation that changed the structure of a table.

You could make use of the following SQL to know the proper SCN of a specific point-in-time:

```
SELECT TIMESTAMP_TO_SCN(TO_
DATE('2013-07-07:16:04:45','YYYY-MM-
DD:HH24:MI:SS')) FROM v$database;
```

Of course, remember to change the date and time used in the SQL for the correct point-in-time you need.

Monitoring Data Pump job status

As we have seen earlier, the Data Pump export and import client utilities can be easily attached to a job that is currently running or stopped in either logging mode or interactive-command mode.

In the logging mode, a real-time detailed status about the job is automatically displayed during the execution of the job. The information displayed can include all or something of the following: job and parameter descriptions, an estimate of the amount of data to be processed, a description of the current operation or item being processed, the files used during the job, any errors encountered, and the final job state (Stopped or Completed).

In interactive-command mode, the job status can be displayed only by request by using the STATUS command. The information displayed can include the job description and state, a description of the current operation or item being processed, files being written, and a cumulative status of the job.

Another possible alternative that we have available to determine a job status or to get other information about any Data Pump job would be to query one of the following views:

- DBA_DATAPUMP_JOBS: All active Data Pump jobs and the state of each job
- USER_DATAPUMP_JOBS: Summary of the user's active Data Pump jobs
- DBA_DATAPUMP_SESSIONS: All active user sessions that are attached to a Data Pump job
- V$SESSION_LONGOPS: Shows all progress on each active Data Pump job, where the progress is indicated in an estimation of megabytes of table data transferred

The use of the COMPRESSION, ENCRYPTION, ENCRYPTION_ ALGORITHM, ENCRYPTION_MODE, ENCRYPTION_PASSWORD, QUERY, and REMAP_DATA parameters will not be reflected in the determination of the estimate values.

The following V$SESSION_LONGOPS columns are relevant to a Data Pump job:

- USERNAME: The job owner
- OPNAME: The job name
- TARGET_DESC: The job operation
- SOFAR: Megabytes transferred so far during the job
- TOTALWORK: Estimated number of megabytes in the job
- UNITS: Megabytes (MB)
- MESSAGE: A formatted status message of the form:

  ```
  job_name: operation_name: nnn out of mmm MB done
  ```

You can also use the parameter METRICS=YES when executing an export or import operation, and then the number of objects and the elapsed time will be recorded in the Data Pump log file.

Some performance tuning tips

I would like to finish this chapter talking very briefly about how you can improve the performance of your export and import operations. My recommendations are:

- Always exclude statistics:
    - Exporting and importing statistics were very slow since the introduction of Data Pump (10.1)
    - Exclude from export when possible or if included in the export; exclude them in the import operation
    - Regenerate the statistics after the import operation is completed

- Use Parallelism (requires Enterprise Edition and extra license for this option):
    - ° Use as many resources available to improve Data Pump performance when loading or unloading data
    - ° Remember it can be changed dynamically any time you need using the interactive-command mode; make parallel higher during no-peak times and lower when on peak time
    - ° Never forget to use the wildcard for dump file generation (%U) when using parallelism

- Use Transportable Tablespaces or Full Transportable Export/Import (as we have seen in *Chapter 3, What is New in 12c*):
    - ° Remember that this is the fastest way to move data across databases and platforms
    - ° If not possible, think to use Network mode import

Summary

In this hands-on chapter, we have learned a lot about what we can do when using Data Pump, and how to monitor and tune it. Always remember, Data Pump is your good friend and you will be amazed with all you can do with it to make your life as a DBA easier and productive.

In our next chapter, we will talk about OEM12*c* and SQL Developer and see how to use them for backup and recovery operations.

11
OEM12c and SQL Developer

Many Oracle DBAs are still using traditional methods such as UNIX scripts and crontab to execute a scheduled backup and recovery operation that uses **RMAN** or Data Pump. Most of these operations can also be easily achieved by using Oracle Enterprise Manager 12c (OEM12c R3) Cloud Control. This is a very comprehensive tool capable of managing a whole data center and contains the RMAN and Data Pump GUI console; and in some cases by using the SQL Developer DBA Navigator GUI interface for RMAN and Data Pump that was introduced in version 3.1 of this product. The use of these two products will help you to improve productivity, reduce maintenance costs, achieve centralized management — and what is even more important — help you to reduce any probability of human errors during backup and recovery operations. But, OEM12c and SQL Developer are not only useful for scheduling jobs; they are much more flexible and powerful as we will see in the later stages of this chapter.

In this chapter, we will discuss and understand the following topics:

- Configuring our backup and recovery settings (including catalog settings) in OEM12c
- Scheduling backups in OEM12c
- Creating restore points in OEM12c
- Understanding database Export/Import operations in OEM12c
- Getting familiar with SQL Developer 3.2

Configuring backup, recovery, and catalog settings

In this section, we will learn about how to setup our database backup, recovery, and catalog settings using OEM12c. We will cover only disk backups, as going into the detail of tape backups is outside the scope of this book.

Backup settings

To adjust the database backup settings, you will need to use the following steps:

1. Firstly, navigate to **Availability | Backup & Recovery**, and then click on **Backup Settings** on the **OEM12c Container Database** main menu as shown in the following screenshot:

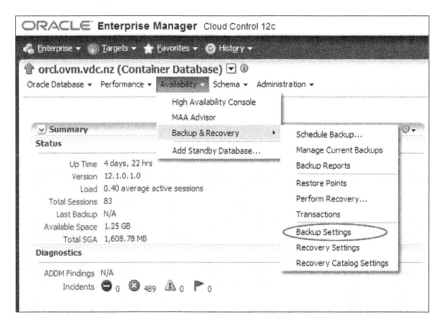

2. In the **Default Settings** page you can easily see and change any **Device**, **Backup Set** or **Policy** related settings. Let's start talking about the **Device** settings. The first section of this page will be the **Disk Settings**, and here you can easily set the following values:

   ○ **Parallelism**: Concurrent streams to disk drivers

   ○ **Disk Backup Location**: The fast recovery area is by default location for disk backups; here you can enter a new disk location to overwrite the previous location

° **Disk Backup Type**: Basically, you can choose between three available options: **Backup Set**, **Compressed Backup Set**, and **Image Copy**

After entering all disk settings, you can test if everything is well set by clicking on the **Test Disk Backup** option.

 You need to have entered the host credentials on the bottom of the page to allow you to test it.

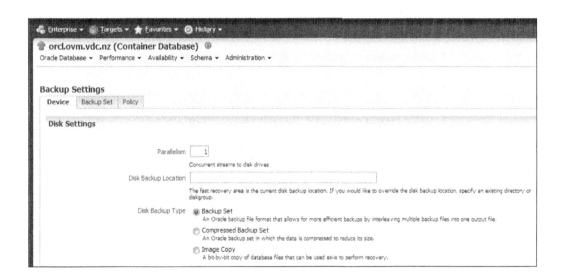

3. Now it's time to go over the tape settings; this step is very similar to the previous one, and if you are not doing tape backups you can skip this section.

4. The **Oracle Secure Backup Domain** section is an optional one, and you should only configure it if using Oracle Secure Backup. In this book we will skip it because it is out of the scope of this book.

5. The last two remaining sections of the **Device** settings are **Media Management Settings** and **Host Credentials**. Please enter the host credentials for the server running the target database.

6. Now that we are ready with all device settings, it's time to move on and select the next tab (**Backup Set**) to continue with all configurations. The important information you need to know about backup set settings are:

 For this scenario we will keep this section set as **DEFAULT**.

- **Maximum Backup Piece (File) Size**: Enter the delimitation value for each backup piece; the value can use KB, MB, or even GB sizes. Only enter an amount here if you really want to restrict the backup pieces' size, if not just leave it blank.

- **Compression Algorithm**: Here you can specify the compression algorithm that will be used for the disk and tape compressed backup sets. Just remember that while selecting an **Algorithm Name**, only the **BASIC** option is free of charge; if you want to select **LOW**, **MEDIUM**, or **HIGH**, you will need to have the Advanced Compression Option licensed.

- **Optimized For Load**: It controls the pre-compression process by ensuring that RMAN optimizes the CPU usage and avoids pre-compression block processing. If not selected, RMAN uses additional CPU resources to perform pre-compression block processing.

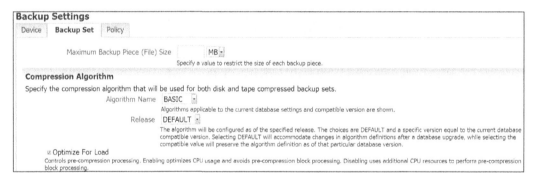

7. Now it's time to move to the last tab (**Policy**) and take a closer look at all options available here. The first section will ask us about the **Backup Policy**, and the options are:

- ◦ **Automatic Backup of control file and SPFILE**: If selected, an automatic backup of our database control file and SPILE will be generated when executing a backup operation or a database structural change happens. When selecting this option, you need to enter an auto backup disk location, only if you want to generate these backups in a different location other than your database fast recovery area location.

- ◦ **Optimize whole database backups**: This option, if selected, will optimize whole backups by skipping unchanged files such as read-only and offline datafiles that have been already backed up.

- ◦ **Enable block change tracking**: By selecting this option, block change tracking will be used to increase the performance of any incremental backup done. If no location and filename is specified, an Oracle managed file will be automatically created for you.

Device	Backup Set	**Policy**

Backup Policy

☐ Automatically backup the control file and server parameter file (SPFILE) with every backup and database structural change

Autobackup Disk Location

An existing directory or diskgroup name where the control file and server parameter file will be backed up. If you do not specify a location, the files will be backed up to the fast recovery area location.

☐ Optimize the whole database backup by skipping unchanged files such as read-only and offline datafiles that have been backed up

☐ Enable block change tracking for faster incremental backups

Block Change Tracking File

Specify a location and file, otherwise an Oracle managed file will be created in the database area.

8. The next section will allow you to specify any tablespace you want to exclude while executing a whole database backup; if a tablespace is included here, you will only be able to generate a backup of it by using the commands `BACKUP TABLESPACE` and `BACKUP DATABASE NOEXCLUDE`.

9. The next step will be to set the retention policy of our backups. The options available here are (and these options are mutually exclusive):

- ◦ **Retain all backups**: When clicking on this option, you will be responsible for manually deleting any backup of your database to release disk space

- ◦ **Specific number of days**: Here you can specify the number of days to retain your backups

- ∘ **Redundancy**: Here you can specify the number of full backups for each datafile that should be retained

---

Tablespaces Excluded From Whole Database Backup

Add the tablespaces you want to exclude from a whole database backup.

Add

Select	Container	Tablespace Name	Tablespace Number	Status	Contents
	No Items Selected				

☑ **TIP** These tablespaces can be backed up separately using tablespace backup.

Retention Policy

○ Retain All Backups

   You must manually delete any backups

○ Retain backups that are necessary for a recovery to any time within the specified number of days (point-in-time recovery)

      Days   31

                Recovery Window

⦿ Retain at least the specified number of full backups for each datafile

      Backups   1

                Redundancy

---

10. The last section in this **Policy** tab is the **Archived Redo Log Deletion Policy** section. Here you can choose between two available options; they are:

- ∘ **None**: No deletion policy will be used for archived redo logfiles.

- ∘ **After been backed up for a specific number of times**: When this option is selected, the number entered will specify when an archived redo logfile can be deleted. It means if we enter 5, an archived redo logfile will only be deleted after been backed up 5 times.

Archived Redo Log Deletion Policy

Specify the deletion policy for archived redo log files. The archived redo log files will be eligible for deletion if the fast recovery area becomes full.

⦿ None

   If a fast recovery area is set, archived redo log files that have been backed up to a tertiary device and are obsolete based on the retention policy will be deleted.

○ Delete archived redo log files after they have been backed up the specified number of times

      Backups   1

If you have data guard, you will see the following three options:

- None
- Delete archived redo logfiles:
    - After they have been applied to all standby databases
    - After they have been shipped to all standby databases
- Delete archived redo logfiles after they have been backed up the specified number of times

Now that we finished with all backup settings, you can click on **OK** to save them.

Recovery settings

Just as we did with the backup settings, we need to setup all recovery settings for our database by performing the following steps:

1. Firstly, navigate to **Availability | Backup & Recovery** and then click on **Recovery Settings** in the **OEM12c Container Database** main menu.

2. Enter a desired mean-time to recover (MTTR) value that will be used to set the database FAST_START_MTTR_TARGET initialization parameter. If a nonzero value is specified, it will control the amount of time the database will take to perform a crash recovery and it will be done by maintaining the speed of the database checkpoints. The value entered can be specified to minutes or seconds.

Recovery Settings

Show SQL Revert Apply

Instance Recovery

The fast-start checkpointing feature is enabled by specifying a non-zero desired mean-time to recover (MTTR) value, which will be used to set the FAST_START_MTTR_TARGET initialization parameter. This parameter controls the amount of time the database takes to perform crash recovery for a single instance. When fast-start checkpointing is enabled, Oracle automatically maintains the speed of checkpointing so that the requested MTTR is achieved. Setting the value to 0 will disable this functionality.

Current Estimated Mean Time To Recover (seconds) 15

Desired Mean Time To Recover 0   Minutes

---

3. The next step will be to specify our media recovery settings. Here you can easily specify whether the database will be running in ARCHIVELOG mode or note the archivelog files' name format and the location where it will be generated. Here you can also enable minimal supplemental logging for LogMiner.

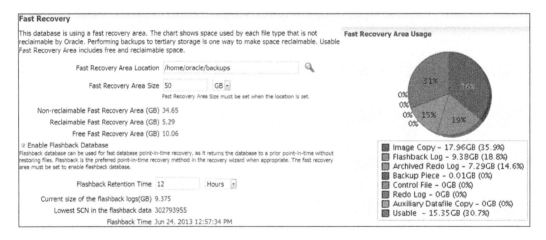

Media Recovery

The database is currently in ARCHIVELOG mode. In ARCHIVELOG mode, hot backups and recovery to the latest time are possible, but you must provide space for archived redo log files. If you change the database to ARCHIVELOG mode, you should perform a backup immediately. In NOARCHIVELOG mode, only cold backups are possible and data may be lost in the event of database corruption.

☑ ARCHIVELOG Mode*

Log Archive Filename Format* orcl_%s_%t_%r.arc

Number	Archived Redo Log Destination	Status	Type
1	USE_DB_RECOVERY_FILE_DEST	VALID	Local

Add Another Row

☑ **TIP** It is recommended that archived redo log files be written to multiple locations spread across the different disks.
☑ **TIP** You can specify up to 10 archived redo log destinations.

☑ Enable Minimal Supplemental Logging
Minimal supplemental logging logs the minimal amount of information needed for LogMiner (and any product building on LogMiner technology) to identify, group, and merge the redo operations associated with DML changes.

4. The last step here will be to set up your FRA, enable flash recovery database, and set up your flashback retention policy (time).

Fast Recovery

This database is using a fast recovery area. The chart shows space used by each file type that is not reclaimable by Oracle. Performing backups to tertiary storage is one way to make space reclaimable. Usable Fast Recovery Area includes free and reclaimable space.

Fast Recovery Area Usage

Fast Recovery Area Location /home/oracle/backups

Fast Recovery Area Size 50   GB

Fast Recovery Area Size must be set when the location is set.

Non-reclaimable Fast Recovery Area (GB) 34.65
Reclaimable Fast Recovery Area (GB) 5.29
Free Fast Recovery Area (GB) 10.06

☑ Enable Flashback Database
Flashback database can be used for fast database point-in-time recovery, as it returns the database to a prior point-in-time without restoring files. Flashback is the preferred point-in-time recovery method in the recovery wizard when appropriate. The fast recovery area must be set to enable flashback database.

Flashback Retention Time 12   Hours

Current size of the flashback logs(GB) 9.375
Lowest SCN in the flashback data 302793955
Flashback Time Jun 24, 2013 12:57:34 PM

- Image Copy – 17.96GB (35.9%)
- Flashback Log – 9.38GB (18.8%)
- Archived Redo Log – 7.29GB (14.6%)
- Backup Piece – 0.01GB (0%)
- Control File – 0GB (0%)
- Redo Log – 0GB (0%)
- Auxiliary Datafile Copy – 0GB (0%)
- Usable – 15.35GB (30.7%)

5. When finished, you can click on **Show SQL** if you want to see all SQL statements that will be executed to apply all changes done in the **Recovery Settings** page, or click on **Revert** if you want to cancel all changes and revert the information in the page as it was before the changes were made, or **Apply** to apply all changes made to the target database.

Catalog settings

As we have learned in *Chapter 7, RMAN Reporting and Catalog Management,* we can use our control file (default) as the main repository for our backup's information or use a RMAN Catalog Repository to manage this information. In the **OEM12c Catalog Settings** page we are able to do the following:

- Setup the retention period for backup information in the control file
- Register our database to an existing recovery catalog, or even create a new catalog in our target database

Now perform the following steps to configure the catalog settings:

1. Firstly, navigate to **Availability | Backup & Recovery,** and then click on **Recovery Catalog Settings** in the **OEM12c Container Database** main menu.
2. The **Recovery Catalog Settings** page has only two available options to choose as the RMAN metadata repository; they are:
   - **Use Control File**: This is the default and if you choose this option, you can specify the retention period in days that the control file will keep RMAN records
   - **Use Recovery Catalog**: If you choose this option, you can register the target database to an existing RMAN recovery catalog (by selecting a recovery catalog from a list of values) or even create a new recovery catalog in this target database or another one available

[As a best practice, I always suggest to create a catalog repository in its own database.]

Recovery Catalog Settings

The Recovery Manager (RMAN) repository is a collection of metadata about the target database that is used by backup and recovery operations. The information can be stored in the control file or in a recovery catalog - a schema in a separate database that can hold information for one or more databases.

If you select a recovery catalog for which this database is not registered, the database will automatically be registered when you click OK.

○ Use Control File

  Keep RMAN Records (days)   7

  Specify how long to keep RMAN records in the control file before they can be reused.

⦿ Use Recovery Catalog

                  Recovery Catalog   orcl.ovm.vdc.nz-system ▾

                  Obsolete recovery catalogs must be edited and their credentials updated before   Add Recovery Catalog
                  use.

      Host username and password is required if your database is not registered with the selected catalog.

---

3. If you choose the option **Add Recovery Catalog**, you can select any database target being managed by OEM12c or even specify a database that is not an OEM12c target to create the RMAN recovery catalog. Choose your selection and click on **Next**.

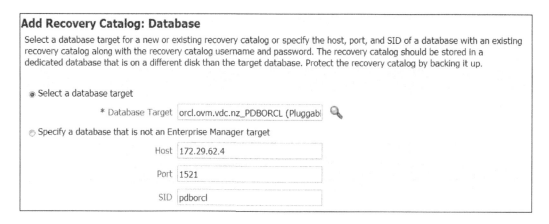

4. The next step will be to add the host and database credentials for the database target that you choose to create in the **Recovery Catalog** and click on **Next**.

5. Now is the time to enter the recovery catalog user credentials. This user should already exist in the target database. When ready please click on **Next**.

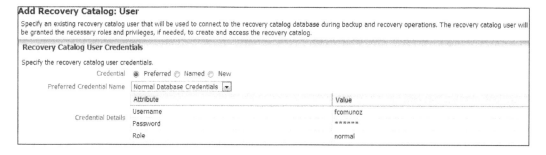

6. Review all the information entered, and click on **Finish** to create the **Recovery Catalog** configured.

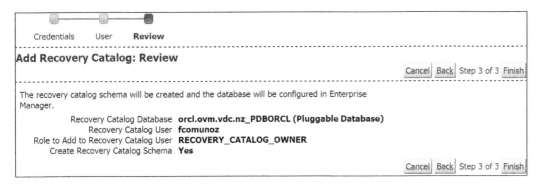

7. Then just click on **OK** in the **Recovery Catalog Settings** page to save all the information entered.

Scheduling an RMAN backup

OEM12*c* is a centralized management tool with its own repository that is able to monitor and manage target hosts by the deployment of an OEM12*c* agent on it. From this centralized console, you will be able to easily run or schedule any RMAN or even Data Pump operations without the need to manually connect to each target server in question to run it, saving you a lot of effort and time. It also monitors the jobs and generates an alert to warn you in case of any job failure. When using OEM12*c* to schedule a backup operation, you can choose between the two options available:

- Oracle-suggested backup
- Customized backup

Now let's take a closer look at how to schedule a backup using both the preceding options.

Using the Oracle-Suggested Backup strategy option

In this first scenario we will use OEM12*c* to schedule our daily backup of the pluggable database PDBORCL by using the Oracle-suggested backup strategy that gives us the following benefits:

- Provides an out-of-the-box backup strategy based on the backup destination
- Sets up the recovery window for backup management
- Schedules recurring and immediate backups
- Automates backup management

Now let's schedule an Oracle-suggested backup by performing the following steps:

1. In the **Container Database** console page, navigate to **Availability | Backup & Recovery | Schedule Backup**.

2. In the **Schedule Backup** page, enter the host credentials and when ready, click on **Schedule Oracle-Suggested Backup**.

Oracle-Suggested Backup

Schedule a backup using Oracle's automated backup strategy.

Schedule Oracle-Suggested Backup

This option will back up the entire database. The database will be backed up on daily and weekly intervals.

If the database is running in NOARCHIVELOG mode, the database will SHUTDOWN and will be placed in MOUNT mode when running this job.

3. In the Destination page, select the destination media where the backup will be generated. You have three options available: **Disk**, **Tape**, or **Both Disk and Tape**. For this example we will click on **Disk**, and then click on **Next**.

Chapter 11

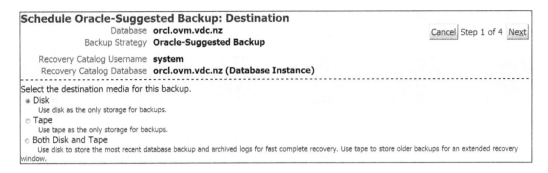

4. In the setup page, you can at first review the Oracle-suggested strategy of a full backup, followed by incremental backups. Here you can also make use of encryption. Please review the information on this page and click on **Next**.

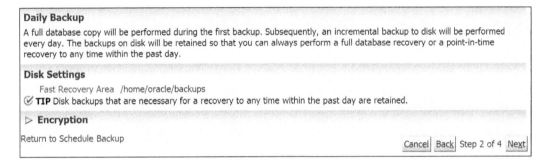

5. In the schedule page, enter the start date, time zone, and daily backup time information to allow the daily job to be created, and then click on **Next**.

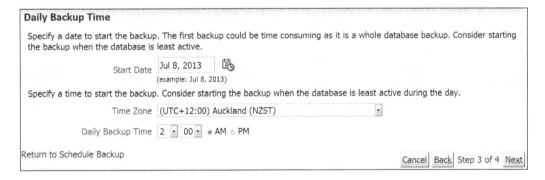

6. Review all the information entered and the RMAN script that will be executed in the target pluggable database and click on **Submit Job**.

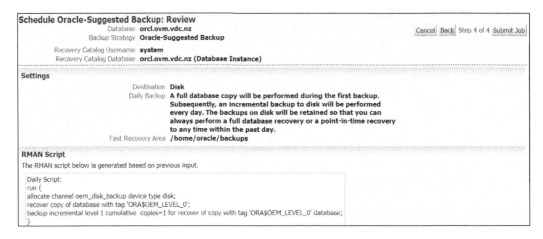

7. A pop-up window will appear saying that the job has been successfully submitted. You can now click on **OK** to finalize this process, or even click on **View Job** to view the status of the submitted job.

Using the Customized Backup option

In this scenario we will schedule our daily backup of the pluggable database PDBORCL by using the customized backup option that allows you to:

*   Specify the objects to be backed up
*   Choose disk or tape backup destinations
*   Overwrite the default backup settings
*   Schedule the backup to run once or periodically

Now let's schedule this backup by performing the following steps:

1. In the **Customized Backup** section, enter the host credentials and click on **Schedule Customized Backup**.

Customized Backup

Select the object(s) you want to back up.   Schedule Customized Backup

- ◉ Whole Database
- ○ Container Database Root
- ○ Pluggable Databases
- ○ Tablespaces
- ○ Datafiles
- ○ Archived Logs
- ○ All Recovery Files on Disk
    Includes all archived logs and disk backups that
  are not already backed up to tape.

Here you can schedule backups at the following levels: **Whole Database**, **Container Database Root**, **Pluggable Databases**, **Tablespaces**, **Datafiles**, **Archived Logs**, and **All Recovery Files on Disk**. For this scenario, we will only execute a Whole Database backup.

The options page allows you to perform the following things:

- ° Selecting the backup type, where you can choose between a full backup and an incremental backup

- ° Selecting the backup mode, where you can choose to perform an online backup or even an offline backup

- ° Choose to back up all archived log on disk and even delete all archived logs from the disk after they are successfully backed up

- ° Delete obsolete backups

- ° Use proxy copy supported by media management software for backups

- ° Specify the maximum number of files per backup set
- ° Specify the section size of a backup (accepts KB/MB/GB)
- ° Use Oracle Encryption Wallet, a user supplied password, or even both options to protect any sensitive data in the backup
- ° Select and enter the options as per your requirements and click on **Next**

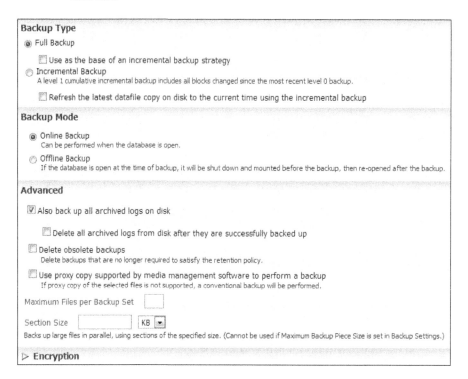

2. In the settings page, select the destination media for the backup. It can be **Disk** or **Tape**, and click on **Next** when ready to proceed.

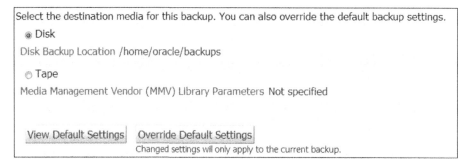

In this page you can also view the default backup settings and overwrite them, if necessary, only for this backup job. This means that all changes done in the settings here will not be saved and will only be used for this specific job.

3. In the schedule page, enter the job name and description of it (or leave the default suggested) and select the job type (**One Time (Immediately)**, **One Time (Later)**, or **Repeating**) and click on **Next**. For this example we are selecting the **One Time (Immediately)** option.

4. Review all options including the RMAN script generated and if all looks ok, click on **Submit Job**.

Restore points

A restore point is a user-defined name for a point-in-time that allows you to rewind your data back in time to solve any problem caused by user errors or data corruption to a specific point-in-time (in this case, a restore point previously created). Oracle has two types of restore points:

- **Normal Restore Point**: Allows the creation of a restore point to a specific SCN, current time, or any point-in-time (that already passed). This type of restore point ages out the control file after it is beyond the point of recoverability.

- **Guaranteed Restored Point**: This type of restore point ensures that flashback can be used to rewind the database to the time of the restore point. It requires the database to have an FRA, be in ARCHIVELOG mode, and the compatibility mode should be 10.2 or greater.

We can easily see all restore points created in our database and create a new one if necessary by navigating in the database console menu to **Availability]** | **Backup & Recovery** | **Restore Points**.

The first page you will see will be the **Manage Restore Points** page that shows us all restore points available in our database and also allows us to create any new restore point. Let's click on **Create** to create a restore point.

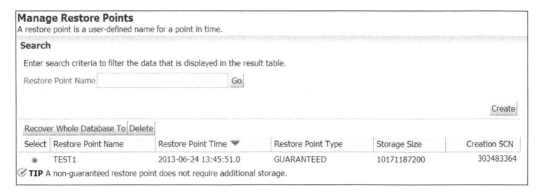

Point-in-time recovery and flashbacks are the data protection features of Oracle that let you rewind your data back to a restore point or a specified time/SCN.

Now in the **Create Restore Point** page, we will need to first enter the restore point name and then select the restore point type we want to create; it can be:

- Normal Restore Point
- Guarantee Restore Point

For this example, I will enter Test2 in the **Restore Point name** field, and click on the **Normal Restore Point** type and **Current Time** and then click on **OK**.

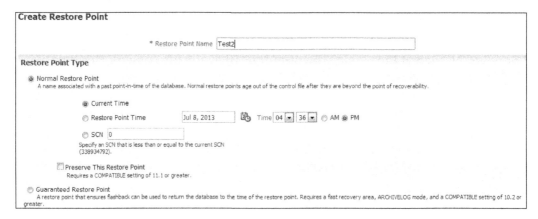

Next in the **Confirmation** page, we will enter the host credentials and click on **Yes** to have the restore point created.

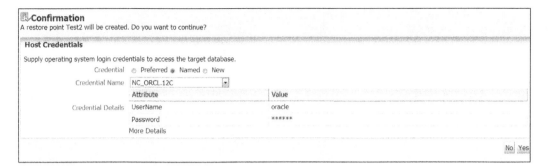

Export/Import with OEM12c

OEM12*c* is also the GUI tool for Data Pump; here we can easily perform the following operations with Data Pump:

- Transport tablespaces
- Export to an export file (dump file)
- Import from an export file (dump file)
- Import from a database (using database link)
- Load data from user files (external tables)
- View export and import jobs

As you can see, OEM12*c* allows us to basically do almost all of the most important operations available with Data Pump. For this chapter, we will only take a closer look at how to execute an export operation via OEM12*c* and how to view its job execution.

Executing an export operation

To perform an export via OEM12*c*, firstly we will need to navigate in the database console (for this example, we will use the pluggable database `pdborcl`) main menu to **Schema** | **Database Export/Import** | **Export** to export files.

In the export page, firstly we will need to select the type of export operation; in other words, what we want to be included in the export. The options are:

- **Database**: Exports the whole database.
- **Schemas**: Allows you to select one or more schemas to be included in the export operation.
- **Tables**: Allows you to select one or more table from a selected schema to be exported.
- **Tablespace**: Allows you to select one or more tablespaces. In this option, only tables in the tablespaces will be exported.

In this example, we will enter our host credentials, click on the option **Database**, and click on **Continue**.

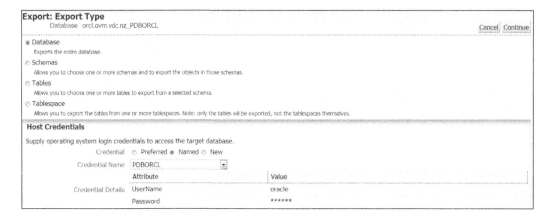

In the options page, we can enter the following (these are optional):

- 1 for the maximum number of threads in export job; remember that parallelism option is only available within the Oracle Database Enterprise Edition (EE) and needs to be licensed as an extra option. If not licensed or not using EE, you should leave this value as 1.
- Blocks for estimated disk space (here you can also click on **Estimate Disk Space Now** to calculate the estimated space that will be used by the export operation without performing the export operation).
- We will select the **Generate Log File** option and use the directory object DATA_PUMP_DIR to generate the dump file and the logfile EXPDAT.LOG.

For this example, we will not make use of the **Advanced Options** and we will click on **Next** to continue.

If **Advanced Option** is selected, it will allow you to:

- Select the content you want to export from the source database (all/data only/metadata only) and it includes all objects, only objects specified, or only objects that are not excluded

- Use Flashback to export a read-consistent view of the data to a specific SCN or point-in-time

- Specify a SELECT statement predicate clause to be applied to the tables being exported

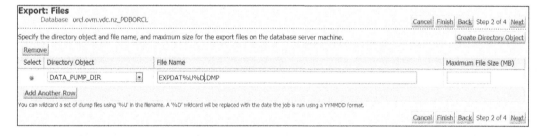

In the **Files** page, we will select **DATA_PUMP_DIR** as the directory object to be used to create the dump file EXPDP%U%D.DMP file and click on **Next**. I'm using the wildcard %D in the dump file name to include the date of the job (YY/MM/DD) on it to make it easier to be identified later. Here you can also add a maximum file size for the dump files if necessary (MB).

Export: Files
Database orcl.ovm.vdc.nz_PDBORCL   Cancel Finish Back Step 2 of 4 Next

Specify the directory object and file name, and maximum size for the export files on the database server machine.   Create Directory Object

Remove

Select	Directory Object	File Name	Maximum File Size (MB)
⦿	DATA_PUMP_DIR	EXPDAT%U%D.DMP	

Add Another Row

You can wildcard a set of dump files using '%U' in the filename. A '%D' wildcard will be replaced with the date the job is run using a YYMMDD format.

Cancel Finish Back Step 2 of 4 Next

In the **Job Schedule** page, we will enter the name of the job to be DATAPUMPTEST and schedule it to be executed immediately (one time only) and click on **Next**. In this page, you can also choose to execute the job later at a specific date and time and allow it to be executed periodically.

Now it's time to look at the **Review** page; here we will review the information entered and click on **Submit Job**. You can also click on **Show PL/SQL** to see the PL/SQL that will be executed by the database.

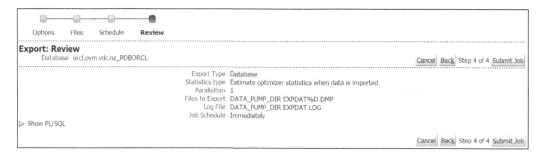

> When executing Data Pump with OEM12c, always ensure that the `STREAMS_POOL_SIZE` initialization parameter is not set to 0. If it is set to 0, it could give you an error at OEM12c saying that it was unable to allocate memory for the streams pool.

Monitoring the job

We can easily monitor the job execution of our just launched DATAPUMPTEST job by navigating to **Schema** | **Database Export/Import** | **View Export & Import Jobs** in the PDBORCL database console.

It will automatically show us all Data Pump jobs in the database and its status, as you can see in the following screenshot, our **DATAPUMPTEST** job has a status of **EXECUTING**.

And if we need more details of the job, all we will need to do will be to click on the name of the job we want more details, and that's it.

This page will only show you **EXECUTING** and **STOPPED** jobs. When a Data Pump job is completed, it will disappear from this page.

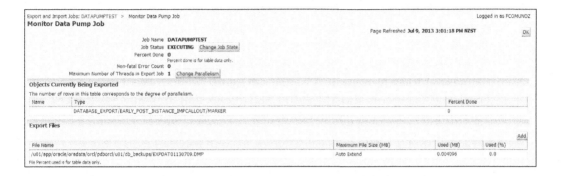

SQL developer 3.2

The SQL Developer DBA Navigator GUI interface for RMAN and Data Pump is a very flexible option available for performing backup and recovery operations, and incredibly many DBAs do not have idea that it exists. In this section, we will take a closer look at some of the options available with this tool.

RMAN operations

The DBA Navigator allows us to have the following RMAN options available:

- **Backup Jobs**: We can view backup jobs that have been previously executed. It also permits us to create and run a new backup job from here; for example, using the right-click you can execute the following actions: Backup operations such as tablespaces backup, datafiles backup, archivelog backup, and recovery files backup, Restore/Recovery operations such as recover a whole database, restore a whole database, recover a tablespace, restore a tablespace, recover datafiles, restore datafiles, block recovery, restore archived logs, and Flashback database, create disk backups, create tape backups, and create disk/tape backups.

- **Backup Sets**: Shows backup sets that have been created by previous backup jobs and are available for a recovery operation. If using right-click here, you will be able to perform the following actions: **Catalog Recovery Area**, **Crosscheck All**, **Delete all obsolete**, and **Delete all Expired**.

- **Image Copies**: Shows image copies made by previous backup jobs and are available for a recovery operation. If using right-click here, you will be able to perform the same actions previously mentioned for **Backup Sets**.

- **RMAN Settings**: Displays current RMAN settings stored in the database server for Backup and Recovery. If using right-click here, you will be able to edit: disk devices settings, tape devices settings, compression algorithm settings, tape backup set settings, backup policies, log deletion policies, and switch archived log mode and flashback database using RMAN.

- **Scheduled RMAN Actions**: Displays all DBMS_SCHEDULER jobs that have been used to execute RMAN scripts and allows you to review the logfiles. This option is only available for database 11.1 and higher.

Now let's play with this GUI tool and, for start, we will proceed to execute a whole backup of our pluggable database PDBORCL. We will be able to do this job by navigating to **Backup Jobs** | **Action** | **Custom Backups** | **Create Custom Whole Database Backup** from the **Backup Jobs** option, as shown in the following screenshot:

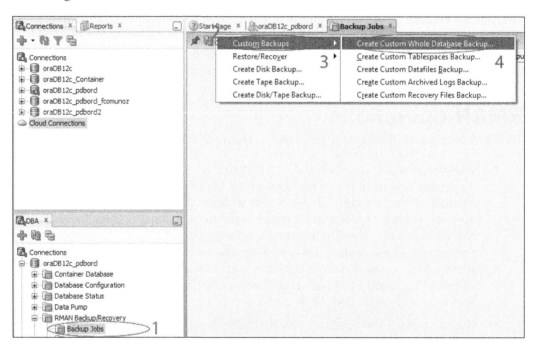

When the **Create Whole Database Backup** page appears, we need to first check if all the information in the tabs **Properties and Options**, **Compression**, **Disk**, **Backup Set**, and **Policy** are correct. If all looks good, click on **Apply** to execute it. When the job is completed, you will see a window saying that the RMAN script was successfully processed and recommends you to see the latest action job log for processing details.

Data Pump operations

The DBA Navigator allows us to have the following Data Pump options available:

- **Export Jobs**: Shows any Data Pump Export job that is currently running or stopped; it also allows us to create a new Data Pump Export job from here by using the right-click and selecting **Data Pump Export Wizard**
- **Import Jobs**: Shows any Data Pump Import job that is currently running or stopped; it also allows us to create a new Data Pump Import job from here by using the right-click and selecting **Data Pump Import Wizard**

Summary

In this chapter, we have learned a hands-on format on how to use some important features for backup and recovery using OEM12*c* and SQL Developer. I recommend you to take your time and explore these two GUI interfaces in detail to discover the complete potential that they have to simplify your daily activities, making your life incredibly easy.

Following this chapter, there is an appendix that has various scenarios and examples so that you can learn the concept that we provide in this book. Remember that you can download all scripts and examples in this book from the Packt Publishing website (http://www.packtpub.com).

Scenarios and Examples – A Hands-on Lab

The main idea of this hands-on appendix is to allow you to practice some of the scenarios you saw in this book (step-by-step) and learn by practice. If you have any doubt about a command of what it will be doing, for more information please refer to the corresponding chapter in this book for the scenario.

To be able to execute the exercises in this appendix, you should first create a test environment performing the following steps:

1. Download the Oracle VirtualBox (free virtualization tool) at
   `https://www.virtualbox.org/wiki/Downloads`.

2. Download Oracle Enterprise Linux 6.4 (`https://edelivery.oracle.com/linux`) and Oracle 12*c* database for Linux at `http://www.oracle.com/technetwork/database/enterprise-edition/downloads/database12c-linux-download-1959253.html`.

> You do not need to use explicitly Linux to be able to run this lab. You can also use Solaris (SPARK and x86) or even Windows 64 bits. The use of VirtualBox with Linux is just a suggestion.

3. Follow the instructions in my blog to do the installation of the products you downloaded (`http://oraclenz.org/?p=3069`).

4. Create the following directories for the examples:

   ```
   $ mkdir /data/pdborcl
   $ mkdir /data/pdborcl/backups
   $ mkdir /data/pdborcl/backups/controlfile
   ```

```
$ mkdir /data/pdborcl/backups/archivelogs

$ mkdir /data/orcl/fast_recovery_area

$ mkdir /data/orcl/redologs

$ chown -R oracle:oinstall /data/pdborcl

$ chown -R oracle:oinstall /data/orcl
```

5. Create a test user and tablespace test.

 Because this is an Oracle 12*c* book, all scenarios will be for Oracle 12*c* in this appendix.

```
$ sqlplus / as sysdba

SQL> ALTER SESSION SET CONTAINER=pdborcl;

SQL> CREATE TABLESPACE test DATAFILE '/data/pdborcl
  /test_01_tbs.dbf' SIZE 100m;

SQL> CREATE USER test IDENTIFIED BY test DEFAULT TABLESPACE
  test QUOTA UNLIMITED ON test;

SQL> GRANT connect, resource TO test;
```

6. Create a table employee and load data on the schema test using the following command:

```
SQL> CREATE TABLE TEST.EMPLOYEE
( EMP_ID    NUMBER(10) NOT NULL,
  EMP_NAME VARCHAR2(30),
  EMP_SSN  VARCHAR2(9),
  EMP_DOB  DATE
);


SQL> INSERT INTO test.employee VALUES (101,'Francisco
  Munoz',123456789,'30-JUN-73');


SQL> INSERT INTO test.employee VALUES (102,'Gonzalo
  Munoz',234567890,'02-OCT-96');


SQL> INSERT INTO test.employee VALUES (103,'Evelyn
  Aghemio',659812831,'02-OCT-79');


SQL> COMMIT;
```

Now that you are all set, please perform the following hands-on exercises.

 Explanation of the examples is out of the scope of this appendix. These are only practical examples to be executed by the reader to understand how each one works.

Configuring the database

In this section we will configure our database to allow us to run all the scenarios in this appendix.

Making sure an spfile is used to start the database

Log on to the database as `sysdba` and verify if an `spfile` is used:

```
SQL> CONNECT sys AS sysdba
SQL> SHOW PARAMETER spfile;
```

```
NAME     TYPE         VALUE
------   -----------  -----------------------------------------
spfile   string       /u01/app/oracle/conf/orcl/spfileorcl.ora
```

If an `spfile` is used, a value is returned with the `spfile` location. If the `spfile` is not used, the string is empty. In that case, carry out the following command in order to start the database with the `spfile`:

```
SQL> CREATE spfile FROM pfile;
SQL> STARTUP FORCE;
```

Placing the database in the archivelog mode and activating Flashback

In order to make hot backups, the database needs to be in the archivelog mode.

Connect to your database and set the following parameters:

 Firstly, please be sure that paths used in this demo exist in your environment; if not, you can change it for existing paths in your machine.

```
SQL> ALTER SYSTEM SET db_recovery_file_dest_size=2G;
SQL> ALTER SYSTEM SET db_recovery_file_dest
  ='/data/orcl/fast_recovery_area';
SQL> ALTER SYSTEM SET  log_archive_dest_1
  ='LOCATION=/data/pdborcl/backups/archivelogs;
SQL> ALTER SYSTEM SET log_archive_dest_10
  ='LOCATION=USE_DB_RECOVERY_FILE_DEST';
SQL> ALTER SYSTEM SET log_archive_format="orcl_%s_%t_%r.arc"
  SCOPE=spfile;
SQL> ALTER SYSTEM SET db_flashback_retention_target=720 SCOPE=spfile;
SQL> SHUTDOWN IMMEDIATE
SQL> STARTUP MOUNT
SQL> ALTER DATABASE ARCHIVELOG;
SQL> ALTER DATABASE FLASHBACK ON;
SQL> ALTER DATABASE OPEN;
```

Creating a new redo log group and associated files

As I have mentioned in *Chapter 1, Understanding the Basics of Backup and Recovery*, of this book, each group of redo log files needs to have at least two members in it; we will now create a new redo log group with two members in it.

Firstly, we will check the redo log groups and logfiles that already exist in the database. Have a look at the following command:

```
SQL> SET LINESIZE 200
SQL> SET PAGESIZE 200
SQL> COLUMN member FORMAT a50
SQL> COLUMN bytes FORMAT 999,999,999
SQL> SELECT group#, sequence#, bytes, members FROM v$log;
SQL> SELECT group#, member FROM v$logfile;
SQL> ALTER DATABASE ADD LOGFILE GROUP 4 '/data/orcl/redologs
/redo_04a.rdo' SIZE 50m;
SQL> ALTER DATABASE ADD LOGFILE MEMBER'/data/orcl/redologs
/redo_04b.rdo' TO GROUP 4;
```

Configuring RMAN

Now is the time to configure our RMAN environment to allow us to run all RMAN scenarios.

Creating the target DB RMAN backup account

Have a look at the following command:

```
SQL> CREATE USER backup_admin IDENTIFIED BY bckpwd DEFAULT TABLESPACE
  users;


SQL> GRANT sysbackup TO backup_admin;


$ rman target=backup_admin/bckpwd@pdborcl
```

Configure RMAN using the configure command

Have a look at the following command:

```
RMAN> CONFIGURE DEVICE TYPE DISK BACKUP TYPE TO COMPRESSED BACKUSET;

RMAN> CONFIGURE CHANNEL 1 DEVICE TYPE DISK FORMAL
  '/data/pdborcl/backups /bck_orcl_%U';

RMAN> CONFIGURE CHANNEL 1 DEVICE TYPE DISK MAXPIECESIZE 200m
  MAXOPENFILES 8 RATE 150m;

RMAN> CONFIGURE BACKUP OPTIMIZATION ON;

RMAN> CONFIGURE CONTROLFILE AUTOBACKUP ON;

RMAN> CONFIGURE CONROLFILE AUTOBACKUP FORMAT FOR DEVICE TYPE DISK TO
  '/data/pdborcl/backups/controlfile/ctl_orcl_%F';

RMAN> CONFIGURE RETENTION POLICY TO RECOVERY WINDOW OF 1 DAYS;

RMAN> CONFIGURE ARCHIVELOG DELETION POLICY TO BACKED UP 1 TIMES TO
  DISK;
```

Backup database

Have a look at the following command:

```
RMAN> BACKUP DATABASE PLUS ARCHIVELOG;
```

Checking and deleting obsolete backups

Have a look at the following command:

```
RMAN> REPORT OBSOLETE;

RMAN> DELETE OBSOLETE;
```

Creating RMAN catalog user

Have a look at the following command:

```
SQL> CREATE TABLESPACE catalog_tbs DATAFILE '/data/pdborcl
  /catalog_01_tbs.dbf' SIZE 100m;

SQL> CREATE USER catalog_bck IDENTIFIED BY rmancatalog DEFAULT
  TABLESPACE catalog_tbs QUOTA UNLIMITED ON catalog_tbs;

SQL> GRANT connect, resource, recovery_catalog_owner TO catalog_bck;
```

Creating recovery catalog

Have a look at the following command:

```
$ rman target / catalog=catalog_bck/rmancatalog@pdborcl


RMAN> CREATE CATALOG tablespace catalog_tbs;
```

Register your DB in the recovery catalog

Have a look at the following command:

```
$ rman target=backup_admin/bckpwd catalog=catalog_bck/rmancatalog@pdborcl

RMAN> REGISTER DATABASE;

RMAN> REPORT SCHEMA;
```

Creating a virtual private catalog

Have a look at the following command:

```
SQL> CREATE USER fmunoz IDENTIFIED BY alvarez DEFAULT TABLESPACE
  catalog_tbs;

SQL> GRANT recovery_catalog_owner TO fmunoz;


$ rman catalog=catalog_bck/rmancatalog@pdborcl
```

```
RMAN> GRANT CATALOG FOR DATABASE pdborcl TO fmunoz;
RMAN> GRANT REGISTER DATABASE TO fmunoz;


rman catalog=fmunoz/alvarez@pdborcl


RMAN> CREATE VIRTUAL CATALOG;
```

Enabling Block Change tracking

Have a look at the following command:

```
SQL> ALTER DATABASE ENABLE BLOCK CHANGE TRACKING;
SQL> SELECT status FROM v$block_change_tracking;
```

Playing with RMAN, FRA, and catalog views

Now that we have all configured for RMAN (including our catalog), let's play with our environment.

Monitoring a backup

Of course, to be able to monitor a backup running in our database, we will need to first run our scripts using the following command:

```
RMAN> BACKUP DATABASE PLUS ARCHIVELOG;
```

Now that we have our backup running, open a new terminal, connect to SQL*Plus, and execute the following command:

```
SQL> SELECT sid, serial#, context, sofar, totalwork,
  round(sofar/totalwork*100,2) "%_COMPLETE"
  2   FROM    v$session_longops
  3   WHERE   opname like 'RMAN%'
  4   AND     opname not like '%aggregate%'
  5   AND     totalwork !=0
  6   AND     sofar <> totalwork
/
```

This script will show the completed percentage of the current channels, not of the complete job.

Incremental backups

Here are some examples of incremental backup statements:

```
RMAN> BACKUP INCREMENTALLEVEL=0 DATABASE PLUS ARCHIVELOG DELETE
   INPUT;

RMAN> BACKUP INCREMENTALLEVEL=1 DATABASE PLUS ARCHIVELOG DELETE
   INPUT;

RMAN> BACKUP INCREMENTALLEVEL=0 CUMULATIVE DATABASE PLUS ARCHIVELOG
   DELETE INPUT;
```

Multisection backups

Have a look at the following command:

```
RMAN> BACKUP SECTION SIZE 10M TABLESPACE users;
```

FRA – checking number of redo switches

Have a look at the following command:

```
SQL> ALTER SESSION SET nls_date_format='dd/mm/yyyy hh24:mi:ss';

SQL> SELECT sequence#, first_time log_started,
lead(first_time, 1,null) over (order by first_time) log_ended
  2    FROM (SELECT DISTINCT sequence#, first_time
  3          FROM    dba_hist_log
  4          WHERE   archived='YES'
  5          AND     sequence#!=0
  6          ORDER BY first_time)
  7    ORDER BY sequence#;
```

Check for alerts

Have a look at the following command:

```
SQL> SELECT reason FROM dba_outstanding_alerts;
```

Check FRA usage

Have a look at the following command:

```
SQL> SELECT * FROM v$recovery_file_dest;
SQL> ALTER SYSTEM SWITCH LOGFILE;
SQL> SELECT * FROM v$recovery_file_dest;
SQL> SELECT * FROM v$flash_recovery_area_usage;
```

See the archived log generated by the DB target

Have a look at the following command:

```
SQL> SET PAGESIZE 200
SQL> SET LINESIZE 200
SQL> COLUMN name FORMAT a50
SQL> COLUMN completion_time FORMAT a25
SQL> ALTER SESSION SET nls_date_format= 'DD-MON-YYYY:HH24:MI:SS';
SQL> SELECT name, sequence#, status, completion_time
  2    FROM    CATALOG_BCK.rc_archived_log;
```

See the control file backups

Have a look at the following command:

```
SQL> SET PAGESIZE 200
SQL> SET LINESIZE 200
SQL> SELECT file#, creation_time, resetlogs_time
blocks, block_size, controlfile_type
  2    FROM    v$backup_datafile where file#=0;

SQL> COLUMN completion_time FORMAT a25
SQL> COLUMN autobackup_date FORMAT a25
SQL> ALTER SESSION SET nls_date_format= 'DD-MON-YYYY:HH24:MI:SS';
SQL> SELECT db_name, status, completion_time, controlfile_type,
autobackup_date
  2    FROM    CATALOG_BCK.rc_backup_controlfile;

SQL> SELECT creation_time, block_size,
  status,completion_time,autobackup_date, autobackup_sequence
  2    FROM    CATALOG_BCK.rc_backup_controlfile;
```

See the corrupted list that exists in datafile backups

Have a look at the following command:

```
SQL> SELECT db_name, piece#, file#, block#, blocks, corruption_type
  2  FROM    CATALOG_BCK.rc_backup_corruption where db_name='ORCL';
```

See block corruption in the DB, populated when backup or backup validate

Have a look at the following command:

```
SQL> SELECT file#, block#, corruption_type
  2  FROM    v$database_block_corruption;
```

See all RMAN configurations (equivalent to show all)

Have a look at the following command:

```
SQL> COLUMN value FORMAT a60
SQL> SELECT db_key,name, value
  2  FROM    CATALOG_BCK.rc_rman_configuration;
```

Monitor backup outputs (RMAN)

Have a look at the following command:

```
SQL> SELECT output FROM v$rman_output ORDER BY stamp;
```

Offline backups with RMAN

Have a look at the following command:

```
$ rman target / catalog=catalog_bck/rmancatalog@pdborcl
RMAN> SHUTDOWN IMMEDIATE
RMAN> STARTUP MOUNT
RMAN> BACKUP AS COMPRESSED BACKUPSET DATABASE;
RMAN> ALTER DATABASE OPEN;
```

Offline backup without using configured defaults

Have a look at the following command:

```
SHUTDOWN IMMEDIATE

STARTUP MOUNT

RUN

{

ALLOCATE CHANNEL c1 DEVICE TYPE DISK FORMAT
  '/DB/u02/backups/other/bck1/orcl_%U';

ALLOCATE CHANNEL c2 DEVICE TYPE DISK FORMAT
  '/DB/u02/backups/other/bck2/orcl_%U';

BACKUP AS COMPRESSED BACKUPSET DATABASE;

BACKUP CURRRENT CONTROLFILE;

}
```

Using backup limits (duration)

Have a look at the following command:

```
RMAN> BACKUP DURATION 00:05 DATABASE;

RMAN> BACKUP DURATION 00:05 MINIMIZE TIME DATABASE;

RMAN> BACKUP DURATION 00:05 MINIMIZE LOAD DATABASE;
```

Modifying the retention policy for a backup set (archival backups)

Have a look at the following command.

 In Oracle 11*g*, the KEEP command overrides the default criteria; this cannot use the FRA.

```
RMAN> BACKUP DATABASE KEEP FOREVER;

RMAN> BACKUP DATABASE FORMAT '/DB/u02/backups/other/bck1/orcl_%U'
  KEEP untiltime='sysdate+180' TAG keep_backup;
```

Archive deletion policy

Have a look at the following command:

```
RMAN> CONFIGURE ARCHIVELOG DELETION POLICY TO BACKED UP 2 TIMES TO
    DEVICE TYPE DISK;
```

Using RMAN to scan DB for physical and logical errors

Have a look at the following command:

```
RMAN> BACKUP VALIDATE CHECK LOGICAL DATABASE;
```

Configuring tablespaces for exclusion from whole database backups

Have a look at the following command:

```
RMAN> CONFIGURE EXCLUDE FOR TABLESPACE example;

RMAN> BACKUP DATABASE;

# backs up the whole database, including example

RMAN> BACKUP DATABASE NOEXCLUDE;

RMAN> BACKUP TABLESPACE example;   # backs up only  example

RMAN> CONFIGURE EXCLUDE FOR TABLESPACE example CLEAR;
```

Skipping offline, inaccessible, or read-only datafiles

Have a look at the following command:

```
RMAN> BACKUP DATABASE SKIP READONLY;

RMAN> BACKUP DATABASE SKIP OFFLINE;

RMAN> BACKUP DATABASE SKIP INACCESSIBLE;

RMAN> BACKUP DATABASE SKIP READONLY SKIP OFFLINE SKIP INACCESSIBLE;
```

Forcing backups of read-only datafiles

Have a look at the following command:

```
RMAN> BACKUP DATABASE FORCE;
```

Backup of newly added datafiles

Add a new datafile for the tablespace example and execute using the following command:

```
RMAN> BACKUP DATABASE NOT BACKED UP;
```

Backup files not backed up during a specific period

Have a look at the following command:

```
RMAN> BACKUP DATABASE NOT BACKED UP SINCE time='sysdate-2';

RMAN> BACKUP ARCIVELOG ALL NOT BACKED UP 1 TIMES;

RMAN> BACKUP AS COMPRESSED BACKUPSET DATABASE PLUS ARCHIVELOG NOT
  BACKED UP 1 TIMES DELETE INPUT;
```

General backup examples

Have a look at the following command:

```
RMAN> BACKUP TABLESPACE USERS INCLUDE CURRENT CONTROLFILE PLUS
  ARCHIVELOG;

RMAN> BACKUP DATAFILE 2;

RMAN> BACKUP ARCHIVELOG ALL;

RMAN> BACKUP ARCHIVELOG FROM TIME 'sysdate-1';

RMAN> BACKUP ARCHIVELOG FROM SEQUENCE 123; (Enter here a valid
  sequence from your database)

RMAN> BACKUP ARCHIVELOG ALL DELETE INPUT;

RMAN> BACKUP ARCHIVELOG FROM SEQUENCE xxx DELETE INPUT;

RMAN> BACKUP ARCHIVELOG NOT BACKED UP 3 TIMES;

RMAN> BACKUP ARCHIVELOG UNTIL TIME 'sysdate - 2' DELETE ALL INPUT;
```

Backup copies

Have a look at the following command.

RMAN will use FRA if it is configured.

```
RMAN> BACKUP AS COPY DATABASE;
RMAN> BACKUP AS COPY TABLESPACE USERS;
RMAN> BACKUP AS COPY DATAFILE 1;
RMAN> BACKUP AS COPY ARCHIVELOG ALL;
```

Advanced RMAN

Now is time to play with some more advanced RMAN scenarios.

Information about fully-completed backups

Have a look at the following command:

```
SQL> ALTER SESSION SET nls_date_format= 'DD-MON-YYYY:HH24:MI:SS';
SQL> SELECT /*+ RULE */ session_key, session_recid,
start_time, end_time, output_bytes, elapsed_seconds, optimized
  2    FROM    v$rman_backup_job_details
  3    WHERE   start_time >= sysdate-180
  4    AND     status='COMPLETED'
  5    AND     input_type='DB FULL';
```

Summary of the active session history

A summary of the active session history might help (make sure you are licensed to use it by acquiring the Oracle Diagnostic Pack!). Have a look at the following command:

```
SQL> SELECT sid, serial#, program
  2    FROM    v$session
  3    WHERE   lower(program) like '%rman%';


SQL> SET LINES 132
```

```
SQL> COLUMN session_id FORMAT 999 HEADING "SESS|ID"
SQL> COLUMN session_serial# FORMAT 9999 HEADING "SESS|SER|#"
SQL> COLUMN event FORMAT a40
SQL> COLUMN total_waits FORMAT 9,999,999,999 HEADING
  "TOTAL|TIME|WAITED|MICRO"
SQL> SELECT session_id, session_serial#, Event, sum(time_waited)
  total_waits
  2    FROM    v$active_session_history
  3    WHERE   session_id||session_serial# in (403, 476, 4831)
  4    AND     sample_time > sysdate -1
  5    AND     program like '%rman%'
  6    AND     session_state='WAITING' And time_waited > 0
  7    GROUP BY session_id, session_serial#, Event
  8    ORDER BY session_id, session_serial#, total_waits desc;
```

How long does it take?

Have a look at the following command:

```
RMAN> BACKUP DATABASE PLUS ARCHIVELOG;
```

Open a new terminal and execute:

```
$ sqlplus / as sysdba
```

```
SQL> ALTER SESSION SET CONTAINER=pdborcl;
```

```
SQL> SELECT sid, serial#, program
  2    FROM    v$session
  3    WHERE   lower(program) like '%rman%';
```

```
SQL> SELECT sid, serial#, opname, time_remaining
  2    FROM    v$session_longops
  3    WHERE   sid||serial# in (<XXX>, <XXX>, <XXX>)
  4    AND     time_remaining > 0;
```

 Remember to replace the values <XXX> with the sid and serial# from the first query. For example, sid=4 and serial#=20 enter 420.

V$BACKUP_ASYNC_IO

Have a look at the following command:

```
SQL> SELECT sid, serial#, program
  2    FROM   v$session
  3    WHERE  lower(program) like '%rman%';


SQL> COLUMN filename FORMAT a60
SQL> SELECT sid, serial, effective_bytes_per_second, filename
  2    FROM   V$BACKUP_ASYNC_IO
  3    WHERE  sid||serial in (<XXX>, <XXX>, <XXX>);


SQL> SELECT LONG_WAITS/IO_COUNT, FILENAME
  2    FROM   V$BACKUP_ASYNC_IO
  3    WHERE  LONG_WAITS/IO_COUNT > 0
  4    AND    sid||serial in (<XXX>, <XXX>, <XXX>)
  5    ORDER BY LONG_WAITS/IO_COUNT DESC;
```

 Remember to replace the values <XXX> with the `sid` and `serial#` from the first query. For example, `sid=4 and serial#=20` enter `420`.

Tablespace Point-in-time Recovery (TSPITR)

Firstly, we will check if the tablespace TEST is fully self-contained.

 Remember that you should have the EXECUTE_CATALOG_ROLE granted to be able to execute the TRANSPORT_SET_CHECK procedure.

```
SQL> EXECUTE DBMS_TTS.TRANSPORT_SET_CHECK('test', TRUE);


SQL> SELECT * FROM transport_set_violations;
```

Look for object that will be lost during the recovery using the following command:

```
SQL> SELECT OWNER, NAME, TABLESPACE_NAME,
  2    TO_CHAR(CREATION_TIME, 'YYYY-MM-DD:HH24:MI:SS')
  3    FROM  TS_PITR_OBJECTS_TO_BE_DROPPED
```

```
4    WHERE TABLESPACE_NAME IN ('TEST')
5    AND CREATION_TIME >
6    TO_DATE('07-OCT-08:22:35:30','YY-MON-DD:HH24:MI:SS')
7    ORDER BY TABLESPACE_NAME, CREATION_TIME;
```

Execute the TSPITR.

```
RMAN>RECOVER TABLESPACE pdborcl:test UNTIL SCN <XXXX> AUXILIARY
DESTINATION '/tmp';
```

 Replace <XXXX> for any previous SCN of the database.

Reporting from a catalog

Here is a script that displays databases that are registered in the catalog and the last date they were backed up (full backup or level 0):

```
SQL> SELECT a.db_key, a.dbid, a.name db_name,
b.backup_type, b.incremental_level,
b.completion_time, max(b.completion_time)
over (partition by a.name, a.dbid) max_completion_time
  2 FROM    catalog_bck.rc_database a, catalog_bck.rc_backup_set b
  3 WHERE   b.status = 'A'
  4 AND     b.backup_type = 'D'
  5 AND     b.db_key = a.db_key;
```

Duplex backup

Have a look at the following command:

```
RMAN> CONFIGURE DATAFILE BACKUPCOPIES FOR DEVICE TYPE DISK TO 2;

RMAN> CONFIGURE ARCHIVELOG BACKUp COPIES FOR DEVICE TYPE DISK TO 2;

RMAN> BACKUP DATAFILE 1 FORMAT
  '/DB/u02/backups/bck_orcl_%U','/Data/backup/bck_orcl_%U' PLUS
  ARCHIVELOG;
```

Check if the database is recoverable

Have a look at the following command:

```
RMAN> RESTORE DATABASE PREVIEW;
```

Recover advisor

Firstly, let's create a tablespace and a user for this scenario:

```
SQL> CREATE TABLESPACE test3_tbs DATAFILE '/data/pdborcl
  /test3_01.dbf' SIZE 100m;

SQL> CREATE USER test3 IDENTIFIED BY test3 DEFAULT TABLESPACE
  test3_tbs QUOTA UNLIMITED ON test3_tbs;

SQL> GRANT CONNECT, RESOURCE to test3;

SQL> CREATE TABLE test3.EMPLOYEE

( EMP_ID    NUMBER(10) NOT NULL,

  EMP_NAME VARCHAR2(30),

  EMP_SSN  VARCHAR2(9),

  EMP_DOB  DATE

);


SQL> INSERT INTO test.employee VALUES (101,'Francisco
  Munoz',123456789,'30-JUN-73');


SQL> INSERT INTO test.employee VALUES (102,'Gonzalo
  Munoz',234567890,'02-OCT-96');


SQL> INSERT INTO test.employee VALUES (103,'Evelyn
  Aghemio',659812831,'02-OCT-79');

$ Cd /data/pdborcl

$ echo > test3_01_dbf.dbf

$ ls -lrt


RMAN> VALIDATE DATABASE;

RMAN> LIST FAILURE;

RMAN> ADVISE FAILURE;

RMAN> REPAIR FAILURE PREVIEW;

RMAN> REPAIR FAILURE;
```

Magic with Data Pump

Now is the time to play with Data Pump. Firstly, we will set up the environment, and then we will start playing with it.

Preparing Data Pump

```
$ sqlplus / as sysdba

SQL> ALTER SESSION SET CONTAINER=pdborcl;

SQL> CREATE USER fcomunoz IDENTIFIED BY alvarez DEFAULT TABLESPACE
  users QUOTA UNLIMITED ON users;

SQL> GRANT CREATE SESSION, RESOURCE, DATAPUMP_EXP_FULL_DATABASE,
  DATAPUMP_IMP_FULL_DATABASE TO fcomunoz;

SQL> CREATE DIRECTORY datapump AS '/data/pdborcl/backups;

SQL> GRANT READ, WRITE ON DIRECTORY datapump to fcomunoz;
```

Data masking

Have a look at the following command:

```
SQL> CREATE TABLE fcomunoz.EMPLOYEE
( EMP_ID   NUMBER(10) NOT NULL,
  EMP_NAME VARCHAR2(30),
  EMP_SSN  VARCHAR2(9),
  EMP_DOB  DATE
)
/

SQL> INSERT INTO fcomunoz.employee VALUES (101,'Francisco
  Munoz',123456789,'30-JUN-73');

SQL> INSERT INTO fcomunoz.employee VALUES (102,'Gonzalo
  Munoz',234567890,'02-OCT-96');

SQL> INSERT INTO fcomunoz.employee VALUES (103,'Evelyn
  Aghemio',659812831,'02-OCT-79');

SQL> CREATE OR REPLACE PACKAGE fcomunoz.pkg_masking
 as
 FUNCTION mask_ssn (p_in VARCHAR2) RETURN VARCHAR2;
```

```
END;
/

SQL> CREATE OR REPLACE PACKAGE BODY fcomunoz.pkg_masking
 2    AS
 3      FUNCTION mask_ssn (p_in varchar2)
 4      RETURN VARCHAR2
 5      IS
 6    BEGIN
 7      RETURN LPAD (
 8      ROUND(DBMS_RANDOM.VALUE (001000000,999999999)),9,0);
 9    END;
10    END;
11    /

SQL> SELECT * FOM fcomunozemployees;

$expdp fcomunoz/alvarez@pdborcl tables=fcomunoz.employee
  dumpfile=mask_ssn.dmp directory=datapump remap_data=fcomunoz.employee.
emp_ssn:pkg_masking.mask_ssn

$ impdp fcomunoz/alvarez@pdborcl table_exists_action=truncate
  directory=datapump dumpfile=mask_ssn.dmp

SQL> SELECT * FROM fcomunoz.employees;
```

Metadata repository

Have a look at the following command:

```
$ expdp fcomunoz/alvarez@pdborcl content=metadata_only full=y
  directory=datapump dumpfile=metadata_06192013.dmp

$ impdp fcomunoz/alvarez@pdborcl directory=datapump dumpfile=
  metadata_06192013.dmp sqlfile=metadata_06192013.sql

$ expdp fcomunoz/alvarez@pdborcl content=metadata_only
  tables=fcomunoz.employee directory=datapump dumpfile=
    refresh_of_table_employee_06192013.dmp

$ impdp fcomunoz/alvarez@pdborcl table_exists_action=replace
  directory=datapump dumpfile= refresh_of_table_name_06192013.dmp
```

Cloning a user

Have a look at the following command:

```
$ expdp fcomunoz/alvarez@pdborcl schemas=fcomunoz
  content=metadata_only directory=datapump dumpfile=
    fcomunoz_06192013.dmp


SQL> CREATE USER fcomunoz2 IDENTIFIED BY alvarez DEFAULT TABLESPACE
  users QUOTA UNLIMITED ON users;

SQL> GRANT connect,resource TO fcomunoz2;


$ impdp fcomunoz/alvarez@pdborcl remap_schema=fcomunoz:fcomunoz2
  directory=datapump dumpfile= fcomunoz_06192013.dmp
```

And, your new user `fcomunoz2` is now created like your existing user `fcomunoz` that easily!

Creating smaller copies of production

Let us see how this cab be done for metadata-only and metadata and data:

- Metadata only:

    Have a look at the following command:

    ```
    $ expdp fcomunoz/alvarez@pdborcl content=metadata_
    only tables=fcomunoz.employee directory=datapump
    dumpfile=example_206192013.dmp


    $ impdp fcomunoz/alvarez@pdborcl content=metadata_
    only directory=datapump dumpfile=example_206192013.dmp
    sqlfile=employee_06192013.sql


    $ cat /data/pdborcl/backups/employee_06192013.sql


    $ impdp fcomunoz/alvarez@pdborcl transform=pctspace:70
    content=metadata_only directory=datapump dumpfile=
    example_206192013.dmp sqlfile=transform_06192013.sql


    $ cat /data/pdborcl/backups/transform_06192013.sql
    ```

- Metadata and data:

  Have a look at the following command:

  ```
  $ expdp fcomunoz/alvarez@pdborcl sample=70 full=y
  directory=datapump dumpfile=expdp_70_06192013.dmp


  $ impdp fcomunoz/alvarez@pdborcl2 transform=pctspace:70
  directory=datapump dumpfile=expdp_70_06192013.dmp
  ```

Creating your database in a different structure

Have a look at the following command:

```
$ expdp fcomunoz/alvarez@pdborcl full=y directory=datapump
dumpfile=expdp_full_06192013.dmp


$ impdp fcomunoz/alvarez@pdborcl directory=datapump dumpfile= expdp_
full_06192013.dmp remap_datafile='/u01/app/oracle/oradata/pdborcl/
datafile_01.dbf':'/u01/app/oracle/oradata/pdborcl2/datafile_01.dbf'
```

Time-based flashback

Have a look at the following command:

```
SQL> conn / as sysdba


SQL> SELECT dbms_flashback.get_system_change_number
  2    FROM dual;


SQL> SELECT SCN_TO_TIMESTAMP(dbms_flashback.get_system_change_number)
  2    FROM dual;


SQL> exit


$ expdp fcomunoz/alvarez@pdborcl directory=datapump
  tables=fcomunoz.employee dumpfile=employee_flashback_06192013.dmp
flashback_time="to_timestamp('19-06-2013 14:30:00', 'dd-mm-yyyy
  hh24:mi:ss')"


$ expdp fcomunoz/alvarez@pdborcl directory=datapump
  tables=fcomunoz.employee dumpfile=employee_flashback_06192013.dmp
flashback_scn=123
```

In the preceding example with FLASHBACK_SCN, please replace 123 with a valid SCN from your database, where you are running this scenario.

Backup and recovery scenarios

Now is the time to play with some backup and recovery scenarios. Due to the limitations of pages in this book, we will cover only a few scenarios. Remember that you have many scenarios available in the chapters of this book.

Active duplication of a database to a different server with the same structure (non-OMF and non-ASM)

When executing an active duplication, RMAN automatically copies the server parameter file to the destination host from the source, restarts the auxiliary instance using the server parameter file, copies all necessary database files and archived redo logs over the network to the destination host, and recovers the destination database. Finally, RMAN will open the destination (target) database with the RESETLOGS option to be able to create all online redo logs.

The following steps are required:

1. Create a new virtual machine using Oracle database 12.1.0.1 and Oracle Linux 6.4 (without creating a database). Set up the virtual machine with a proper **IP** and **HOSTNAME**.

2. Follow the Oracle installation guide for Linux (http://docs.oracle.com/cd/E16655_01/install.121/e17720/toc.htm), and prepare this machine for the installation of the Oracle database. When creating the Oracle user, please create it to use the password oracle.

3. Clone the newly created virtual machine and give to it a new IP and HOSTNAME. It will be used as the auxiliary server (target).

4. Create a non-CDB database called (in the Virtual Machine created in step 1) orcl using DBCA. This will be the source database.

5. If the source database is open, archiving must be enabled. If the source database is not open, the database does not require instance recovery.

6. In the auxiliary server, create the same directory structure used by the source database created in step 3. For example:

      - ° mkdir /u01/app/oracle/fast_recovery_area
      - ° mkdir /u01/app/oracle/fast_recovery_area/orcl
      - ° mkdir /u01/app/oracle/admin/orcl/adump
      - ° mkdir /u01/app/oracle/oradata/orcl

The steps for the active duplication will be:

1. In the auxiliary server (target), create a new password file to be used by the cloned database (connected as the OS user Oracle).

    ```
    $ orapwd file=/u01/app/oracle/product/12.1/db_1/dbs/orapworcl
      password=oracle entries=10
    ```

2. Add the auxiliary database information to the source database TNSNAMES. ORA file (located at $ORACLE_HOME/network/admin). For example:

    ```
    ORCL_DEST =
      (DESCRIPTION =
        (ADDRESS = (PROTOCOL = TCP) (HOST=172.28.10.62) (PORT =
    1521)
        (CONNECT_DATA)
          (SERVER = DEDICATED)
          (SERVICE_NAME = orcl)
        )
      )
    ```

 Remember to replace the example IP address used above for the correct IP of your virtual machine (auxiliary server).

3. Create the LISTENER.ORA file in the auxiliary server. For example:

    ```
    SID_LIST_LISTENER =
      (SID_LIST =
        (SID_DESC =
          (ORACLE_HOME = /u01/app/oracle/product/12.1/db_1)
          (SID_NAME = orcl)
        )
      )
    ```

```
LISTENER =
  (DESCRIPTION_LIST =
    (DESCRIPTION =
      (ADDRESS = (PROTOCOL = TCP) (HOST = 172.28.10.62) (PORT
= 1521))
    (DESCRIPTION =
      (ADDRESS = (PROTOCOL = IPC) (KEY = EXTPROC1521))
    )
  )

ADR_BASE_LISTENER = /u01/app/oracle
```

 Remember to replace the example IP address used above for the correct IP of your virtual machine (auxiliary server)

4. Add source and auxiliary databases to the auxiliary TNSNAMES.ORA file. For example:

```
LISTENER_ORCL =
  (ADDRESS = (PROTOCOL = TCP) (HOST = 172.28.10.62) (PORT =
  1521))
ORCL =
  (DESCRIPTION =
    (ADDRESS = (PROTOCOL = TCP) (HOST = 172.29.62.11) (PORT =
    1521))
    (CONNECT_DATA =
      (SERVER = DEDICATED)
      (SERVICE_NAME = orcl)
    )
  )


ORCL_DEST =
  (DESCRIPTION =
    (ADDRESS = (PROTOCOL = TCP) (HOST = 172.28.10.62) (PORT =
    1521))
    (CONNECT_DATA =
      (SERVER = DEDICATED)
      (SERVICE_NAME = orcl)
    )
  )
```

Remember to replace example IP addresses by the ones you used on your virtual machines.

5. Create a basic PFILE for the auxiliary database. To make it easy, create a PFILE from SPFILE in the source database and copy it to the auxiliary database.

6. Using SQL*Plus, start up the auxiliary database in NOMOUNT mode; for example:

```
SQL> STARTUP NOMOUNT
```

7. Start the LISTENER for the auxiliary database; for example:

```
$ lsnrctl start
```

8. In the auxiliary server, start your RMAN session connecting to the source database and the auxiliary database; for example:

```
$ rman TARGET sys/oracle@orcl auxiliary sys/oracle@orcl_dest
```

9. Run the DUPLICATE command to make the magic happen, for example:

```
RMAN> DUPLICATE DATABASE TO ORCL

FROM ACTIVE DATABASE

SPFILE

NOFILENAMECHECK;
```

 RMAN uses the pull method (using backup sets) by default.

You can also use COMPRESSED BACKUPSET when performing an active duplication. In this case the DUPLICATE command would be:

```
DUPLICATE TARGET DATABASE TO orcl

FROM ACTIVE DATABASE

PASSWORD FILE

USING COMPRESSED BACKUPSET;
```

By default, when the active duplication is completed, the new database will be open; if you do not want the database to be open, after the duplication, please use the following command:

```
RMAN> DUPLICATE DATABASE TO ORCL

FROM ACTIVE DATABASE

SPFILE

NOFILENAMECHECK

NOOPEN;
```

Duplicating a PDB

If you want to duplicate a PDB, please create a multitenant container database called orcl with a PDB called pdborcl using DBCA, and follow all steps in the previous scenario and replace the DUPLICATE command with the following one:

```
RMAN> DUPLICATE TARGET DATABASE TO orcl

PLUGGABLE DATABASE pdborcl

FROM ACTIVE DATABASE

PASSWORD FILE

SPFILE

NOFILENAMECHECK;
```

> The root and seed database are automatically included in the duplication. The auxiliary instance must have been started with an initialization parameter file that includes the declaration enable_pluggable_database=TRUE.

ASM backup and restore

Perform the following steps:

1. Take an RMAN backup of the USERS tablespace:

    ```
    RMAN> BACKUP TABLESPACE users;
    ```

2. Create a new directory called abc in the disk group DATA. Once you create the directory, create an alias called +DATA/abc/users.f. This alias will point to the ASM datafile in which the USERS tablespace is stored:

    ```
    ASMCMD> mkdir +DATA1/abc

    ASMCMD> mkalias TBSJFV.354.323232323    +DATA1/abc/users.f
    ```

3. Backup the ASM metadata for the DATA disk group:

```
ASMCMD> md_backup -g  data1
```

The md_backup command will produce a restore script named ambr_backup_intermediate_file in the current directory. You'll need this file to perform the restore operation later.

4. Drop the disk group DATA to simulate the failure. You can use the dismount force clause to dismount the disk group and then force drop it:

```
SQL> ALTER DISKGROUP data1 DISMOUNT FORCE;

SQL> DROP DISKGROUP data1 FORCE INCLUDING CONTENTS;
```

5. Edit the ambr_backup_intermideate_file to remove the au_size entry. Once you make the change and save the restore file, run the md_restore command to restore the ASM metadata for the dropped disk group:

```
ASMCMD> md_restore -b ambr_backup_intermediate_file -t full
-g data
```

6. Once you restore the ASM metadata for the disk group, you must restore the USERS tablespace that was in the dropped disk group. You can use the backup that you made earlier of the USERS tablespace for this:

```
RMAN> RESTORE TABLESPACE users;
```

Recovering from the loss of the SYSTEM tablespace

We are running this scenario with the assumption that you have a current backup of your database and all archived redo log files since your last backup are available. To recover your SYSTEM tablespace, please follow these steps:

1. Connect to RMAN:

```
$ rman target /
```

2. Start your DB in mount mode and restore your SYSTEM tablespace:

```
RMAN> STARTUP MOUNT;

RMAN> RESTORE TABLESPACE SYSTEM;
```

3. Recover and open your DB:

```
RMAN> RECOVER TABLESPACE SYSTEM;

RMAN> ALTER DATABASE OPEN;
```

If you do not have a current backup of your database and all archive redo log files are unavailable, you should perform a point-in-time recovery of your database and open it using the RESETLOGS option.

Recovering a lost datafile using an image from an FRA

We are running this scenario with the assumption that you have a current image copy of the datafile 7 on the FRA. To recover your datafile 7 from the FRA, perform the following steps:

1. Create a copy backup of your database.

2. Let's first put the datafile offline to simulate that we lost the datafile:

    ```
    SQL> ALTER DATABASE DATAFILE 7 OFFLINE;
    ```

3. Now let's do the trick; we will switch to the copy of the datafile available on our FRA:

    ```
    $ rman target /
    RMAN> SWITCH DATAFILE 7 TO COPY;
    RMAN> RECOVER DATAFILE 7;
    ```

4. All you need to do now is to put the datafile online and you are ready to go, without losing your time waiting for a backup to be retrieved from tape.

    ```
    RMAN> ALTER DATABASE DATAFILE 7 ONLINE;
    ```

 Remember to switch from datafile copy in the FRA to disk again; if not, you will have issues again.

```
$ rman target /
RMAN> BACKUP AS COPY DATAFILE 7 FORMAT '/Data/data/test3_tbs_01.
dbf';
RMAN> SWITCH DATAFILE 7 TO COPY;
RMAN> RECOVER DATAFILE 7;
RMAN> ALTER DATABASE DATAFILE 7 ONLINE;
```

Index

Symbols

%a variable 23
%d variable 23
%r variable 23
%s variable 22
%S variable 22
%t variable 23
%T variable 23

A

Active Duplicate feature 87
Active/Inactive 23
ADD_FILE command 316
Add Recovery Catalog option 355-357
Advanced Compression Option (ACO)
    license 162
advanced Data Pump
  database, creating in different file structure
    335
  data masking 326-329
  data, migrating for upgrade 336-338
  metadata repository, creating 330, 331
  objects, moving from one tablespace to
    another 336
  objects, moving to different schema 336
  Oracle Database, downgrading 338, 339
  performance tuning tips 345, 346
  smaller copies, creating of production
    environment 333-335
  SOURCE_EDITION, using 332
  tablespace, transporting 340-343
  TARGET_EDITION, using 332
  user, cloning 332
  version control, creating 330, 331

advanced RMAN
  active session history, summary 386
  catalog, reporting 389
  completed backup 386
  database recovery, checking 390
  duplex backup 389
  recover advisor 390
  time, calculating 387
  TSPITR 388, 389
  V$BACKUP_ASYNC_IO 388
alert log file
  using 273, 274
alerts
  checking 380
ALTER DATABASE BACKUP
    CONTROLFILE command 111
ALTER DATABASE FORCE LOGGING
    command 31
application error 10
architecture, Data Pump 299, 300
architecture, RMAN
  about 130
  ARCHIVELOG mode, configuring 135-137
  auxiliary database 132
  channels 132
  EM Cloud Control 12c 133
  FRA, configuring 135-137
  Media Management Library (MML) 134
  memory requisites 134, 135
  Oracle secure backup (OSB) 134
  Recovery Catalog 132, 133
  RMAN client 133
  Target Control File 132
  target database 131

archived log deletion policy
   configuring 195
archived redo logs
   backups, performing 159, 160
ARCHIVELOG mode
   about 18-20, 101
   archival destinations status, viewing 23
   configuring 135-137
   database, placing into 24, 25
   excessive redo generation 26
   hot backup mode 27
   parameters, specifying 22
   preparing 20, 21
   redo 25, 26
   status, checking 22
   undo 25
ASM (Automatic Storage Management) 277
asynchronous IO mode 278, 279
AU (Allocation Unit) 277
auto backup configuration
   for control file 181, 182
   for SPFILE 181, 182
Automatic Diagnostic Repository (ADR)
      160, 273
Automatic Memory Management (AMM)
      280
Automatic Shared Memory Management
      (ASMM) 280
auxiliary database 132

B

backup
   copies 386
   device type, configuration 181
   examples 385
   logical backup 11
   monitoring 379
   performing 146-148
   performing, of backups 168, 169
   physical backup 11
   purpose 7
   strategy 12
   testing 8, 9
   types 11
BACKUP command 146, 147, 157

backup formats
   about 137
   backup set 138
   image copy 139
Backup Jobs option 370
backup limits (duration)
   using 383
backup optimization
   about 178, 179
   configuring 178-180
backup piece 139
backup privileges
   about 80-84
   SYSBACKUP 80
   SYSDBA 80
backup retention policy
   configuring 174
   recovery window 178
   redundancy 175-177
backup retention policy configuration
      174-178
backups
   about 44
   and NOLOGGING 60
   compression, configuring 193, 194
   performing, of archived redo logs 159, 160
   performing, of control file 159, 160
   performing, of pluggable database 167, 168
   performing, of root 167, 168
   performing, of SPFILE 159
   restricting 169
   RMAN compression, using for 161-163
   updating, incrementally 156, 157
backup set 138
backup settings 348-353
backups outputs (RMAN)
   monitoring 382
BEGIN BACKUP option 104
benefits, incremental backups 140
BigFile tablespaces 150
binary backup 111
Block Change Tracking (BCT) 152
block change tracking (BCT) file
   used, for performing incremental backups
      152-155
block corruption, in DB
   checking 382

Block Media Recovery. *See* BMR
blocks
  corrupting, due to NOLOGGING 63
Block Written Record (BWR) 206
BMR
  about 221, 222
  performing 221, 222
bulk deletes 45, 58, 59
bulk inserts 44, 58
bulk updates 46, 59

C

CATALOG option 130
catalog settings 355, 356
CDB
  about 31, 76, 163
  complete recovery 216
Change Tracking Writer (CTWR) 154
channels
  configuring 182, 183
checkpoint 204
CHECKSYNTAX command
  about 268
  using 268-270
cold backup 101
Command Line Interface (CLI) 239
commands, RMAN 145, 146
compression
  configuring, for backups 193, 194
configuration, ARCHIVELOG mode
    135-137
Configuration Assistant (DBCA) 239
configuration, FRA 135, 137
CONFIGURE command 138
container database. *See* CDB
container database, hot backup
  datafile status, checking 109
  root only or individual pluggable database
    108
  whole container database 107, 108
CONTINUE_CLIENT command 316
control file
  auto backup, configuring 181, 182
  backups, performing 159
  using, for RMAN metadata 233-236

control file backup
  about 110
  binary backup 111
  checking 381
  text file backup 111, 112
CONTROLFILE_RECORD_KEEP_TIME
  (CFRKT) parameter 236, 237
control file recovery
  performing 218-221
conventional path method
  used, for moving data 303
copies
  creating, of production environment
    333-335
crash recovery
  about 201
  in container 207, 208
  steps 206, 207
Create Restore Point page 364
CREATE TABLE AS SELECT. *See* CTAS
Create Whole Database Backup page 371
CTAS 40
cumulative incremental backup 142
Customized Backup option
  using 360-363

D

data
  exporting, from data vault 96
  importing, via data link 320-322
  migrating, for upgrade 336-338
  protecting 9
database
  backing up, steps 101, 102
  configuring 375, 376
  creating, in different file structure 335
database configuration
  Flashback, activating 375
  in archivelog mode 375
  new redo log group, creating 376
  spfile, using 375
database duplication
  ASM backup 399, 400
  ASM restore 399, 400
  lost datafile, recovering from 401
  PDB 399

steps 395-399
SYSTEM tablespace loss, recovering from
    400, 401
Database Identifier. *See* **DBID**
Database Point-in-time Recovery.
    See **DBPITR**
database startup
stage overview 204, 205
data definition language (DDL) 91
datafile copy method
used, for moving data 301
datafiles
about 304
working on 384
data masking 326-329
data protection
application error 10
hardware failure 10
human error 10
media failure 9
Data Pump
about 391
database, creating 394
data masking 391
export operations 304
import operations 304
metadata repository 392
preparing 391
time based flashback 394
user, cloning 393
Data Pump API 299
Data Pump commands
auditing 96
DATAPUMP_EXP_FULL_DATABASE role
    304, 321
Data Pump flashback 343, 344
DATAPUMP_IMP_FULL_DATABASE role
    304, 321
Data Pump operations
Export Jobs 371
Import Jobs 371
Data Pump utility
about 297
architecture 299, 300
features 298, 299
files 304

job status, monitoring 344, 345
methods 301
new concepts 301
scenarios 306
Data Recovery Advisor. *See* **DRA**
data vault
data, exporting from 96
DBID 129
DBMS_DATAPUMP package 299, 300
DBMS_METADATA package 299, 300
DBMS_REPAIR package 127
DBPITR
about 91, 223-226
performing, over PDB 225, 226
recovering, steps 121
DBWR (database writer) 278
DEBUG clause
used, for debugging RMAN 272, 273
deletion policy
archiving 384
device type configuration
for backup 180, 181
dictionary views
used, for monitoring RMAN IO
    performance 281
differential incremental backup 141, 142
Direct Memory Access (DMA) 284
directory objects
about 301, 305
creating 305
Direct Path API 300
direct path inserts 54-57
direct path load
using, in SQL*Loader 68, 69
direct path method
used, for moving data 302
disaster recovery plan. *See* **DRP**
DRA
about 228
commands 228-231
DR (Disaster and Recovery) 133
DRP 8
dump files 304
duplexed backups
creating 184, 185
DUPLICATE command 87, 399

E

EM Cloud Control 12c 133
encrypted backups
  configuring 186
encrypted backups configuration
  about 186
  modes 186
  modes, dual mode encryption 192
  modes, Password encryption 191, 192
  modes, Transparent Data Encryption (TDE)
    187
  Oracle Software Keystore, creating 187-190
encryption password feature 95
enhancements, Data Pump
  about 92
  data, exporting from data vault 96
  Data Pump commands, auditing 96, 97
  encryption password 95
  extended character data types 94
  full transportable Export/Import 93
  LOGGING, disabling on Data Pump Import
    92, 93
  SecureFile LOBs, creating on Import 96
  tables, compressing on import 95
  views, exporting as tables 94
enhancements, RMAN
  about 78
  Active Duplicate feature 87
  backup and restore, for container database
    78, 79
  backup and restore, for pluggable database
    78, 79
  backup privileges 80-84
  cross-platform data transport 89, 90
  DESCRIBE 84
  Enterprise Manager Database Express 79
  multi-section backups, for incremental
    backups 86
  network-based recovery 86
  SQL commands 84
  support, for third-party snapshot 88
  table recovery 91, 92
Enterpise Edition (EE) option 221
Enterprise Manager Database Express 79
error stack
  reading 270, 271

Exadata 78
EXECUTE_CATALOG_ROLE role 103
execute command 256
exercise
  test environment, creating 373-375
EXIT_CLIENT command 316
exp utility 12, 298
extended character data types 94
External Table API 300
external tables method
  used, for moving data 303

F

Fast Recovery Area. *See* FRA
features, RMAN 126, 127
files, Data Pump
  datafile 304
  dump files 304
  log file 304
  SQL files 304
file sections
  for backups, of large data files 150, 151
FILESIZE command 316
Flashback Database
  about 112
  enabling, steps 113-115
FLASHBACK DATABASE command
  options 116
FLASHBACK DROP functionality 91
FORCE LOGGING mode 31
FRA
  about 113, 137, 278
  configuring 135-137, 196-199
  enabling, parameters 197
FRA usage
  checking 381
full backup
  about 139, 293
  performing, of multitenant CDB 164, 165

G

generated archived log, by DB target
  checking 381
Graphical User Interface (GUI) 239

H

Hardware, Security Module (HSM) 188
HCC (Hybrid Columnar Compression) 127
HELP command 316
high water mark (HWM) 31
hot backup
  about 104
  of container database 107
  performing, of tablespaces 106, 107
  performing, of whole database 105, 106
human error. *See* user error

I

image copy
  about 139
  full backup 139
  incremental backups 140
  power of one 143-145
impdp tool 331
Import
  SecureFile LOBs, creating on 96
imp utility 12, 298
incremental backups
  about 140, 293, 380
  benefits 140
  cumulative incremental backup 142
  differential incremental backup 141, 142
  multi-section backups 86
  performing, block change tracking (BCT)
    file used 152-155
  performing, RMAN used 151
index-organized table (IOT) 40-43
instance recovery. *See* crash recovery
interactive command-line mode 301
IO
  and RMAN 275, 276
IO operation
  copy phase 275
  read phase 275
  write phase 275

J

job
  monitoring 368, 369

K

key terms, recovery
  change vectors 202
  checkpoin 204
  data block 202
  dirty block 202
  redo log buffer 203
  redo log files 203
  redo records 203
  redo stream 203
  redo thread 203
KILL_JOB command 316

L

Large Object (LOB) technology 94
Large Pool memory
  setting 279, 280
Least Recently Used (LRU) algorithm 279
LGWR 30, 137
LIST BACKUP command 259
LIST command
  used, for reporting 263
LOG_ARCHIVE_DEST_n parameter 22
LOG_ARCHIVE_FORMAT parameter 22
LOG_ARCHIVE_MIN_SUCCEED_DEST
    parameter 23
log buffer space event 63
log file 304
log file parallel write event 60, 62
log file sync event 62
LOGGING
  disabling, on Data Pump Import 92, 93
LOGGING operations
  tips 44
  versus NOLOGGING operations 31-33
logical backup 11
Log Writer. *See* LGWR
log writer (LGWR) process 14

M

md_backup command 400
Mean Time To Recovery (MTTR) 206
Media Management Library (MML)
    134, 273

media recovery
  about 201
  performing 208, 209
memory requisites, RMAN 134, 135
Metadata API 299
metadata repository
  building 330, 331
methods, Data Pump utility
  conventional path 303
  datafile copy 301
  direct path 302
  external tables 303
  network link 303
MOS (My Oracle Support) 274
multiplexing 293
multi-section backups 293
  for incremental backups 86
multi section incremental backups 155
multisections' backups 380
multitenant CDB
  full backup, performing 164, 165
Multitenant Container Database (CDB)
  31, 75, 78
multitenant container databases, RMAN
  about 163
  backup, performing of backups 168, 169
  backup, performing of pluggable database
    167, 168
  backup, performing of root 167, 168
  backups, restoring 169
  full backup, performing of multitenant CDB
    164, 165
  partial backup, performing of multitenant
    CDB 165-167
  RMAN views, related to backups 169

N

NBC 161
need backup option 264
Netbackup 127
network-based recovery 86
Network Configuration Assistant (NETCA)
  242
network link
  data, importing via 320-322

network link method
  used, for moving data 303
Network Manager (NETMGR) 242
newly added datafiles
  backups 385
NOARCHIVELOG mode
  about 16, 18, 101
  recovery 210, 211
NOLOGGING operations
  about 29-39
  and backups 60
  blocks, corrupting 63
  changes, repairing on physical standby
    database 64
  versus LOGGING operations 31-33
non-system data files
  recovery, ways 212, 213
NO UNREGISTER option 251
Null Block Compression. *See* **NBC**

O

objects
  moving, from one tablespace to another 336
  moving, to different schema 336
OEM12c
  export operation, performing 365-367
  export, performing 367, 368
  operations performing, with Data Pump
    365
offline backups
  about 102, 103
  configured defaults, avoiding 383
  RMAN, using 382
offline tablespaces
  backing up, steps 103, 104
operating system trace file
  using 273, 274
ORA-600 273
ORA-4031 268
ORA-19511 273
Oracle Database
  downgrading 338, 339
Oracle Database 12c
  enhancements 75
  features 75

Oracle Debugger (oradebug) 235
Oracle Enterprise Manager 12c (OEM12c R3)
        Cloud Control 347
Oracle Enterprise Manager Cloud Control
        79
Oracle Enterprise Manager (OEM) 21
Oracle Enterprise MOEM12c
    backup settings 348
    catalog settings 355
    recovery settings 353
Oracle Manage File (OMF) 199
Oracle Secure Backup (OSB) 284
Oracle-Suggested Backup strategy option
    using 358-360
OSB (Oracle Secure Backup) 134

P

PARALLEL command 316
parallelism 293
partial backup
    performing, of multitenant CDB 165-167
partitioning 46-54
PDB
    about 76, 163
    upgrading 76, 77
PGA (Program Global Area) 275
physical backup 11
physical standby database
    NOLOGGING changes. repairing on 64
pluggable database
    about 75
    complete recovery 216
    exporting 311, 312
    importing 311, 312
    key points 77, 78
point-in-time recovery
    performing 223, 226
point-in-time recovery, performing
    DBPITR 223-226
    TSPITR 226, 227
POR (Point Of Recovery) 178
production environment
    smaller copies, creating 333-335

R

read-only datafiles
    backups 385
Real Application Cluster (RAC) 201
RedoByte Address (RBA) 203
RECOVER command 86, 89, 157
recovery
    NOARCHIVELOG mode 210, 211
    purpose 7
    versus, restore 13
recovery catalog
    availability, checking 258
    catalog owner schema, creating 241
    creating 239, 242
    database, creating 239
    database, sizing 239, 240
    databases, unregistering from 259
    default tablespace, creating for catalog
        owner 240
    dropping 260
    features 238
    merging, into single 247-251
    privileges, granting to catalog owner 241
    protecting, methods 258
    related views 260, 263
    resynchronizing, with control file 245-247
    stored scripts, creating 255-258
    stored scripts, managing 255-258
    upgrading 259
    using 242-245
    virtual private catalogs, using 252-254
Recovery Catalog 126, 132, 133
Recovery Catalog Settings page 355, 357
Recovery Point Objective (RPO) 13
recovery scenarios 122
recovery settings 353, 354
Recovery Time Objective (RTO) 13
recovery window retention policy 178
redo
    about 14
    log files 14-16
    log groups, using 14
Redo Apply 64
redo_current_status.sql script 72

redo, facts
  direct path load, using in SQL*Loader
    68, 69
  Flashback, and NOLOGGING 67, 68
  materialized view 67
  performance, considerations 68
  recovery, considerations 68
  redo, and temporary tables 67
  redo, for DML 66
  redo generation 67
  undo, for DML 66
redo_generated_by_session.sql script 71
redo generating sessions
  searching 65
redo generation
  about 16
  disabling 34
  reducing 44
redo logs
  archiving 19
redo log space request event 62
redo related wait events
  about 60
  log buffer space 63
  log file parallel write 60, 62
  log file sync 62
  redo log space request 62
redo, scripts
  NOLOGGING objects, in database 72
  redo_current_status.sql 72
  redo_generated_by_session.sql 71
  redo_since_session_started.sql 71
  redo_since_startup.sql 69
  redo_switch_info.sql 72
redo_since_session_started.sql script 71
redo_since_startup.sql script 69
redo stream 203
redo switches time
  checking 380
redo_switch_info.sql script 72
redo thread 203
redundancy 352
redundancy retention policy 175-177
REMAP_DATA parameter 326
REPORT command
  used, for reporting 264

RESETLOGS option 395
restore
  versus recovery 13
restore point
  guaranteed restored point 363
  normal restore point 363
  using 363, 364
Retain all backups option 351
retention policy, for backup set
  modifying 383
REUSE_DUMPFILES command 316
Review page 368
RMAN
  about 268, 347
  and IO 275, 276
  architecture 130
  authentication configuration 199
  backup formats 137
  configuring 377
  controlling 290, 292
  debugging, DEBUG clause used 272, 273
  features 126, 127
  for multitenant container databases 163
  reporting option 263
  reporting option, LIST command used 263
  reporting option, REPORT command used
    264
  starting with 128-130
  used, for performing incremental backups
    151
  used, for performing table partitions
    recovery 91
  using, for DB scan 384
RMAN authentication configuration
  about 199
  OS authentication 199
  password file authentication 200
RMAN backup
  Customized Backup option, using 360-363
  Oracle-Suggested Backup strategy option,
    using 358-360
  scheduling 357
  table partition-level recovery 227
RMAN channels 132
RMAN client 133
RMAN commands 145, 146

RMAN compression
 using, for backups 161-163
RMAN configuration
 about 171
 Block Change tracking, enabling 379
 catalog user, creating 378
 checking 382
 configure command, using 377
 database, backing up 377
 DB, registering in recovery catalog 378
 obsolete backups, checking 378
 recovery catalog, creating 378
 SHOW ALL command 172-174
 target DB RMAN backup account, creating
  377
 V$RMAN_CONFIGURATION view using
  172
 virtual private catalog, creating 378
RMAN IO performance
 monitoring, dictionary views used 281
RMAN metadata
 control file, using 233-236
RMAN operations
 monitoring 285-289
RMAN options
 Backup Jobs 369
 Backup Sets 369
 Image Copies 370
 RMAN Settings 370
 Scheduled RMAN Actions 370
rmanoutput.log file 130
RMAN performance
 troubleshooting, tracing used 294, 295
RMAN performance tuning 274, 275
RMAN session
 monitoring 285-289
RMAN troubleshooting 268
RMAN views, related to backups
 V$BACKUP_CONTROLFILE_DETAILS
  170
 V$BACKUP_COPY_DETAILS 170
 V$BACKUP_DATAFILE_DETAILS 170
 V$BACKUP_FILES 169
 V$BACKUP_PIECE 170
 V$BACKUP_REDOLOG 170
 V$BACKUP_SET_SUMMARY 170
 V$RMAN_BACKUP_JOB_DETAILS 170

 V$RMAN_OUTPUT 170
 V$RMAN_STATUS 170
rollback segments 66
root container
 complete recovery 217, 218
RPC (Remote Procedure Calls) 134

S

SaaS (Software as a Service) 77
SBT performance
 tuning 283, 284
SBTTEST utility 274
scenarios, Data Pump utility
 data, importing via network link 320-322
 Export, used for estimating space 313
 interactive-command mode 314-316
 parallel full database export 314-316
 pluggable database, exporting 311, 312
 pluggable database, importing 311, 312
 schema export 306-309
 schema import 306-309
 tables, exporting 310
 tables, importing 310
 tables, importing with only metadata 317
 views, exporting as tables 318-320
SCN (System Change Number) 27, 68, 152
SecureFile LOBs
 creating, on Import 96
SEED 76
SGA (System Global Area) 275
Shared Pool 134
SHOW command 175
SHOW ALL command
 using 172-174
SID (System ID) 285
Single Tenant Container Database 75
SLAs (Service Level Agreement) 12
snapshot control file
 configuring 194
Social Security Number. *See* **SSN**
SOURCE_EDITION parameter
 using 332
Specific number of days option 351
SPFILE
 auto backup, configuring 181, 182
 backups, performing 159

SQL developer 3.2
  about 369
  Data Pump operations 371
  RMAN Operations 369, 370
SQL files 304
SQL*Loader
  direct path loader, using in 68, 69
SSN 326
START_JOB command 316
Statspack report 60
STATUS command 316
STOP_JOB command 317
Symmetric Binary Tape (SBT) 180
synchronous IO mode 278, 279
SYSBACKUP administrative privilege 80
SYSBACKUP privilege 128
SYSDBA privilege 80, 128
system data files
  recovery, steps 214, 215

T

TABLE_EXISTS_ACTION parameter 318
table partition-level recovery
  RMAN backups 227
table partitions recovery
  performing, RMAN used 91
tables
  compressing, on import 95
  exporting 310
  importing 310
  importing, with only metadata 317
  views, exporting as 94, 318, 320
tablespace
  transporting 340-343
Tablespace Point-in-time Recovery. See
  TSPITR
tablespaces
  configuring, for exclusion 384
Target Control File 132
target database 131
TARGET_EDITION parameter
  using 332
tee command 130
temporary file
  recovery, ways 211
text file backup 111, 112

tips, LOGGING operations
  backups 44
  bulk deletes 45
  bulk inserts 44
  bulk updates 46
  for developers 48-51
  partitioning 46, 47
tips, NOLOGGING operations
  bulk deletes 58, 59
  bulk inserts 58
  bulk updates 59
  direct path inserts 54-57
  partitioning 51-54
Tivoli 127
tracing
  used, for troubleshooting RMAN
    performance 294, 295
Transparent Data Encryption (TDE) key 187
Transparent Network Substrate (TNS) 243
transportable tablespace set 340
TSPITR 86, 226, 227

U

UBC 161
UNREGISTER command 259
Unused Block Compression. See UBC
UPGRADE CATALOG command 259
user
  cloning 332
user error 10
user-managed backup
  considerations 100
  recovering from 119-122

V

V$BACKUP_ASYNC_IO view 282
V$BACKUP_CONTROLFILE_DETAILS
  view 170
V$BACKUP_COPY_DETAILS view 170
V$BACKUP_DATAFILE_DETAILS view
  170
V$BACKUP_FILES view 169
V$BACKUP_PIECE view 170
V$BACKUP_REDOLOG view 170
V$BACKUP_SET_SUMMARY view 170

V$BACKUP_SYNC_IO view 282, 283
v$pwfile_users view 81
V$RECOVERY_AREA_USAGE view
  options 118, 119
V$RECOVERY_FILE_DEST view
  options 117
V$RMAN_BACKUP_JOB_DETAILS view
  170
V$RMAN_CONFIGURATION view
  using 172
V$RMAN_OUTPUT view 170
V$RMAN_STATUS view 170

Valid/Invalid 23
version control
  creating 331
views
  exporting, as tables 94, 318, 320
VLDB (Very Large Databases) 127

X

X$KCCBP (Kernel Cache Control Backup
  Piece) 234

Thank you for buying
Oracle Database 12c Backup and Recovery Survival Guide

About Packt Publishing

Packt, pronounced 'packed', published its first book "Mastering phpMyAdmin for Effective MySQL Management" in April 2004 and subsequently continued to specialize in publishing highly focused books on specific technologies and solutions.

Our books and publications share the experiences of your fellow IT professionals in adapting and customizing today's systems, applications, and frameworks. Our solution based books give you the knowledge and power to customize the software and technologies you're using to get the job done. Packt books are more specific and less general than the IT books you have seen in the past. Our unique business model allows us to bring you more focused information, giving you more of what you need to know, and less of what you don't.

Packt is a modern, yet unique publishing company, which focuses on producing quality, cutting-edge books for communities of developers, administrators, and newbies alike. For more information, please visit our website: www.packtpub.com.

About Packt Enterprise

In 2010, Packt launched two new brands, Packt Enterprise and Packt Open Source, in order to continue its focus on specialization. This book is part of the Packt Enterprise brand, home to books published on enterprise software – software created by major vendors, including (but not limited to) IBM, Microsoft and Oracle, often for use in other corporations. Its titles will offer information relevant to a range of users of this software, including administrators, developers, architects, and end users.

Writing for Packt

We welcome all inquiries from people who are interested in authoring. Book proposals should be sent to author@packtpub.com. If your book idea is still at an early stage and you would like to discuss it first before writing a formal book proposal, contact us; one of our commissioning editors will get in touch with you.

We're not just looking for published authors; if you have strong technical skills but no writing experience, our experienced editors can help you develop a writing career, or simply get some additional reward for your expertise.

PUBLISHING

professional expertise distilled

**Oracle WebLogic Server 12c
Advanced Administration
Cookbook**

Dalton Iwazaki

Oracle WebLogic Server 12c Advanced Administration Cookbook

ISBN: 978-1-84968-684-6   Paperback: 284 pages

Over 60 advanced recipes to configure, troubleshoot, and tune Oracle WebLogic Server

1. Learn how to set a WebLogic environment with stability, high availability and performance

2. Premature optmization is the root of all evil. Configure and tune only what really matters

3. Understand what are you doing and why. Every recipe covers the theory behind the practice

**Oracle Enterprise Manager
12c Administration Cookbook**

Oracle Enterprise Manager 12c Administration Cookbook

ISBN: 978-1-84968-740-9   Paperback: 324 pages

Over 50 practical recipes to install, configure, and monitor your Oracle setup using Oracle Enterprise manager

1. Recipes for installing, configuring, and getting up and running with Oracle Enterprise Manager

2. Set up automatic discovery, create and clone databases, and perform provisioning

3. Monitor Oracle Fusion Middleware, and remotely use incident and problem management using iPad/iPhone

Please check **www.PacktPub.com** for information on our titles

Oracle Enterprise Manager Cloud Control 12c: Managing Data Center Chaos

ISBN: 978-1-84968-478-1   Paperback: 394 pages

Get to grips with the latest innovative techniques for managing data center chaos including performance tuning, security compliance, patching, and more

Oracle Enterprise Manager Cloud Control 12c: Managing Data Center Chaos

Get to grips with the latest innovative techniques for managing data center chaos including performance tuning, security compliance, patching, and more

Porus Homi Havewala
Oracle Certified Master

1. Learn about the tremendous capabilities of the latest powerhouse version of Oracle Enterprise Manager 12c Cloud Control

2. Take a deep dive into crucial topics including Provisioning and Patch Automation, Performance Management and Exadata Database Machine Management

3. Take advantage of the author's experience as an Oracle Certified Master in this real world guide including enterprise examples and case studies

Securing WebLogic Server 12c [Instant]

ISBN: 978-1-84968-778-2   Paperback: 100 pages

Learn to develop, administer, and troubleshoot your WebLogic Server

Securing WebLogic Server 12c

Learn to develop, administer, and troubleshoot your WebLogic Server

Luca Masini   Rinaldi Vincenzo

1. Discover Authentication providers

2. Configure security for WebLogic applications and develop your own security providers

3. Step by step guide to administer and configure WebLogic security providers

Please check **www.PacktPub.com** for information on our titles

CPSIA information can be obtained
at www.ICGtesting.com
Printed in the USA
BVOW10s0305150617
486943BV00007B/61/P